S itual Police

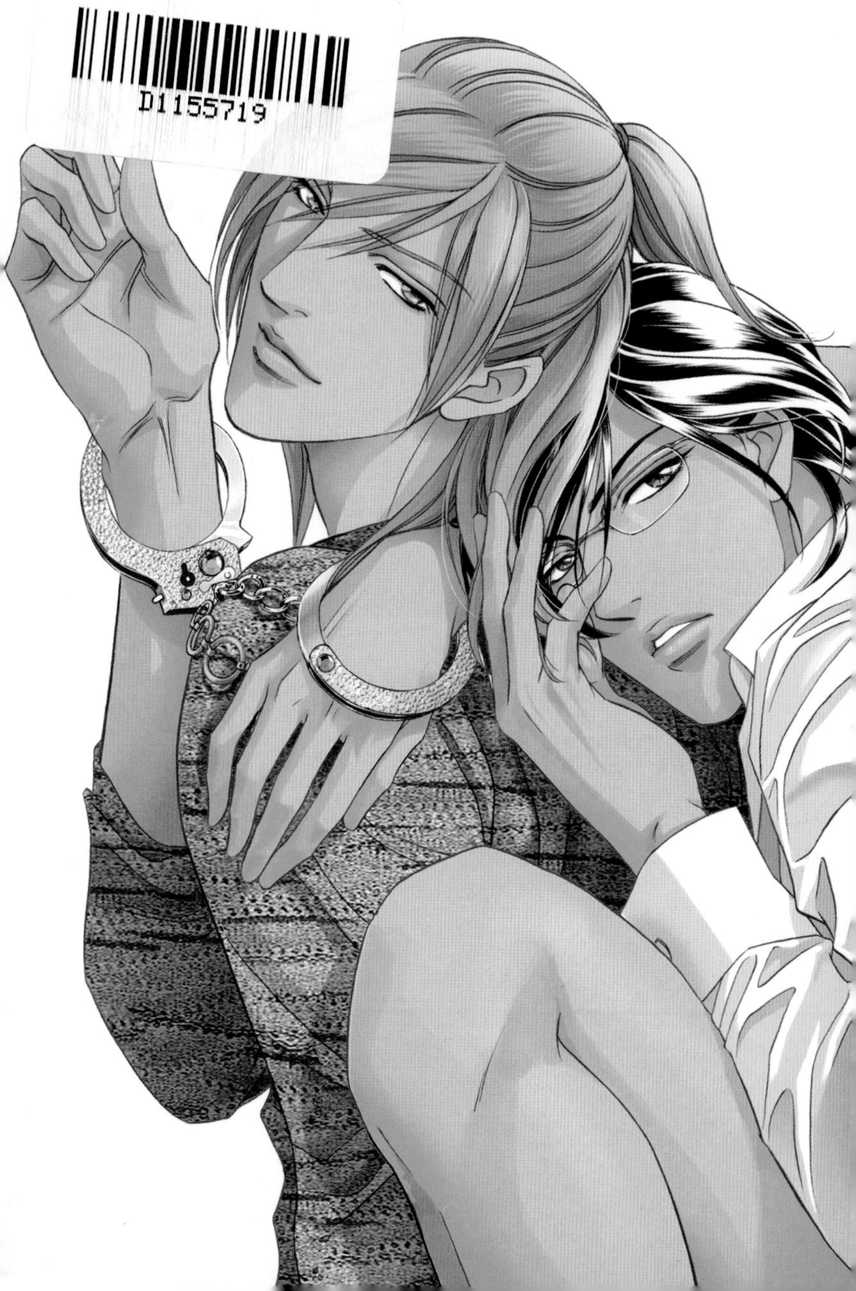

Spiritual Police

Story and Art by **Youka Nitta**　　　volume **1**

CONTENTS

Chapter 1 005

Chapter 2 053

Chapter 3 085

Chapter 4 125

Illustration Collection 163

SUBLIME
SuBLime Manga Edition

スピリチュアルポリス

Spiritual
Police

vol. 1

新田祐克

Youka Nitta presents

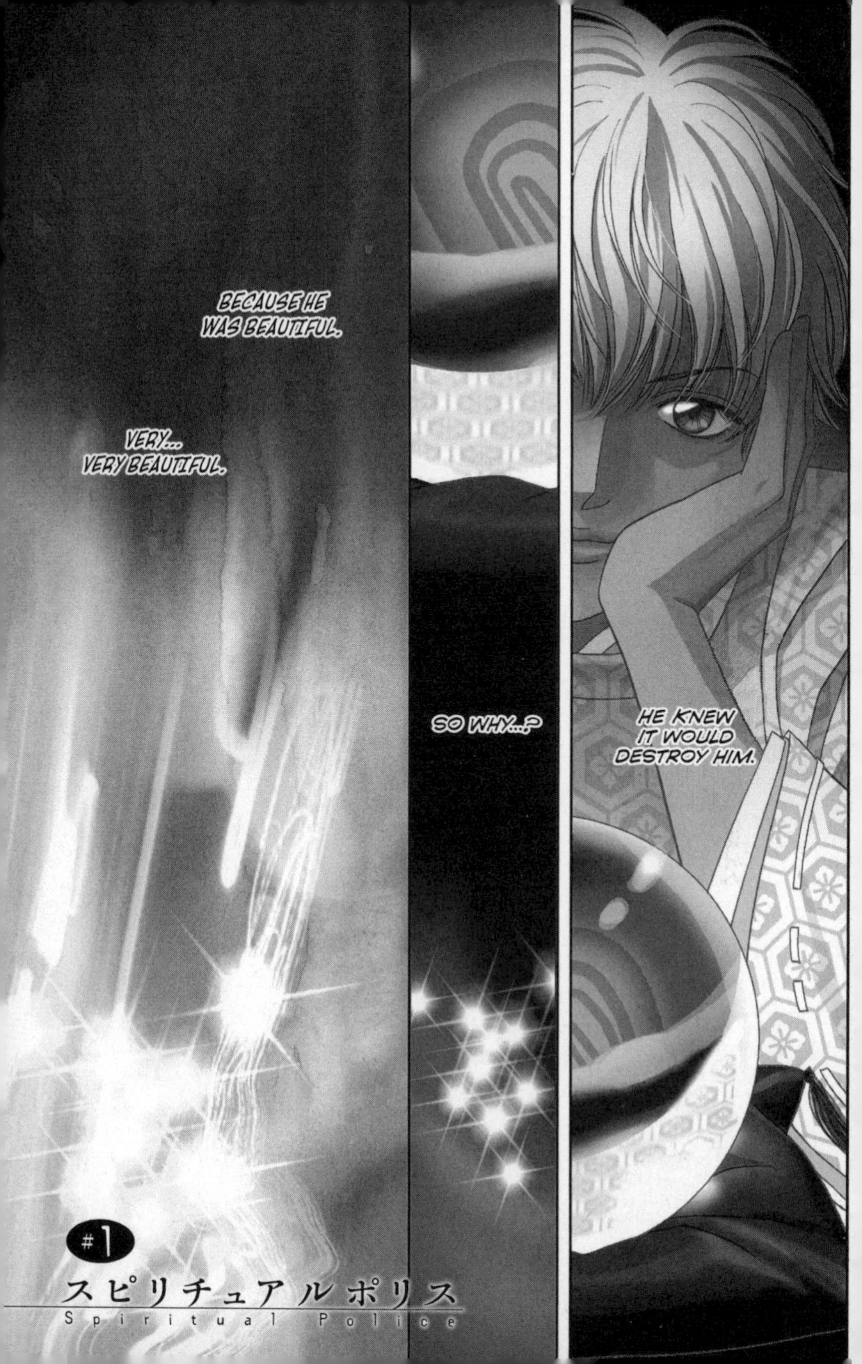
HE KNEW IT WOULD DESTROY HIM.
SO WHY...?
BECAUSE HE WAS BEAUTIFUL.
VERY... VERY BEAUTIFUL.
#1
スピリチュアルポリス
Spiritual Police

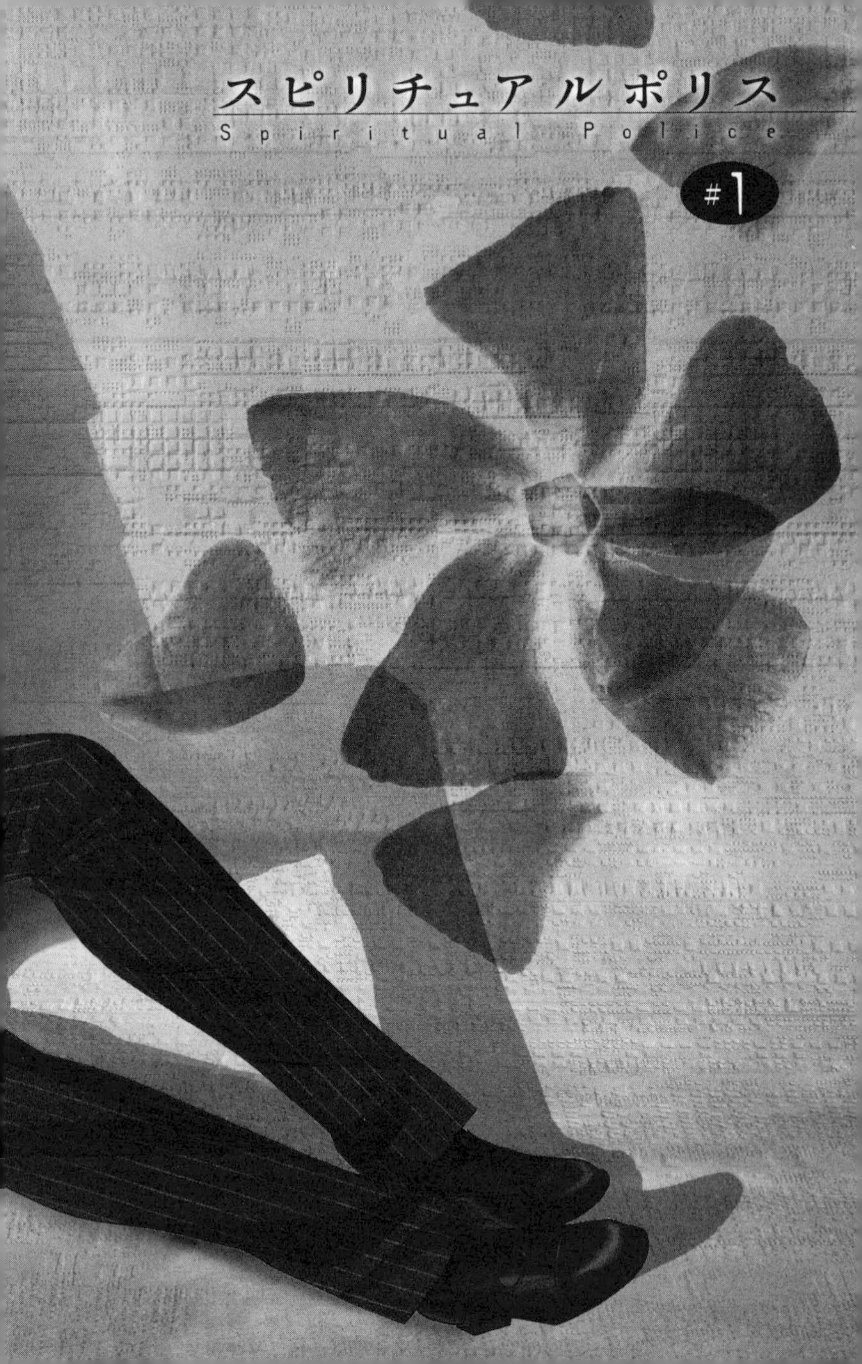
スピリチュアルポリス
Spiritual Police
#1

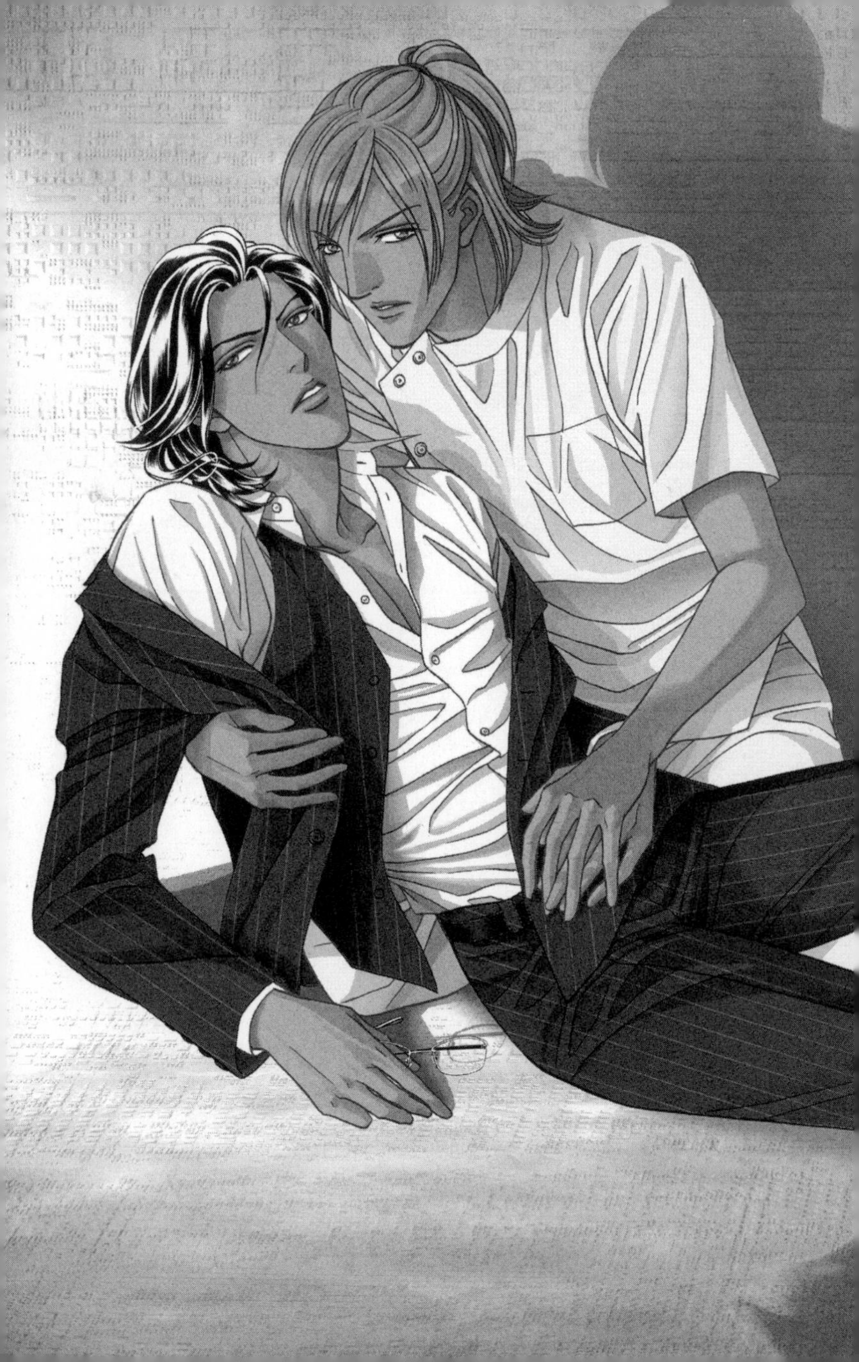

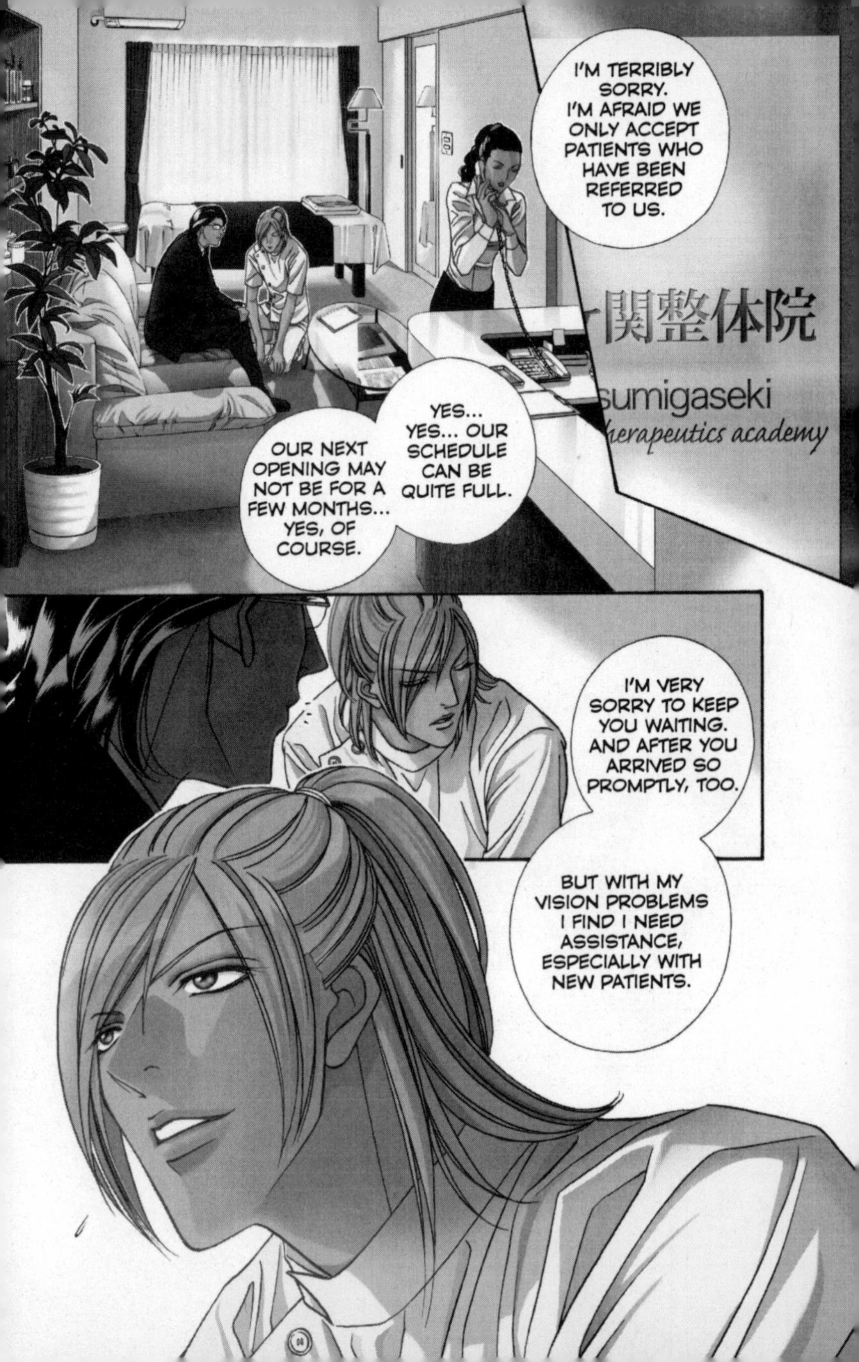
I'M TERRIBLY SORRY. I'M AFRAID WE ONLY ACCEPT PATIENTS WHO HAVE BEEN REFERRED TO US.
関整体院
sumigaseki
herapeutics academy
YES... YES... OUR SCHEDULE CAN BE QUITE FULL.
OUR NEXT OPENING MAY NOT BE FOR A FEW MONTHS... YES, OF COURSE.
I'M VERY SORRY TO KEEP YOU WAITING. AND AFTER YOU ARRIVED SO PROMPTLY, TOO.
BUT WITH MY VISION PROBLEMS I FIND I NEED ASSISTANCE, ESPECIALLY WITH NEW PATIENTS.

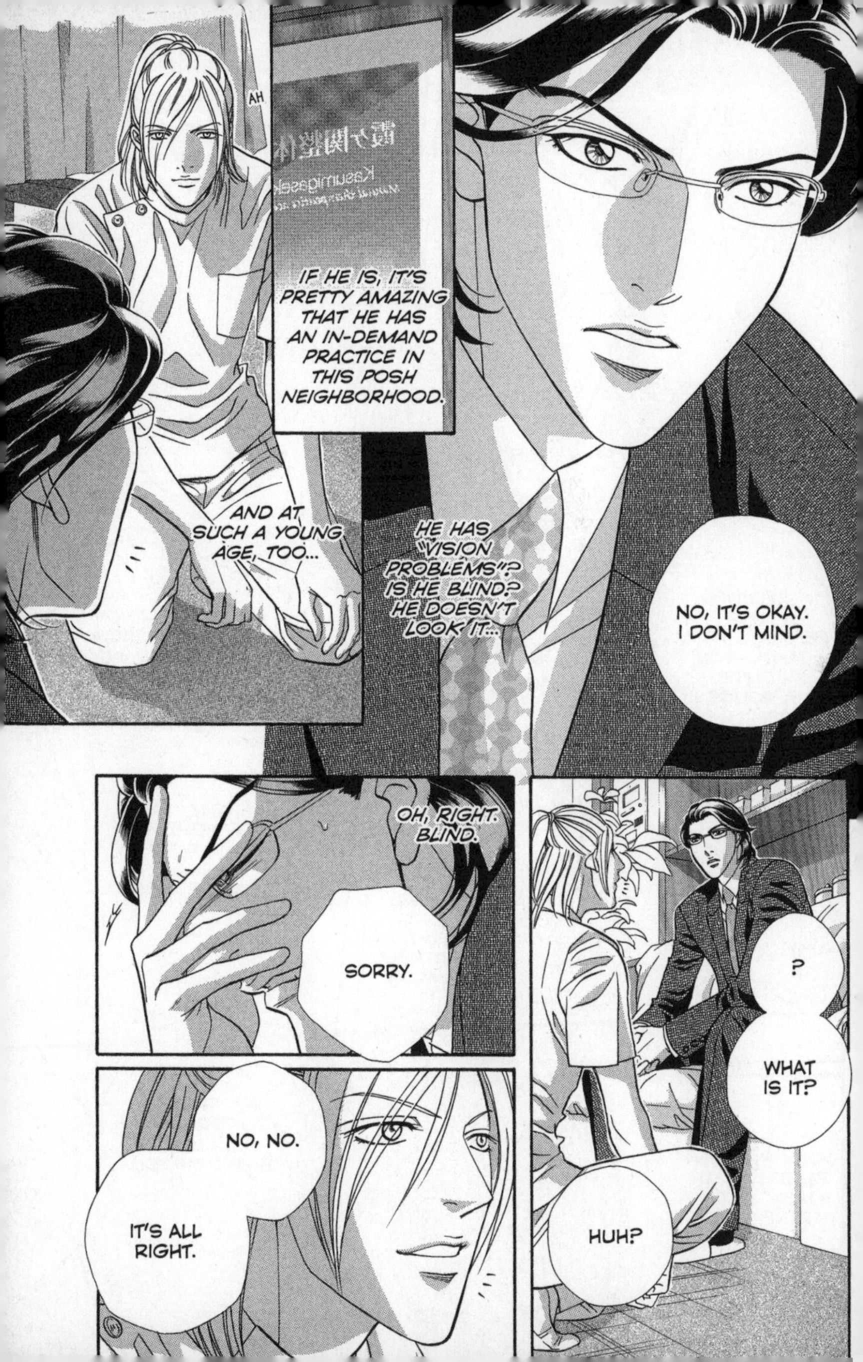
NO, IT'S OKAY. I DON'T MIND.
HE HAS "VISION PROBLEMS"? IS HE BLIND? HE DOESN'T LOOK IT...
IF HE IS, IT'S PRETTY AMAZING THAT HE HAS AN IN-DEMAND PRACTICE IN THIS POSH NEIGHBORHOOD.
AH
AND AT SUCH A YOUNG AGE, TOO...
?
WHAT IS IT?
HUH?
OH, RIGHT. BLIND.
SORRY.
NO, NO.
IT'S ALL RIGHT.

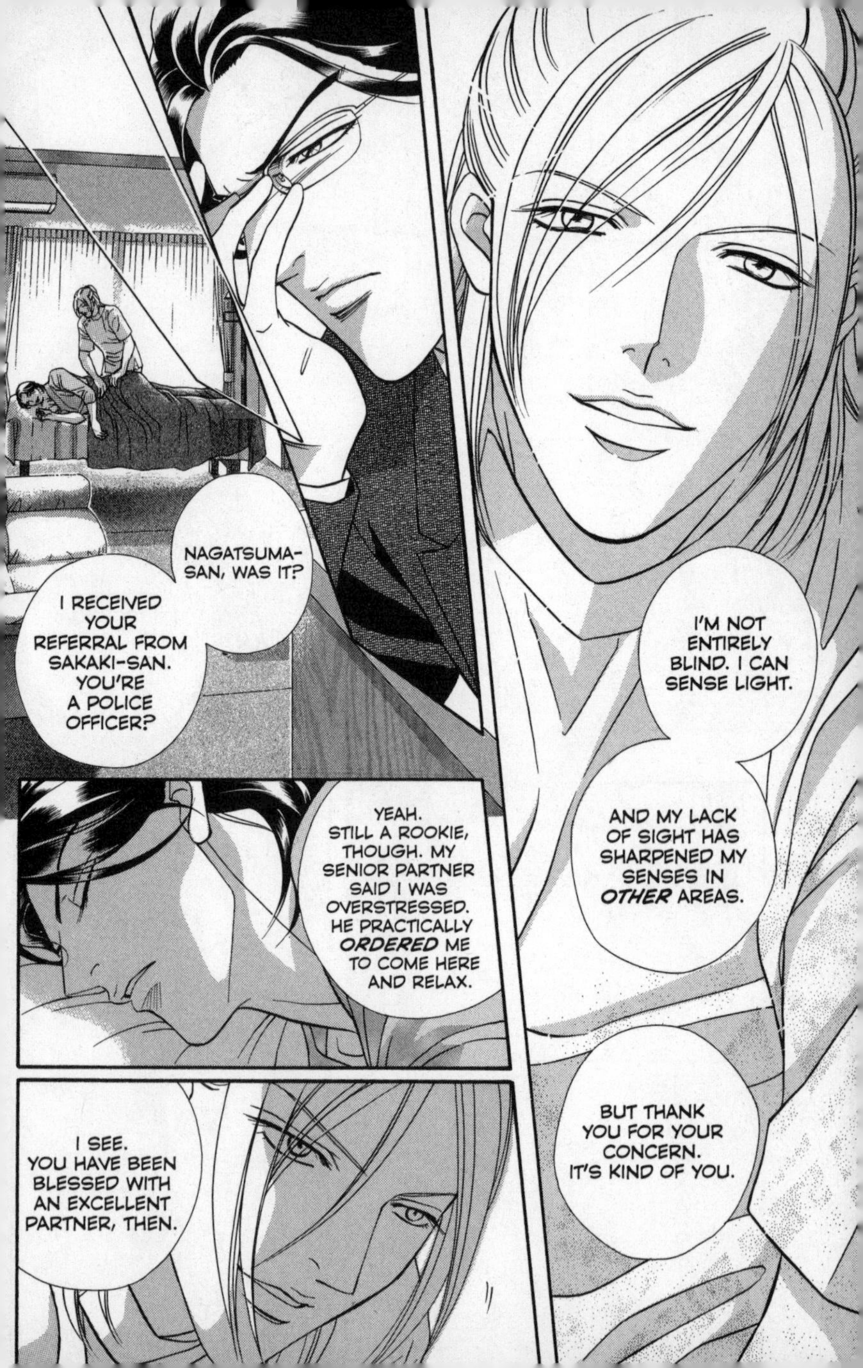
I'M NOT ENTIRELY BLIND. I CAN SENSE LIGHT.
AND MY LACK OF SIGHT HAS SHARPENED MY SENSES IN *OTHER* AREAS.
BUT THANK YOU FOR YOUR CONCERN. IT'S KIND OF YOU.
NAGATSUMA-SAN, WAS IT?
I RECEIVED YOUR REFERRAL FROM SAKAKI-SAN. YOU'RE A POLICE OFFICER?
YEAH. STILL A ROOKIE, THOUGH. MY SENIOR PARTNER SAID I WAS OVERSTRESSED. HE PRACTICALLY *ORDERED* ME TO COME HERE AND RELAX.
I SEE. YOU HAVE BEEN BLESSED WITH AN EXCELLENT PARTNER, THEN.

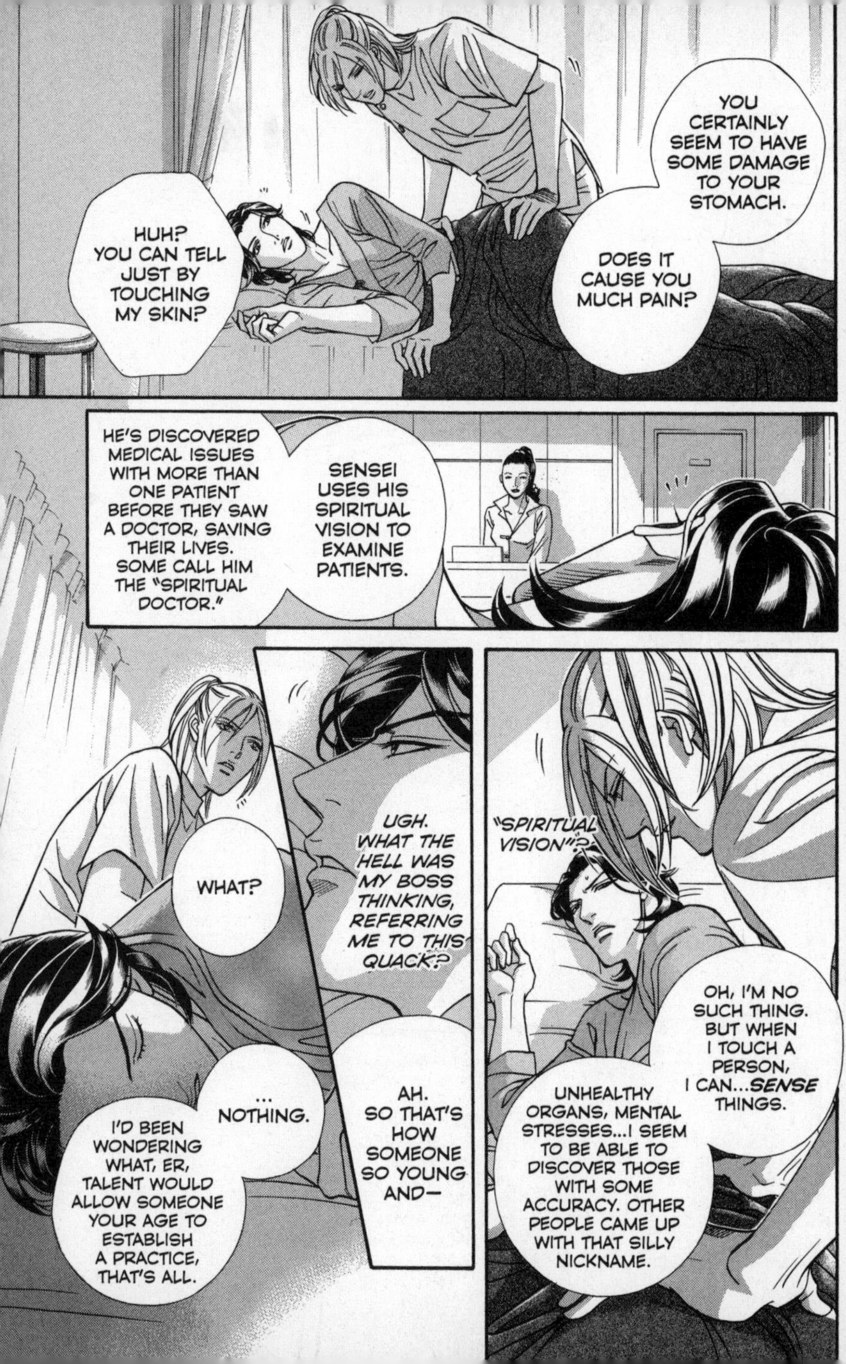
YOU CERTAINLY SEEM TO HAVE SOME DAMAGE TO YOUR STOMACH.
DOES IT CAUSE YOU MUCH PAIN?
HUH? YOU CAN TELL JUST BY TOUCHING MY SKIN?
SENSEI USES HIS SPIRITUAL VISION TO EXAMINE PATIENTS.
HE'S DISCOVERED MEDICAL ISSUES WITH MORE THAN ONE PATIENT BEFORE THEY SAW A DOCTOR, SAVING THEIR LIVES. SOME CALL HIM THE "SPIRITUAL DOCTOR."
"SPIRITUAL VISION"?
OH, I'M NO SUCH THING. BUT WHEN I TOUCH A PERSON, I CAN...*SENSE* THINGS.
UNHEALTHY ORGANS, MENTAL STRESSES...I SEEM TO BE ABLE TO DISCOVER THOSE WITH SOME ACCURACY. OTHER PEOPLE CAME UP WITH THAT SILLY NICKNAME.
UGH. WHAT THE HELL WAS MY BOSS THINKING, REFERRING ME TO THIS QUACK?
AH. SO THAT'S HOW SOMEONE SO YOUNG AND—
WHAT?
... NOTHING.
I'D BEEN WONDERING WHAT, ER, TALENT WOULD ALLOW SOMEONE YOUR AGE TO ESTABLISH A PRACTICE, THAT'S ALL.

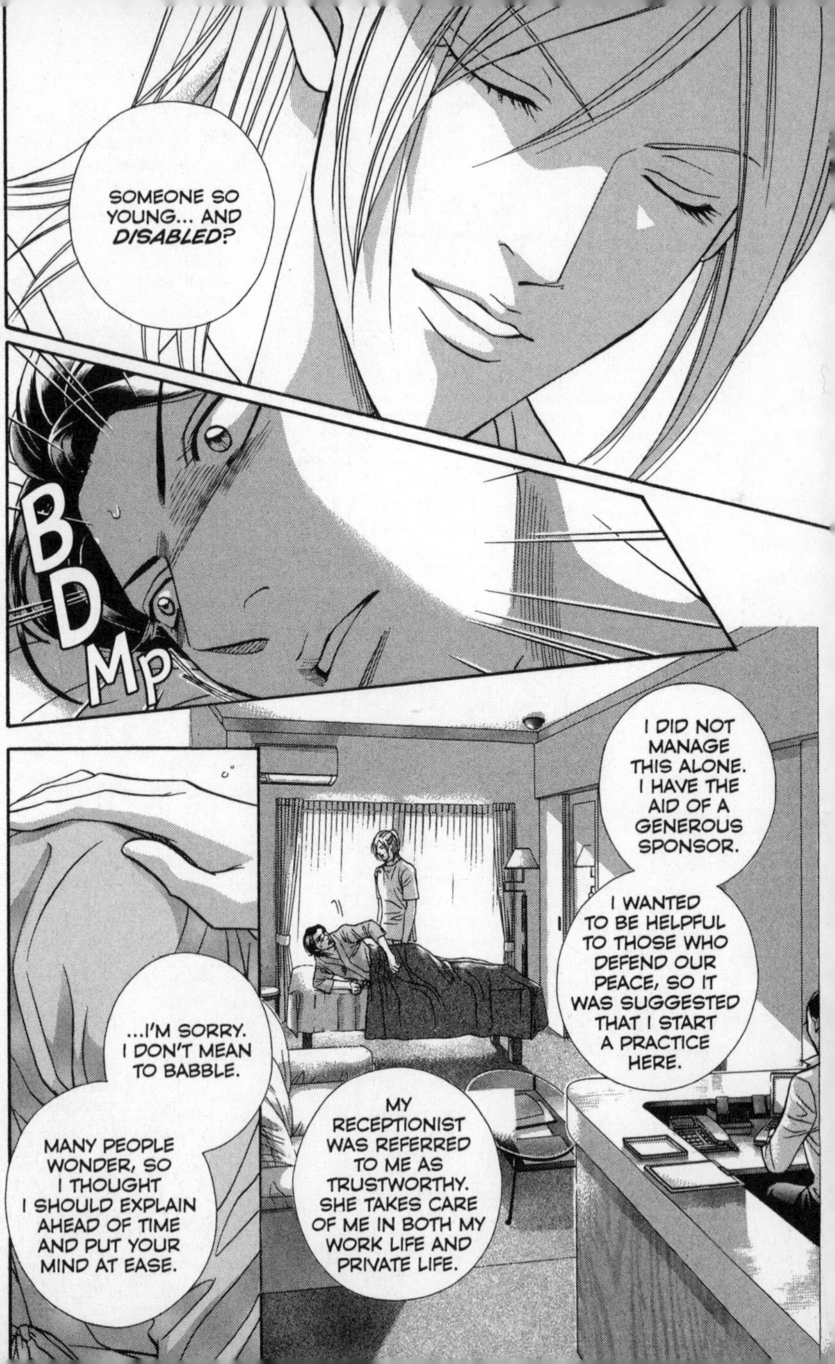
SOMEONE SO YOUNG... AND *DISABLED*?
BDMp
I DID NOT MANAGE THIS ALONE. I HAVE THE AID OF A GENEROUS SPONSOR.
I WANTED TO BE HELPFUL TO THOSE WHO DEFEND OUR PEACE, SO IT WAS SUGGESTED THAT I START A PRACTICE HERE.
MY RECEPTIONIST WAS REFERRED TO ME AS TRUSTWORTHY. SHE TAKES CARE OF ME IN BOTH MY WORK LIFE AND PRIVATE LIFE.
...I'M SORRY. I DON'T MEAN TO BABBLE.
MANY PEOPLE WONDER, SO I THOUGHT I SHOULD EXPLAIN AHEAD OF TIME AND PUT YOUR MIND AT EASE.

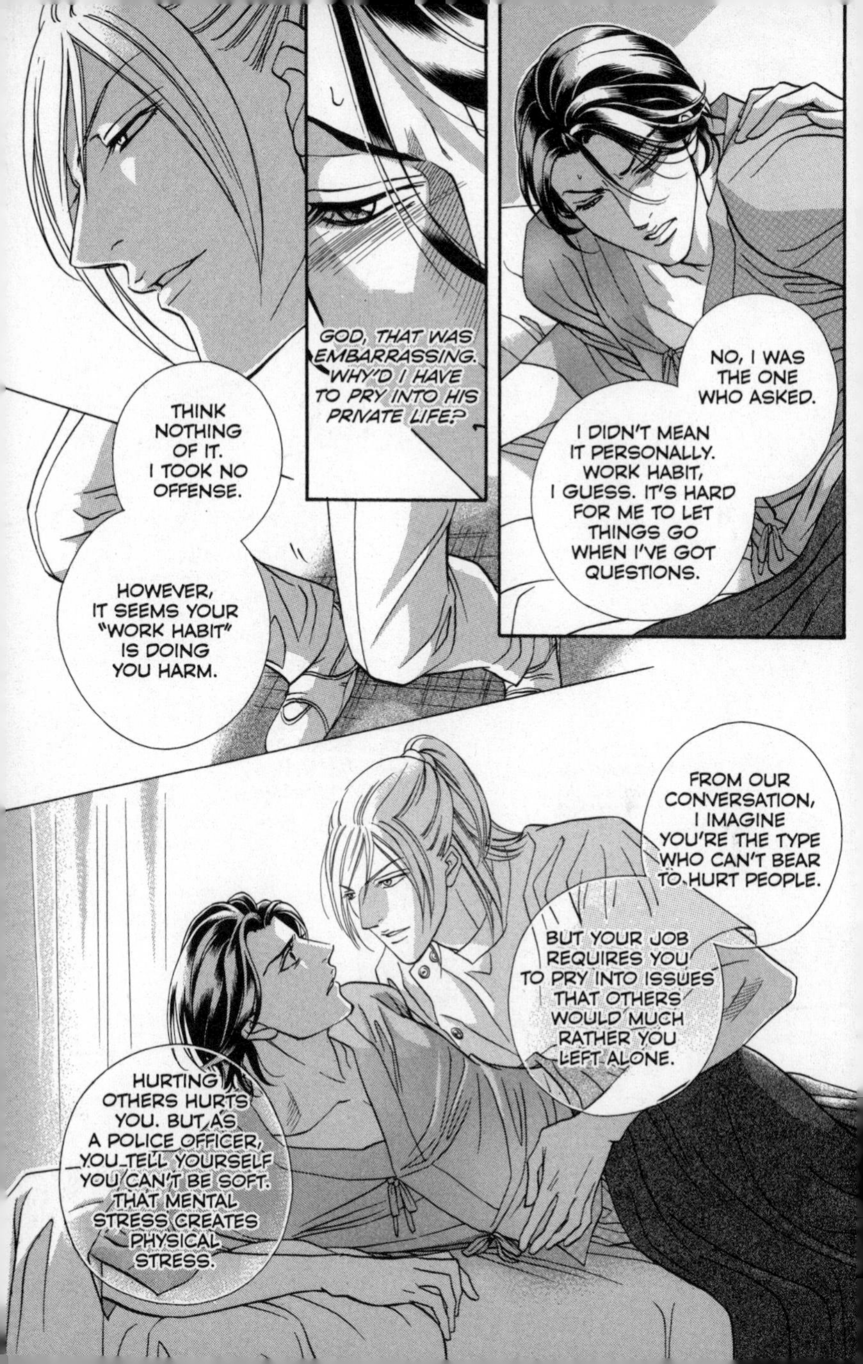
NO, I WAS THE ONE WHO ASKED.
I DIDN'T MEAN IT PERSONALLY. WORK HABIT, I GUESS. IT'S HARD FOR ME TO LET THINGS GO WHEN I'VE GOT QUESTIONS.
GOD, THAT WAS EMBARRASSING. WHY'D I HAVE TO PRY INTO HIS PRIVATE LIFE?
THINK NOTHING OF IT. I TOOK NO OFFENSE.
HOWEVER, IT SEEMS YOUR "WORK HABIT" IS DOING YOU HARM.
FROM OUR CONVERSATION, I IMAGINE YOU'RE THE TYPE WHO CAN'T BEAR TO HURT PEOPLE.
BUT YOUR JOB REQUIRES YOU TO PRY INTO ISSUES THAT OTHERS WOULD MUCH RATHER YOU LEFT ALONE.
HURTING OTHERS HURTS YOU. BUT AS A POLICE OFFICER, YOU TELL YOURSELF YOU CAN'T BE SOFT. THAT MENTAL STRESS CREATES PHYSICAL STRESS.

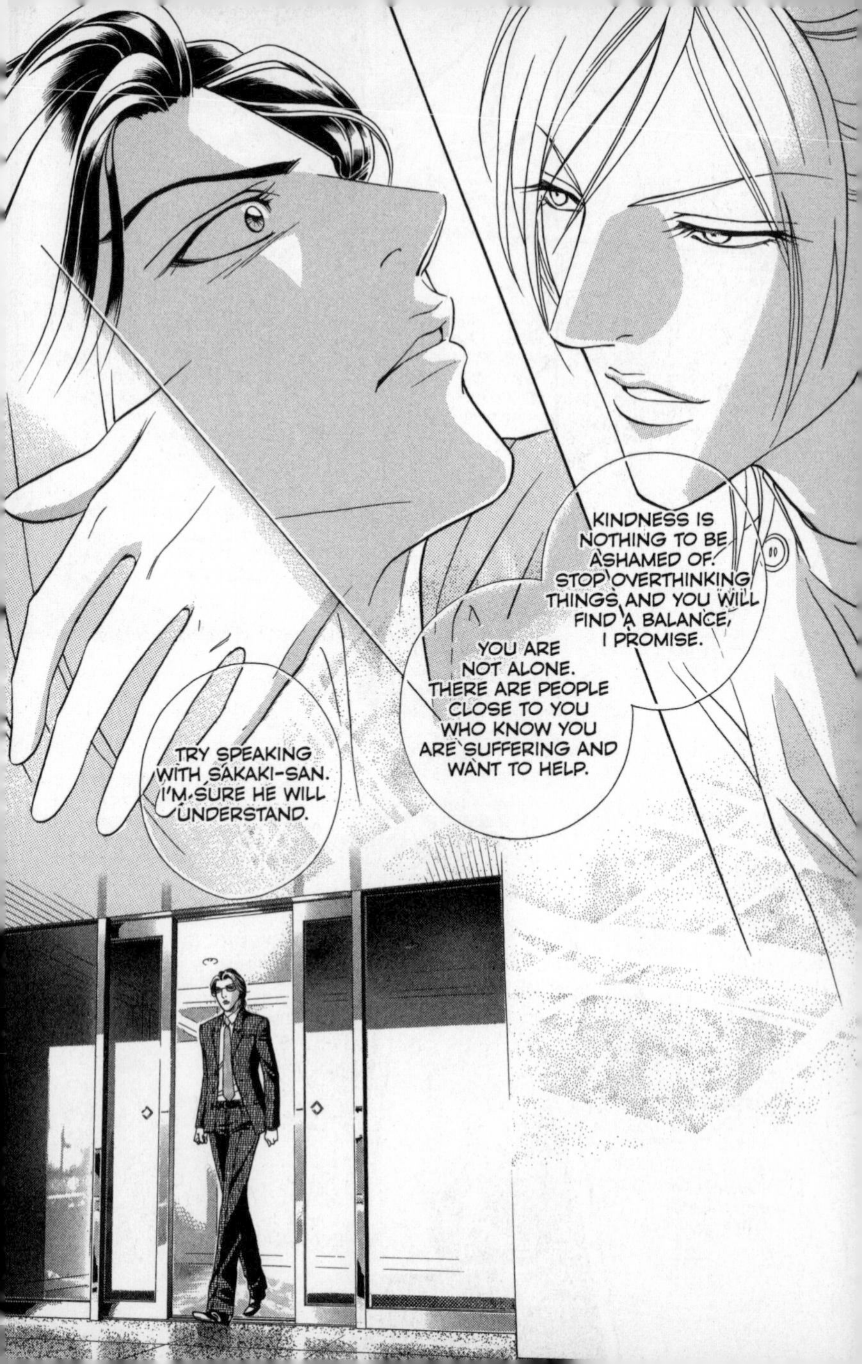
KINDNESS IS NOTHING TO BE ASHAMED OF. STOP OVERTHINKING THINGS AND YOU WILL FIND A BALANCE, I PROMISE.
YOU ARE NOT ALONE. THERE ARE PEOPLE CLOSE TO YOU WHO KNOW YOU ARE SUFFERING AND WANT TO HELP.
TRY SPEAKING WITH SAKAKI-SAN. I'M SURE HE WILL UNDERSTAND.

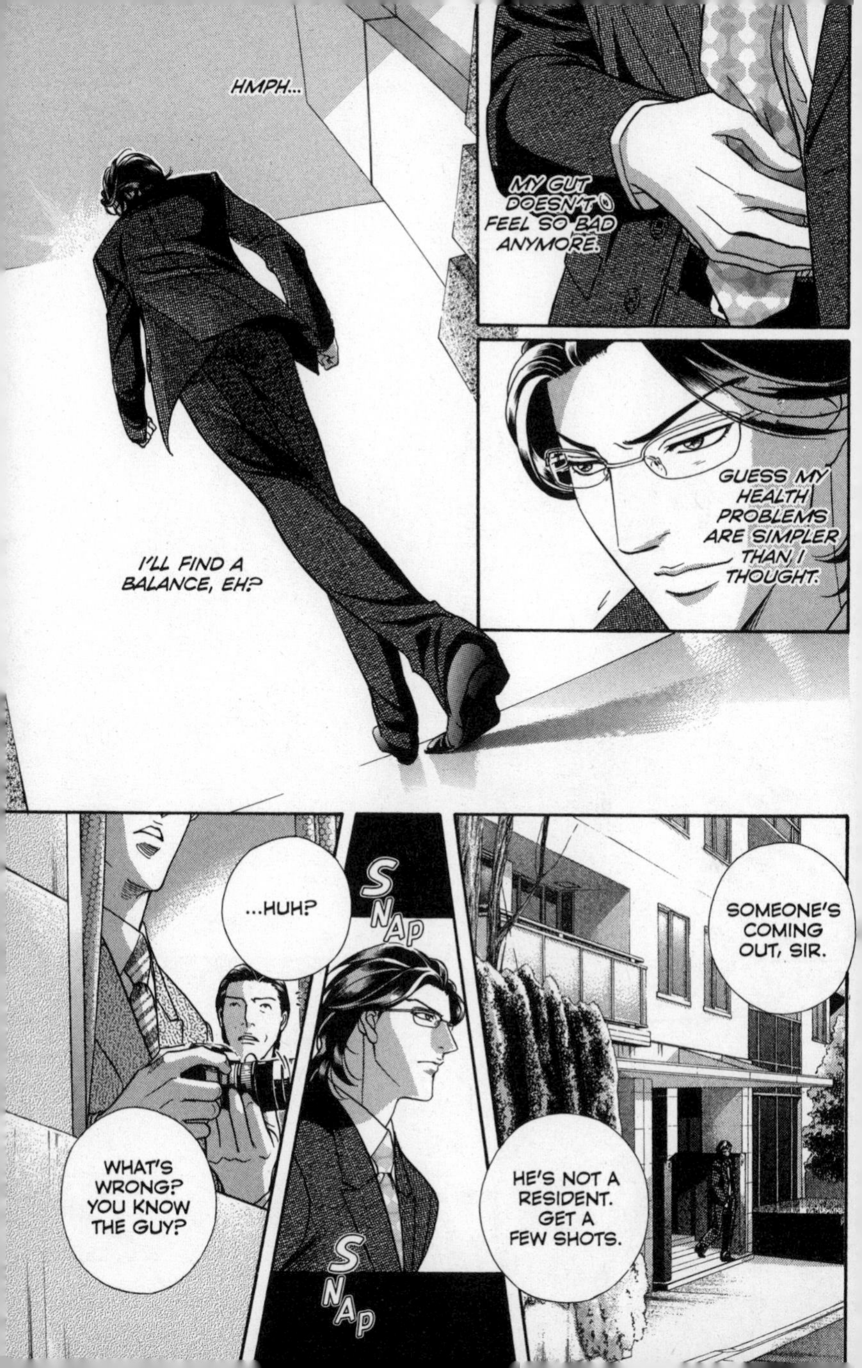
MY GUT DOESN'T FEEL SO BAD ANYMORE.
GUESS MY HEALTH PROBLEMS ARE SIMPLER THAN I THOUGHT.
HMPH...
I'LL FIND A BALANCE, EH?
SOMEONE'S COMING OUT, SIR.
HE'S NOT A RESIDENT. GET A FEW SHOTS.
SNAP
SNAP
...HUH?
WHAT'S WRONG? YOU KNOW THE GUY?

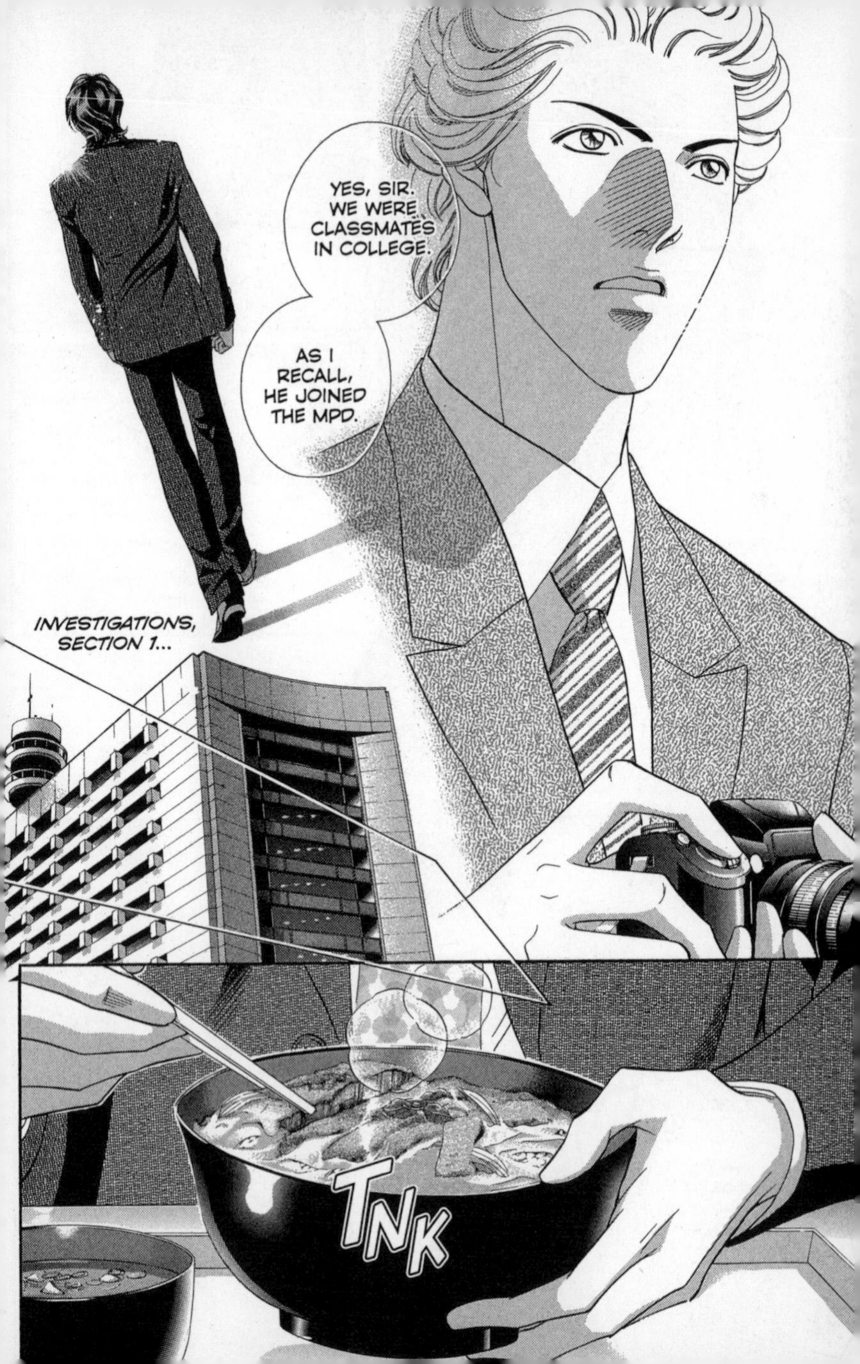
YES, SIR. WE WERE CLASSMATES IN COLLEGE.
AS I RECALL, HE JOINED THE MPD.
INVESTIGATIONS, SECTION 1...
TNK

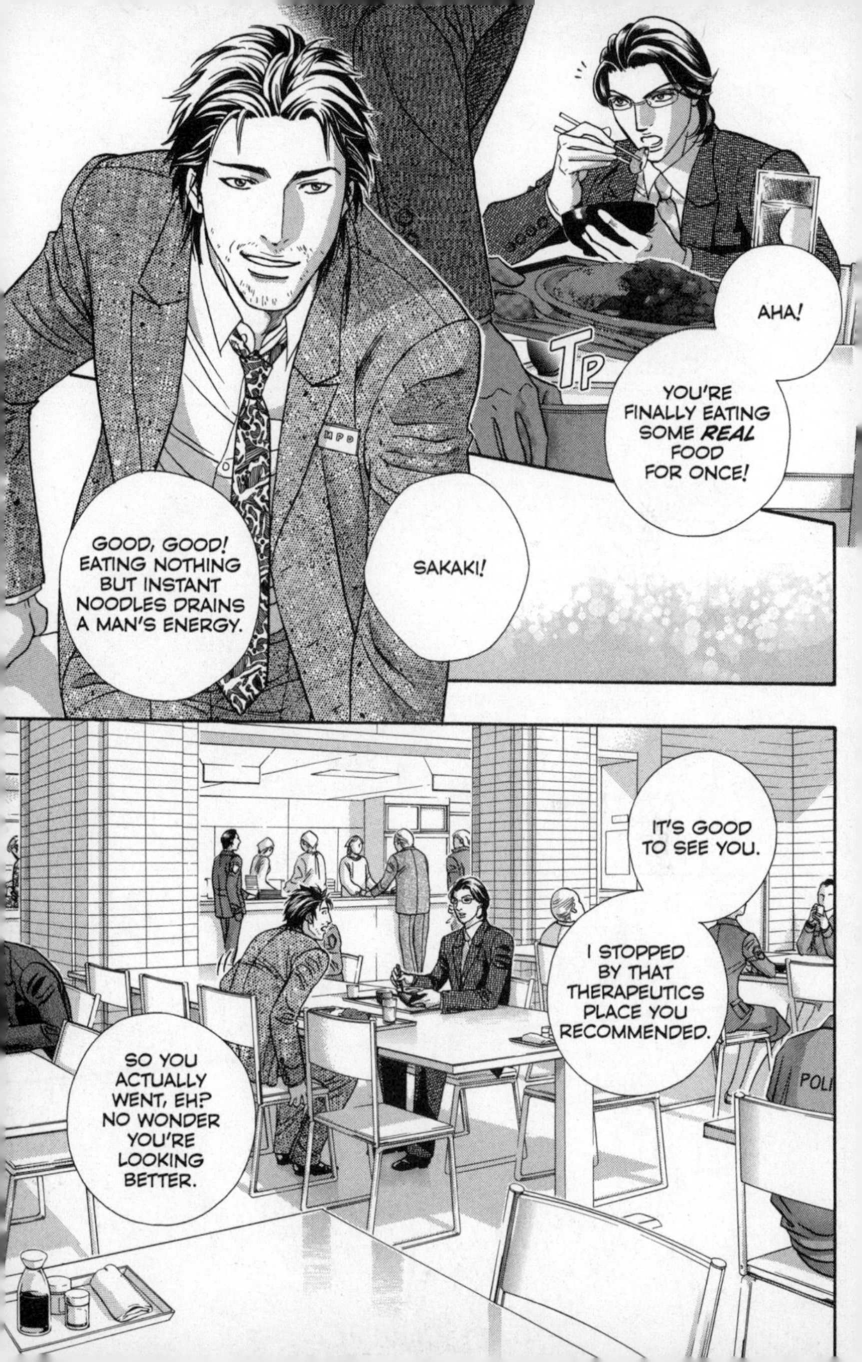
AHA!
TP
YOU'RE FINALLY EATING SOME *REAL* FOOD FOR ONCE!
SAKAKI!
GOOD, GOOD! EATING NOTHING BUT INSTANT NOODLES DRAINS A MAN'S ENERGY.
IT'S GOOD TO SEE YOU.
I STOPPED BY THAT THERAPEUTICS PLACE YOU RECOMMENDED.
SO YOU ACTUALLY WENT, EH? NO WONDER YOU'RE LOOKING BETTER.

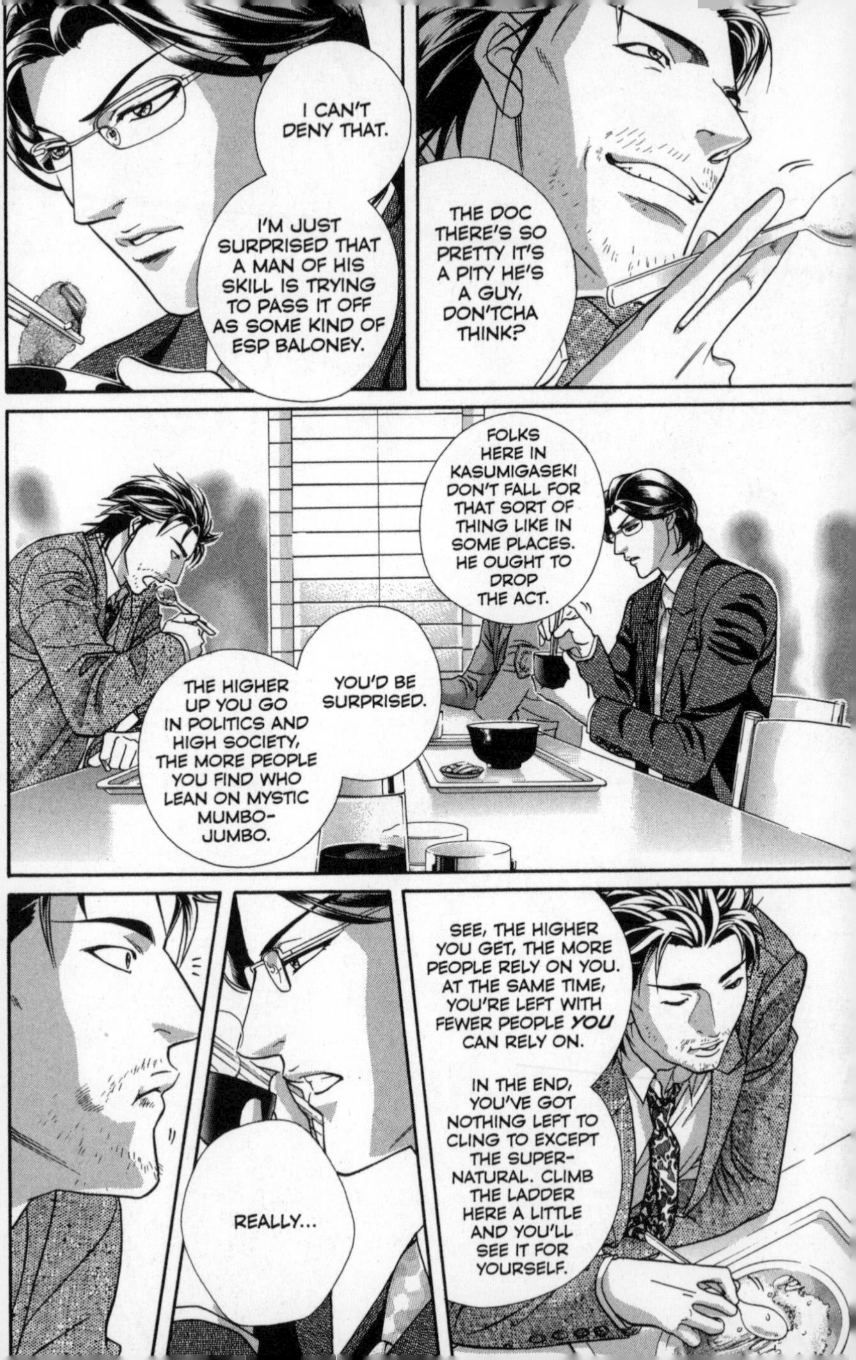
THE DOC THERE'S SO PRETTY IT'S A PITY HE'S A GUY, DON'TCHA THINK?
I CAN'T DENY THAT.
I'M JUST SURPRISED THAT A MAN OF HIS SKILL IS TRYING TO PASS IT OFF AS SOME KIND OF ESP BALONEY.
FOLKS HERE IN KASUMIGASEKI DON'T FALL FOR THAT SORT OF THING LIKE IN SOME PLACES. HE OUGHT TO DROP THE ACT.
YOU'D BE SURPRISED.
THE HIGHER UP YOU GO IN POLITICS AND HIGH SOCIETY, THE MORE PEOPLE YOU FIND WHO LEAN ON MYSTIC MUMBO-JUMBO.
SEE, THE HIGHER YOU GET, THE MORE PEOPLE RELY ON YOU. AT THE SAME TIME, YOU'RE LEFT WITH FEWER PEOPLE *YOU* CAN RELY ON.
IN THE END, YOU'VE GOT NOTHING LEFT TO CLING TO EXCEPT THE SUPER-NATURAL. CLIMB THE LADDER HERE A LITTLE AND YOU'LL SEE IT FOR YOURSELF.
REALLY...

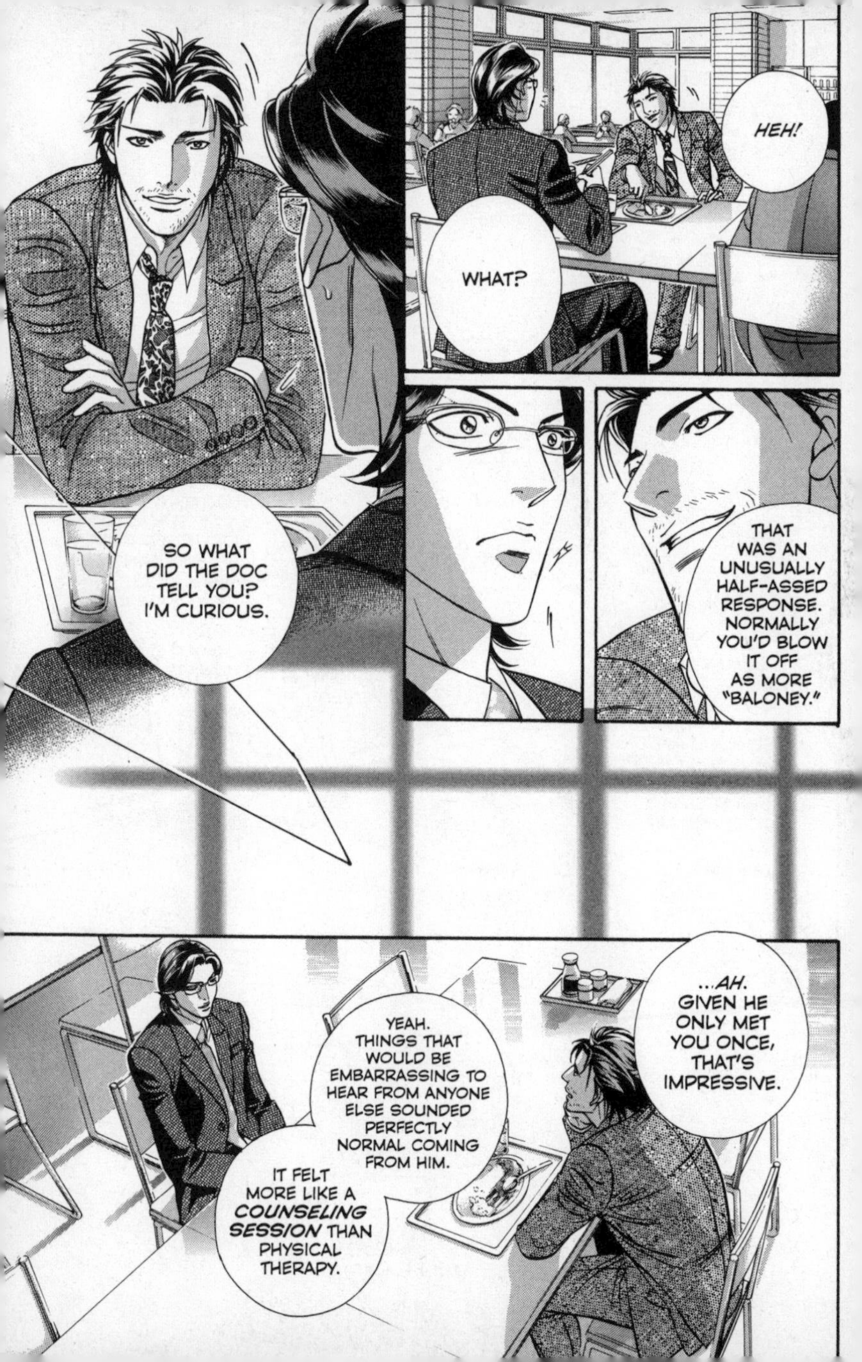
HEH!
WHAT?
THAT WAS AN UNUSUALLY HALF-ASSED RESPONSE. NORMALLY YOU'D BLOW IT OFF AS MORE "BALONEY."
SO WHAT DID THE DOC TELL YOU? I'M CURIOUS.
...*AH*. GIVEN HE ONLY MET YOU ONCE, THAT'S IMPRESSIVE.
YEAH. THINGS THAT WOULD BE EMBARRASSING TO HEAR FROM ANYONE ELSE SOUNDED PERFECTLY NORMAL COMING FROM HIM.
IT FELT MORE LIKE A *COUNSELING SESSION* THAN PHYSICAL THERAPY.

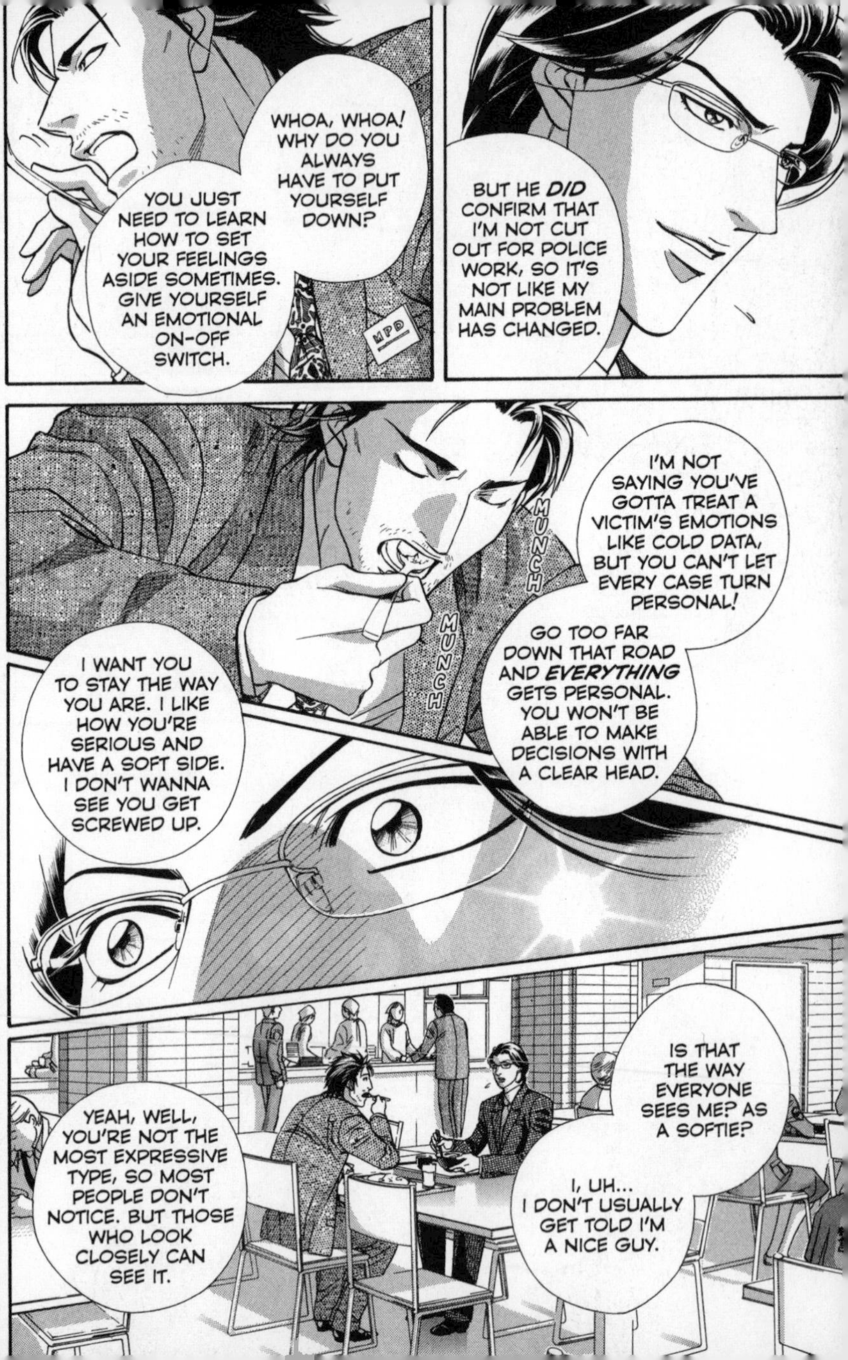
BUT HE *DID* CONFIRM THAT I'M NOT CUT OUT FOR POLICE WORK, SO IT'S NOT LIKE MY MAIN PROBLEM HAS CHANGED.
WHOA, WHOA! WHY DO YOU ALWAYS HAVE TO PUT YOURSELF DOWN?
YOU JUST NEED TO LEARN HOW TO SET YOUR FEELINGS ASIDE SOMETIMES. GIVE YOURSELF AN EMOTIONAL ON-OFF SWITCH.
MPD
I'M NOT SAYING YOU'VE GOTTA TREAT A VICTIM'S EMOTIONS LIKE COLD DATA, BUT YOU CAN'T LET EVERY CASE TURN PERSONAL!
MUNCH
MUNCH
GO TOO FAR DOWN THAT ROAD AND ***EVERYTHING*** GETS PERSONAL. YOU WON'T BE ABLE TO MAKE DECISIONS WITH A CLEAR HEAD.
I WANT YOU TO STAY THE WAY YOU ARE. I LIKE HOW YOU'RE SERIOUS AND HAVE A SOFT SIDE. I DON'T WANNA SEE YOU GET SCREWED UP.
IS THAT THE WAY EVERYONE SEES ME? AS A SOFTIE?
YEAH, WELL, YOU'RE NOT THE MOST EXPRESSIVE TYPE, SO MOST PEOPLE DON'T NOTICE. BUT THOSE WHO LOOK CLOSELY CAN SEE IT.
I, UH... I DON'T USUALLY GET TOLD I'M A NICE GUY.

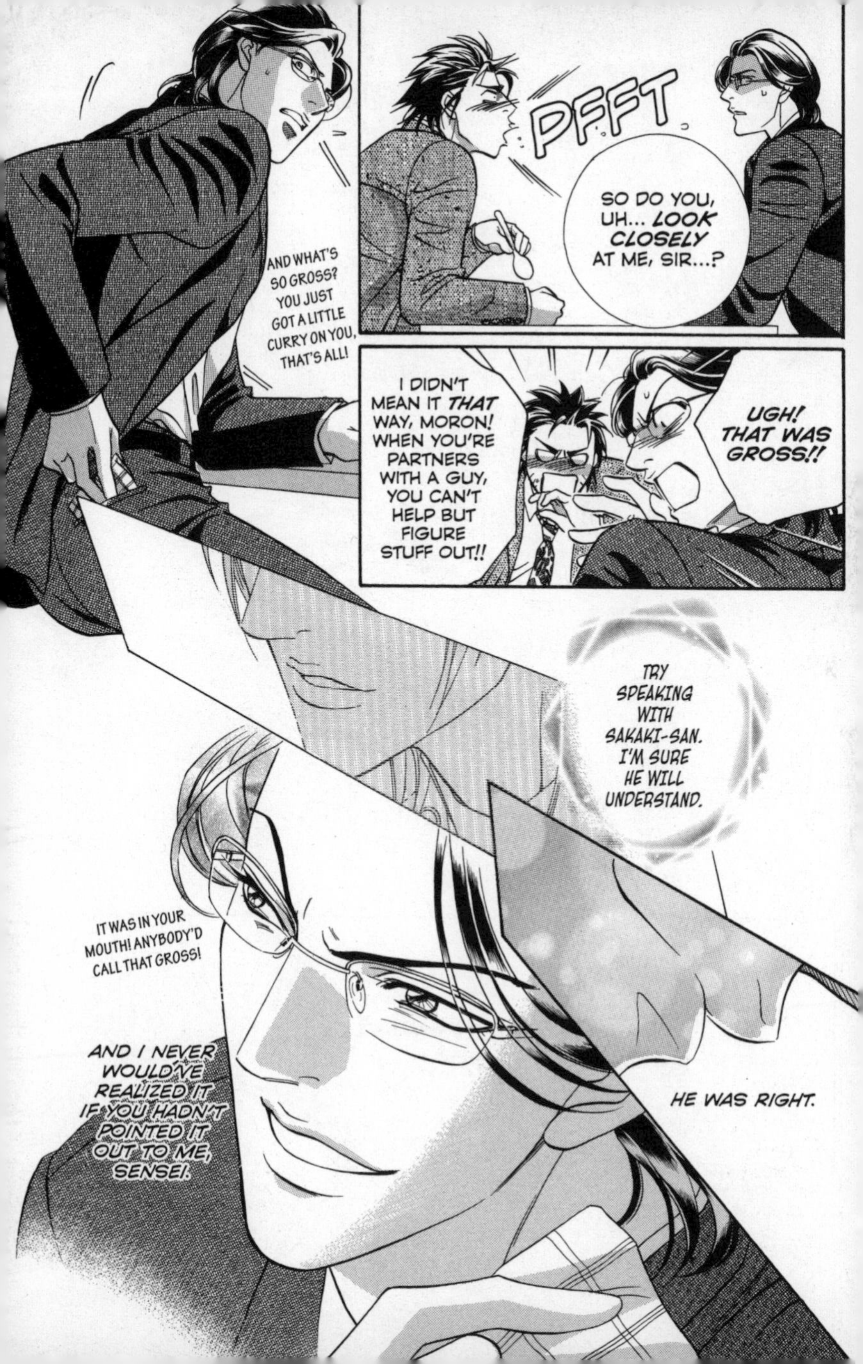
PFFT
SO DO YOU, UH... *LOOK CLOSELY* AT ME, SIR...?
UGH! THAT WAS GROSS!!
I DIDN'T MEAN IT *THAT* WAY, MORON! WHEN YOU'RE PARTNERS WITH A GUY, YOU CAN'T HELP BUT FIGURE STUFF OUT!!
AND WHAT'S SO GROSS? YOU JUST GOT A LITTLE CURRY ON YOU, THAT'S ALL!
IT WAS IN YOUR MOUTH! ANYBODY'D CALL THAT GROSS!
TRY SPEAKING WITH SAKAKI-SAN. I'M SURE HE WILL UNDERSTAND.
HE WAS RIGHT.
AND I NEVER WOULD'VE REALIZED IT IF YOU HADN'T POINTED IT OUT TO ME, SENSEI.

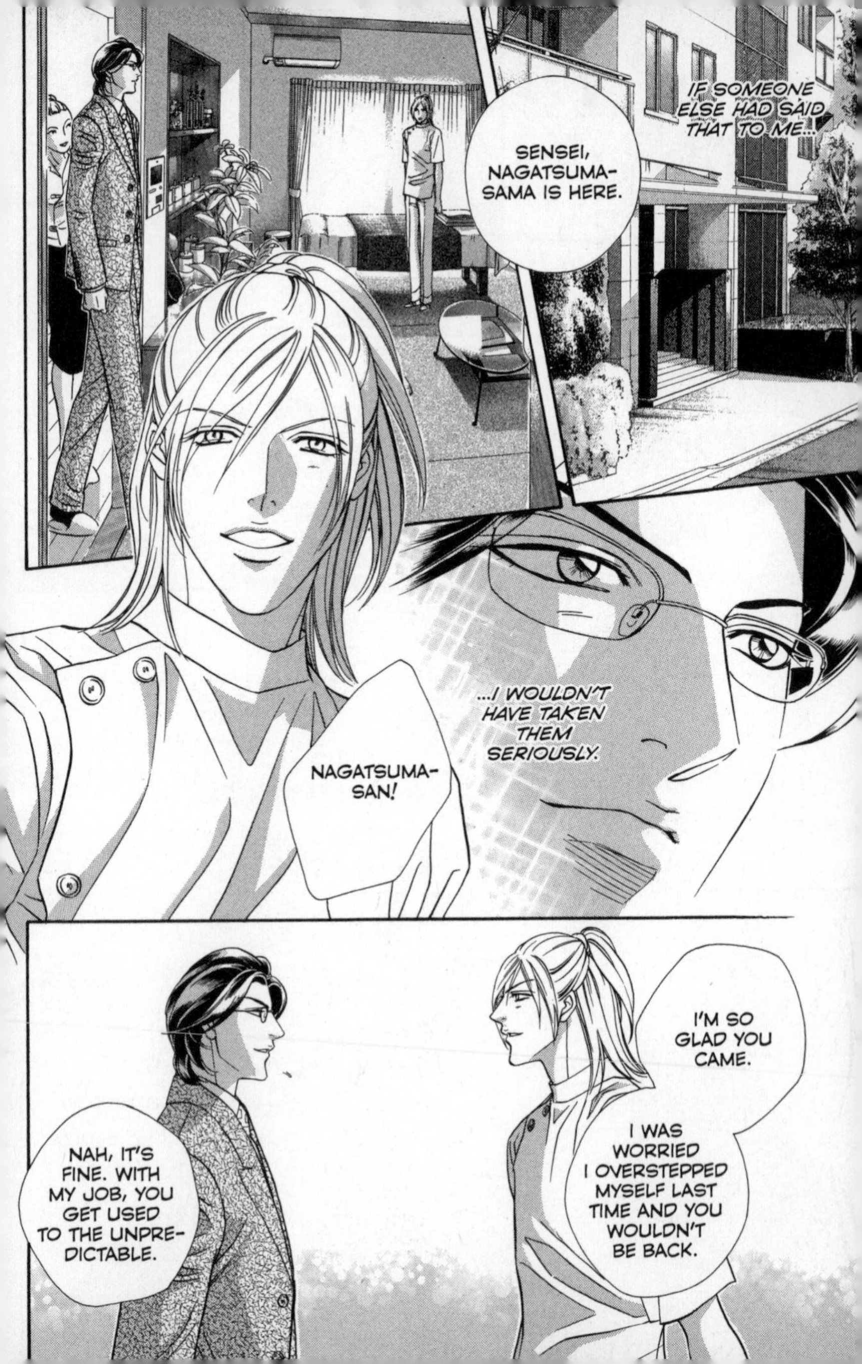
IF SOMEONE ELSE HAD SAID THAT TO ME...
SENSEI, NAGATSUMA-SAMA IS HERE.
...I WOULDN'T HAVE TAKEN THEM SERIOUSLY.
NAGATSUMA-SAN!
I'M SO GLAD YOU CAME.
I WAS WORRIED I OVERSTEPPED MYSELF LAST TIME AND YOU WOULDN'T BE BACK.
NAH, IT'S FINE. WITH MY JOB, YOU GET USED TO THE UNPREDICTABLE.

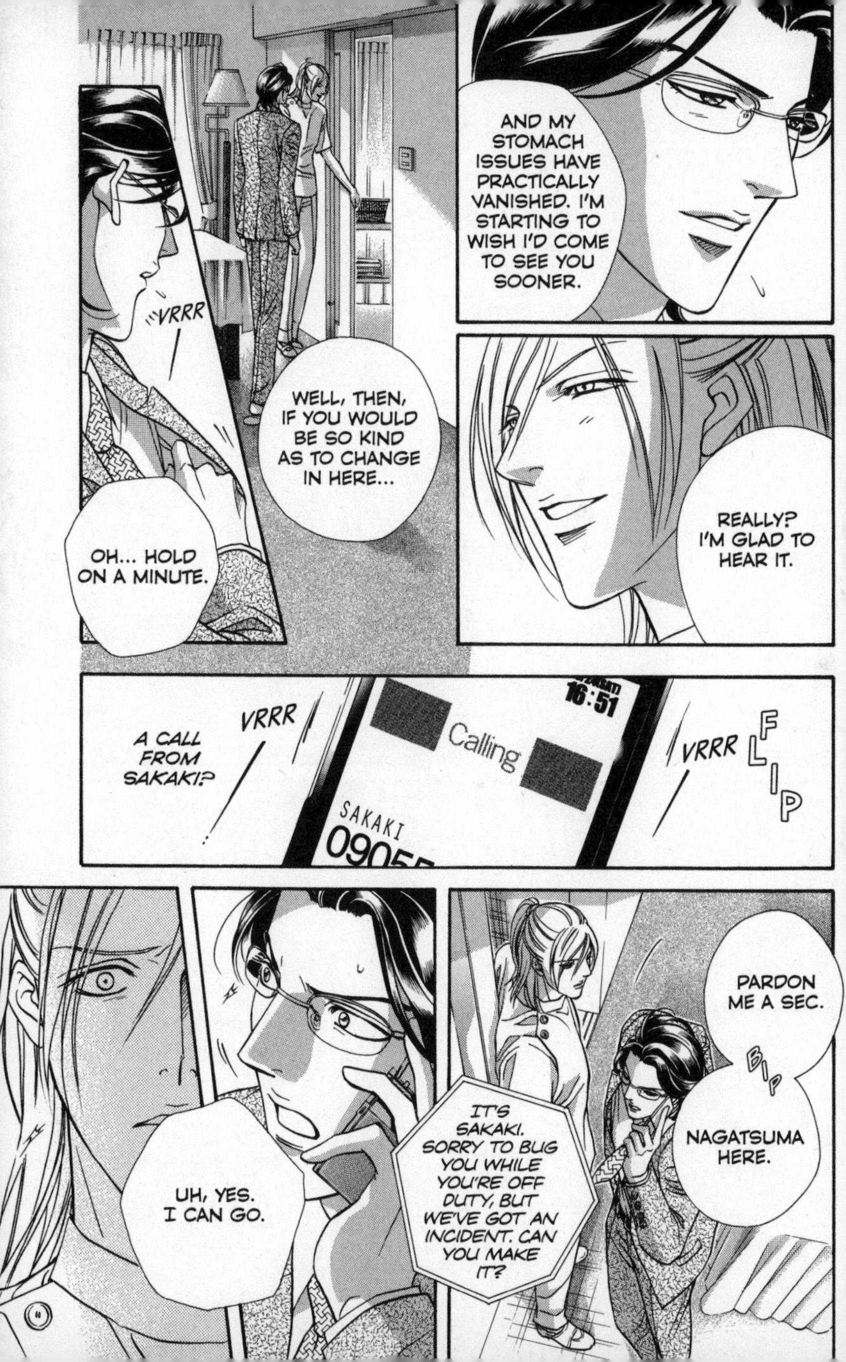

AND MY STOMACH ISSUES HAVE PRACTICALLY VANISHED. I'M STARTING TO WISH I'D COME TO SEE YOU SOONER.
REALLY? I'M GLAD TO HEAR IT.
WELL, THEN, IF YOU WOULD BE SO KIND AS TO CHANGE IN HERE...
VRRR
OH... HOLD ON A MINUTE.
FLIP
VRRR
16:51
Calling
SAKAKI
0905
VRRR
A CALL FROM SAKAKI?
PARDON ME A SEC.
BIP
NAGATSUMA HERE.
IT'S SAKAKI. SORRY TO BUG YOU WHILE YOU'RE OFF DUTY, BUT WE'VE GOT AN INCIDENT. CAN YOU MAKE IT?
UH, YES. I CAN GO.

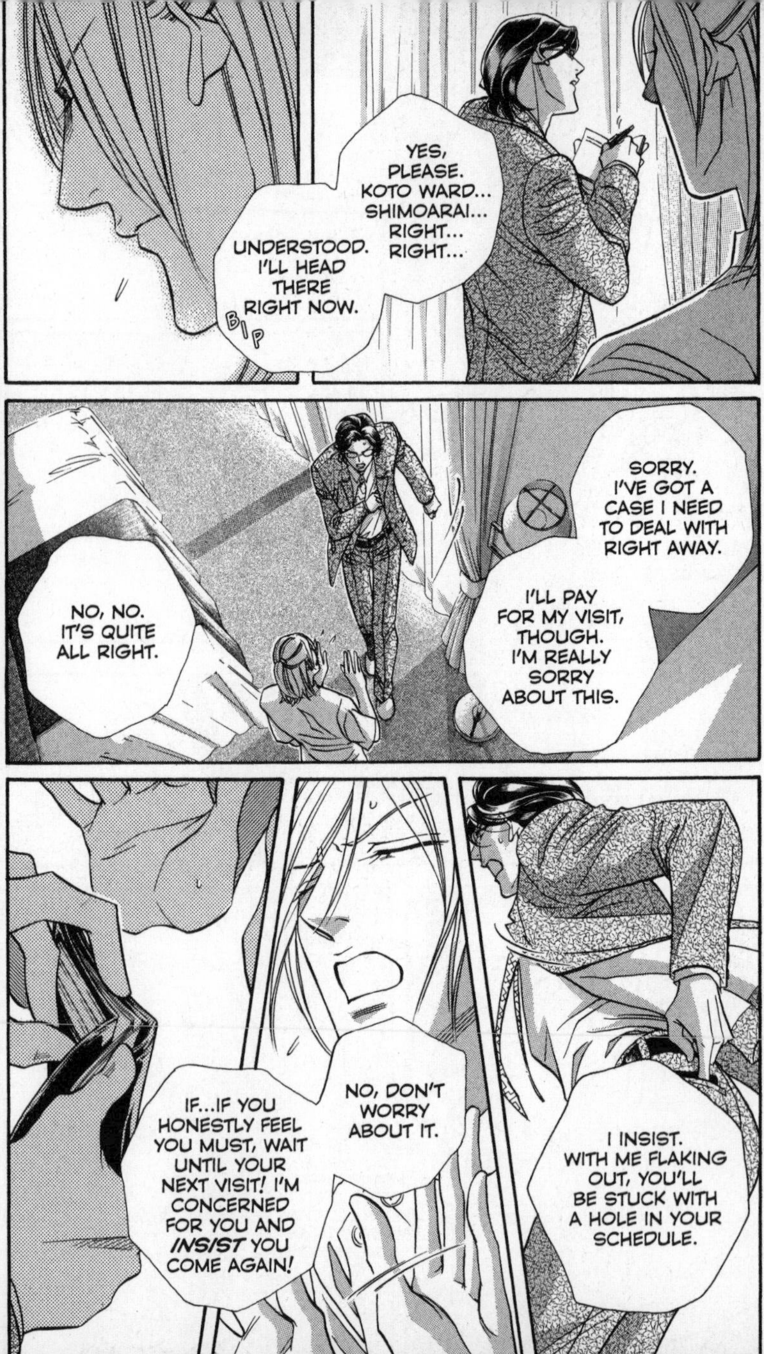
YES, PLEASE. KOTO WARD... SHIMOARAI... RIGHT... RIGHT...
UNDERSTOOD. I'LL HEAD THERE RIGHT NOW.
BIP
SORRY. I'VE GOT A CASE I NEED TO DEAL WITH RIGHT AWAY.
I'LL PAY FOR MY VISIT, THOUGH. I'M REALLY SORRY ABOUT THIS.
NO, NO. IT'S QUITE ALL RIGHT.
I INSIST. WITH ME FLAKING OUT, YOU'LL BE STUCK WITH A HOLE IN YOUR SCHEDULE.
NO, DON'T WORRY ABOUT IT.
IF...IF YOU HONESTLY FEEL YOU MUST, WAIT UNTIL YOUR NEXT VISIT! I'M CONCERNED FOR YOU AND *INSIST* YOU COME AGAIN!

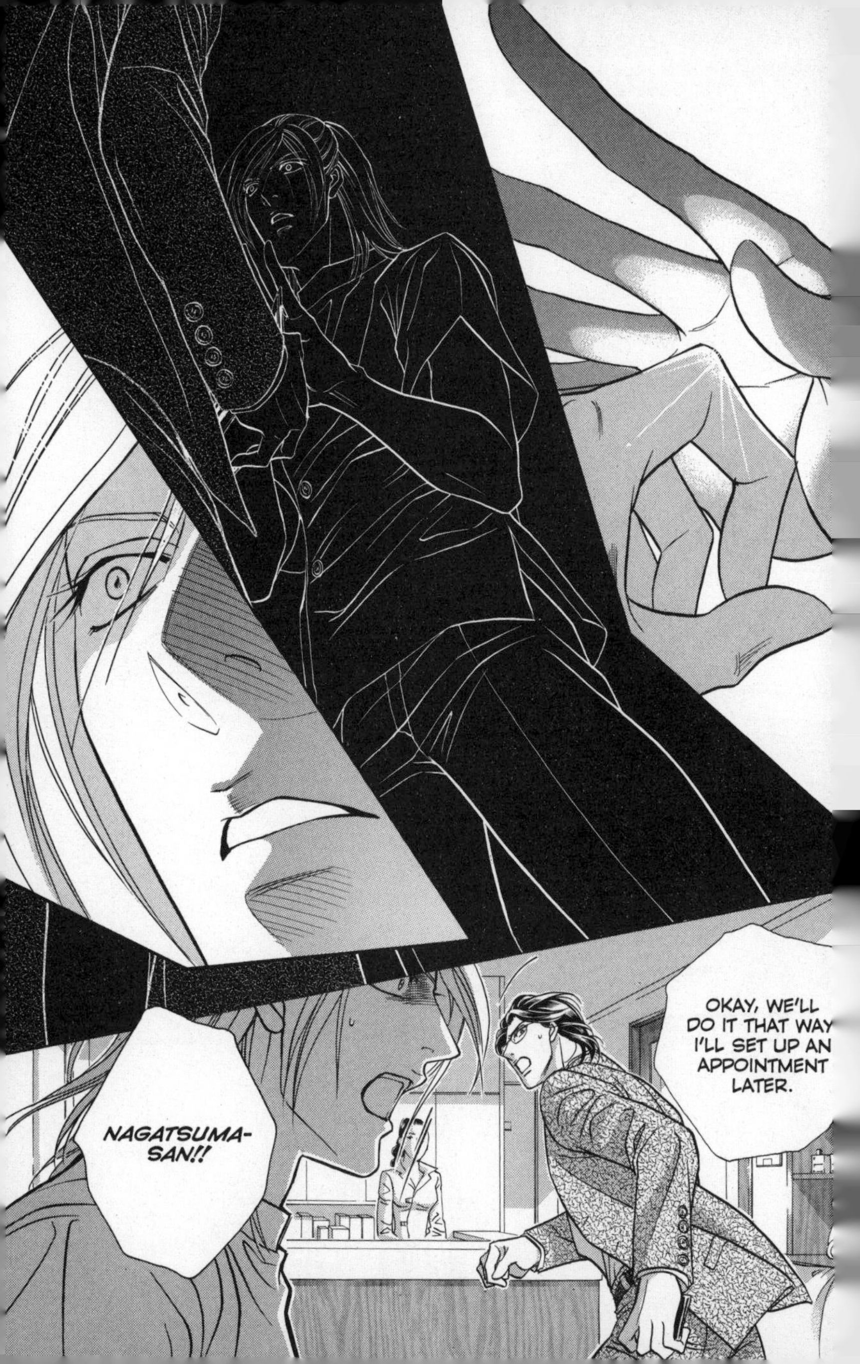
OKAY, WE'LL DO IT THAT WAY I'LL SET UP AN APPOINTMENT LATER.
NAGATSUMA-SAN!!

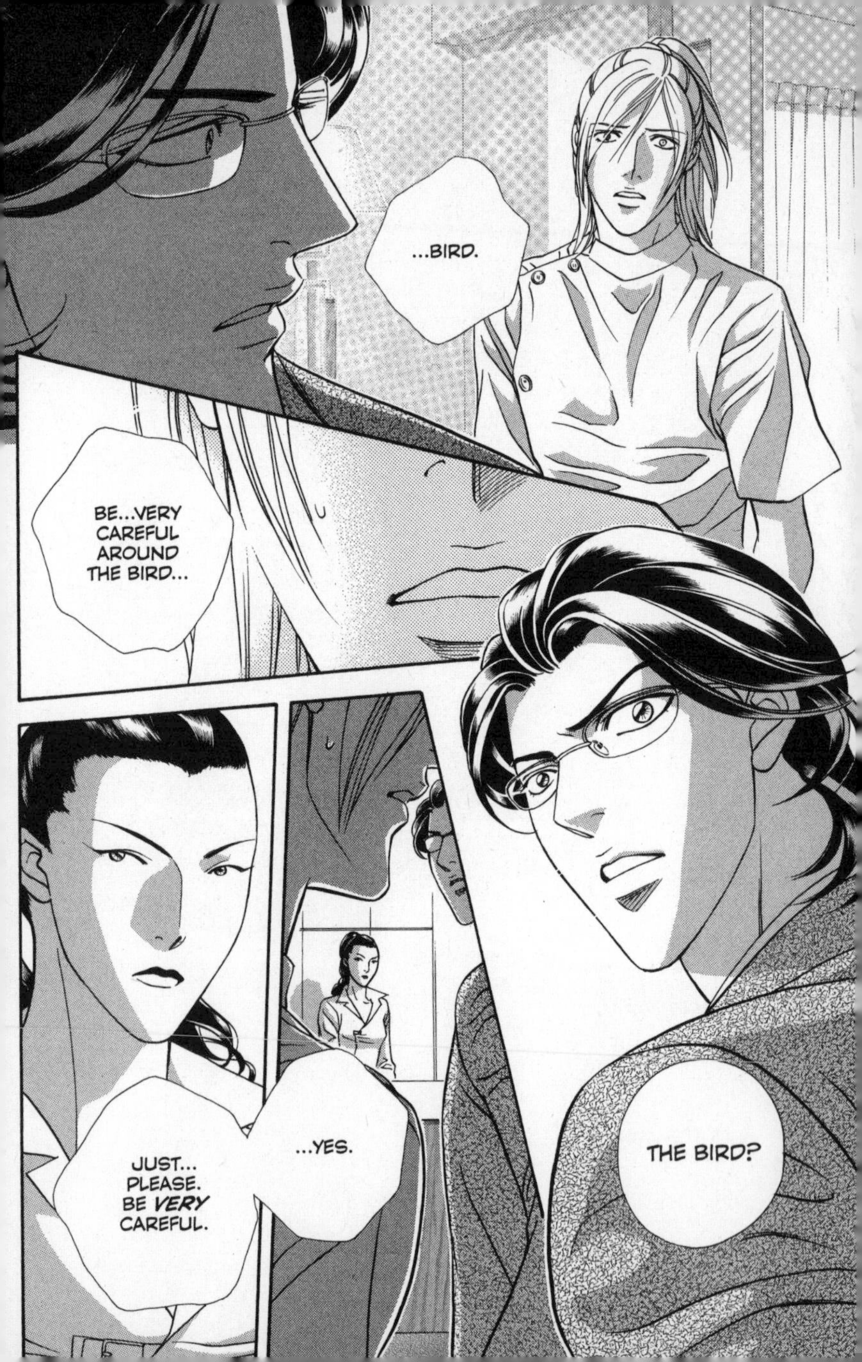
...BIRD.
BE...VERY CAREFUL AROUND THE BIRD...
THE BIRD?
...YES.
JUST... PLEASE. BE VERY CAREFUL.

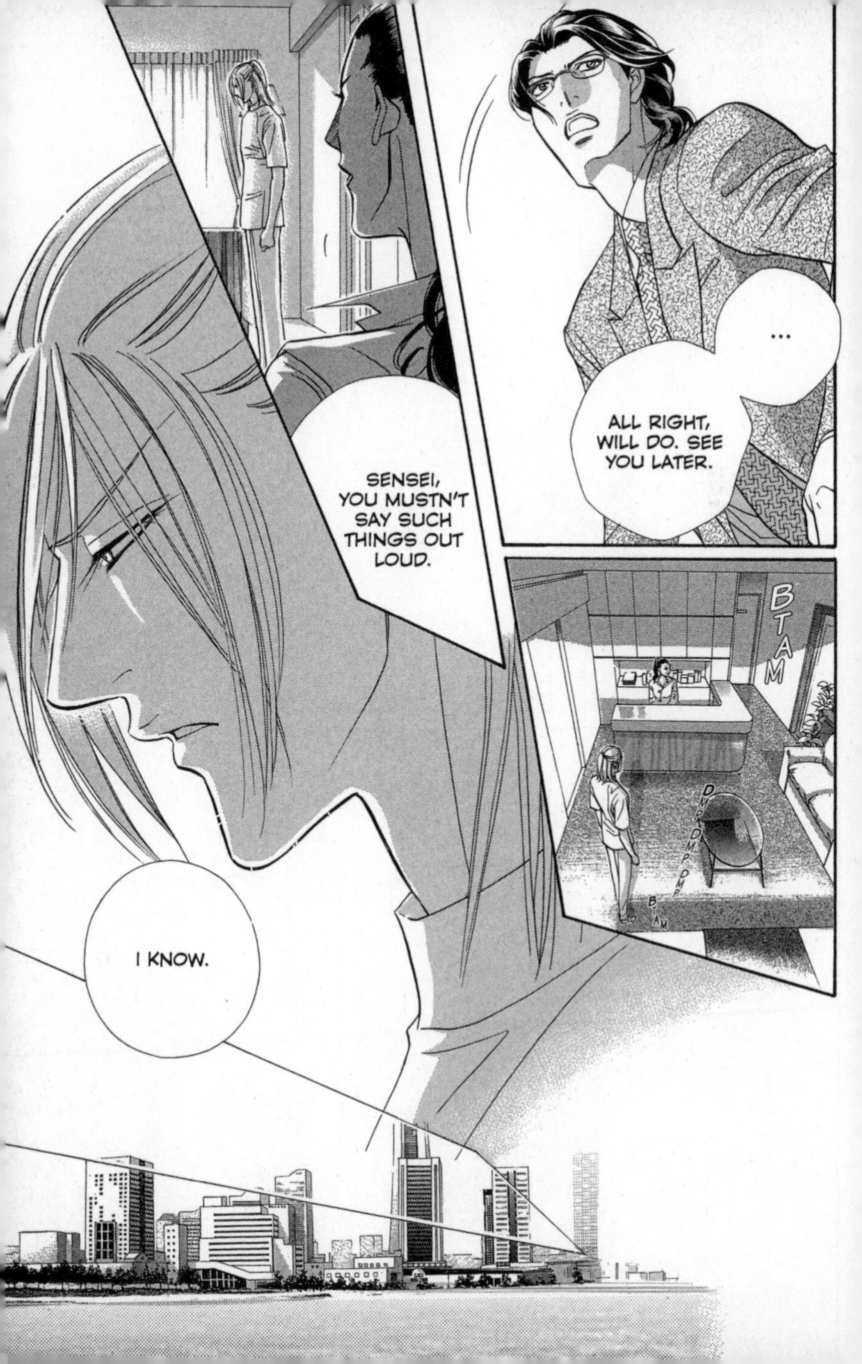
...
ALL RIGHT, WILL DO. SEE YOU LATER.
SENSEI, YOU MUSTN'T SAY SUCH THINGS OUT LOUD.
BTAM
DMP DMP DMP DMP
BTAM
I KNOW.

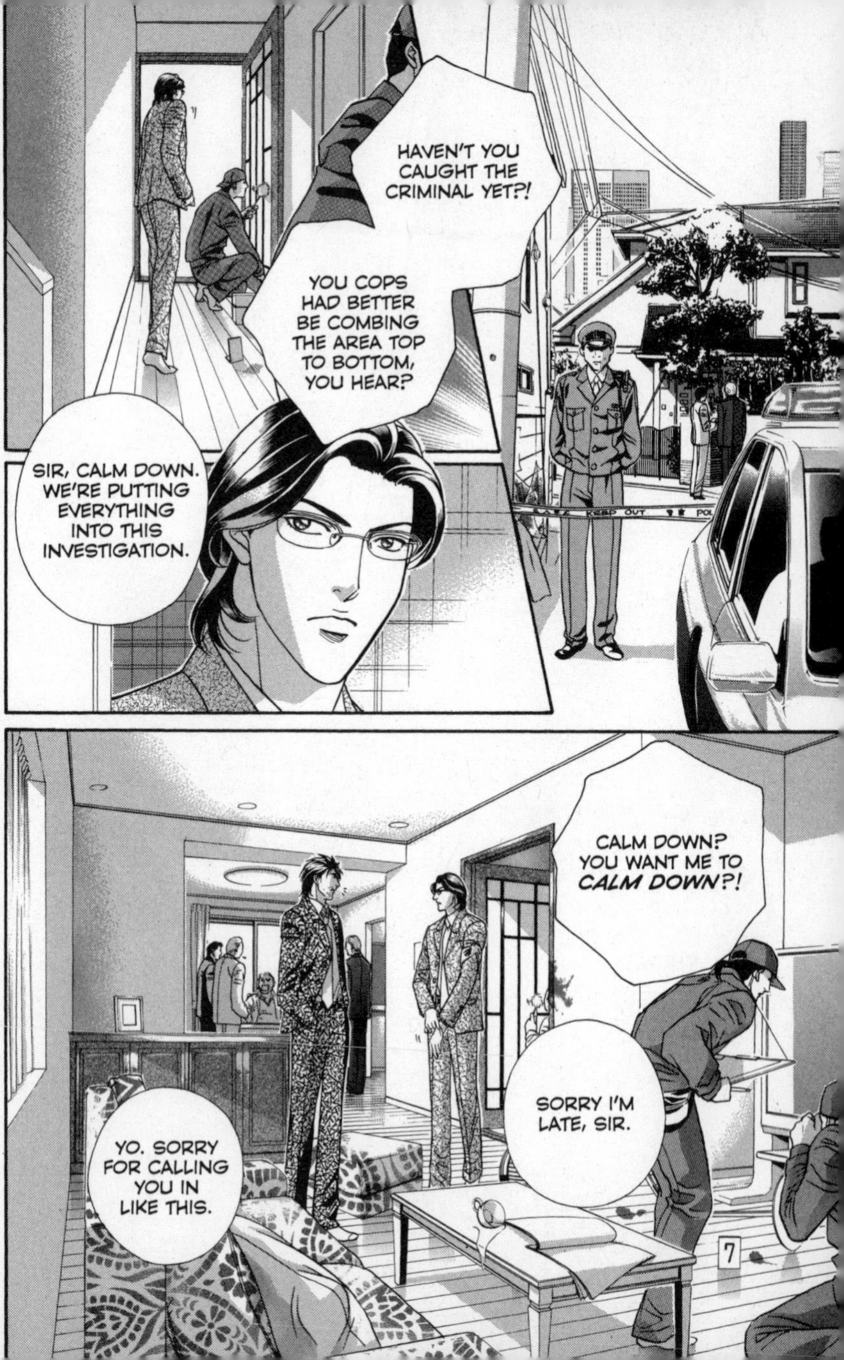
HAVEN'T YOU CAUGHT THE CRIMINAL YET?!
YOU COPS HAD BETTER BE COMBING THE AREA TOP TO BOTTOM, YOU HEAR?
KEEP OUT
SIR, CALM DOWN. WE'RE PUTTING EVERYTHING INTO THIS INVESTIGATION.
CALM DOWN? YOU WANT ME TO *CALM DOWN*?!
SORRY I'M LATE, SIR.
YO. SORRY FOR CALLING YOU IN LIKE THIS.
7

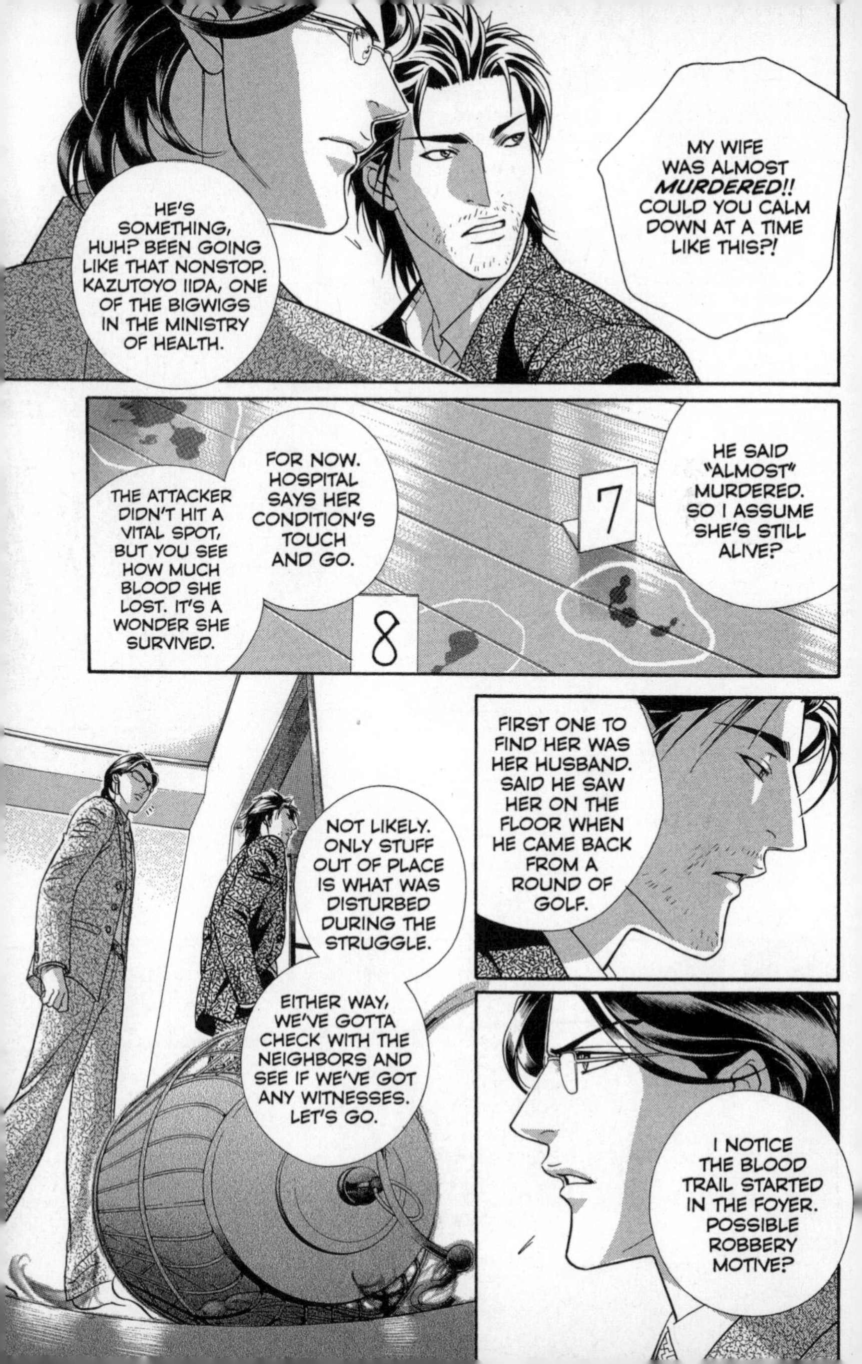
MY WIFE WAS ALMOST ***MURDERED***!! COULD YOU CALM DOWN AT A TIME LIKE THIS?!
HE'S SOMETHING, HUH? BEEN GOING LIKE THAT NONSTOP. KAZUTOYO IIDA, ONE OF THE BIGWIGS IN THE MINISTRY OF HEALTH.
HE SAID "ALMOST" MURDERED. SO I ASSUME SHE'S STILL ALIVE?
7
FOR NOW. HOSPITAL SAYS HER CONDITION'S TOUCH AND GO.
THE ATTACKER DIDN'T HIT A VITAL SPOT, BUT YOU SEE HOW MUCH BLOOD SHE LOST. IT'S A WONDER SHE SURVIVED.
8
FIRST ONE TO FIND HER WAS HER HUSBAND. SAID HE SAW HER ON THE FLOOR WHEN HE CAME BACK FROM A ROUND OF GOLF.
I NOTICE THE BLOOD TRAIL STARTED IN THE FOYER. POSSIBLE ROBBERY MOTIVE?
NOT LIKELY. ONLY STUFF OUT OF PLACE IS WHAT WAS DISTURBED DURING THE STRUGGLE.
EITHER WAY, WE'VE GOTTA CHECK WITH THE NEIGHBORS AND SEE IF WE'VE GOT ANY WITNESSES. LET'S GO.

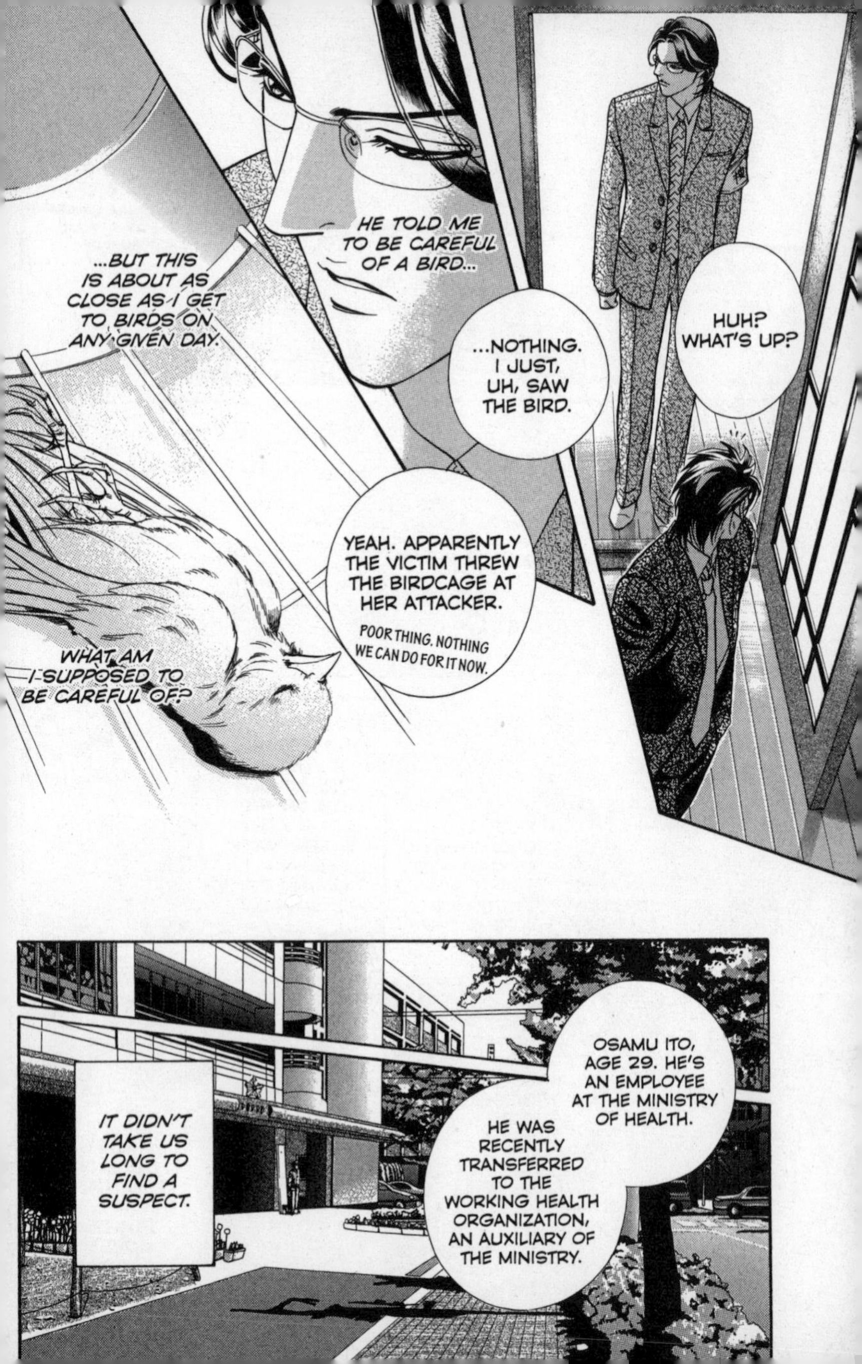
HUH? WHAT'S UP?
...NOTHING. I JUST, UH, SAW THE BIRD.
YEAH. APPARENTLY THE VICTIM THREW THE BIRDCAGE AT HER ATTACKER.
POOR THING. NOTHING WE CAN DO FOR IT NOW.
HE TOLD ME TO BE CAREFUL OF A BIRD...
...BUT THIS IS ABOUT AS CLOSE AS I GET TO BIRDS ON ANY GIVEN DAY.
WHAT AM I SUPPOSED TO BE CAREFUL OF?
OSAMU ITO, AGE 29. HE'S AN EMPLOYEE AT THE MINISTRY OF HEALTH.
HE WAS RECENTLY TRANSFERRED TO THE WORKING HEALTH ORGANIZATION, AN AUXILIARY OF THE MINISTRY.
IT DIDN'T TAKE US LONG TO FIND A SUSPECT.

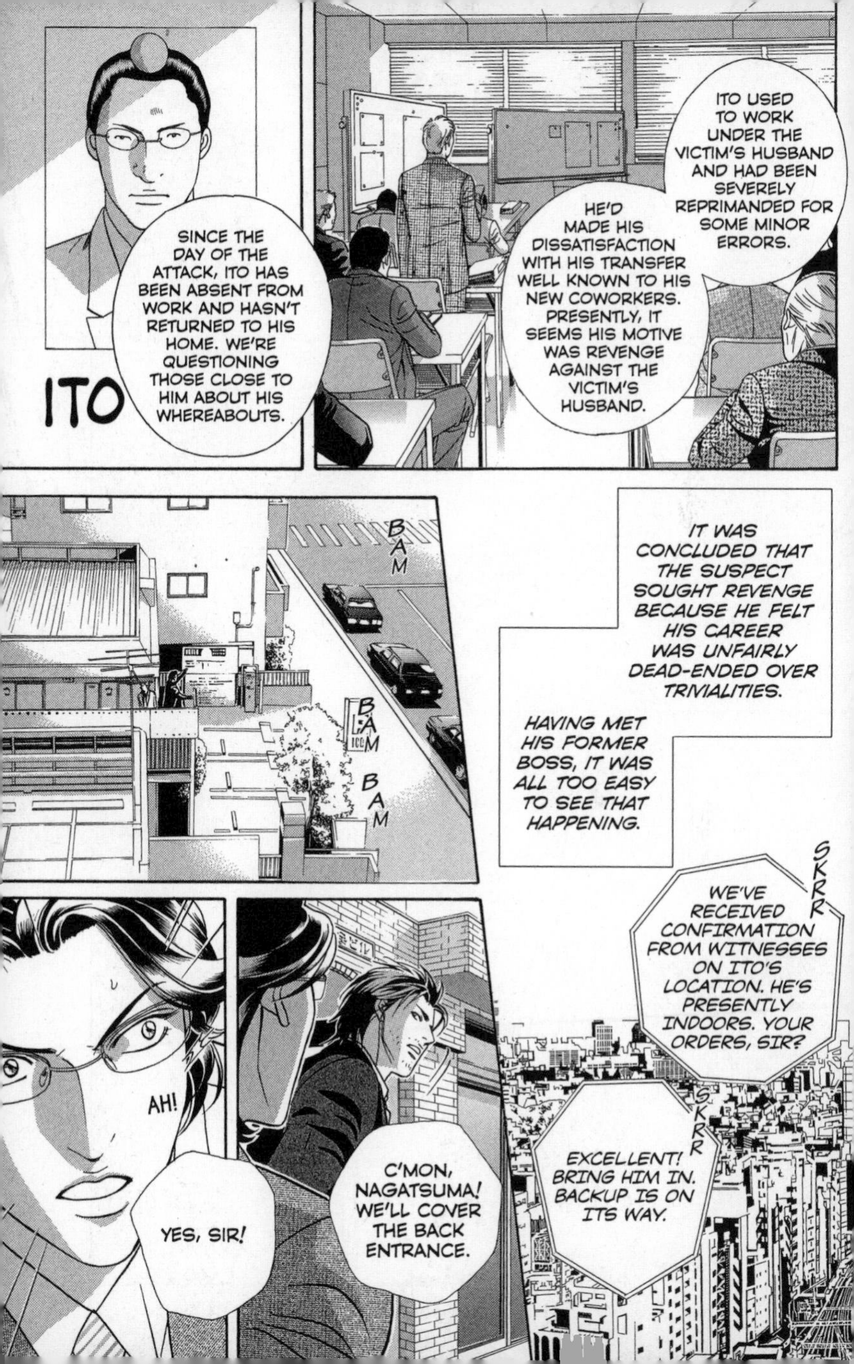
ITO USED TO WORK UNDER THE VICTIM'S HUSBAND AND HAD BEEN SEVERELY REPRIMANDED FOR SOME MINOR ERRORS.
HE'D MADE HIS DISSATISFACTION WITH HIS TRANSFER WELL KNOWN TO HIS NEW COWORKERS. PRESENTLY, IT SEEMS HIS MOTIVE WAS REVENGE AGAINST THE VICTIM'S HUSBAND.
SINCE THE DAY OF THE ATTACK, ITO HAS BEEN ABSENT FROM WORK AND HASN'T RETURNED TO HIS HOME. WE'RE QUESTIONING THOSE CLOSE TO HIM ABOUT HIS WHEREABOUTS.
ITO
IT WAS CONCLUDED THAT THE SUSPECT SOUGHT REVENGE BECAUSE HE FELT HIS CAREER WAS UNFAIRLY DEAD-ENDED OVER TRIVIALITIES.
HAVING MET HIS FORMER BOSS, IT WAS ALL TOO EASY TO SEE THAT HAPPENING.
BAM
BAM
BAM
SKRR
WE'VE RECEIVED CONFIRMATION FROM WITNESSES ON ITO'S LOCATION. HE'S PRESENTLY INDOORS. YOUR ORDERS, SIR?
SKRR
EXCELLENT! BRING HIM IN. BACKUP IS ON ITS WAY.
C'MON, NAGATSUMA! WE'LL COVER THE BACK ENTRANCE.
AH!
YES, SIR!

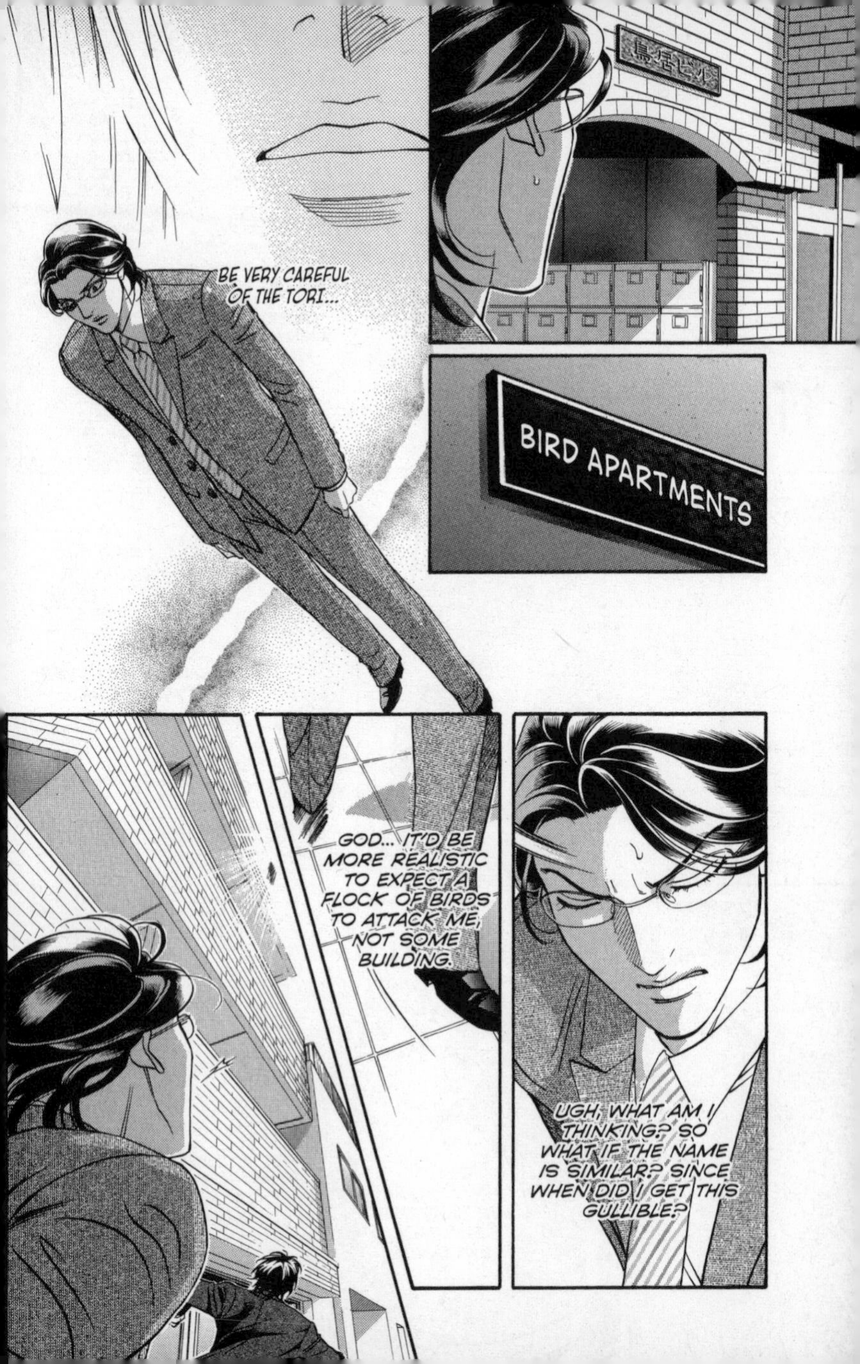
鳥居ビル
BIRD APARTMENTS
BE VERY CAREFUL OF THE TORI...
UGH, WHAT AM I THINKING? SO WHAT IF THE NAME IS SIMILAR? SINCE WHEN DID I GET THIS GULLIBLE?
GOD... IT'D BE MORE REALISTIC TO EXPECT A FLOCK OF BIRDS TO ATTACK ME, NOT SOME BUILDING.

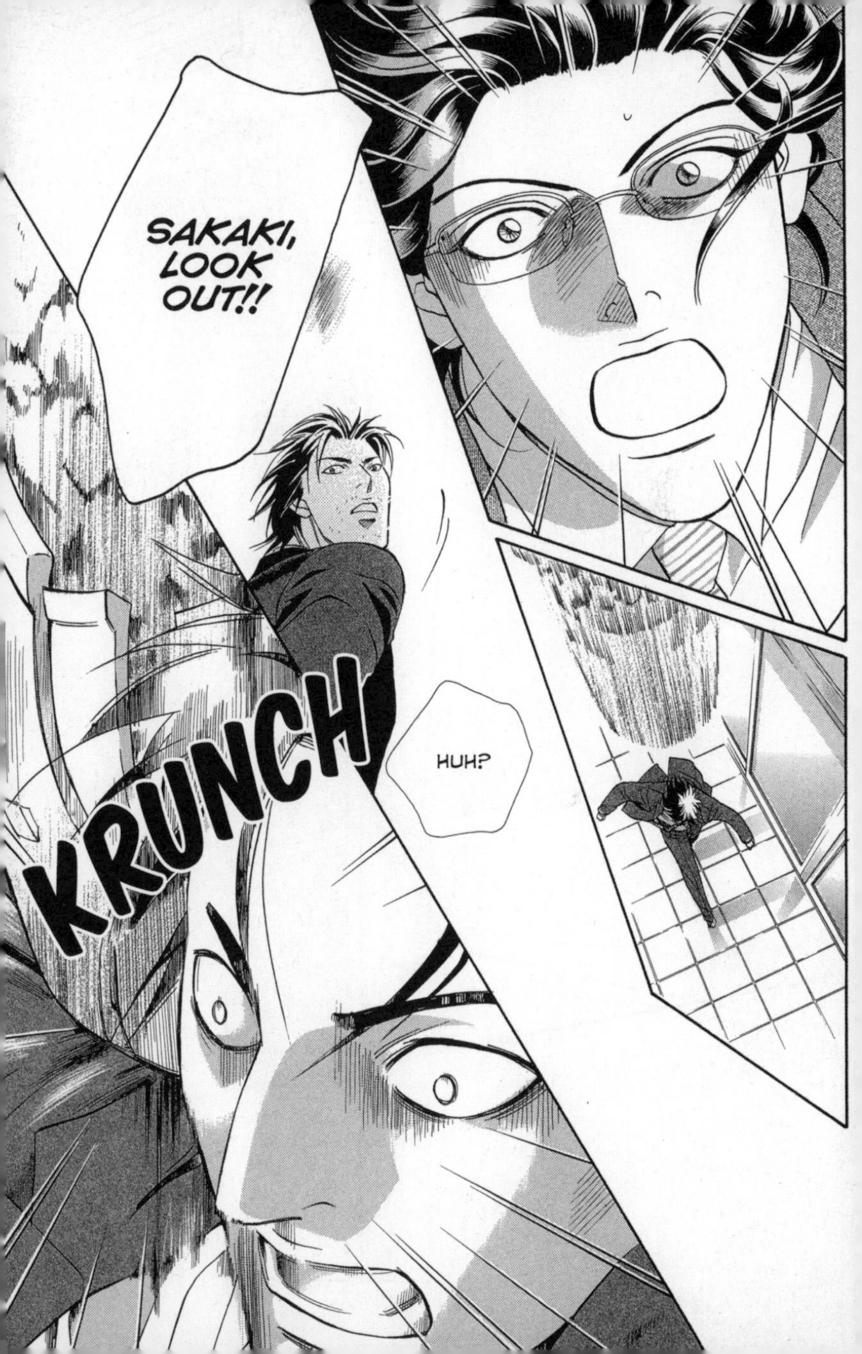
SAKAKI, LOOK OUT!!
HUH?
KRUNCH

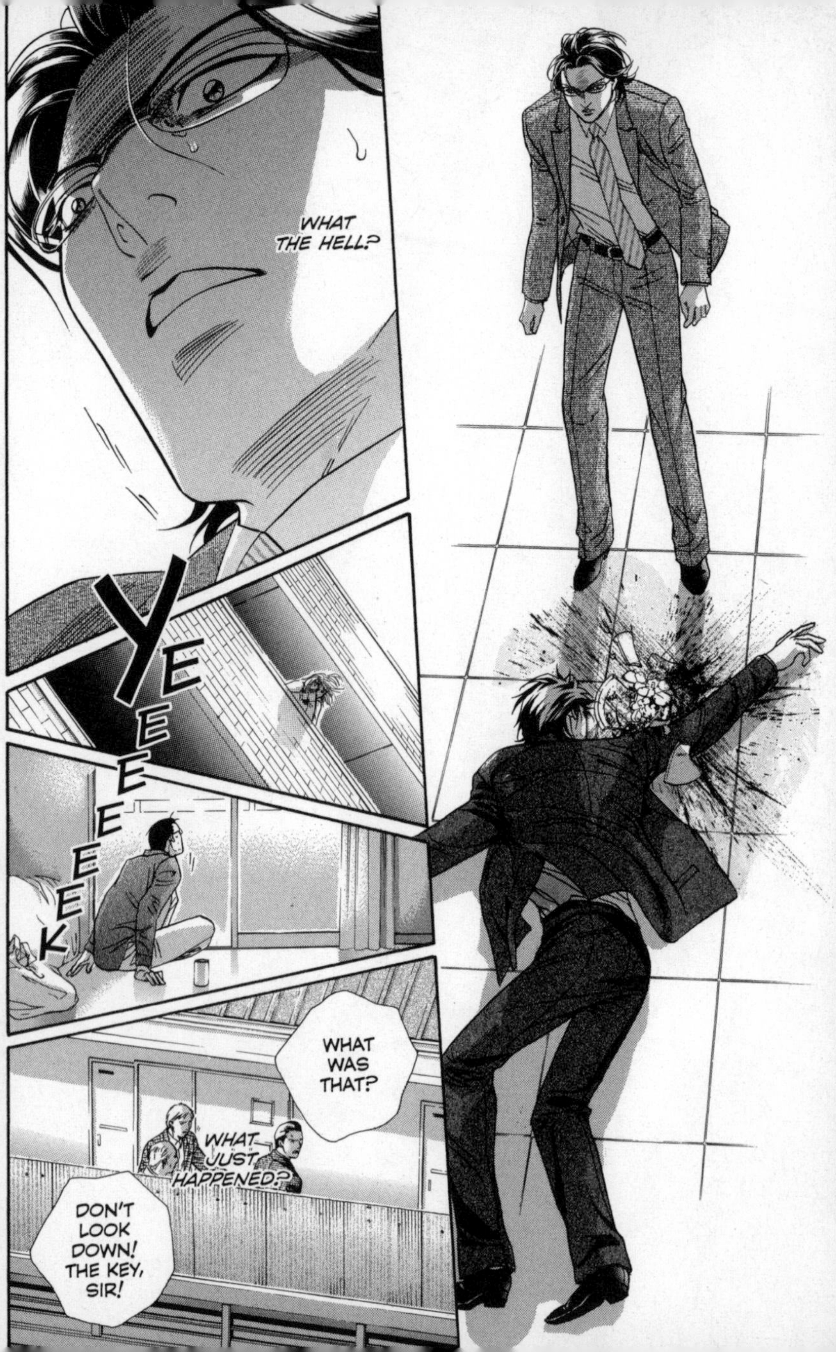
WHAT THE HELL?
YEEEEEEEK
WHAT WAS THAT?
WHAT JUST HAPPENED?
DON'T LOOK DOWN! THE KEY, SIR!

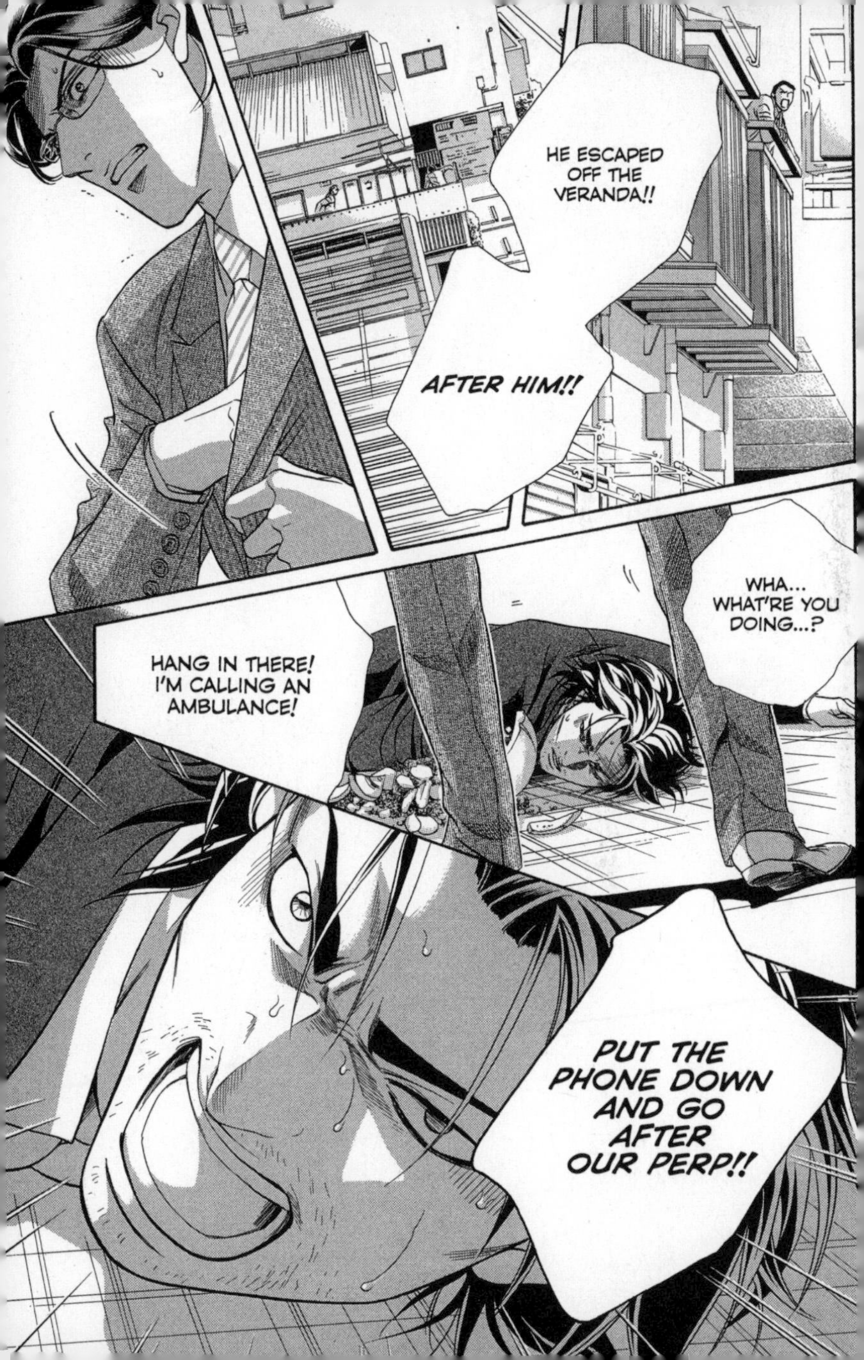
HE ESCAPED OFF THE VERANDA!!
AFTER HIM!!
WHA... WHAT'RE YOU DOING...?
HANG IN THERE! I'M CALLING AN AMBULANCE!
PUT THE PHONE DOWN AND GO AFTER OUR PERP!!

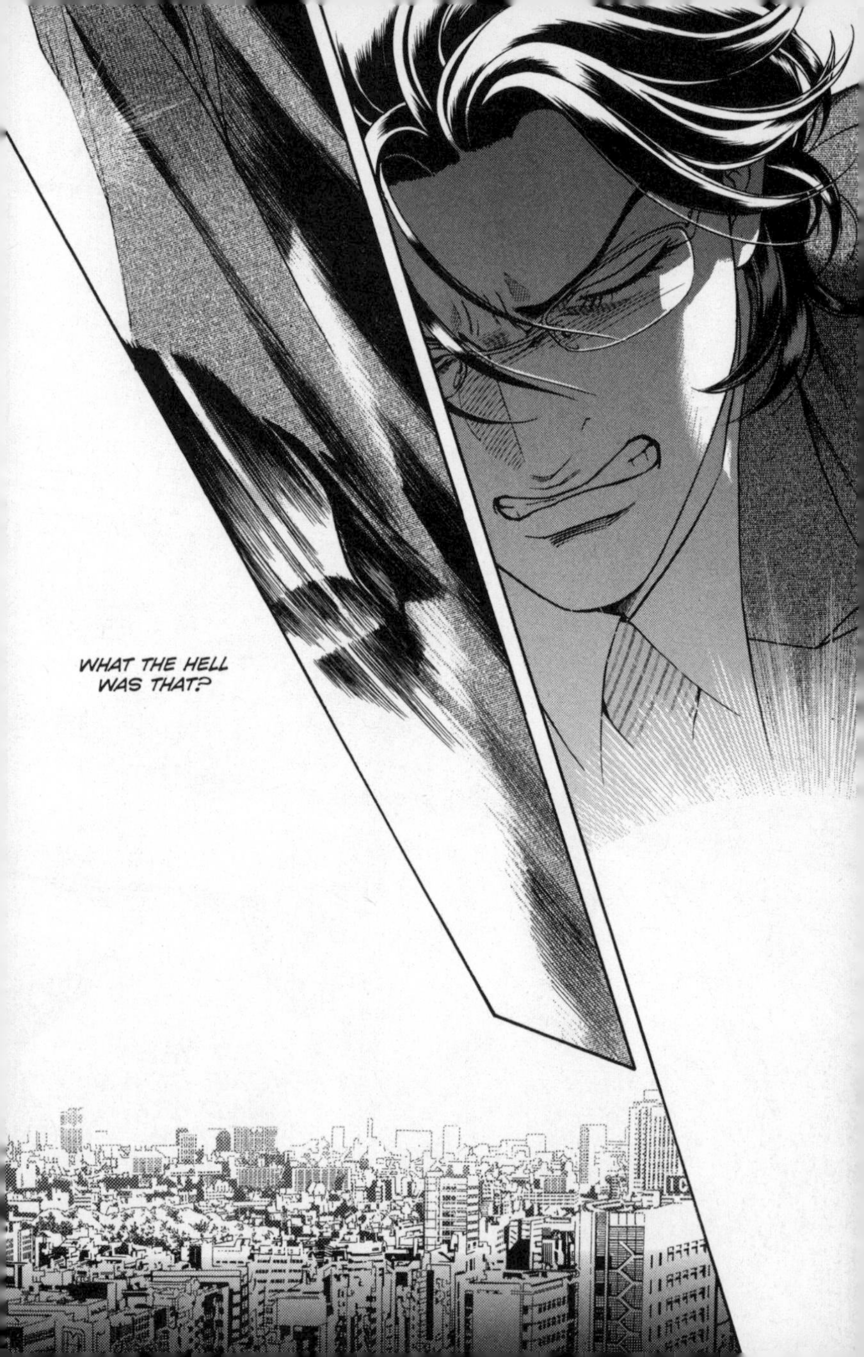
WHAT THE HELL WAS THAT?

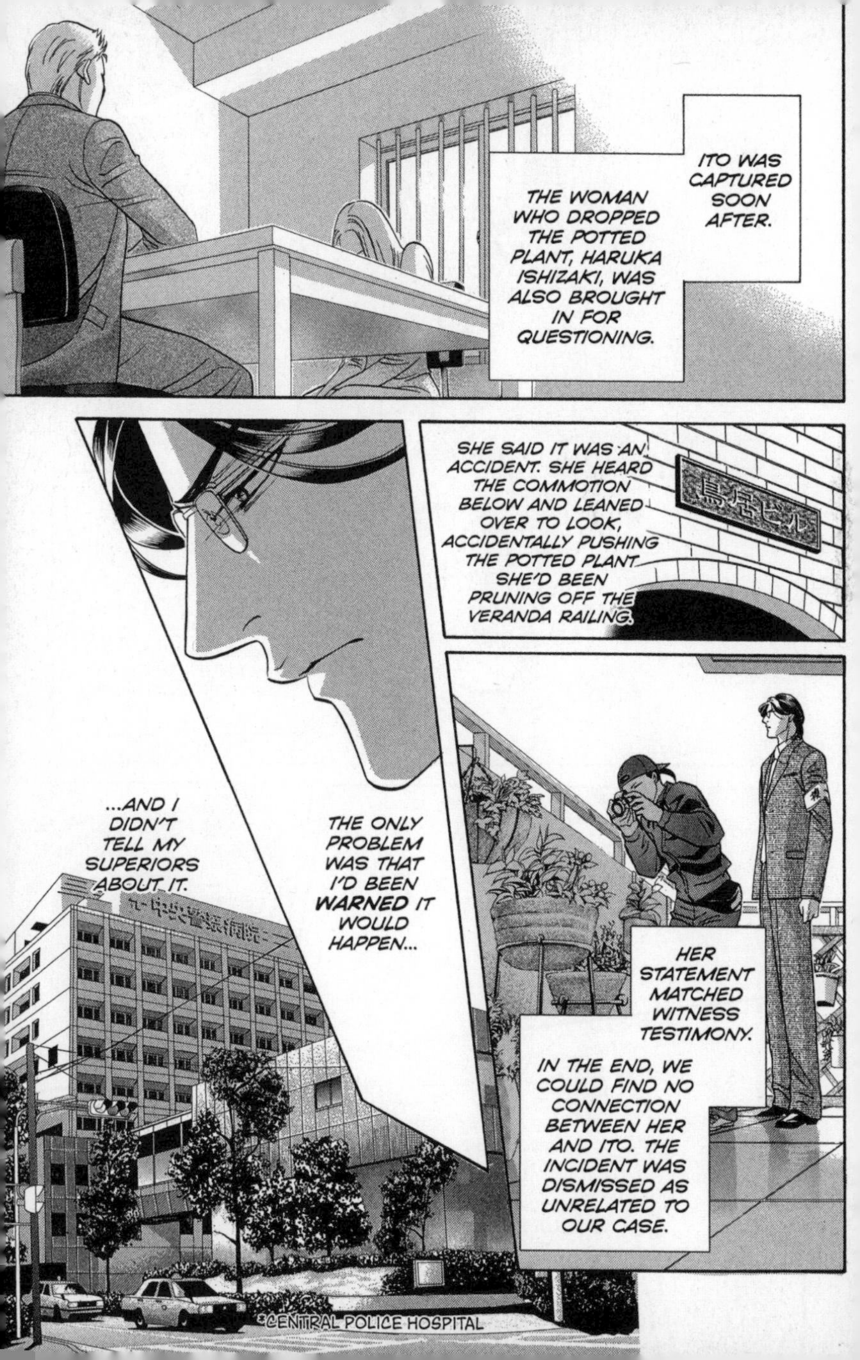
ITO WAS CAPTURED SOON AFTER.
THE WOMAN WHO DROPPED THE POTTED PLANT, HARUKA ISHIZAKI, WAS ALSO BROUGHT IN FOR QUESTIONING.
SHE SAID IT WAS AN ACCIDENT. SHE HEARD THE COMMOTION BELOW AND LEANED OVER TO LOOK, ACCIDENTALLY PUSHING THE POTTED PLANT SHE'D BEEN PRUNING OFF THE VERANDA RAILING.
HER STATEMENT MATCHED WITNESS TESTIMONY.
IN THE END, WE COULD FIND NO CONNECTION BETWEEN HER AND ITO. THE INCIDENT WAS DISMISSED AS UNRELATED TO OUR CASE.
THE ONLY PROBLEM WAS THAT I'D BEEN WARNED IT WOULD HAPPEN...
...AND I DIDN'T TELL MY SUPERIORS ABOUT IT.
*CENTRAL POLICE HOSPITAL

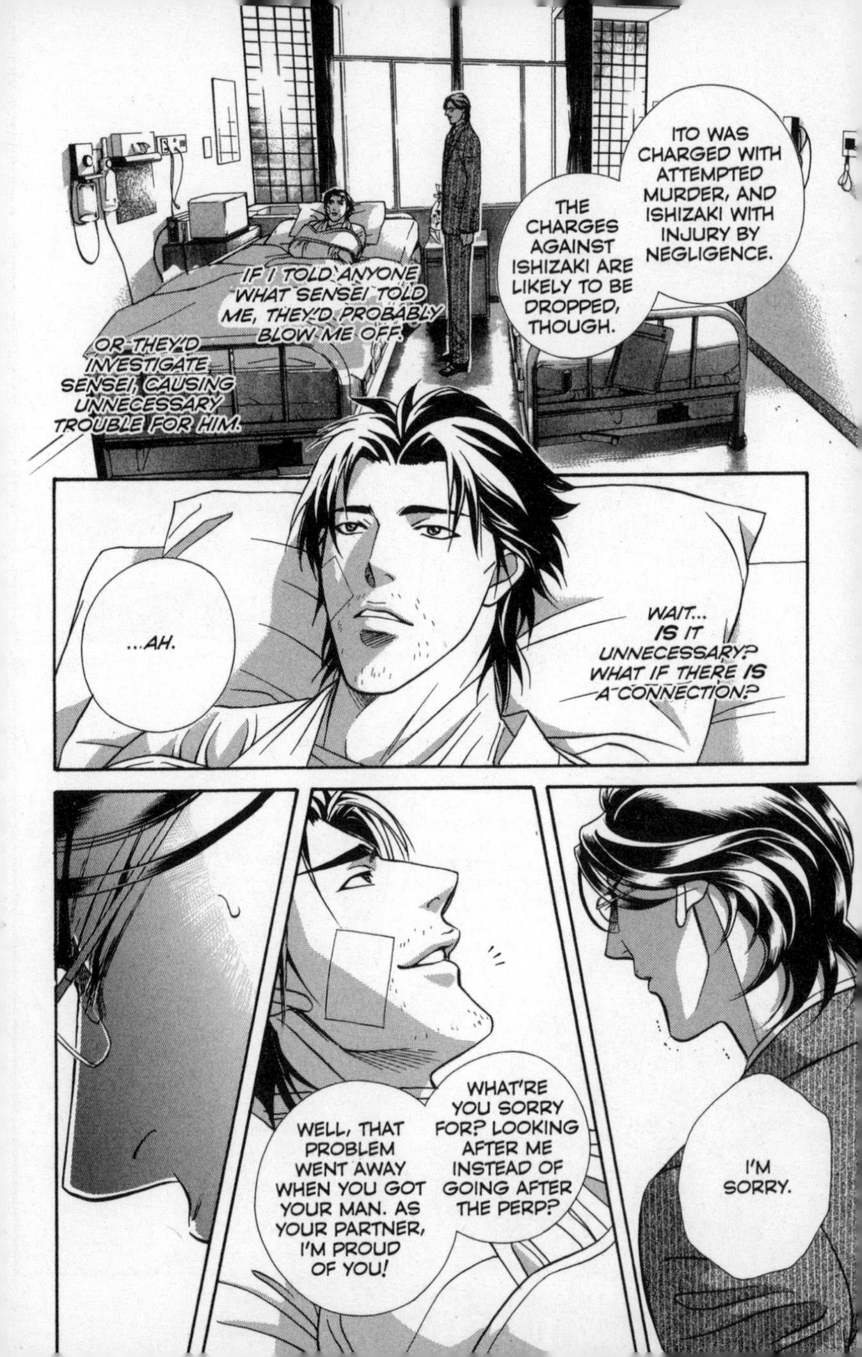

ITO WAS CHARGED WITH ATTEMPTED MURDER, AND ISHIZAKI WITH INJURY BY NEGLIGENCE.
THE CHARGES AGAINST ISHIZAKI ARE LIKELY TO BE DROPPED, THOUGH.
IF I TOLD ANYONE WHAT SENSEI TOLD ME, THEY'D PROBABLY BLOW ME OFF.
OR THEY'D INVESTIGATE SENSEI, CAUSING UNNECESSARY TROUBLE FOR HIM.
WAIT... IS IT UNNECESSARY? WHAT IF THERE IS A CONNECTION?
...AH.
I'M SORRY.
WHAT'RE YOU SORRY FOR? LOOKING AFTER ME INSTEAD OF GOING AFTER THE PERP?
WELL, THAT PROBLEM WENT AWAY WHEN YOU GOT YOUR MAN. AS YOUR PARTNER, I'M PROUD OF YOU!

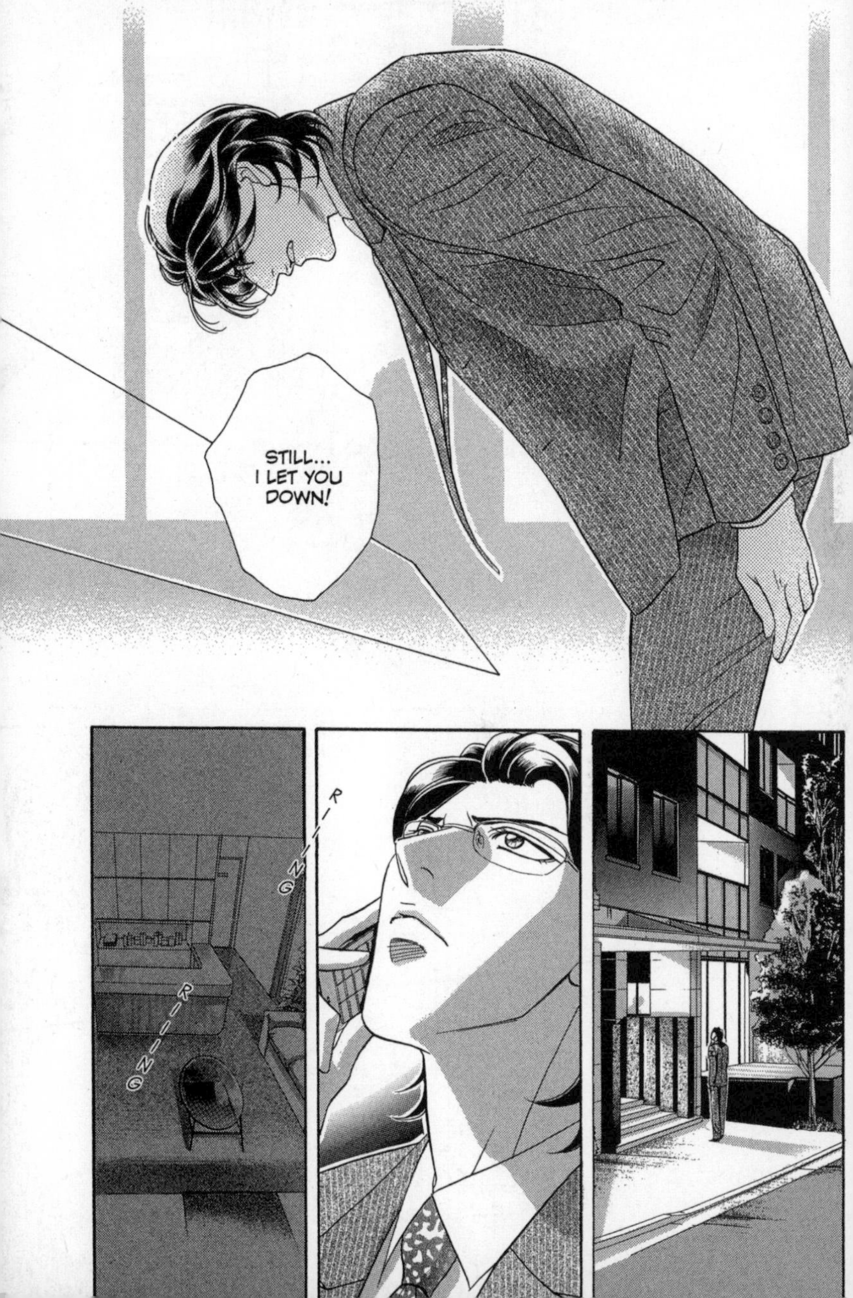
STILL...
I LET YOU
DOWN!
RIIING
RIIING

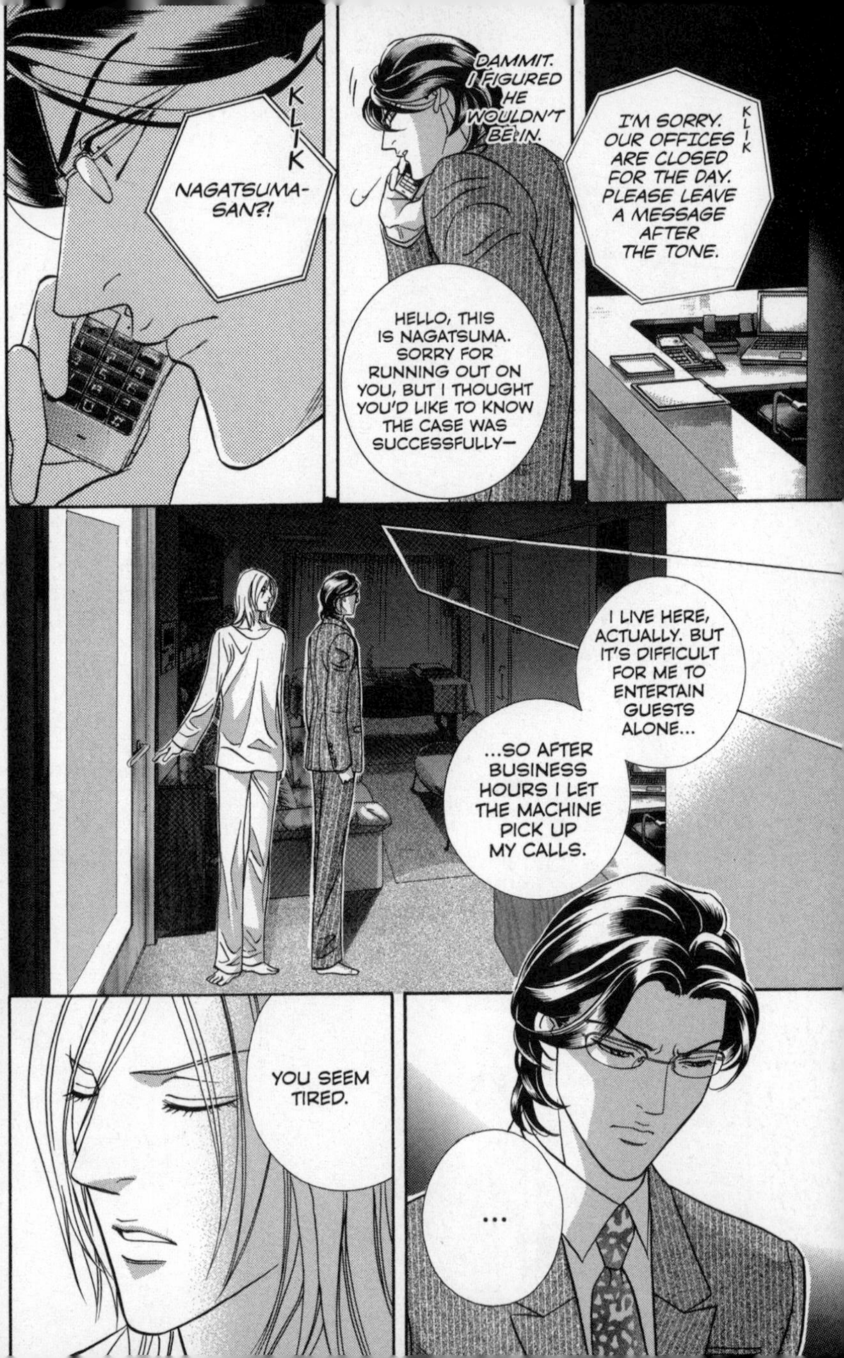
I'M SORRY. OUR OFFICES ARE CLOSED FOR THE DAY. PLEASE LEAVE A MESSAGE AFTER THE TONE.
KLIK
DAMMIT. I FIGURED HE WOULDN'T BE IN.
HELLO, THIS IS NAGATSUMA. SORRY FOR RUNNING OUT ON YOU, BUT I THOUGHT YOU'D LIKE TO KNOW THE CASE WAS SUCCESSFULLY—
KLIK
NAGATSUMA-SAN?!
I LIVE HERE, ACTUALLY. BUT IT'S DIFFICULT FOR ME TO ENTERTAIN GUESTS ALONE...
...SO AFTER BUSINESS HOURS I LET THE MACHINE PICK UP MY CALLS.
...
YOU SEEM TIRED.

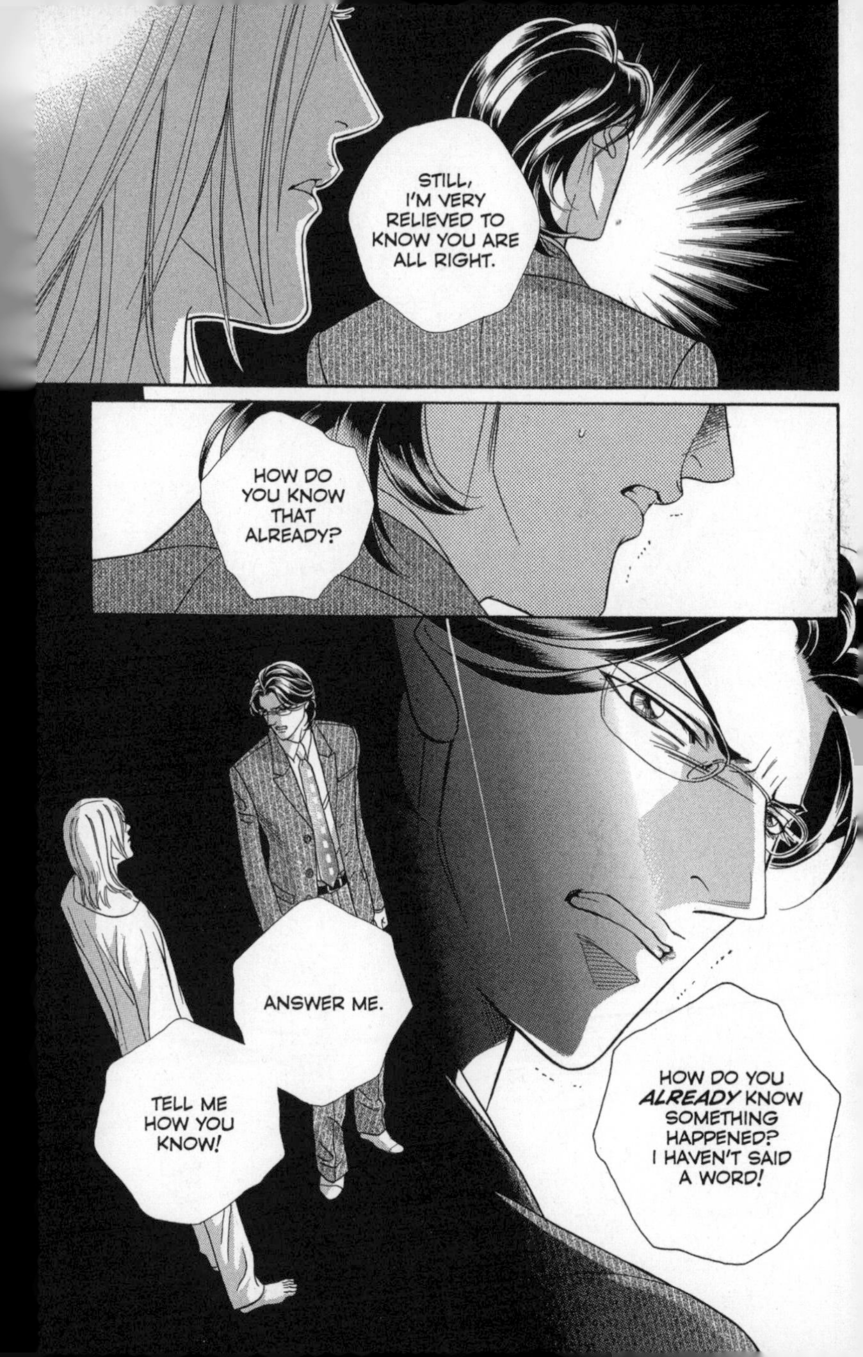
STILL, I'M VERY RELIEVED TO KNOW YOU ARE ALL RIGHT.
HOW DO YOU KNOW THAT ALREADY?
HOW DO YOU *ALREADY* KNOW SOMETHING HAPPENED? I HAVEN'T SAID A WORD!
ANSWER ME.
TELL ME HOW YOU KNOW!

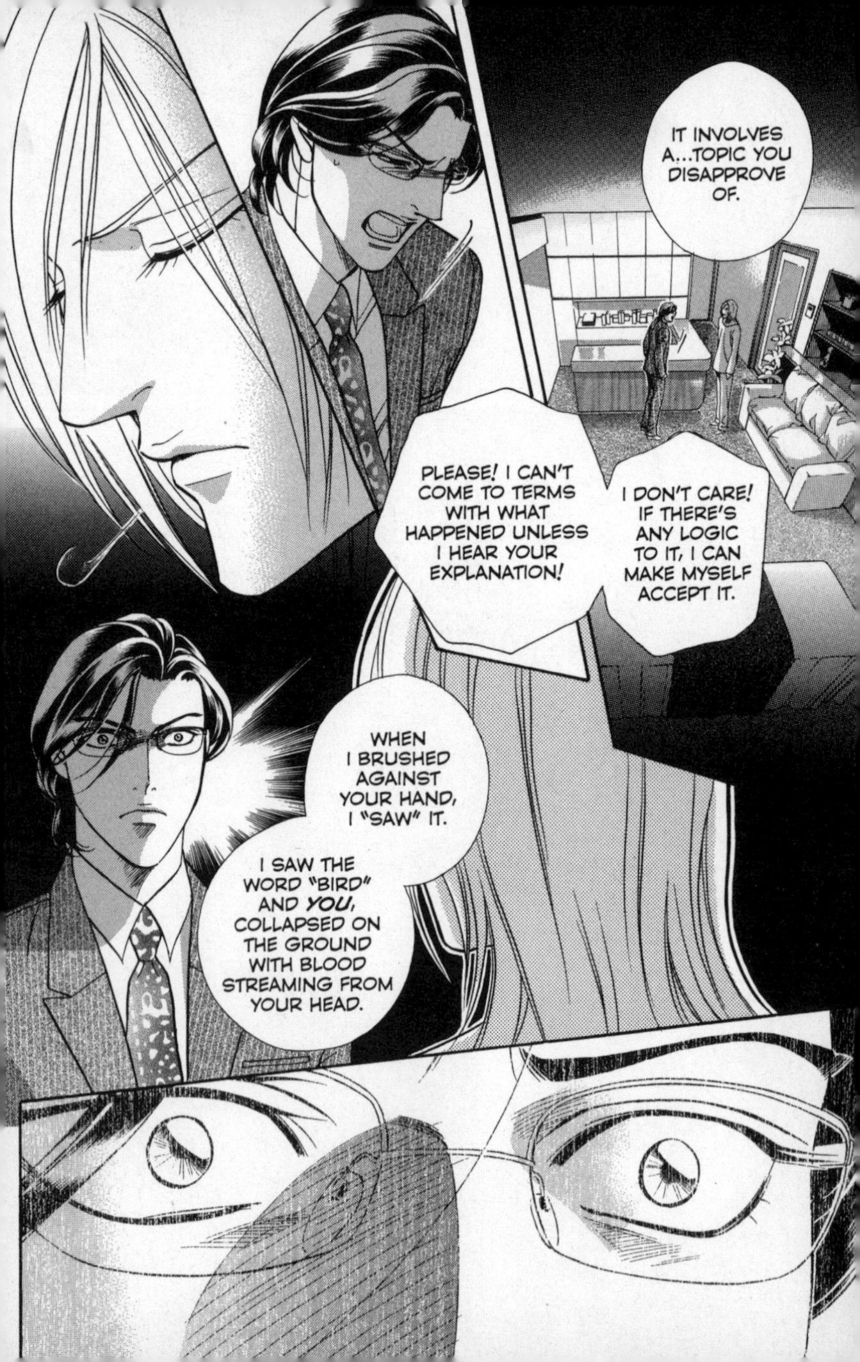
IT INVOLVES A...TOPIC YOU DISAPPROVE OF.
I DON'T CARE! IF THERE'S ANY LOGIC TO IT, I CAN MAKE MYSELF ACCEPT IT.
PLEASE! I CAN'T COME TO TERMS WITH WHAT HAPPENED UNLESS I HEAR YOUR EXPLANATION!
WHEN I BRUSHED AGAINST YOUR HAND, I "SAW" IT.
I SAW THE WORD "BIRD" AND *YOU*, COLLAPSED ON THE GROUND WITH BLOOD STREAMING FROM YOUR HEAD.

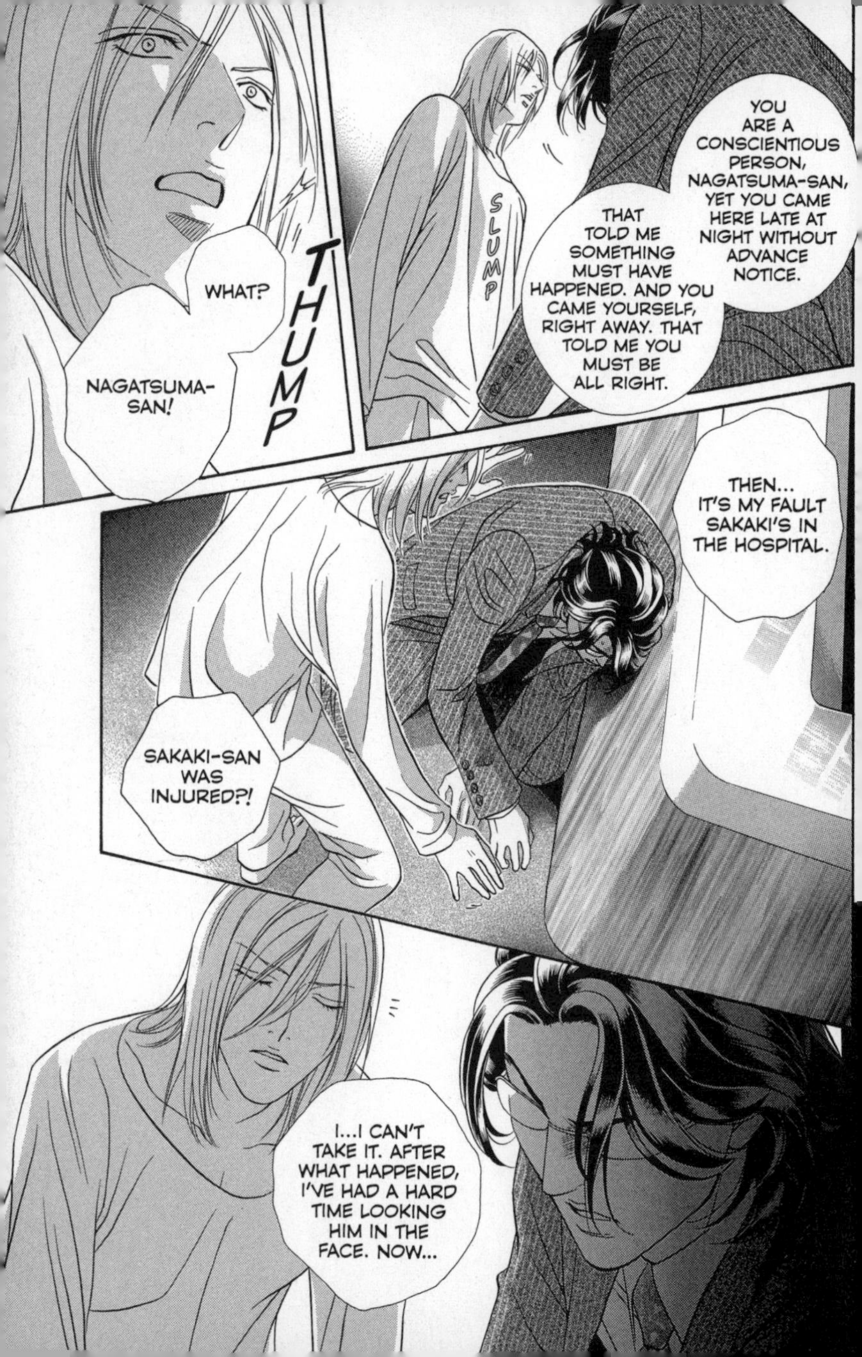
YOU ARE A CONSCIENTIOUS PERSON, NAGATSUMA-SAN, YET YOU CAME HERE LATE AT NIGHT WITHOUT ADVANCE NOTICE.
SLUMP
THAT TOLD ME SOMETHING MUST HAVE HAPPENED. AND YOU CAME YOURSELF, RIGHT AWAY. THAT TOLD ME YOU MUST BE ALL RIGHT.
THUMP
WHAT?
NAGATSUMA-SAN!
THEN... IT'S MY FAULT SAKAKI'S IN THE HOSPITAL.
SAKAKI-SAN WAS INJURED?!
I...I CAN'T TAKE IT. AFTER WHAT HAPPENED, I'VE HAD A HARD TIME LOOKING HIM IN THE FACE. NOW...

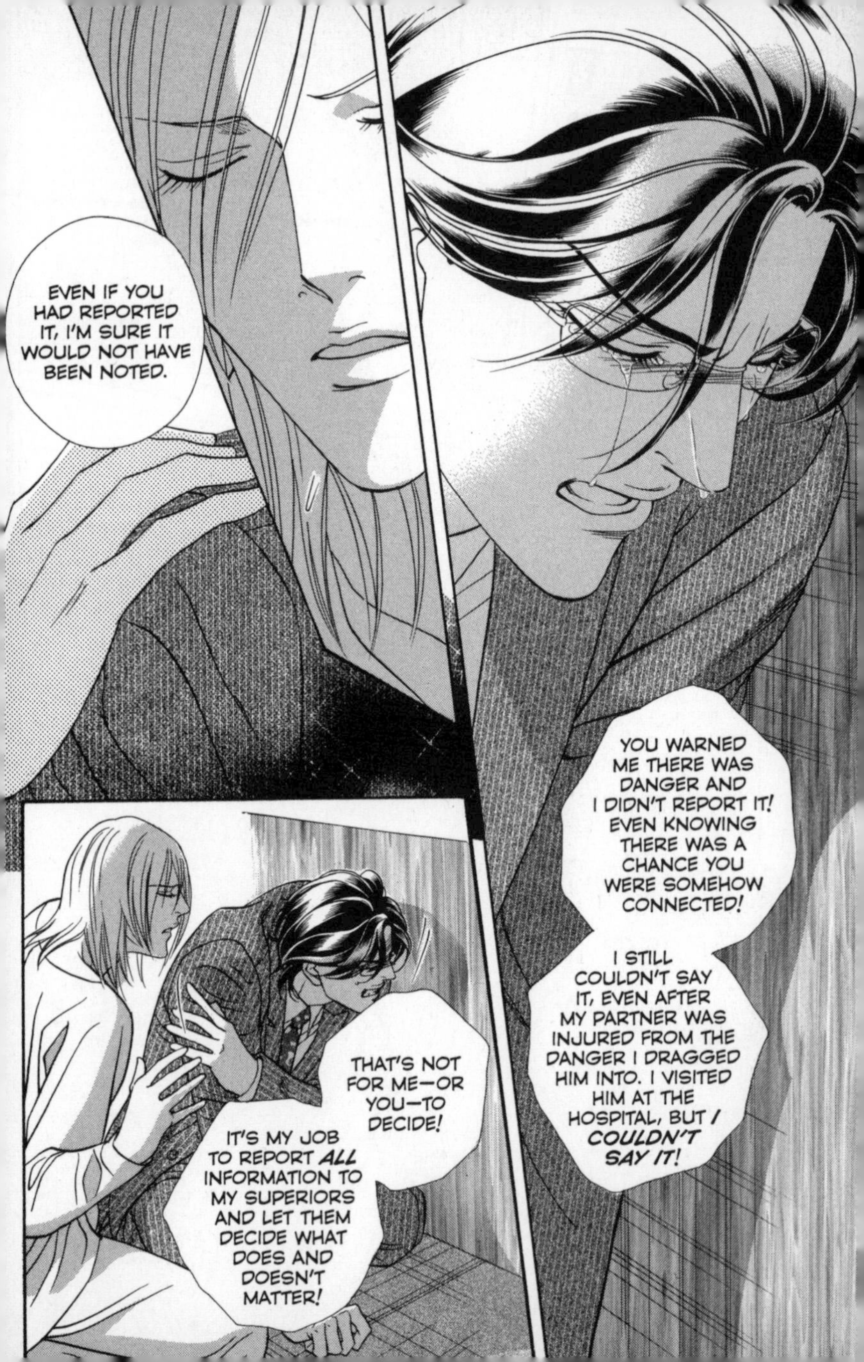

YOU WARNED ME THERE WAS DANGER AND I DIDN'T REPORT IT! EVEN KNOWING THERE WAS A CHANCE YOU WERE SOMEHOW CONNECTED!
I STILL COULDN'T SAY IT, EVEN AFTER MY PARTNER WAS INJURED FROM THE DANGER I DRAGGED HIM INTO. I VISITED HIM AT THE HOSPITAL, BUT *I COULDN'T SAY IT!*
EVEN IF YOU HAD REPORTED IT, I'M SURE IT WOULD NOT HAVE BEEN NOTED.
THAT'S NOT FOR ME—OR YOU—TO DECIDE!
IT'S MY JOB TO REPORT *ALL* INFORMATION TO MY SUPERIORS AND LET THEM DECIDE WHAT DOES AND DOESN'T MATTER!

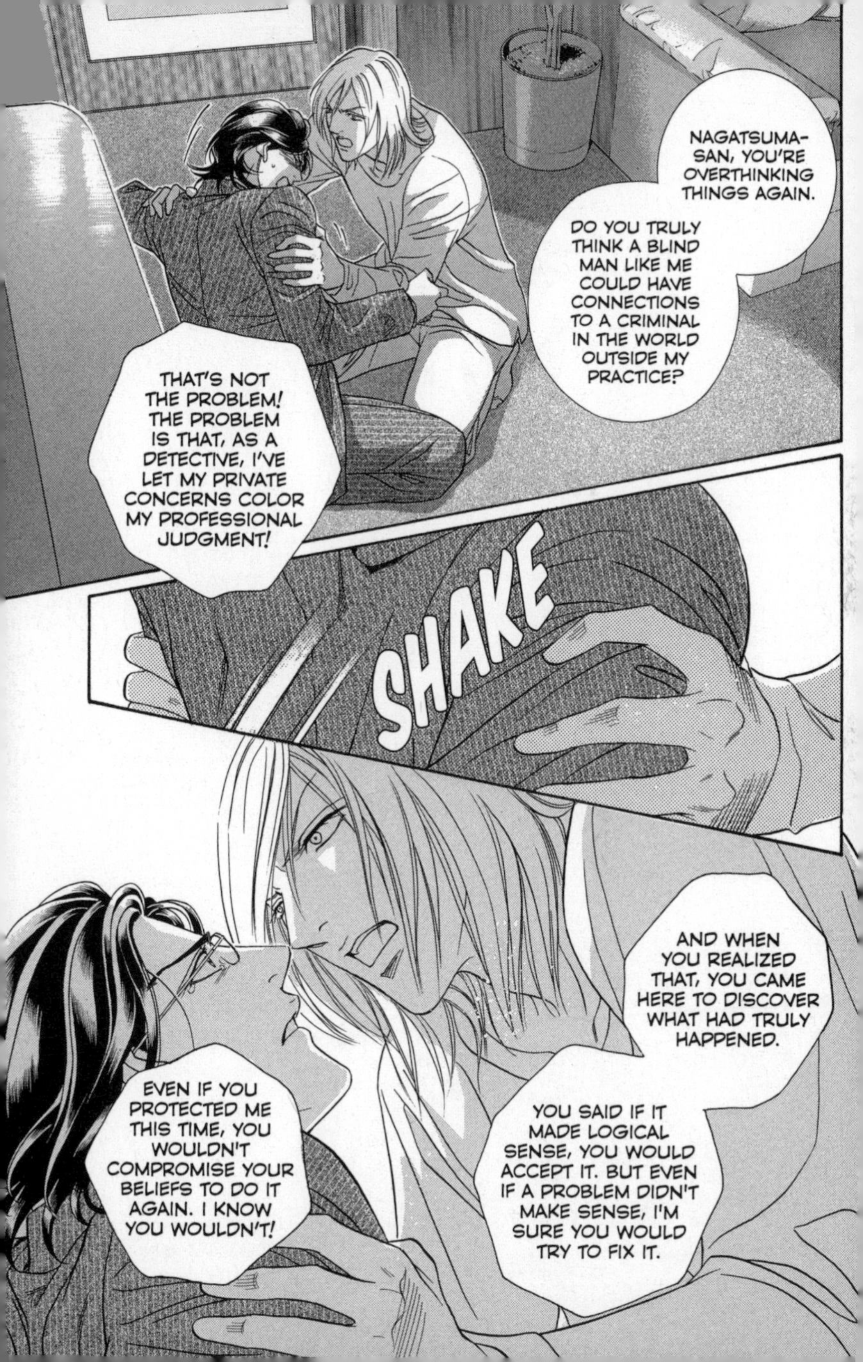
NAGATSUMA-SAN, YOU'RE OVERTHINKING THINGS AGAIN.
DO YOU TRULY THINK A BLIND MAN LIKE ME COULD HAVE CONNECTIONS TO A CRIMINAL IN THE WORLD OUTSIDE MY PRACTICE?
THAT'S NOT THE PROBLEM! THE PROBLEM IS THAT, AS A DETECTIVE, I'VE LET MY PRIVATE CONCERNS COLOR MY PROFESSIONAL JUDGMENT!
SHAKE
AND WHEN YOU REALIZED THAT, YOU CAME HERE TO DISCOVER WHAT HAD TRULY HAPPENED.
YOU SAID IF IT MADE LOGICAL SENSE, YOU WOULD ACCEPT IT. BUT EVEN IF A PROBLEM DIDN'T MAKE SENSE, I'M SURE YOU WOULD TRY TO FIX IT.
EVEN IF YOU PROTECTED ME THIS TIME, YOU WOULDN'T COMPROMISE YOUR BELIEFS TO DO IT AGAIN. I KNOW YOU WOULDN'T!

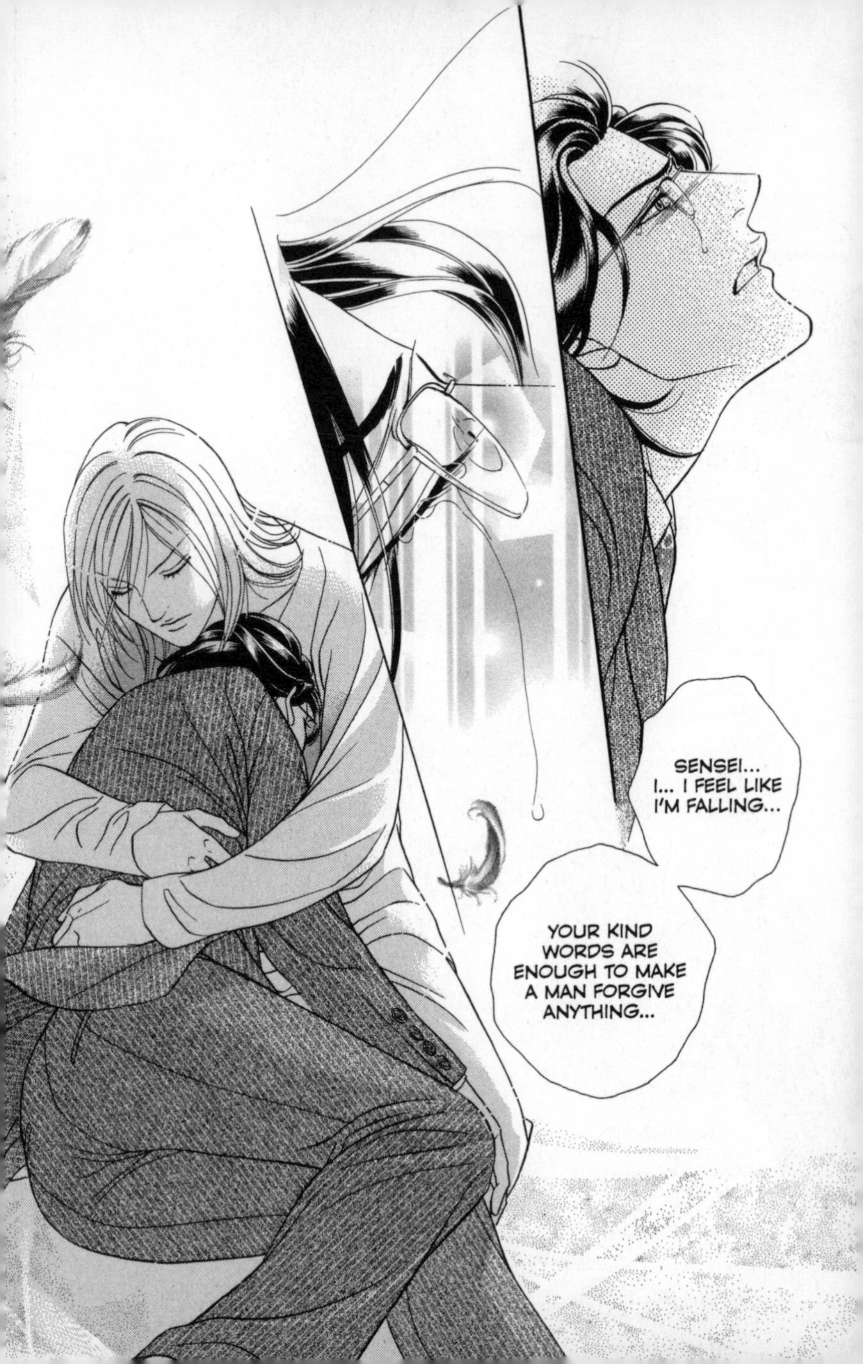
SENSEI... I... I FEEL LIKE I'M FALLING...
YOUR KIND WORDS ARE ENOUGH TO MAKE A MAN FORGIVE ANYTHING...

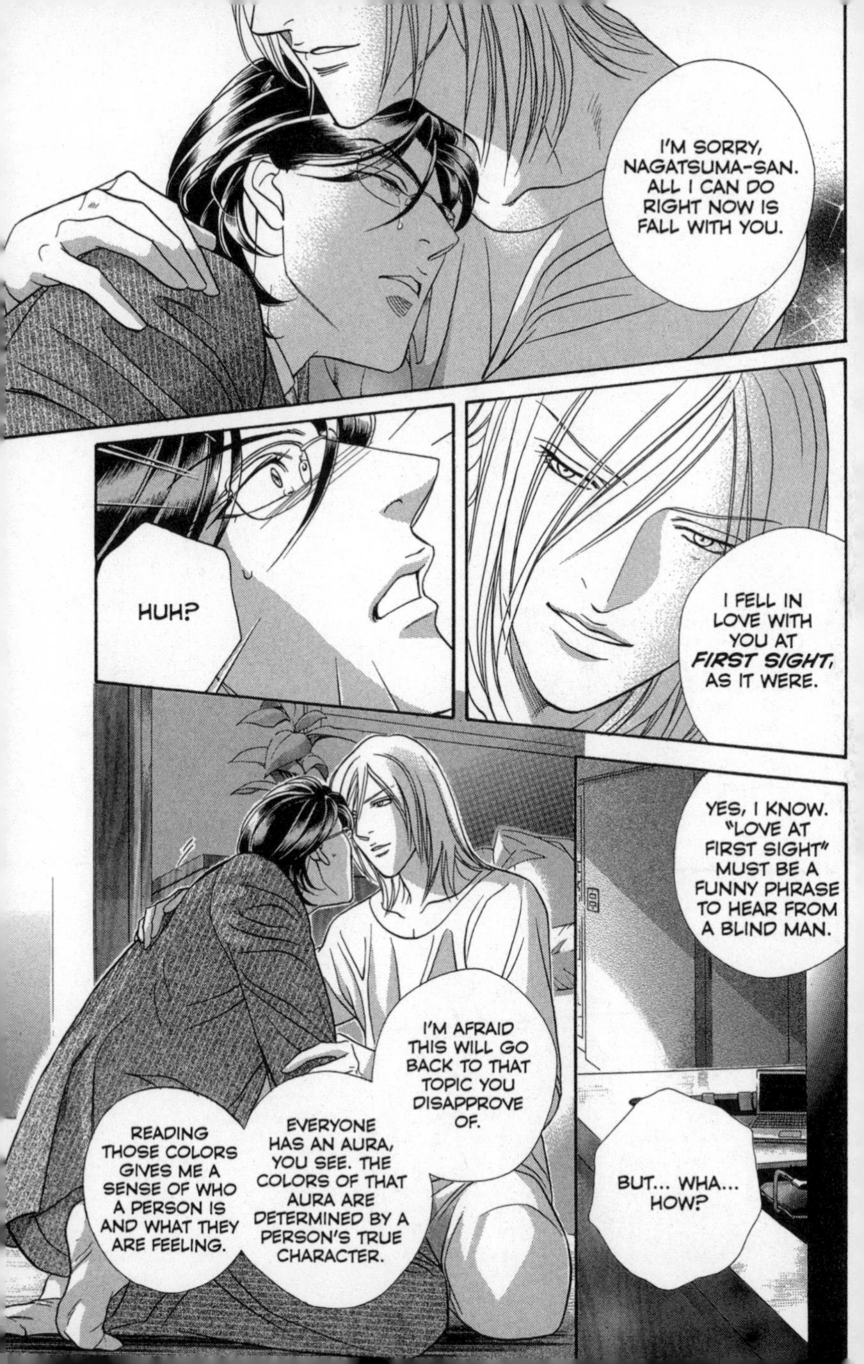
I'M SORRY, NAGATSUMA-SAN. ALL I CAN DO RIGHT NOW IS FALL WITH YOU.
I FELL IN LOVE WITH YOU AT *FIRST SIGHT*, AS IT WERE.
HUH?
YES, I KNOW. "LOVE AT FIRST SIGHT" MUST BE A FUNNY PHRASE TO HEAR FROM A BLIND MAN.
BUT... WHA... HOW?
I'M AFRAID THIS WILL GO BACK TO THAT TOPIC YOU DISAPPROVE OF.
EVERYONE HAS AN AURA, YOU SEE. THE COLORS OF THAT AURA ARE DETERMINED BY A PERSON'S TRUE CHARACTER.
READING THOSE COLORS GIVES ME A SENSE OF WHO A PERSON IS AND WHAT THEY ARE FEELING.

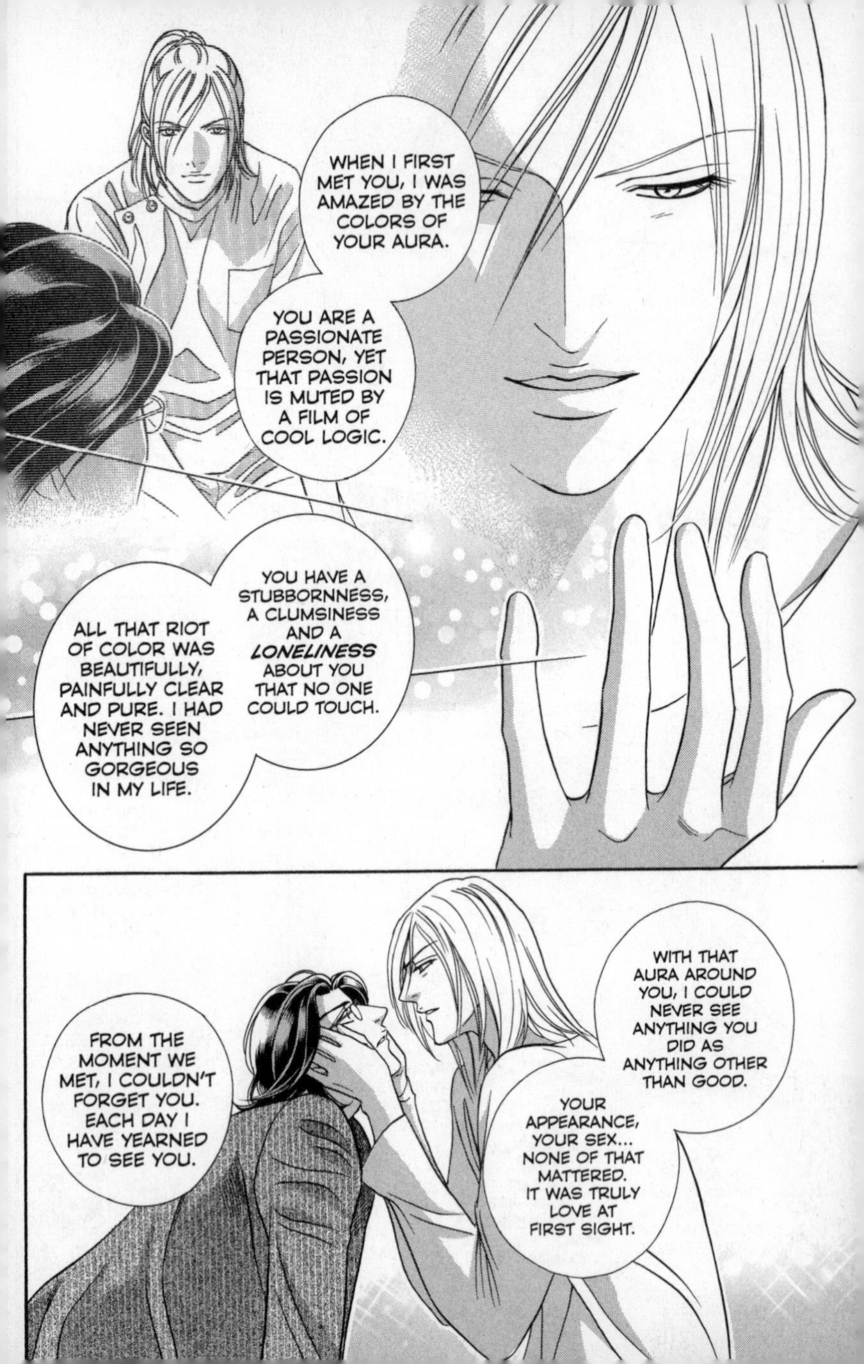
WHEN I FIRST MET YOU, I WAS AMAZED BY THE COLORS OF YOUR AURA.
YOU ARE A PASSIONATE PERSON, YET THAT PASSION IS MUTED BY A FILM OF COOL LOGIC.
YOU HAVE A STUBBORNNESS, A CLUMSINESS AND A *LONELINESS* ABOUT YOU THAT NO ONE COULD TOUCH.
ALL THAT RIOT OF COLOR WAS BEAUTIFULLY, PAINFULLY CLEAR AND PURE. I HAD NEVER SEEN ANYTHING SO GORGEOUS IN MY LIFE.
WITH THAT AURA AROUND YOU, I COULD NEVER SEE ANYTHING YOU DID AS ANYTHING OTHER THAN GOOD.
YOUR APPEARANCE, YOUR SEX... NONE OF THAT MATTERED. IT WAS TRULY LOVE AT FIRST SIGHT.
FROM THE MOMENT WE MET, I COULDN'T FORGET YOU. EACH DAY I HAVE YEARNED TO SEE YOU.

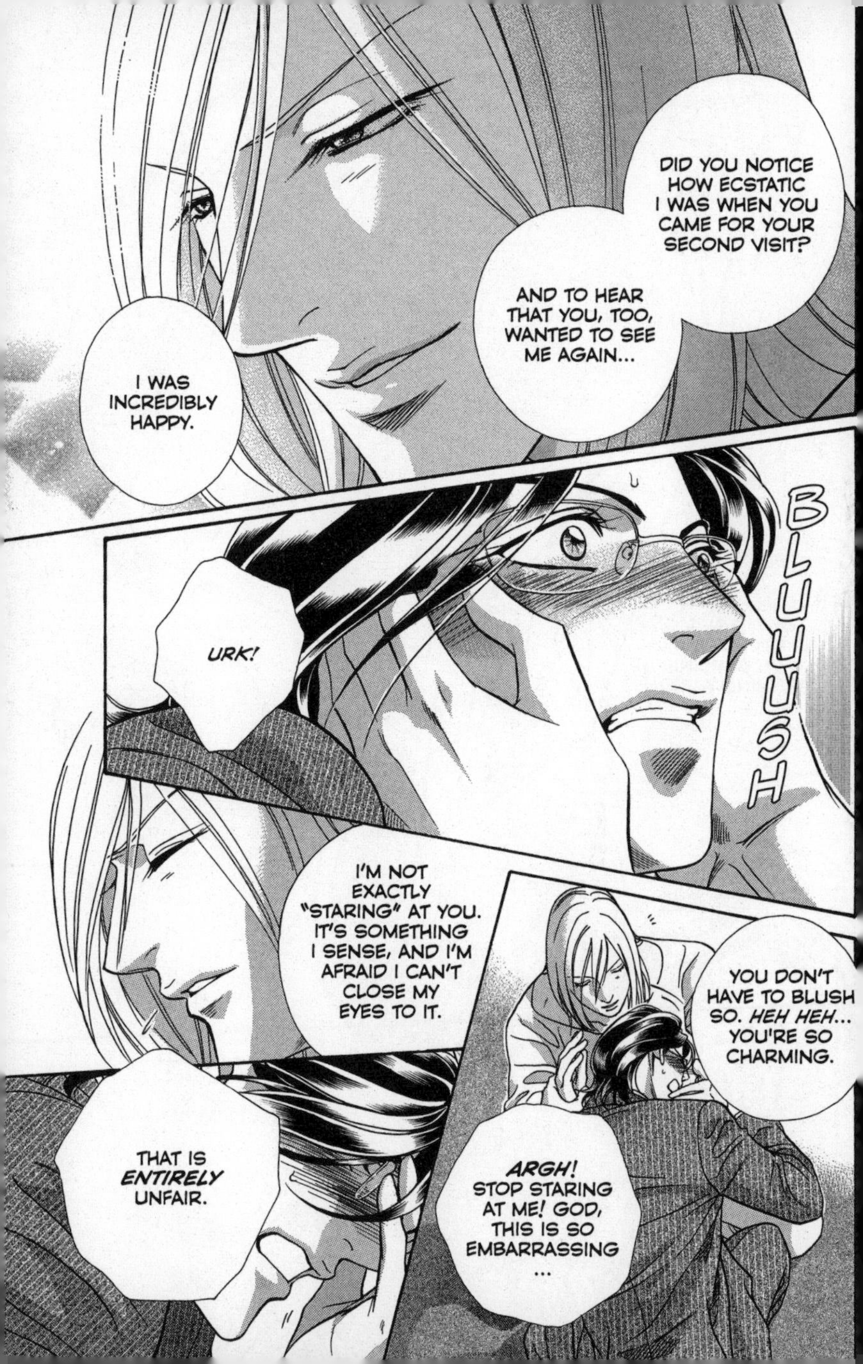
DID YOU NOTICE HOW ECSTATIC I WAS WHEN YOU CAME FOR YOUR SECOND VISIT?
AND TO HEAR THAT YOU, TOO, WANTED TO SEE ME AGAIN...
I WAS INCREDIBLY HAPPY.
BLUUUUSH
URK!
YOU DON'T HAVE TO BLUSH SO. *HEH HEH*... YOU'RE SO CHARMING.
ARGH! STOP STARING AT ME! GOD, THIS IS SO EMBARRASSING ...
I'M NOT EXACTLY "STARING" AT YOU. IT'S SOMETHING I SENSE, AND I'M AFRAID I CAN'T CLOSE MY EYES TO IT.
THAT IS *ENTIRELY* UNFAIR.

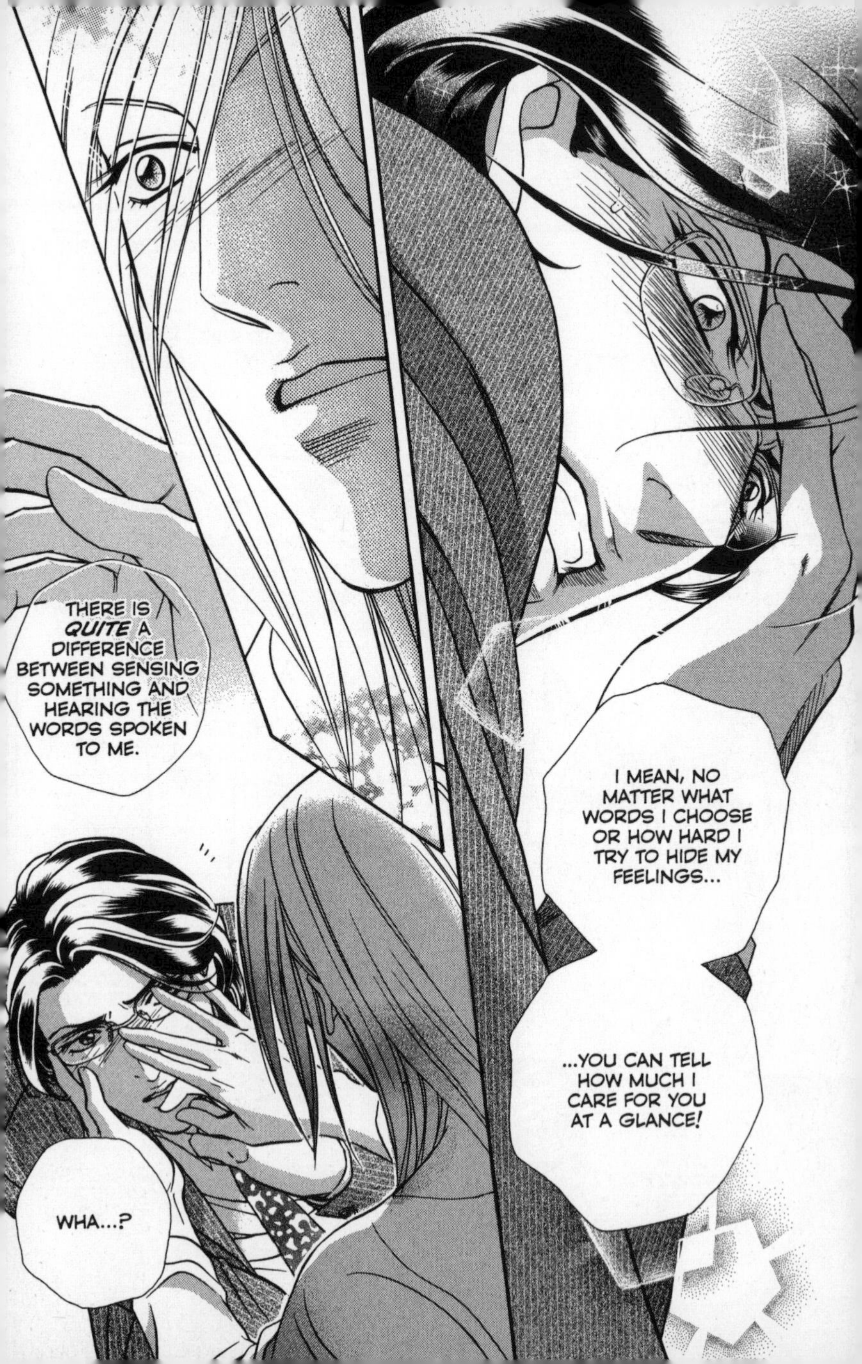
I MEAN, NO MATTER WHAT WORDS I CHOOSE OR HOW HARD I TRY TO HIDE MY FEELINGS...
...YOU CAN TELL HOW MUCH I CARE FOR YOU AT A GLANCE!
THERE IS ***QUITE*** A DIFFERENCE BETWEEN SENSING SOMETHING AND HEARING THE WORDS SPOKEN TO ME.
WHA...?

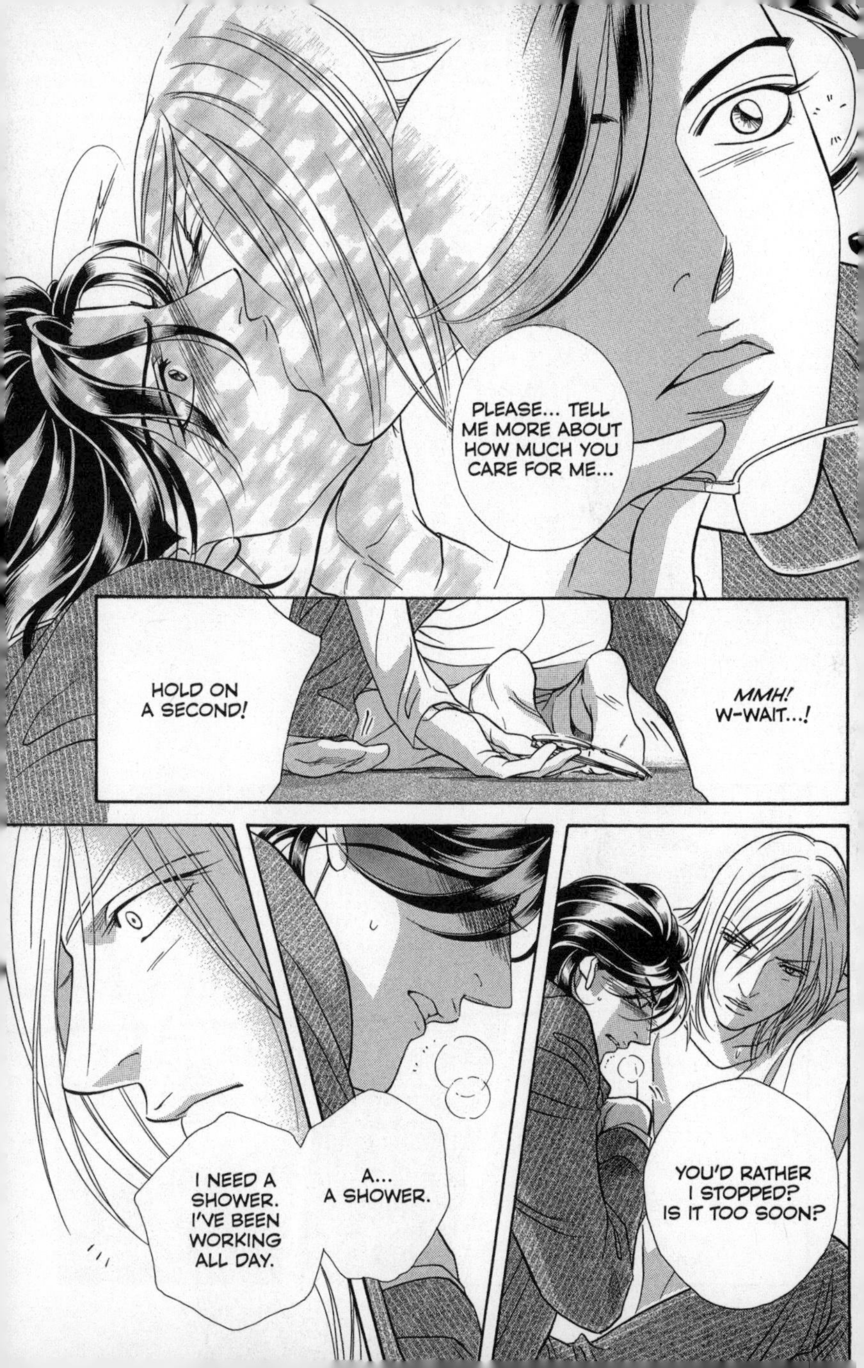
PLEASE... TELL ME MORE ABOUT HOW MUCH YOU CARE FOR ME...
MMH! W-WAIT...!
HOLD ON A SECOND!
YOU'D RATHER I STOPPED? IS IT TOO SOON?
A... A SHOWER.
I NEED A SHOWER. I'VE BEEN WORKING ALL DAY.

HONESTLY.
YOU REALLY *ARE* ADORABLE.

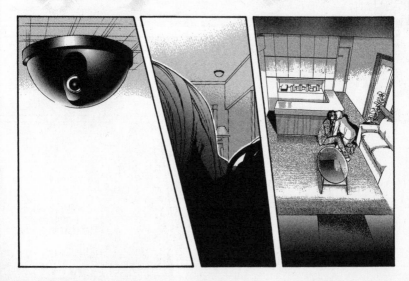

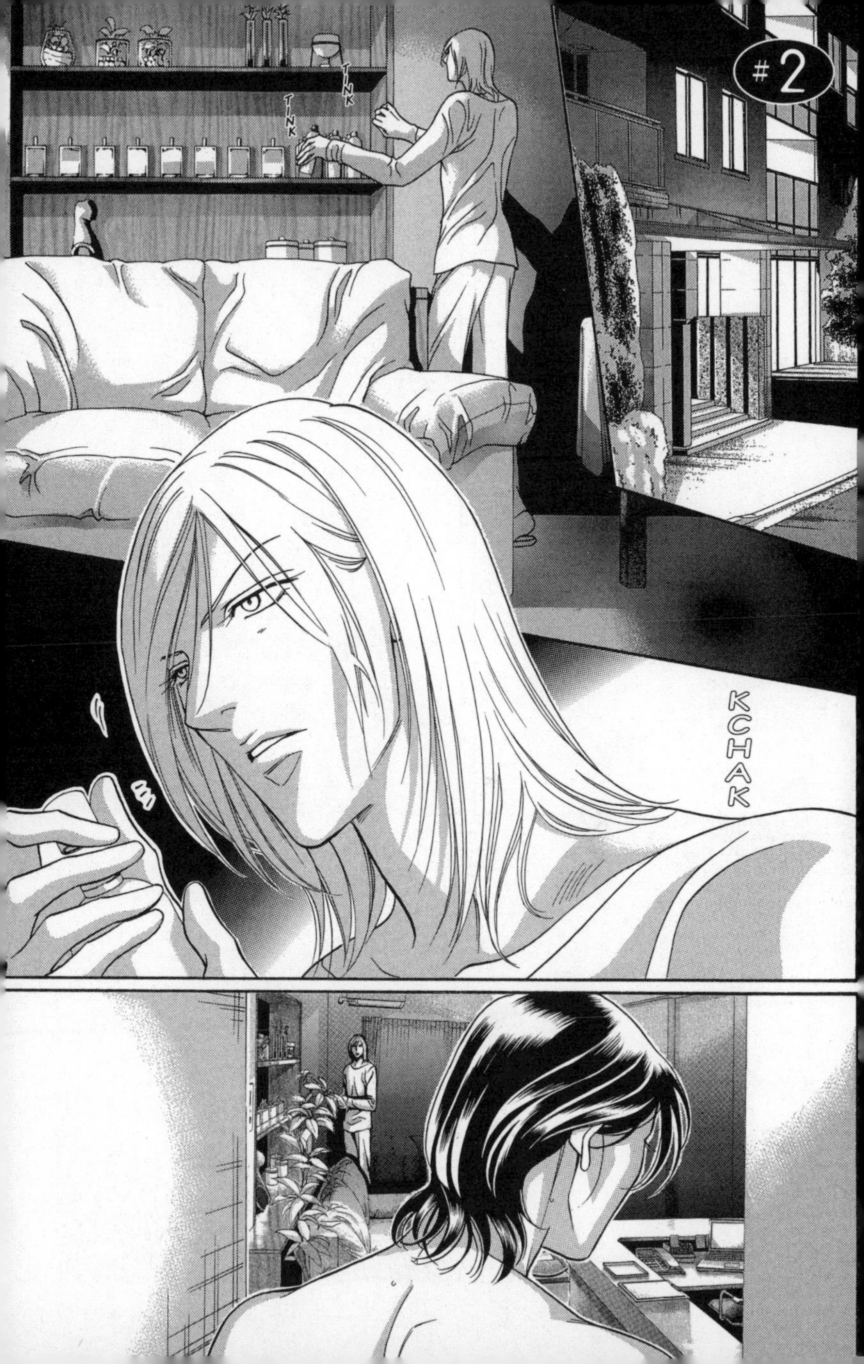
#2
TINK
TINK
KCHAK

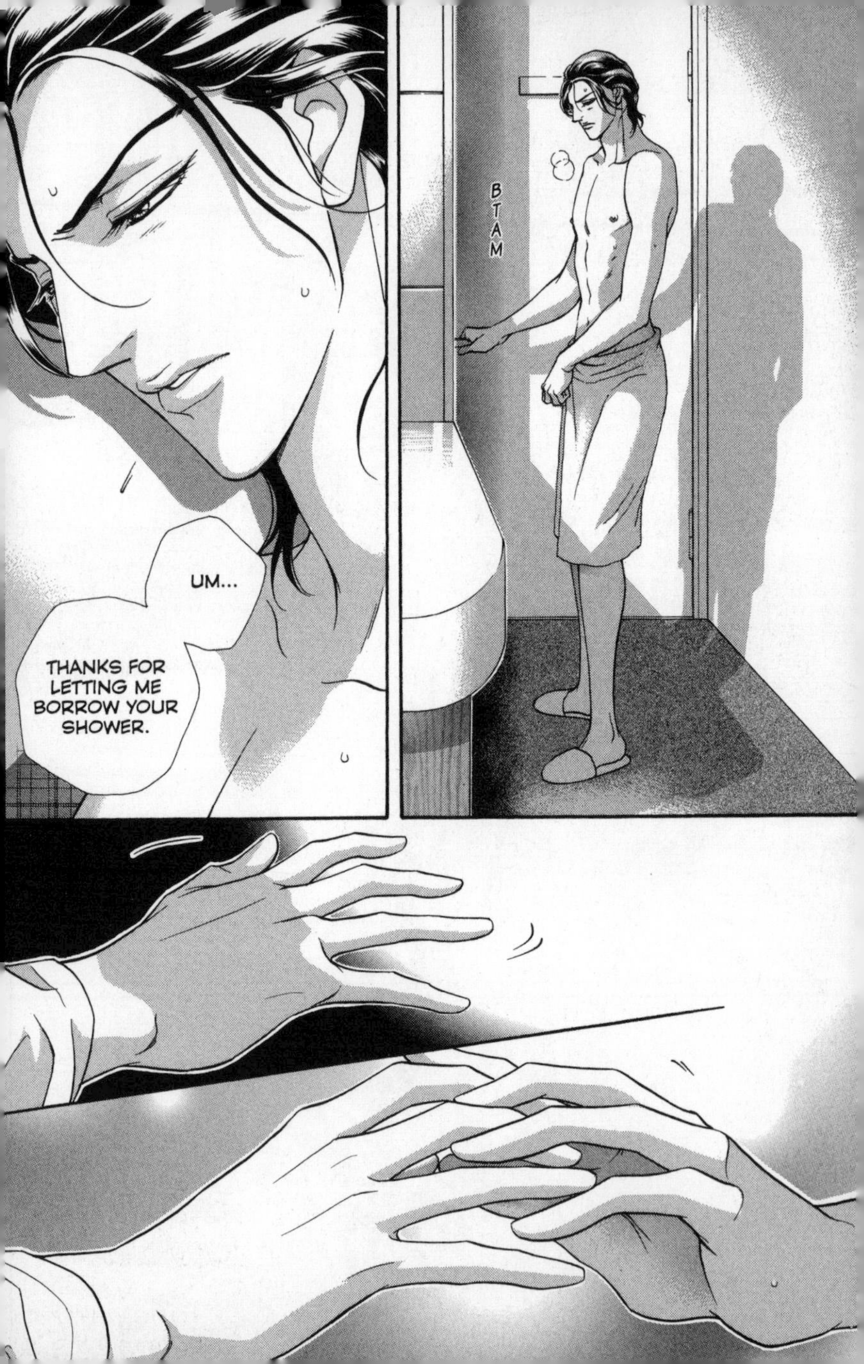
BTAM
UM...
THANKS FOR LETTING ME BORROW YOUR SHOWER.

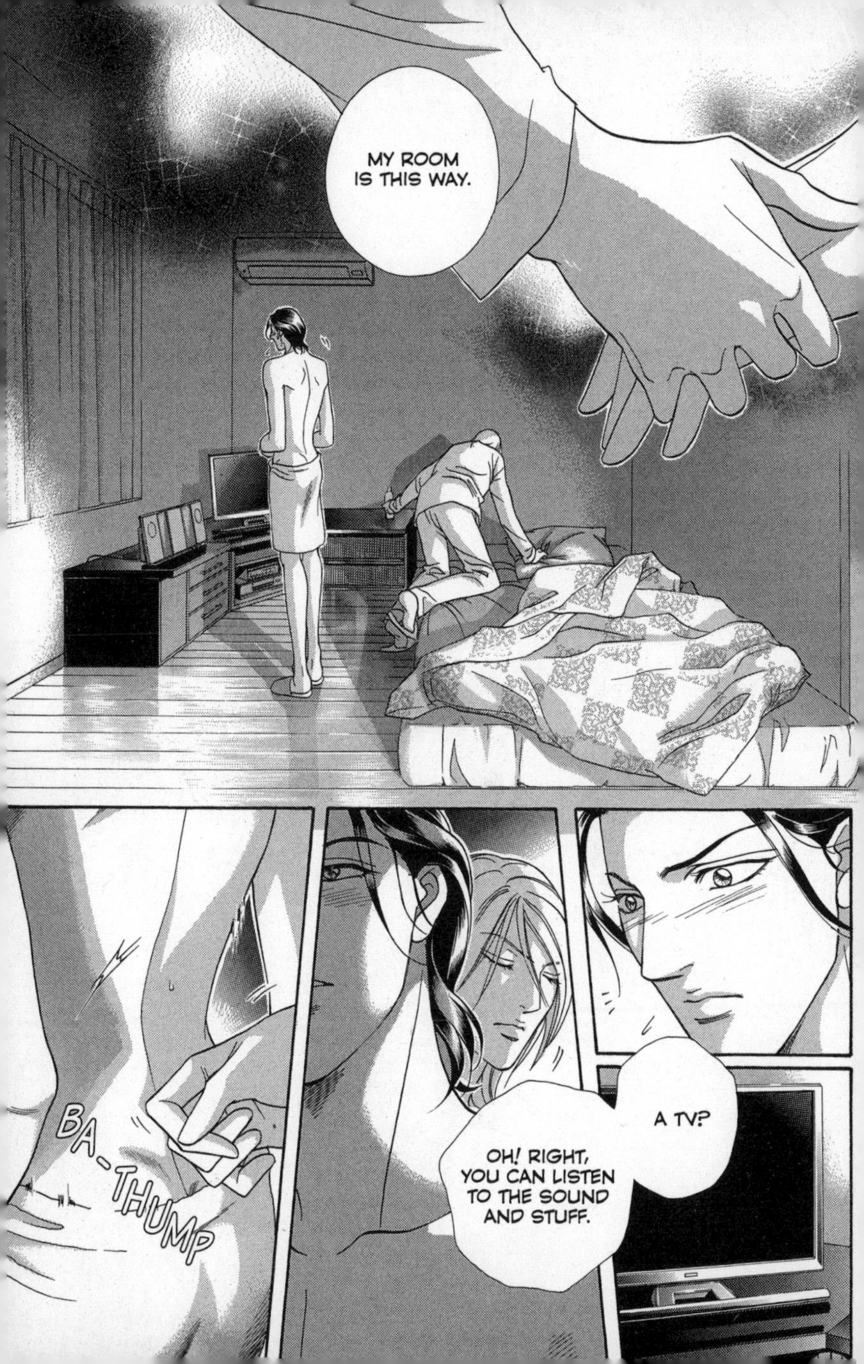
MY ROOM IS THIS WAY.
A TV?
OH! RIGHT, YOU CAN LISTEN TO THE SOUND AND STUFF.
BA-THUMP

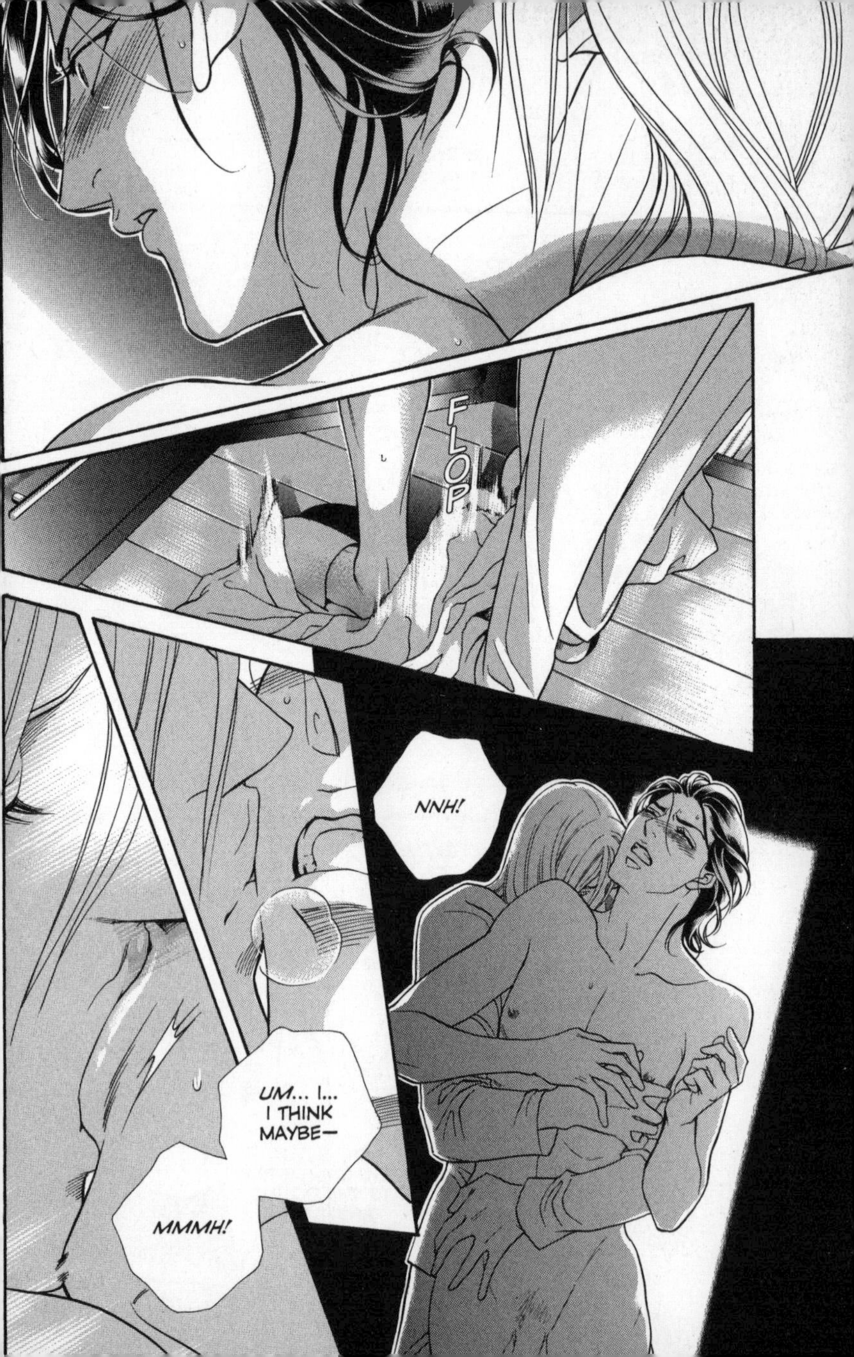
FLOP
NNH!
UM... I... I THINK MAYBE—
MMMH!

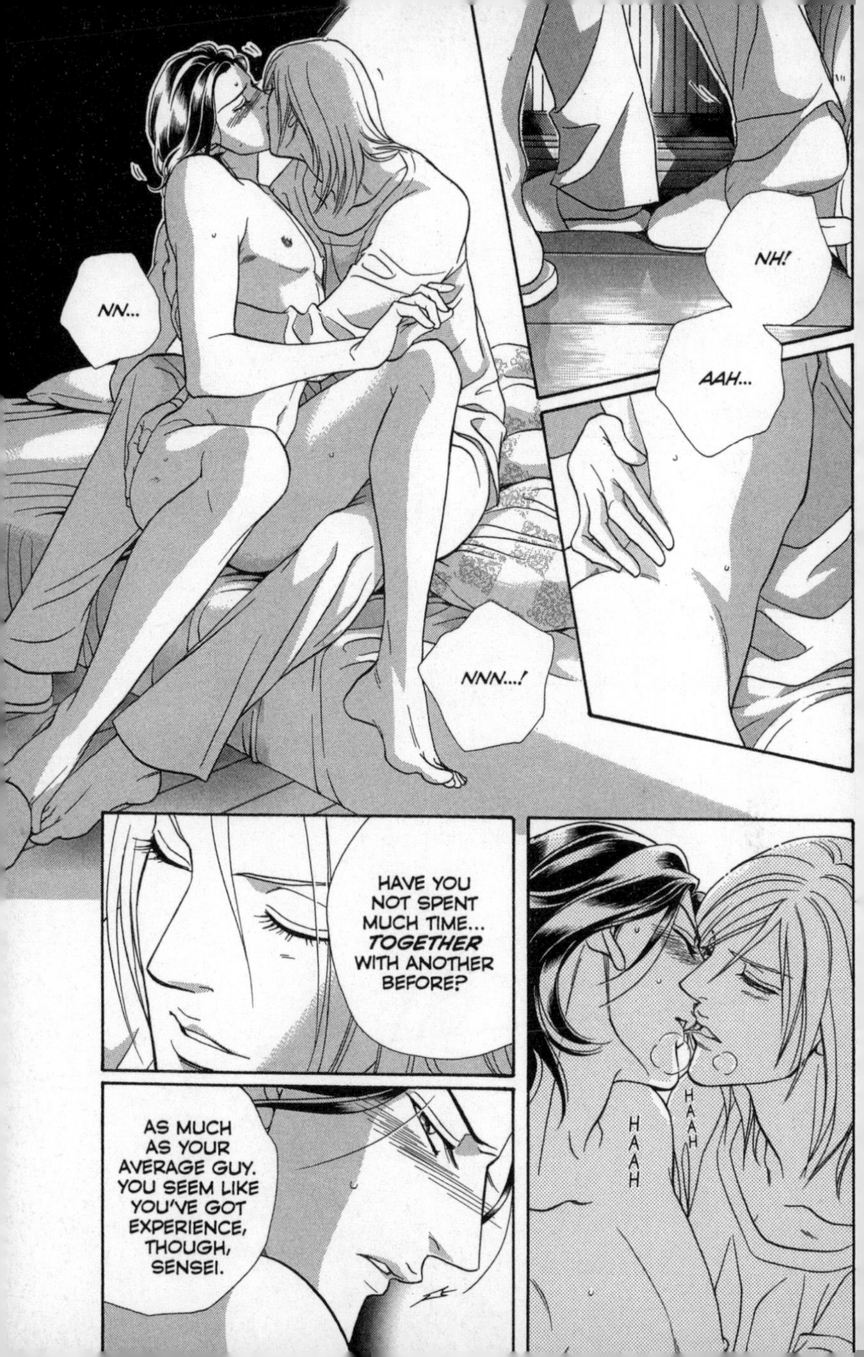
NH!
AAH...
NN...
NNN...!
HAAH
HAAH
HAVE YOU NOT SPENT MUCH TIME... ***TOGETHER*** WITH ANOTHER BEFORE?
AS MUCH AS YOUR AVERAGE GUY. YOU SEEM LIKE YOU'VE GOT EXPERIENCE, THOUGH, SENSEI.

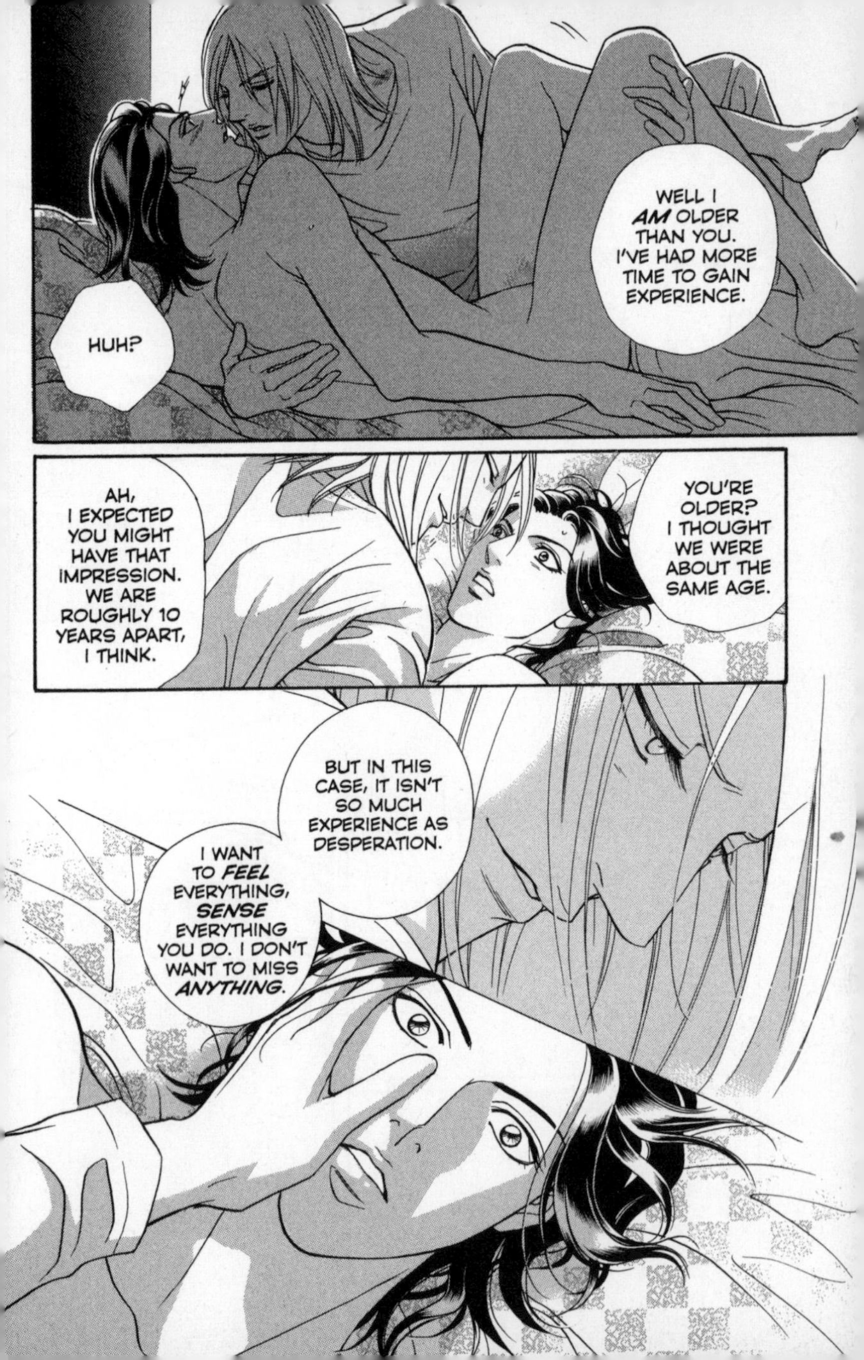
WELL I AM OLDER THAN YOU. I'VE HAD MORE TIME TO GAIN EXPERIENCE.
HUH?
YOU'RE OLDER? I THOUGHT WE WERE ABOUT THE SAME AGE.
AH, I EXPECTED YOU MIGHT HAVE THAT IMPRESSION. WE ARE ROUGHLY 10 YEARS APART, I THINK.
BUT IN THIS CASE, IT ISN'T SO MUCH EXPERIENCE AS DESPERATION.
I WANT TO FEEL EVERYTHING, SENSE EVERYTHING YOU DO. I DON'T WANT TO MISS ANYTHING.

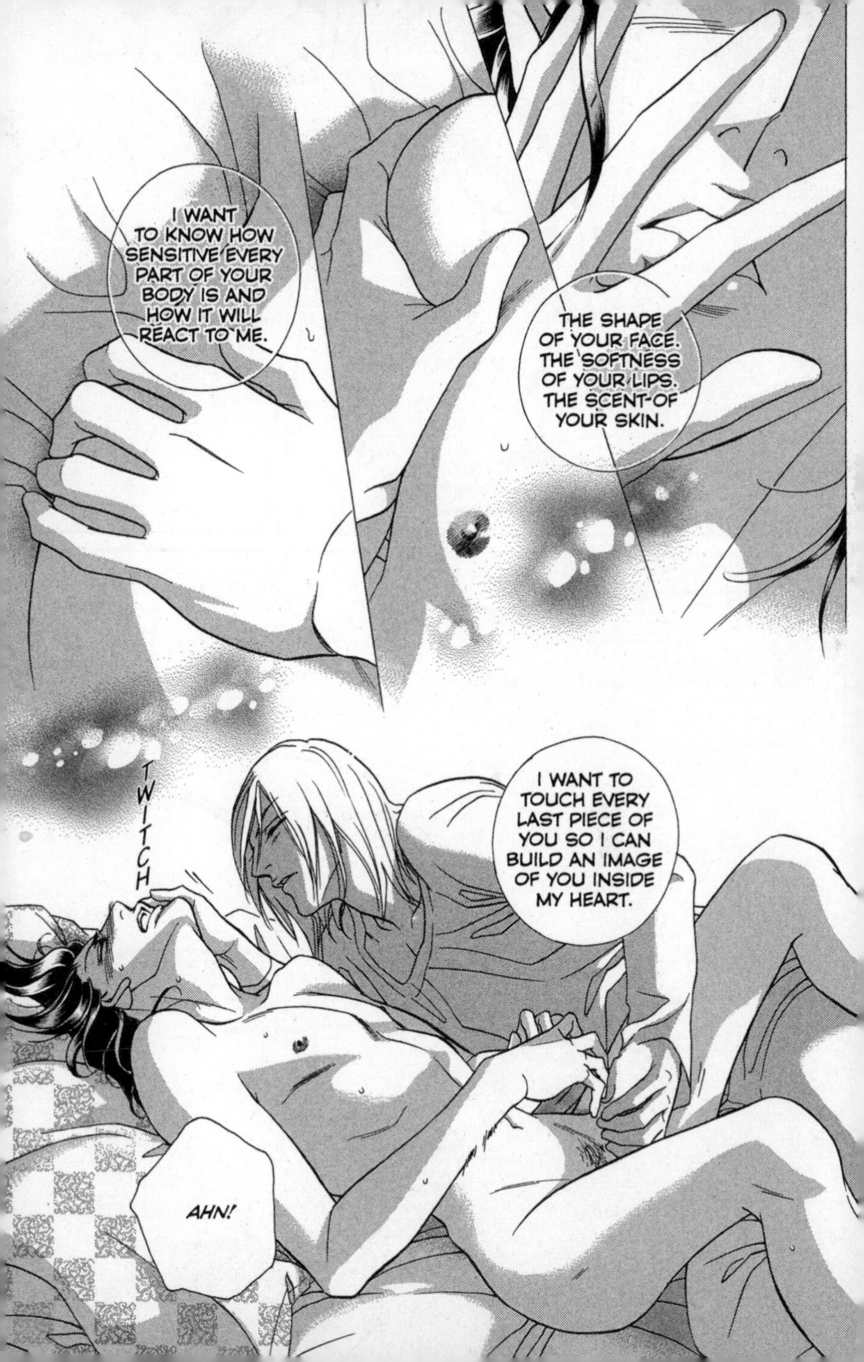
THE SHAPE OF YOUR FACE. THE SOFTNESS OF YOUR LIPS. THE SCENT OF YOUR SKIN.
I WANT TO KNOW HOW SENSITIVE EVERY PART OF YOUR BODY IS AND HOW IT WILL REACT TO ME.
I WANT TO TOUCH EVERY LAST PIECE OF YOU SO I CAN BUILD AN IMAGE OF YOU INSIDE MY HEART.
TWITCH
AHN!

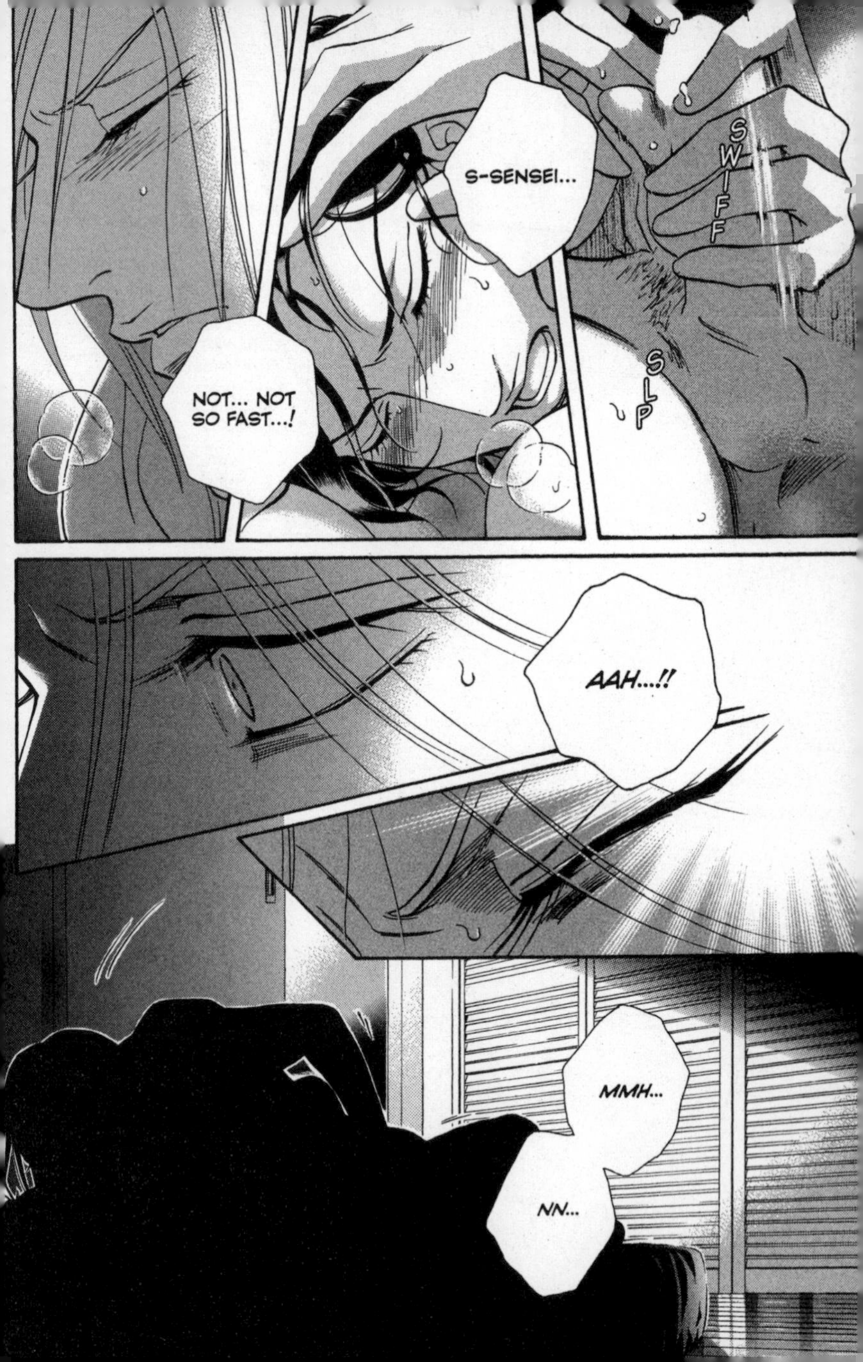
SWIFF
SLP
S-SENSEI...
NOT... NOT SO FAST...!
AAH...!!
MMH...
NN...

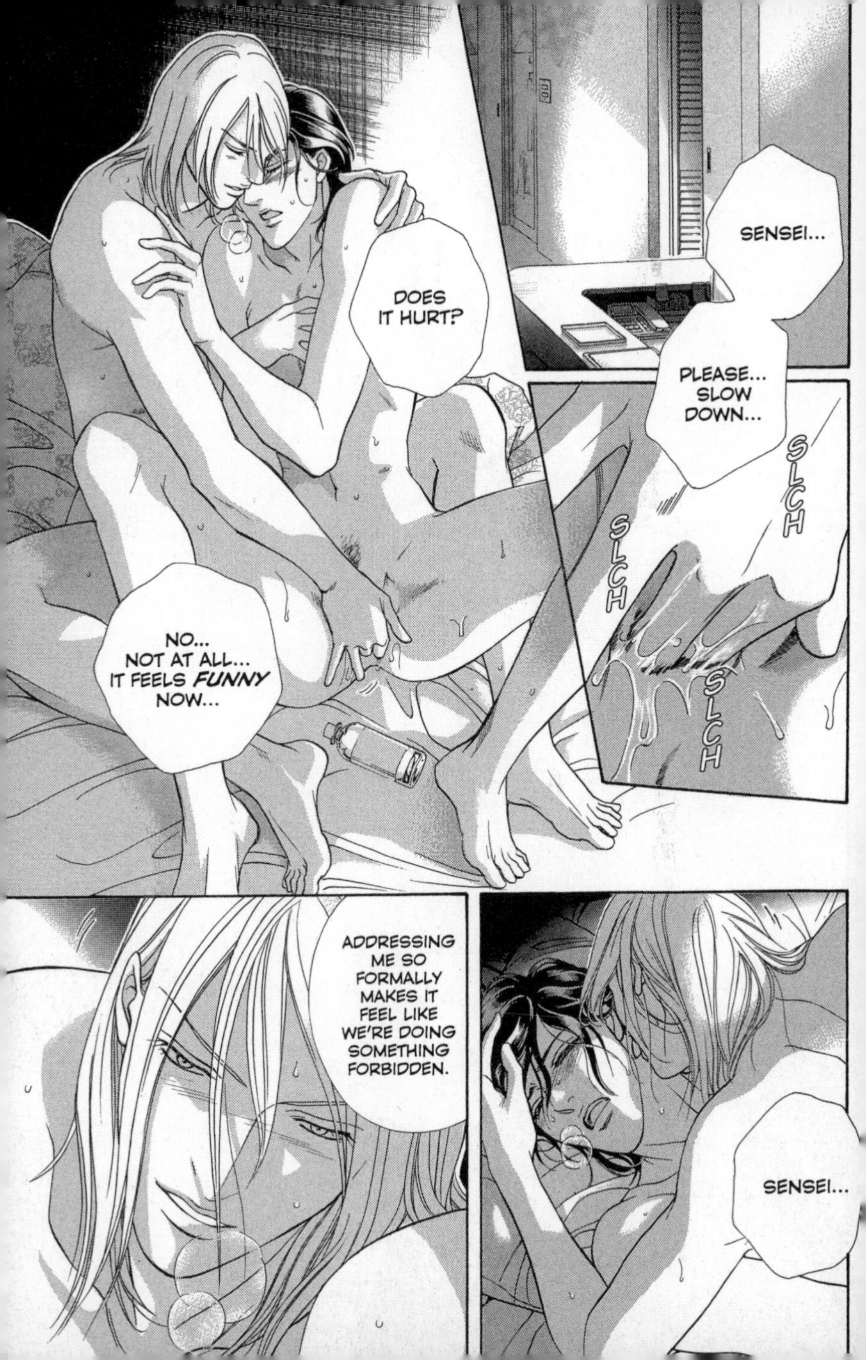
SENSEI...
PLEASE... SLOW DOWN...
SLCH
SLCH
SLCH
DOES IT HURT?
NO... NOT AT ALL... IT FEELS *FUNNY* NOW...
SENSEI...
ADDRESSING ME SO FORMALLY MAKES IT FEEL LIKE WE'RE DOING SOMETHING FORBIDDEN.

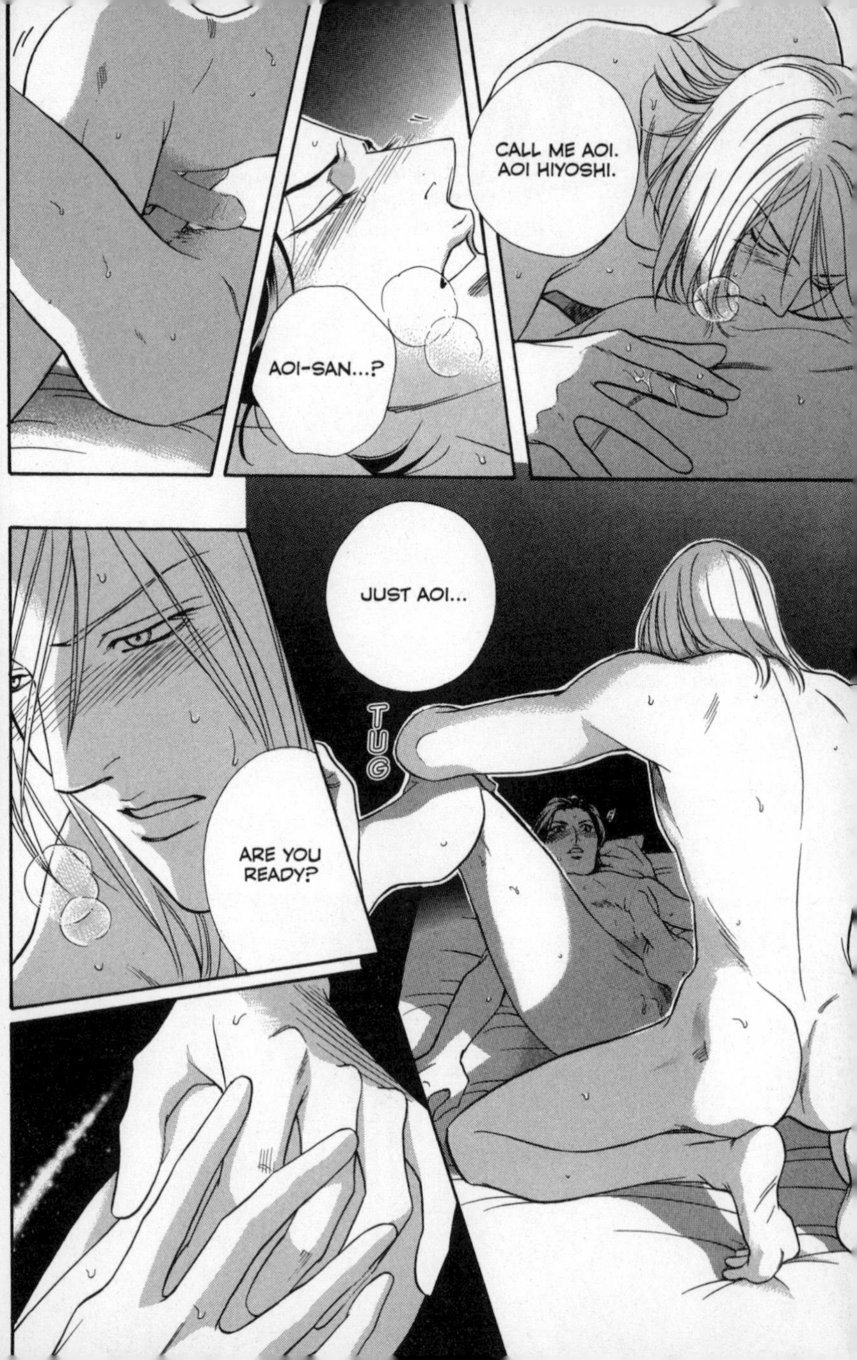
CALL ME AOI. AOI HIYOSHI.
AOI-SAN...?
JUST AOI...
TUG
ARE YOU READY?

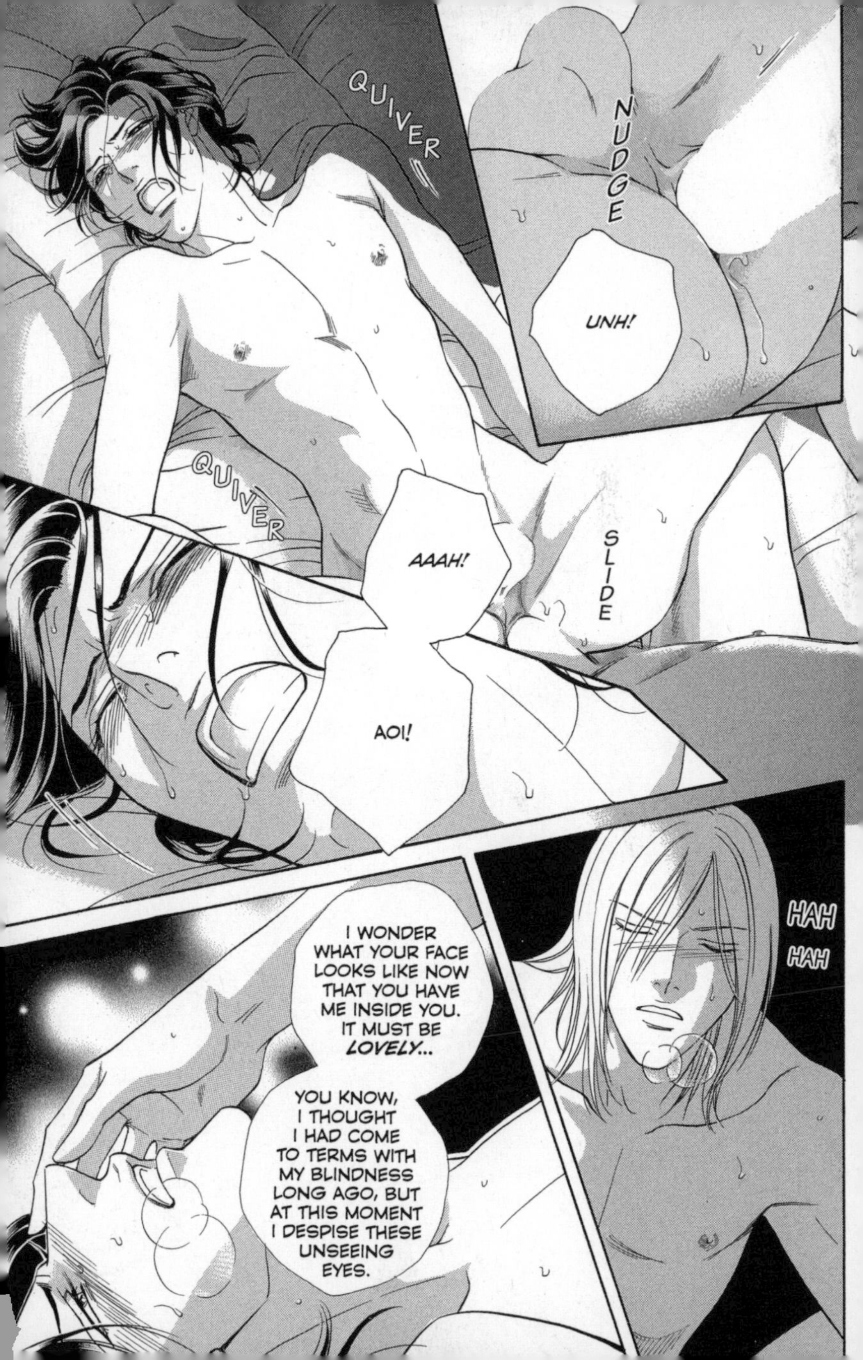
NUDGE
UNH!
QUIVER
QUIVER
SLIDE
AAAH!
AOI!
HAH
HAH
I WONDER WHAT YOUR FACE LOOKS LIKE NOW THAT YOU HAVE ME INSIDE YOU. IT MUST BE ***LOVELY...***
YOU KNOW, I THOUGHT I HAD COME TO TERMS WITH MY BLINDNESS LONG AGO, BUT AT THIS MOMENT I DESPISE THESE UNSEEING EYES.

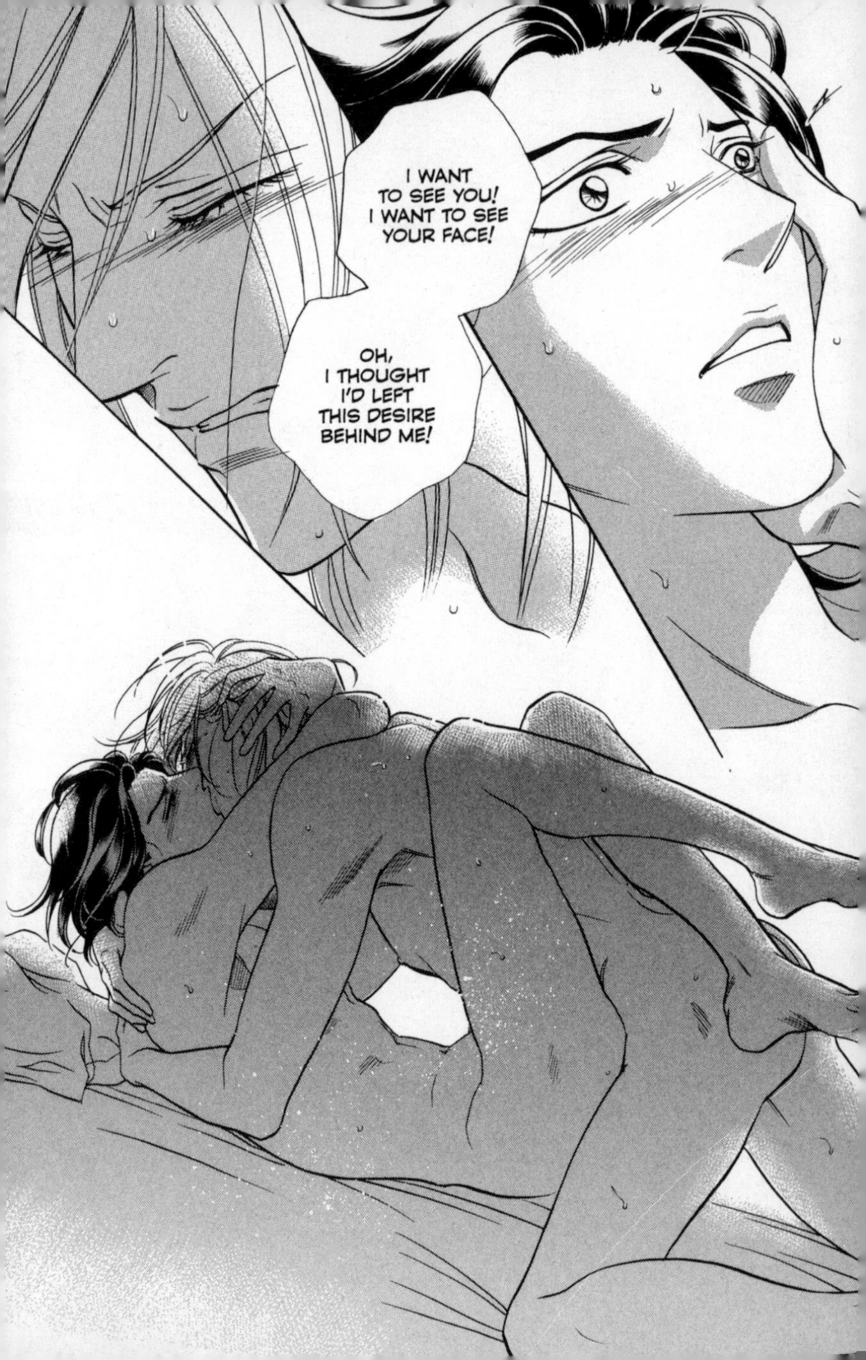
I WANT TO SEE YOU! I WANT TO SEE YOUR FACE!
OH, I THOUGHT I'D LEFT THIS DESIRE BEHIND ME!

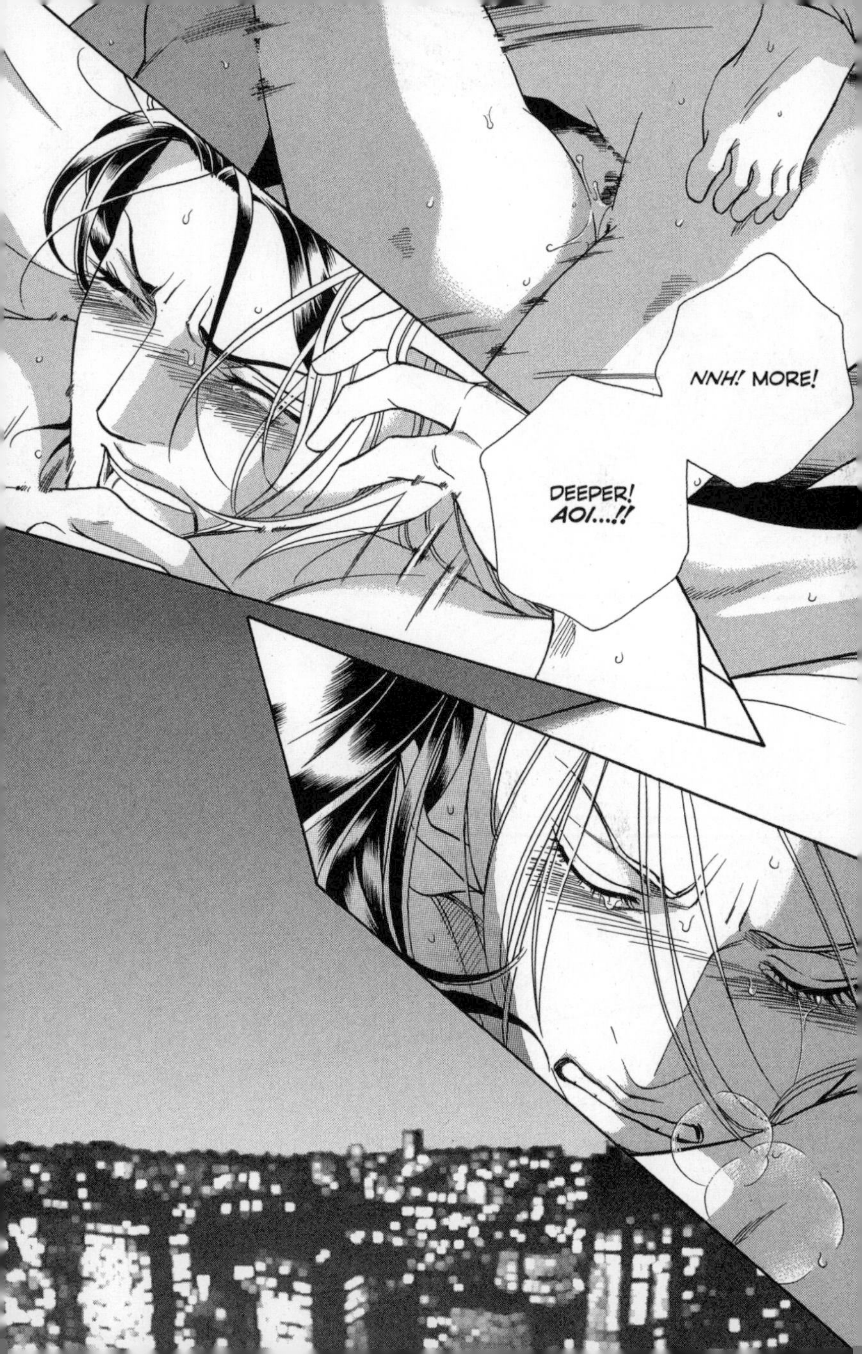
NNH! MORE!
DEEPER! AOI...!!

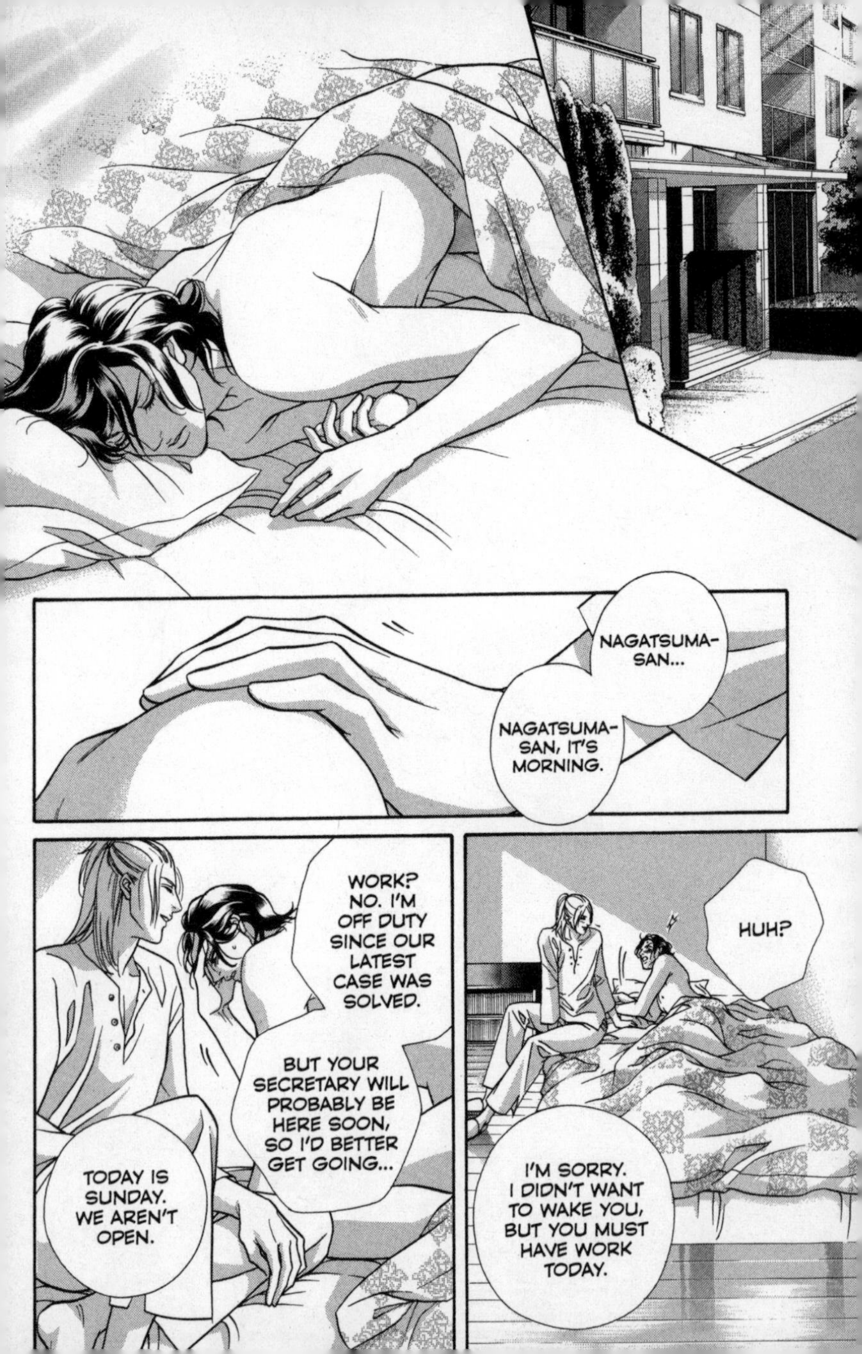
NAGATSUMA-SAN...
NAGATSUMA-SAN, IT'S MORNING.
HUH?
I'M SORRY. I DIDN'T WANT TO WAKE YOU, BUT YOU MUST HAVE WORK TODAY.
WORK? NO. I'M OFF DUTY SINCE OUR LATEST CASE WAS SOLVED.
BUT YOUR SECRETARY WILL PROBABLY BE HERE SOON, SO I'D BETTER GET GOING...
TODAY IS SUNDAY. WE AREN'T OPEN.

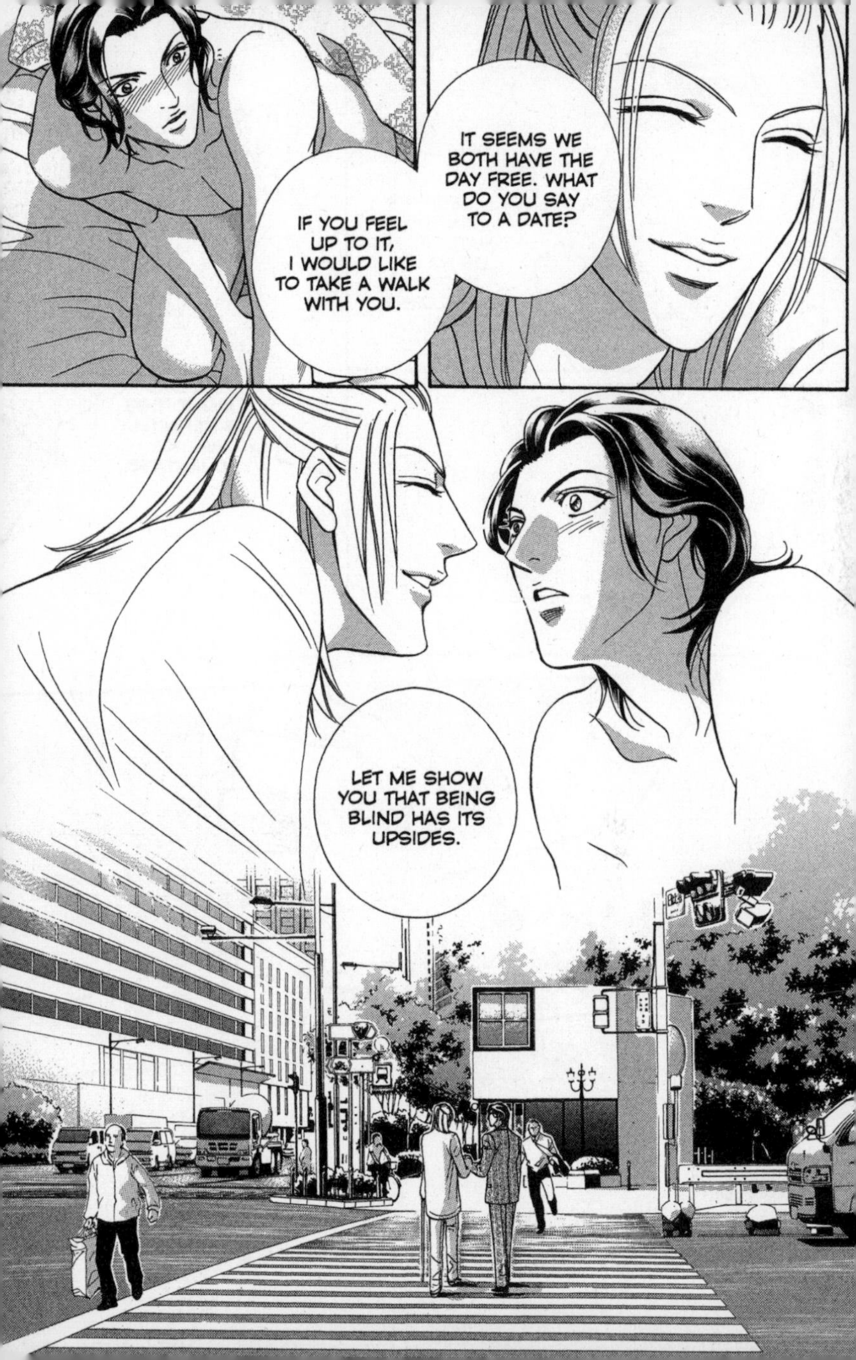
IT SEEMS WE BOTH HAVE THE DAY FREE. WHAT DO YOU SAY TO A DATE?
IF YOU FEEL UP TO IT, I WOULD LIKE TO TAKE A WALK WITH YOU.
LET ME SHOW YOU THAT BEING BLIND HAS ITS UPSIDES.

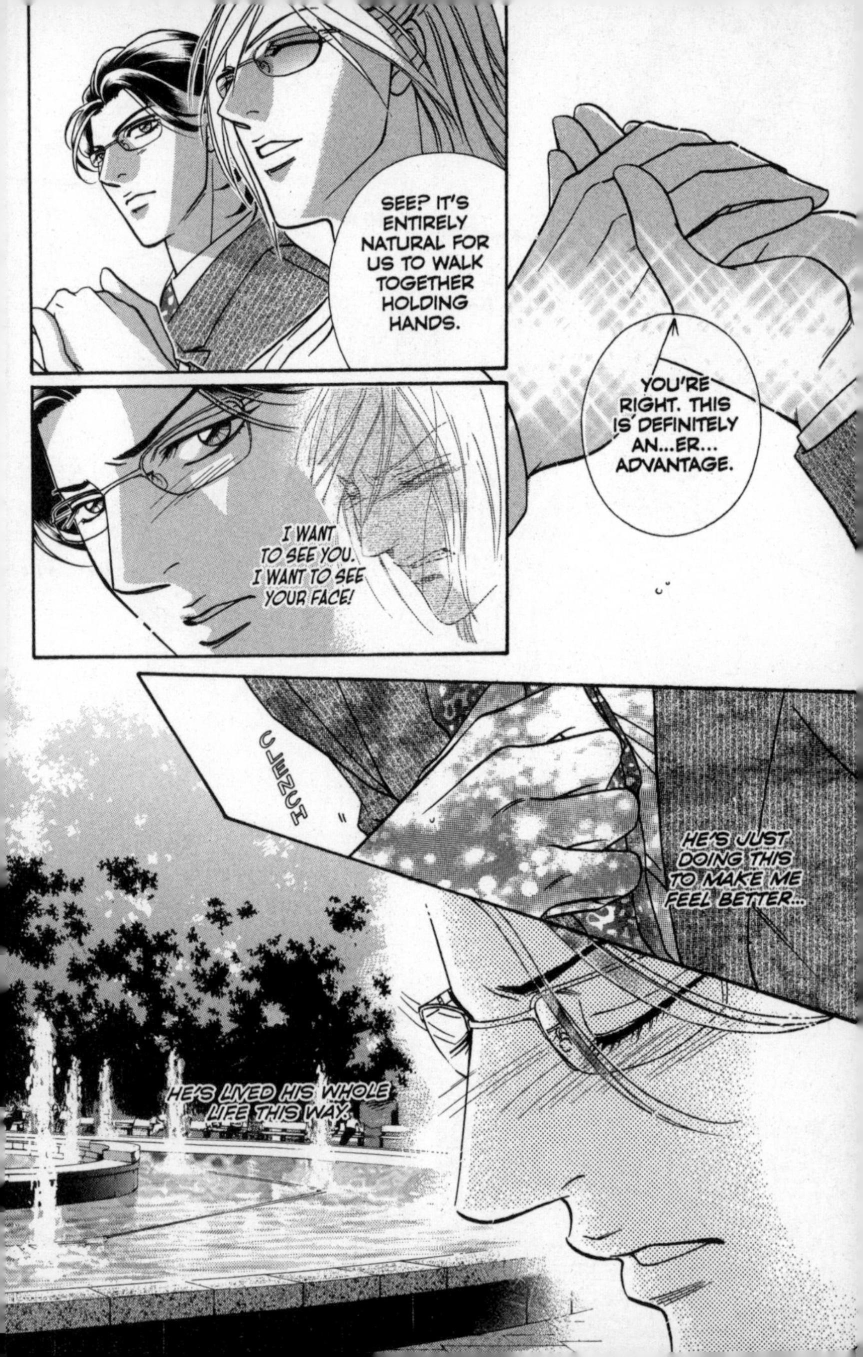
SEE? IT'S ENTIRELY NATURAL FOR US TO WALK TOGETHER HOLDING HANDS.
YOU'RE RIGHT. THIS IS DEFINITELY AN...ER... ADVANTAGE.
I WANT TO SEE YOU. I WANT TO SEE YOUR FACE!
CLENCH
HE'S JUST DOING THIS TO MAKE ME FEEL BETTER...
HE'S LIVED HIS WHOLE LIFE THIS WAY.

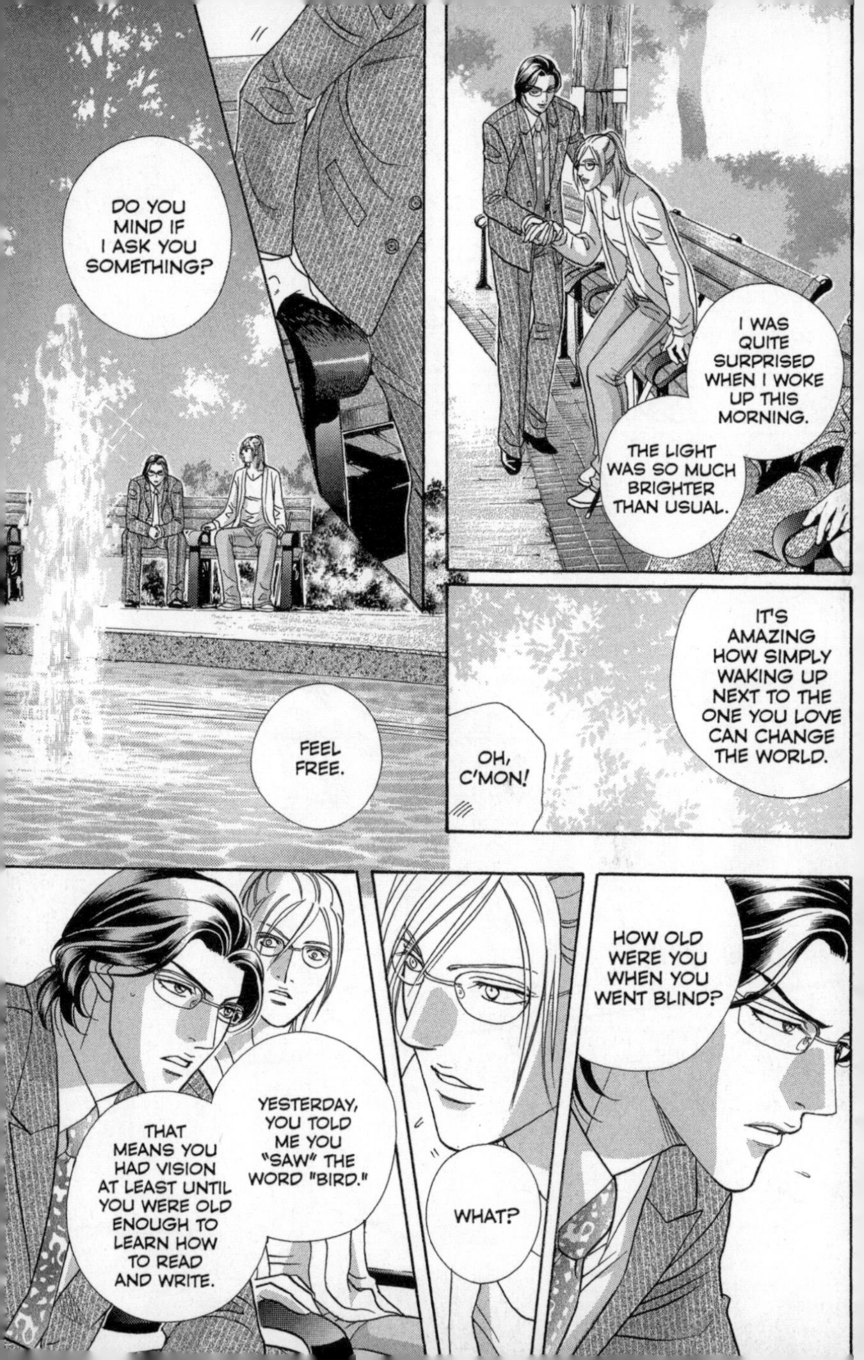

I WAS QUITE SURPRISED WHEN I WOKE UP THIS MORNING.
THE LIGHT WAS SO MUCH BRIGHTER THAN USUAL.
IT'S AMAZING HOW SIMPLY WAKING UP NEXT TO THE ONE YOU LOVE CAN CHANGE THE WORLD.
OH, C'MON!
DO YOU MIND IF I ASK YOU SOMETHING?
FEEL FREE.
HOW OLD WERE YOU WHEN YOU WENT BLIND?
WHAT?
YESTERDAY, YOU TOLD ME YOU "SAW" THE WORD "BIRD."
THAT MEANS YOU HAD VISION AT LEAST UNTIL YOU WERE OLD ENOUGH TO LEARN HOW TO READ AND WRITE.

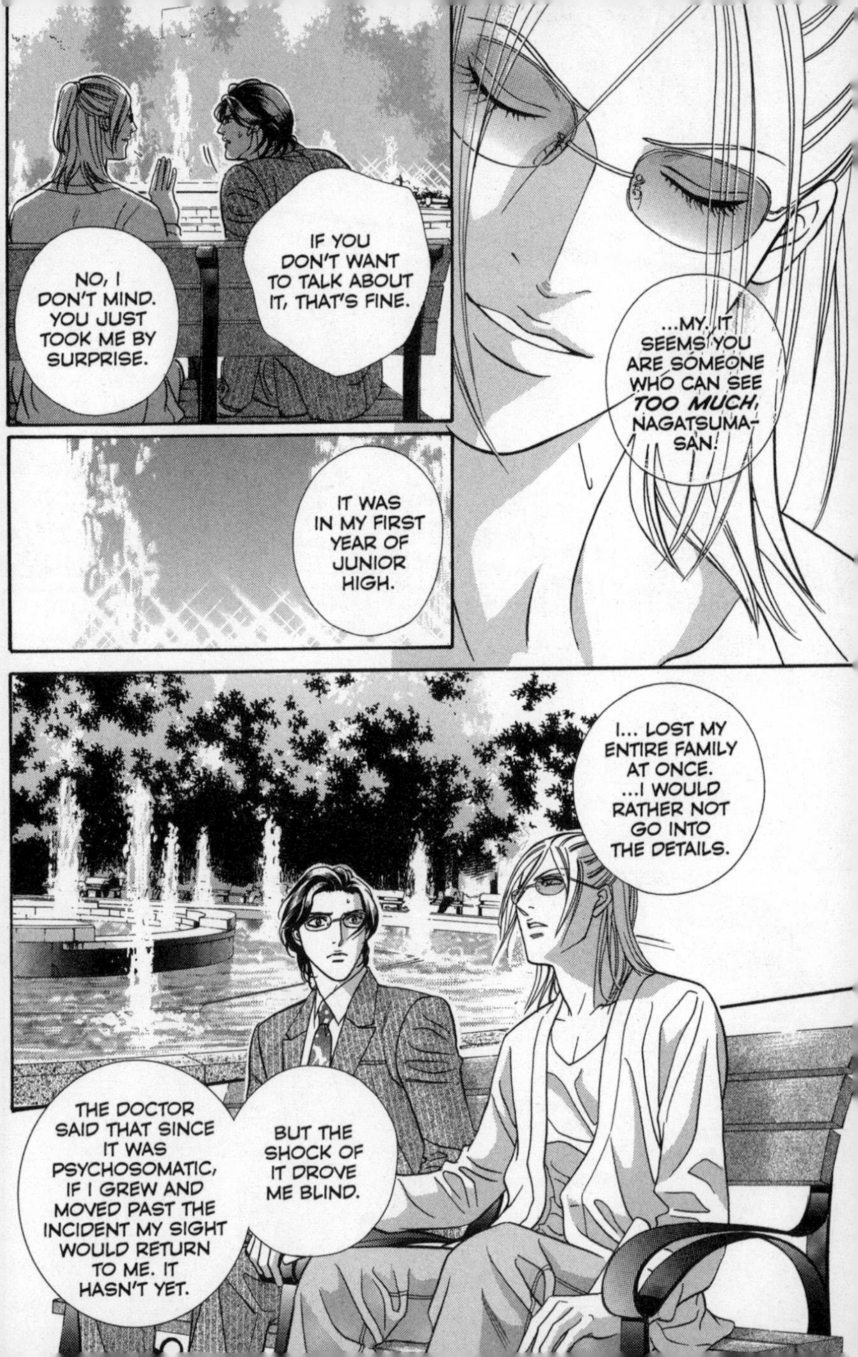
...MY, IT SEEMS YOU ARE SOMEONE WHO CAN SEE *TOO MUCH*, NAGATSUMA-SAN.
IF YOU DON'T WANT TO TALK ABOUT IT, THAT'S FINE.
NO, I DON'T MIND. YOU JUST TOOK ME BY SURPRISE.
IT WAS IN MY FIRST YEAR OF JUNIOR HIGH.
I... LOST MY ENTIRE FAMILY AT ONCE. ...I WOULD RATHER NOT GO INTO THE DETAILS.
BUT THE SHOCK OF IT DROVE ME BLIND.
THE DOCTOR SAID THAT SINCE IT WAS PSYCHOSOMATIC, IF I GREW AND MOVED PAST THE INCIDENT MY SIGHT WOULD RETURN TO ME. IT HASN'T YET.

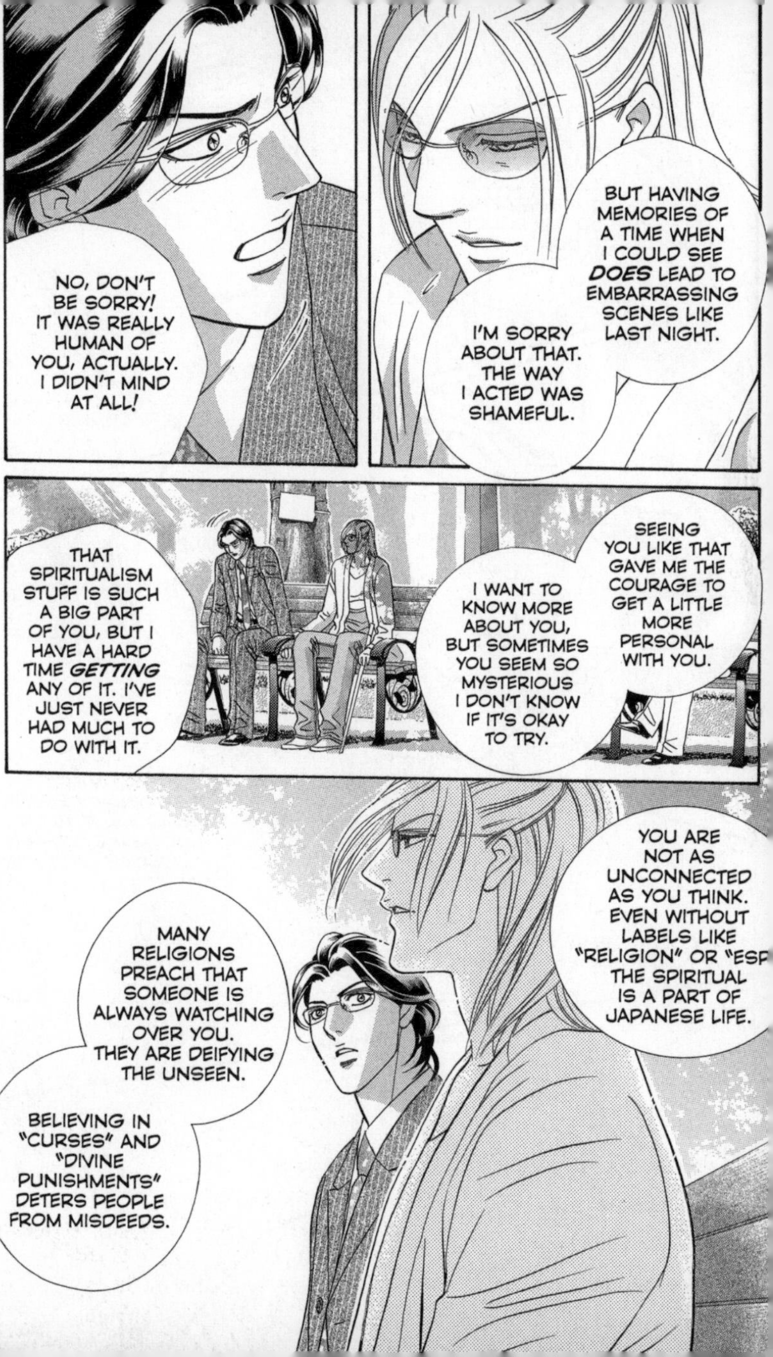
BUT HAVING MEMORIES OF A TIME WHEN I COULD SEE ***DOES*** LEAD TO EMBARRASSING SCENES LIKE LAST NIGHT.
I'M SORRY ABOUT THAT. THE WAY I ACTED WAS SHAMEFUL.
NO, DON'T BE SORRY! IT WAS REALLY HUMAN OF YOU, ACTUALLY. I DIDN'T MIND AT ALL!
SEEING YOU LIKE THAT GAVE ME THE COURAGE TO GET A LITTLE MORE PERSONAL WITH YOU.
I WANT TO KNOW MORE ABOUT YOU, BUT SOMETIMES YOU SEEM SO MYSTERIOUS I DON'T KNOW IF IT'S OKAY TO TRY.
THAT SPIRITUALISM STUFF IS SUCH A BIG PART OF YOU, BUT I HAVE A HARD TIME ***GETTING*** ANY OF IT. I'VE JUST NEVER HAD MUCH TO DO WITH IT.
YOU ARE NOT AS UNCONNECTED AS YOU THINK. EVEN WITHOUT LABELS LIKE "RELIGION" OR "ESP THE SPIRITUAL IS A PART OF JAPANESE LIFE.
MANY RELIGIONS PREACH THAT SOMEONE IS ALWAYS WATCHING OVER YOU. THEY ARE DEIFYING THE UNSEEN.
BELIEVING IN "CURSES" AND "DIVINE PUNISHMENTS" DETERS PEOPLE FROM MISDEEDS.

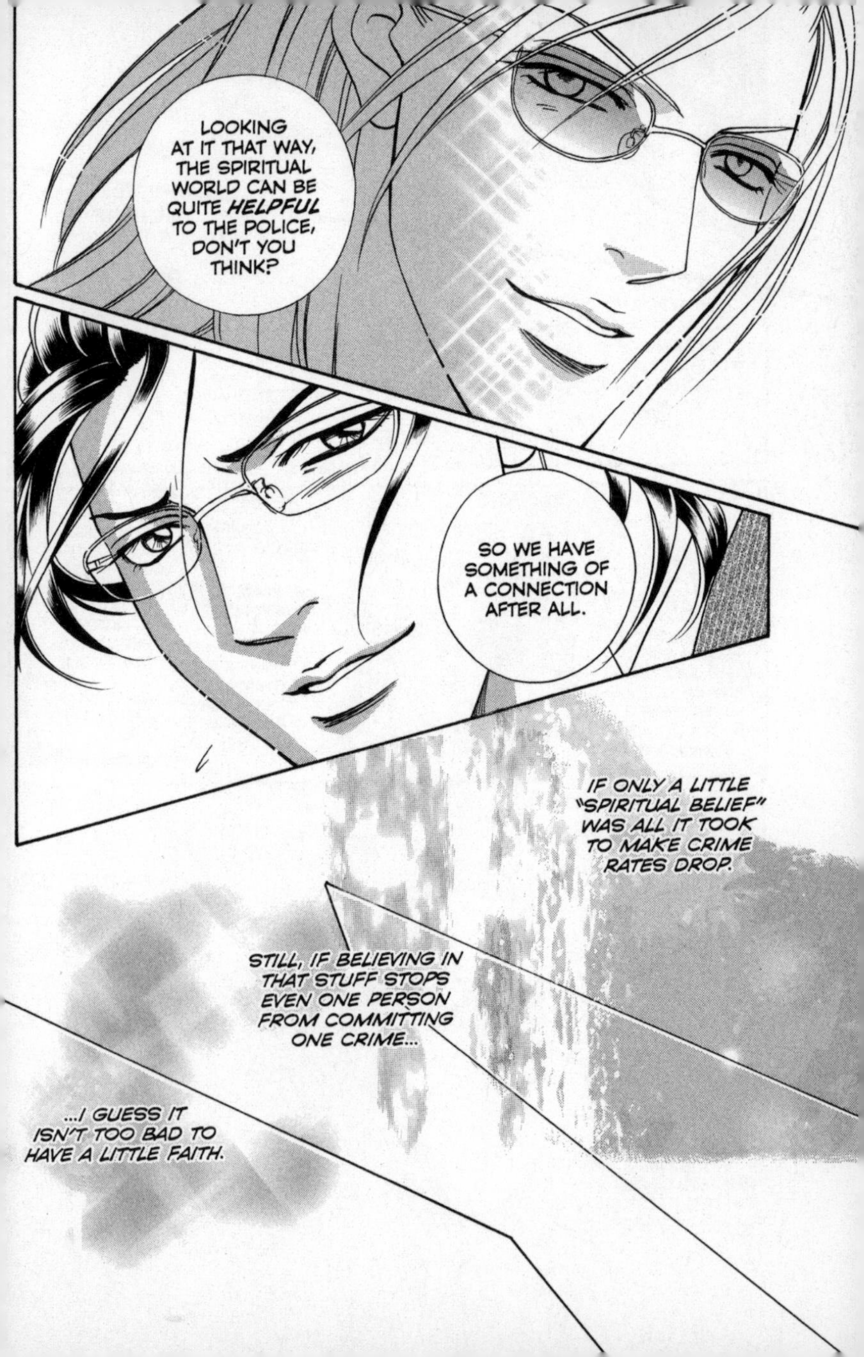
LOOKING AT IT THAT WAY, THE SPIRITUAL WORLD CAN BE QUITE *HELPFUL* TO THE POLICE, DON'T YOU THINK?
SO WE HAVE SOMETHING OF A CONNECTION AFTER ALL.
IF ONLY A LITTLE "SPIRITUAL BELIEF" WAS ALL IT TOOK TO MAKE CRIME RATES DROP.
STILL, IF BELIEVING IN THAT STUFF STOPS EVEN ONE PERSON FROM COMMITTING ONE CRIME...
...I GUESS IT ISN'T TOO BAD TO HAVE A LITTLE FAITH.

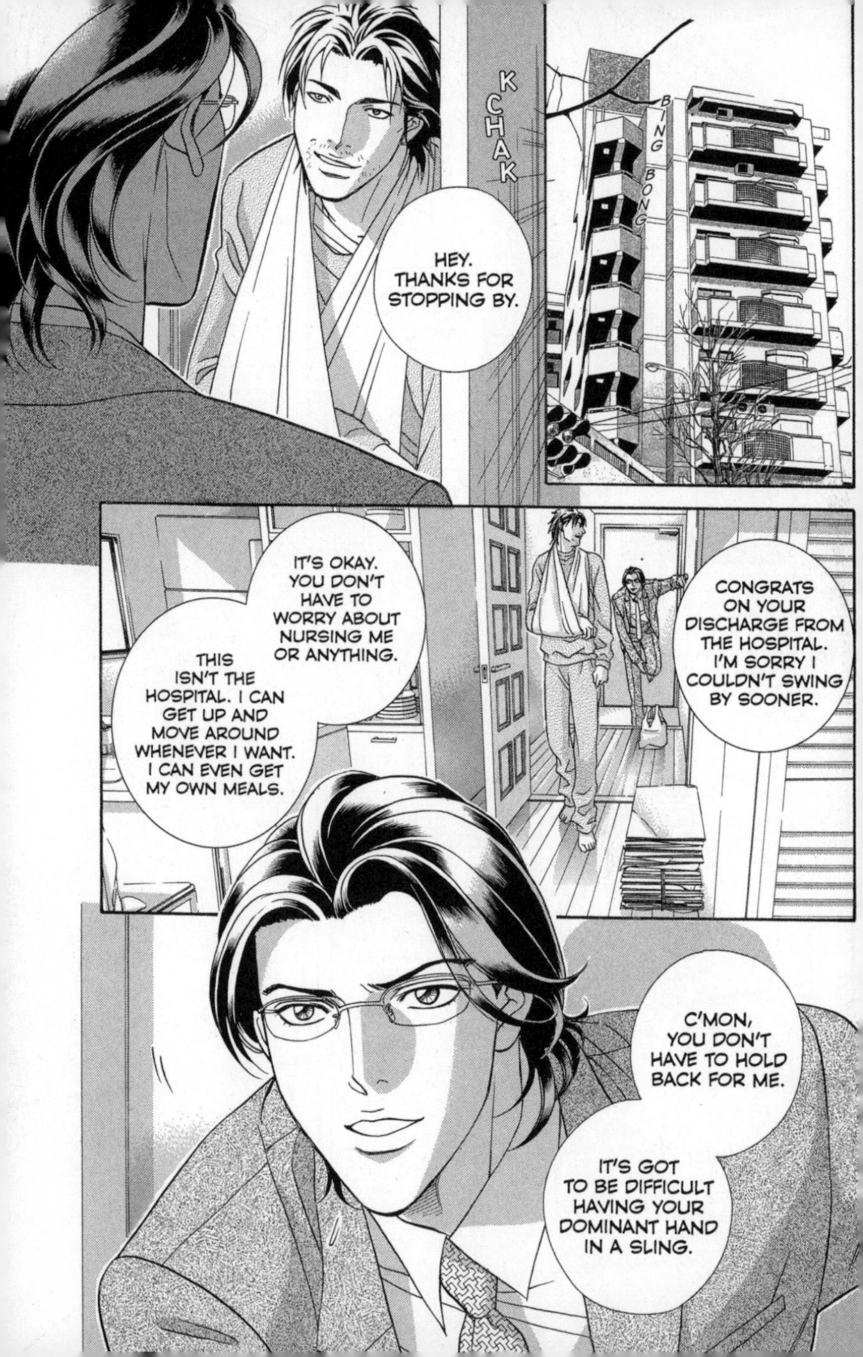
BING BONG
KCHAK
HEY. THANKS FOR STOPPING BY.
CONGRATS ON YOUR DISCHARGE FROM THE HOSPITAL. I'M SORRY I COULDN'T SWING BY SOONER.
IT'S OKAY. YOU DON'T HAVE TO WORRY ABOUT NURSING ME OR ANYTHING.
THIS ISN'T THE HOSPITAL. I CAN GET UP AND MOVE AROUND WHENEVER I WANT. I CAN EVEN GET MY OWN MEALS.
C'MON, YOU DON'T HAVE TO HOLD BACK FOR ME.
IT'S GOT TO BE DIFFICULT HAVING YOUR DOMINANT HAND IN A SLING.

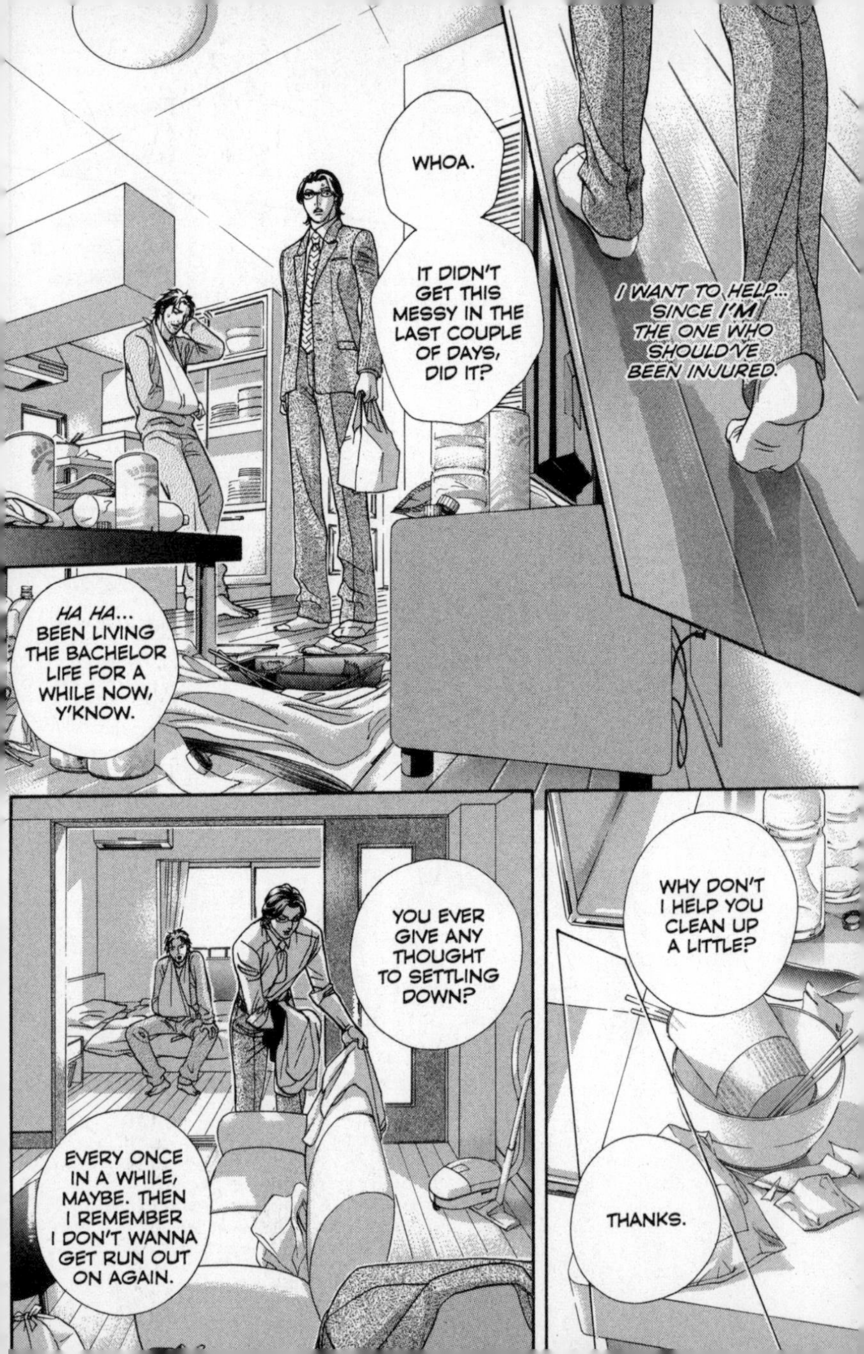
I WANT TO HELP... SINCE I'M THE ONE WHO SHOULD'VE BEEN INJURED.
WHOA.
IT DIDN'T GET THIS MESSY IN THE LAST COUPLE OF DAYS, DID IT?
HA HA... BEEN LIVING THE BACHELOR LIFE FOR A WHILE NOW, Y'KNOW.
WHY DON'T I HELP YOU CLEAN UP A LITTLE?
THANKS.
YOU EVER GIVE ANY THOUGHT TO SETTLING DOWN?
EVERY ONCE IN A WHILE, MAYBE. THEN I REMEMBER I DON'T WANNA GET RUN OUT ON AGAIN.

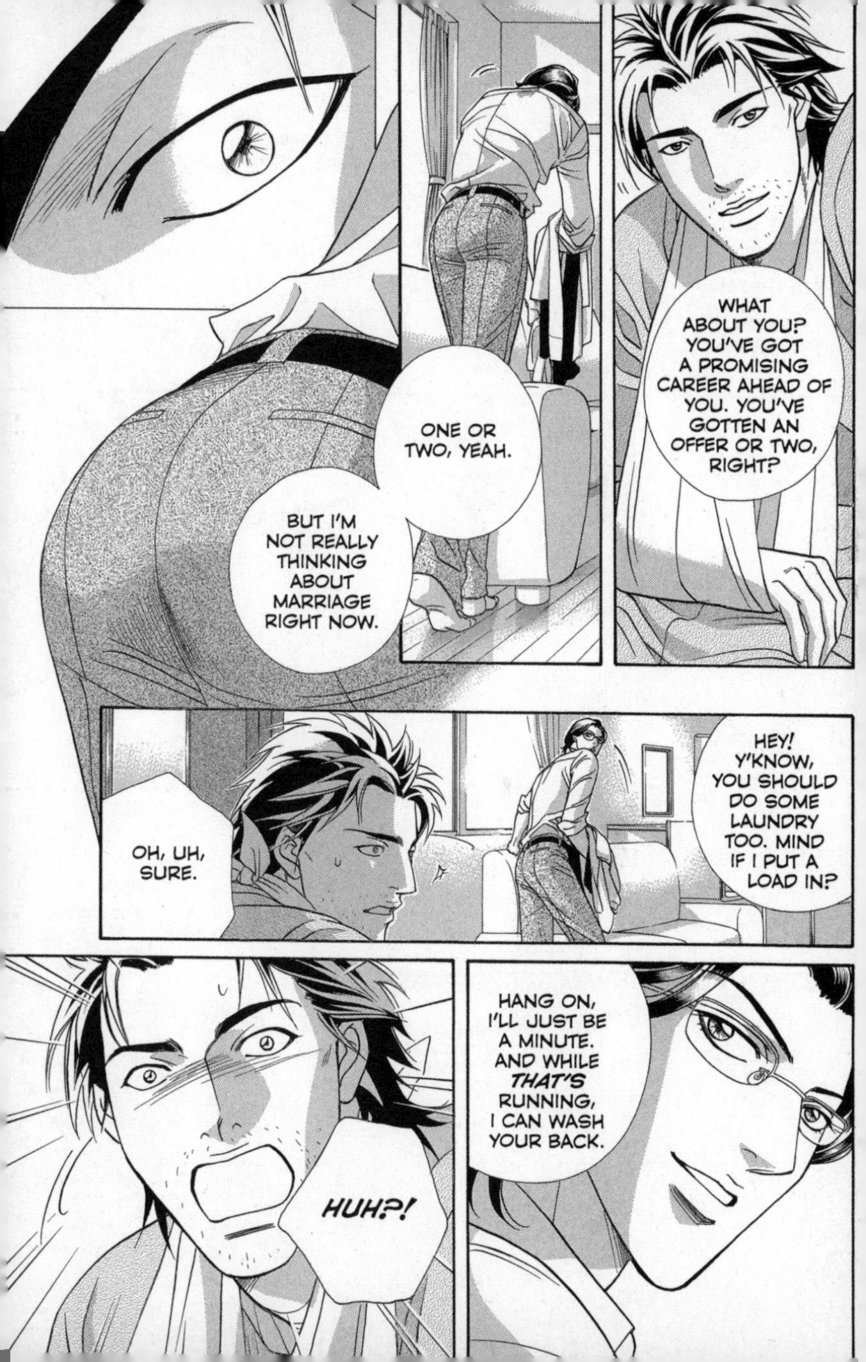
WHAT ABOUT YOU? YOU'VE GOT A PROMISING CAREER AHEAD OF YOU. YOU'VE GOTTEN AN OFFER OR TWO, RIGHT?
ONE OR TWO, YEAH.
BUT I'M NOT REALLY THINKING ABOUT MARRIAGE RIGHT NOW.
HEY! Y'KNOW, YOU SHOULD DO SOME LAUNDRY TOO. MIND IF I PUT A LOAD IN?
OH, UH, SURE.
HANG ON, I'LL JUST BE A MINUTE. AND WHILE *THAT'S* RUNNING, I CAN WASH YOUR BACK.
HUH?!

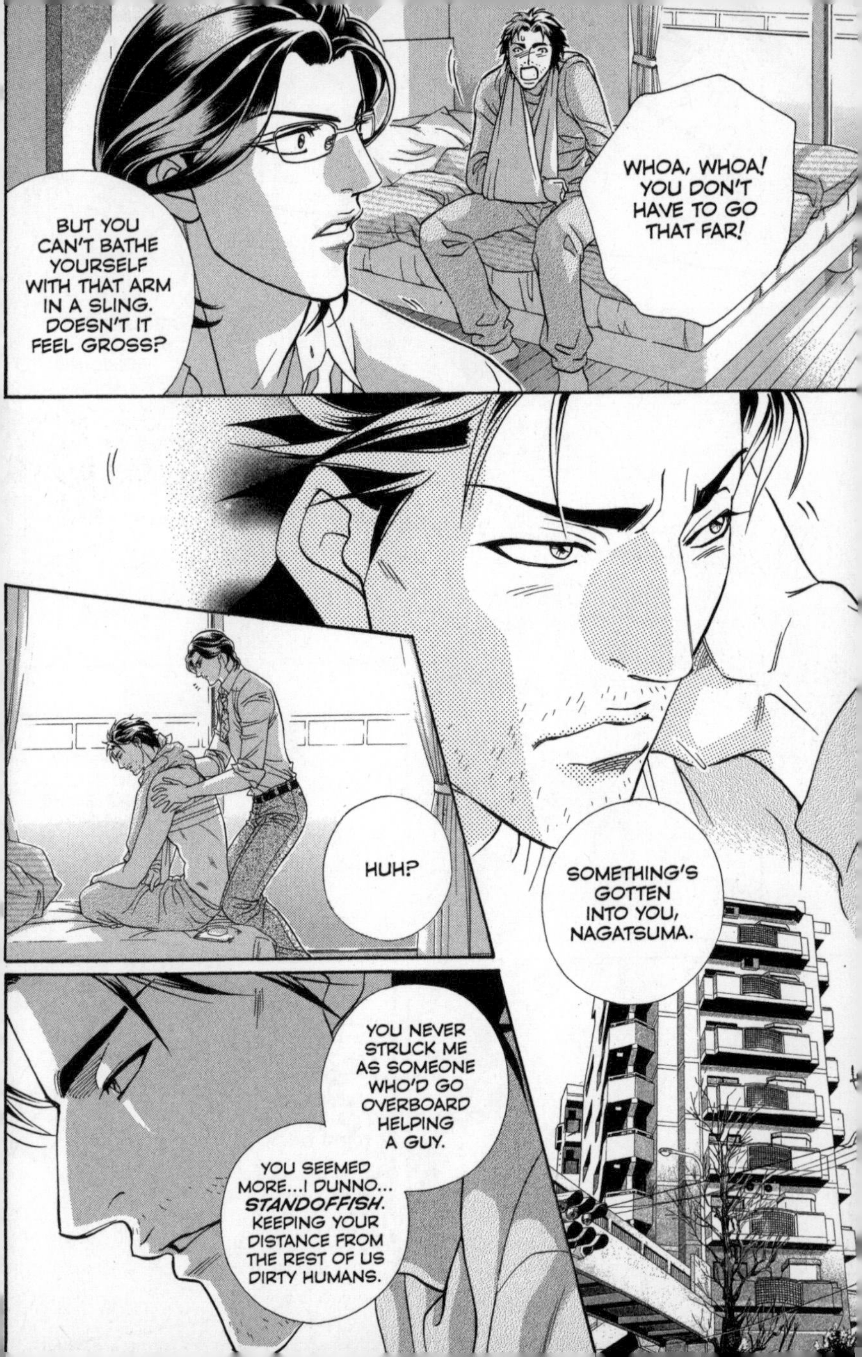
WHOA, WHOA! YOU DON'T HAVE TO GO THAT FAR!
BUT YOU CAN'T BATHE YOURSELF WITH THAT ARM IN A SLING. DOESN'T IT FEEL GROSS?
HUH?
SOMETHING'S GOTTEN INTO YOU, NAGATSUMA.
YOU NEVER STRUCK ME AS SOMEONE WHO'D GO OVERBOARD HELPING A GUY.
YOU SEEMED MORE...I DUNNO... ***STANDOFFISH***. KEEPING YOUR DISTANCE FROM THE REST OF US DIRTY HUMANS.

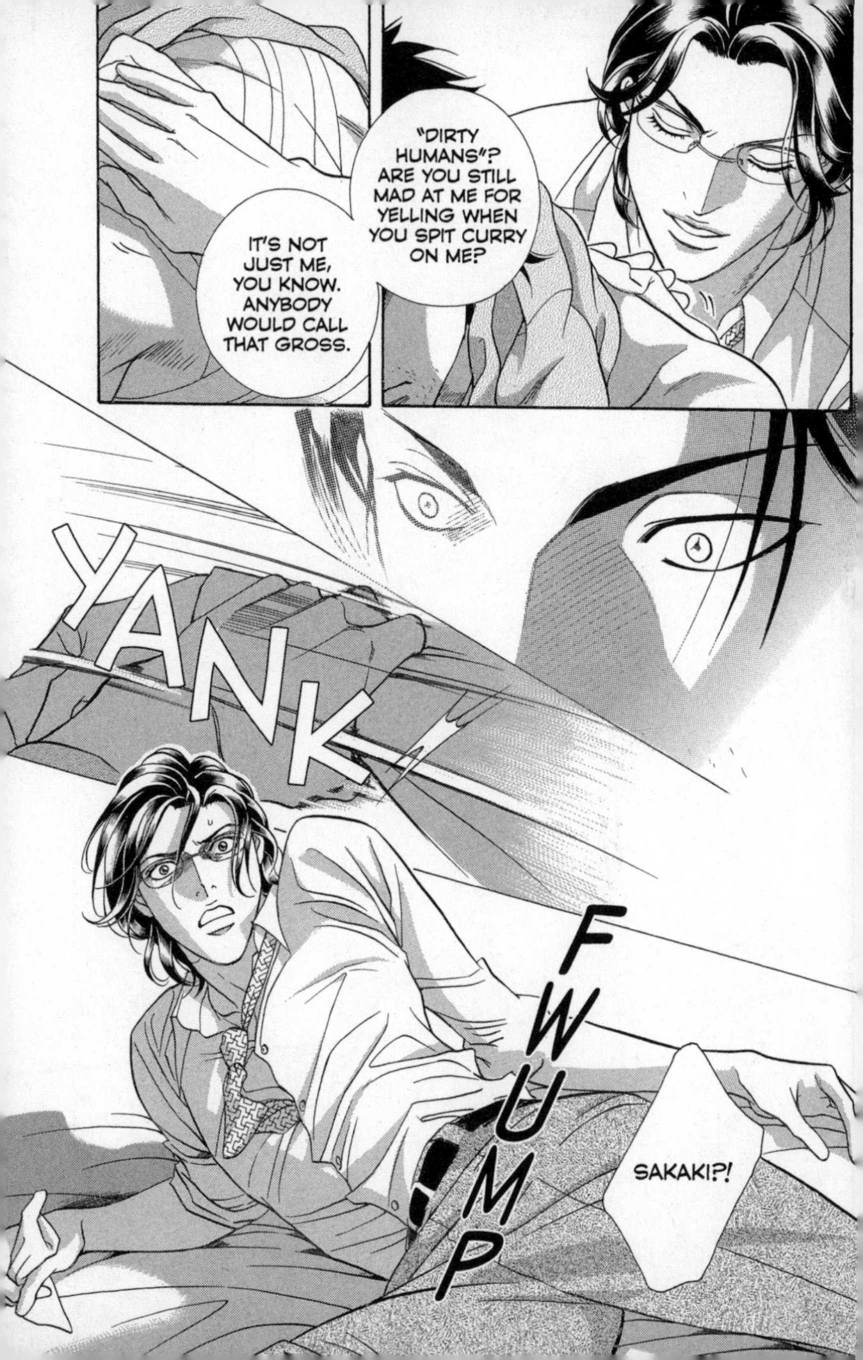
"DIRTY HUMANS"? ARE YOU STILL MAD AT ME FOR YELLING WHEN YOU SPIT CURRY ON ME?
IT'S NOT JUST ME, YOU KNOW. ANYBODY WOULD CALL THAT GROSS.
YANK
FWUMP
SAKAKI?!

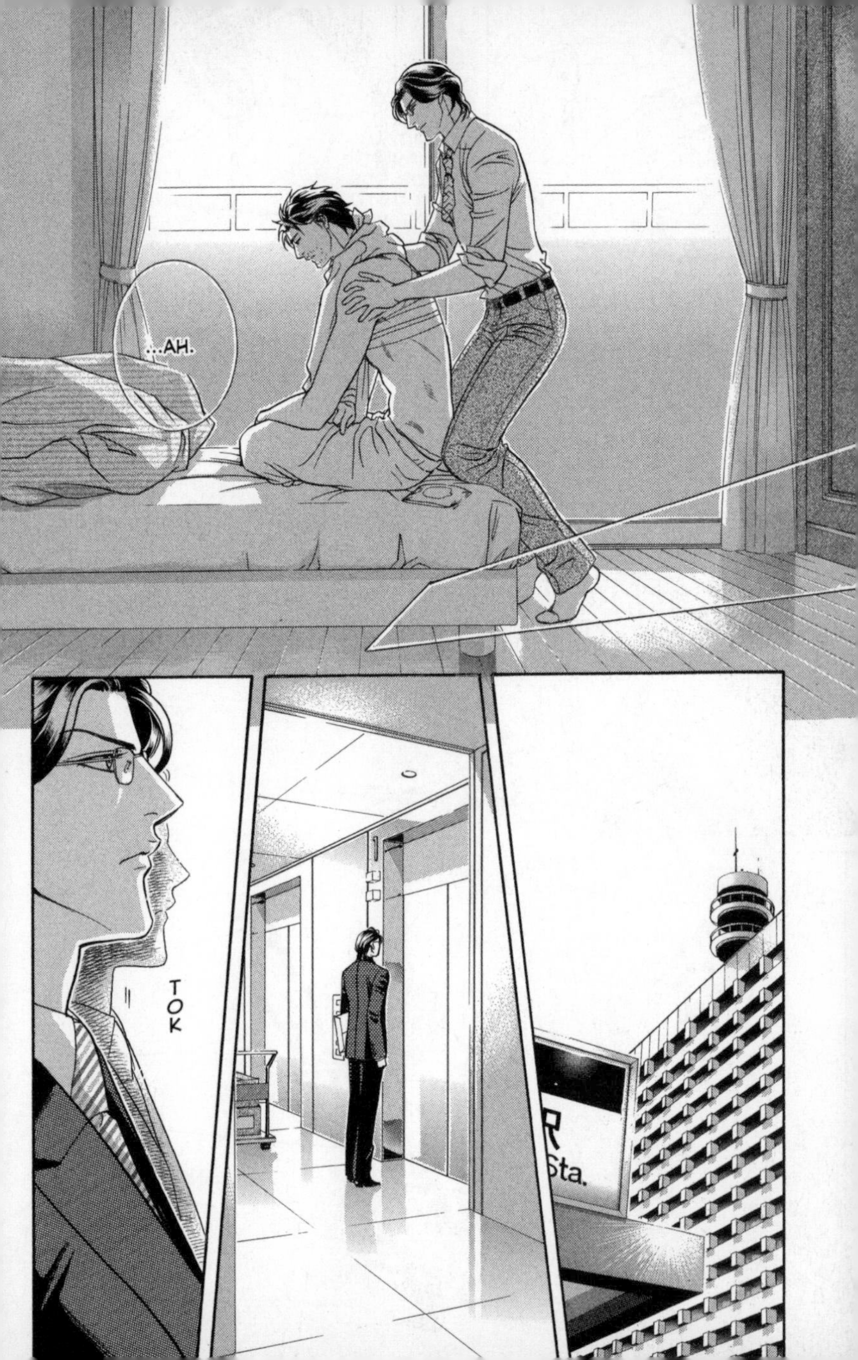
...AH.
Sta.
TOK

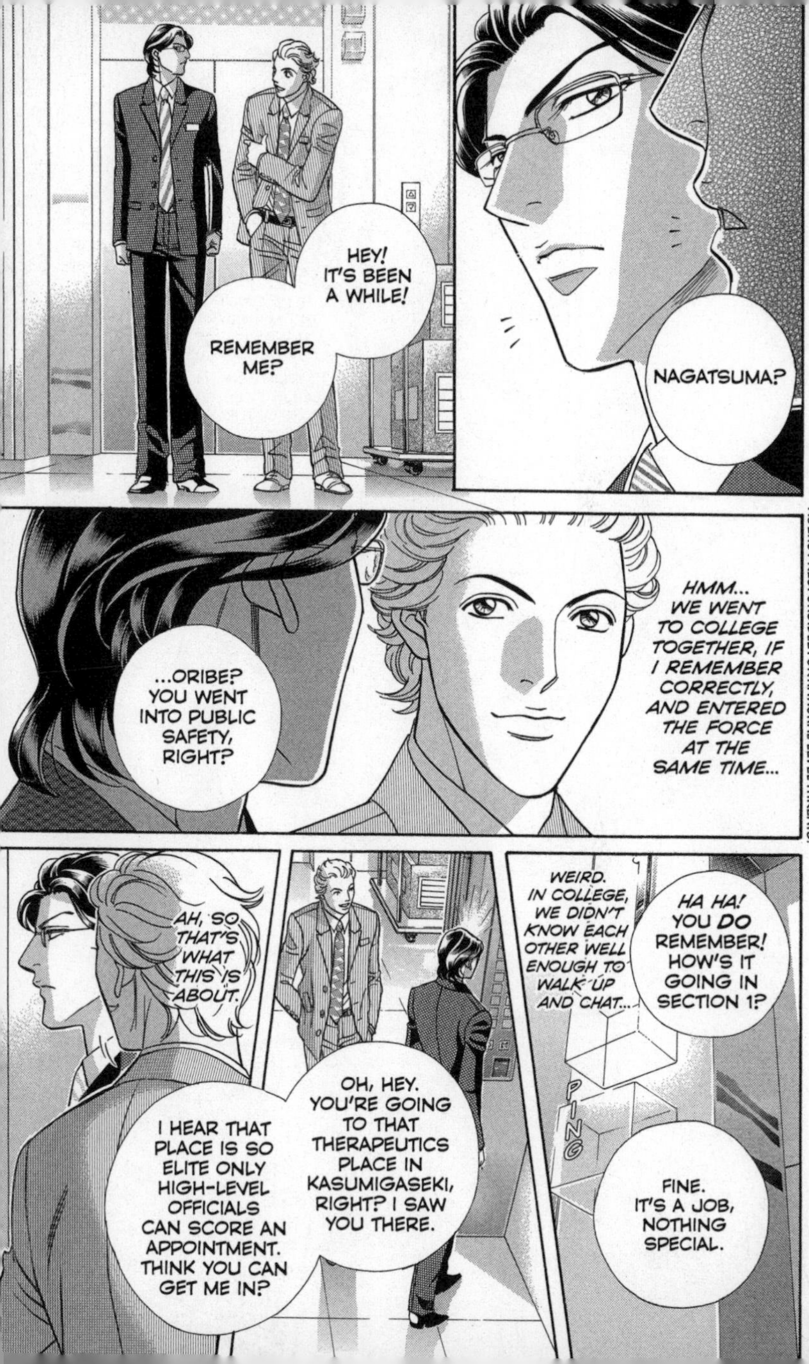
NAGATSUMA?
HEY! IT'S BEEN A WHILE!
REMEMBER ME?
HMM... WE WENT TO COLLEGE TOGETHER, IF I REMEMBER CORRECTLY, AND ENTERED THE FORCE AT THE SAME TIME...
...ORIBE? YOU WENT INTO PUBLIC SAFETY, RIGHT?
HA HA! YOU DO REMEMBER! HOW'S IT GOING IN SECTION 1?
WEIRD. IN COLLEGE, WE DIDN'T KNOW EACH OTHER WELL ENOUGH TO WALK UP AND CHAT...
PING
FINE. IT'S A JOB, NOTHING SPECIAL.
OH, HEY. YOU'RE GOING TO THAT THERAPEUTICS PLACE IN KASUMIGASEKI, RIGHT? I SAW YOU THERE.
I HEAR THAT PLACE IS SO ELITE ONLY HIGH-LEVEL OFFICIALS CAN SCORE AN APPOINTMENT. THINK YOU CAN GET ME IN?
AH, SO THAT'S WHAT THIS IS ABOUT.

*PUBLIC SAFETY: A DIVISION OF THE JAPANESE POLICE AGENCY RESPONSIBLE FOR NATIONAL-LEVEL THREATS.

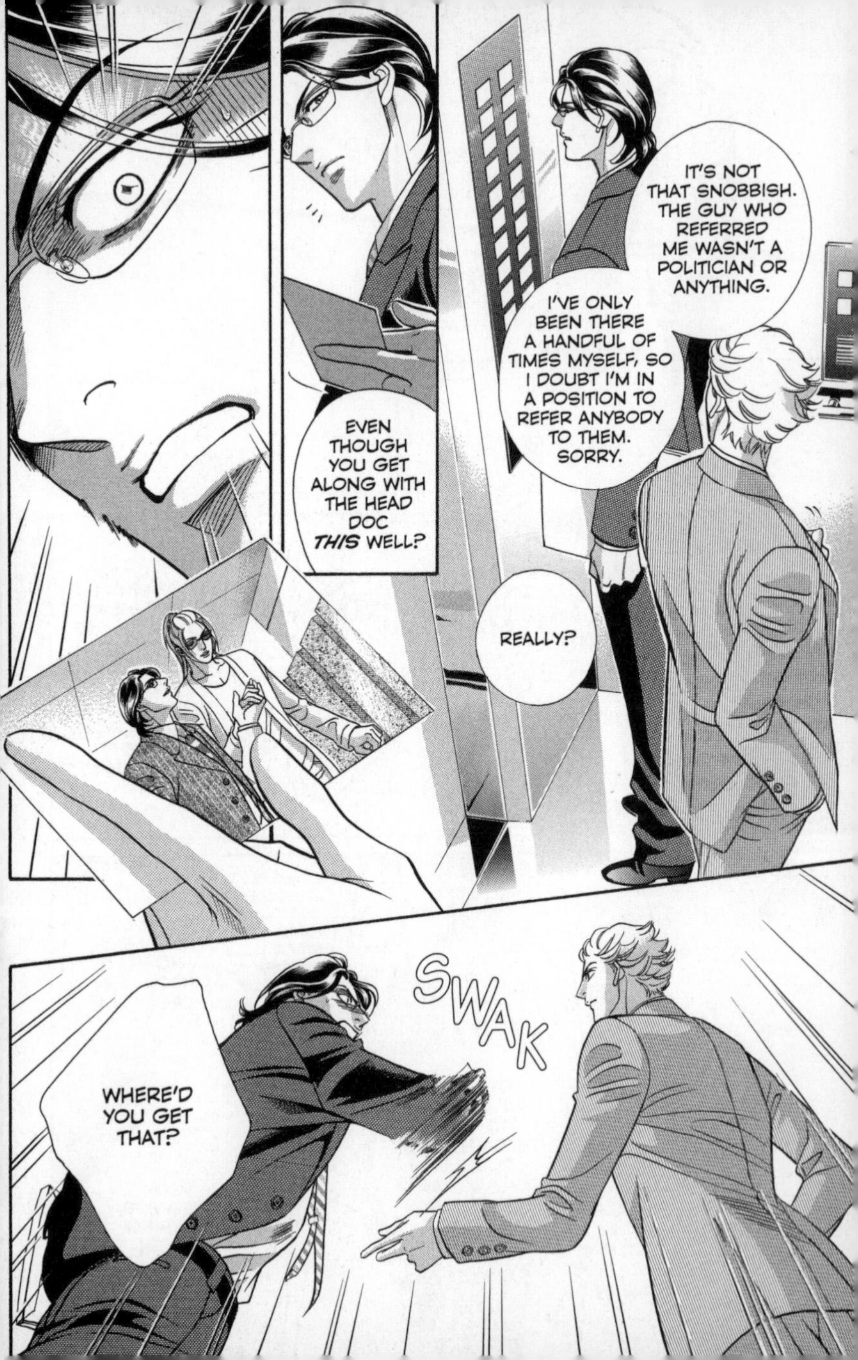
IT'S NOT THAT SNOBBISH. THE GUY WHO REFERRED ME WASN'T A POLITICIAN OR ANYTHING.
I'VE ONLY BEEN THERE A HANDFUL OF TIMES MYSELF, SO I DOUBT I'M IN A POSITION TO REFER ANYBODY TO THEM. SORRY.
REALLY?
EVEN THOUGH YOU GET ALONG WITH THE HEAD DOC *THIS* WELL?
SWAK
WHERE'D YOU GET THAT?

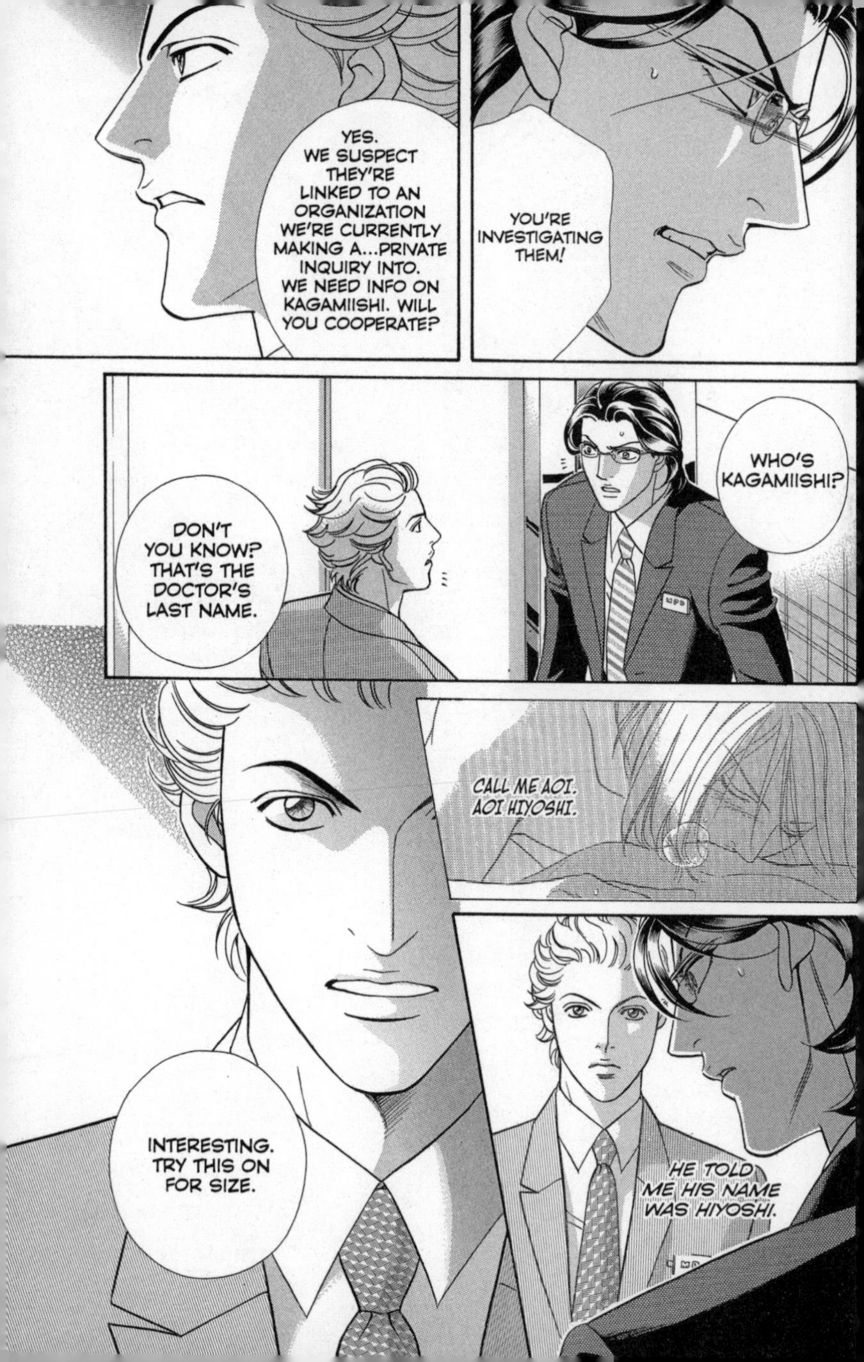
YOU'RE INVESTIGATING THEM!
YES. WE SUSPECT THEY'RE LINKED TO AN ORGANIZATION WE'RE CURRENTLY MAKING A...PRIVATE INQUIRY INTO. WE NEED INFO ON KAGAMIISHI. WILL YOU COOPERATE?
WHO'S KAGAMIISHI?
DON'T YOU KNOW? THAT'S THE DOCTOR'S LAST NAME.
CALL ME AOI. AOI HIYOSHI.
HE TOLD ME HIS NAME WAS HIYOSHI.
INTERESTING. TRY THIS ON FOR SIZE.

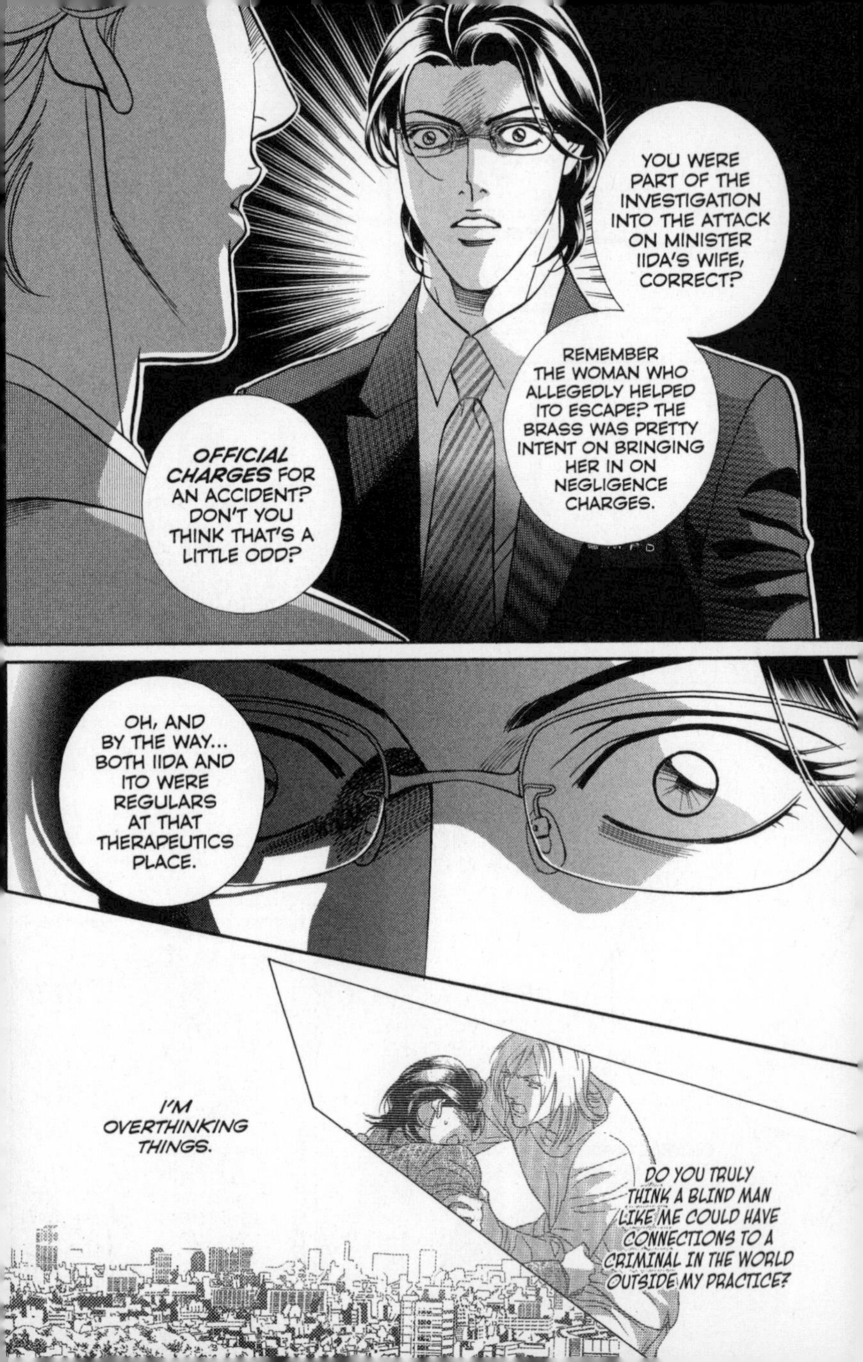
YOU WERE PART OF THE INVESTIGATION INTO THE ATTACK ON MINISTER IIDA'S WIFE, CORRECT?
REMEMBER THE WOMAN WHO ALLEGEDLY HELPED ITO ESCAPE? THE BRASS WAS PRETTY INTENT ON BRINGING HER IN ON NEGLIGENCE CHARGES.
OFFICIAL CHARGES FOR AN ACCIDENT? DON'T YOU THINK THAT'S A LITTLE ODD?
OH, AND BY THE WAY... BOTH IIDA AND ITO WERE REGULARS AT THAT THERAPEUTICS PLACE.
DO YOU TRULY THINK A BLIND MAN LIKE ME COULD HAVE CONNECTIONS TO A CRIMINAL IN THE WORLD OUTSIDE MY PRACTICE?
I'M OVERTHINKING THINGS.

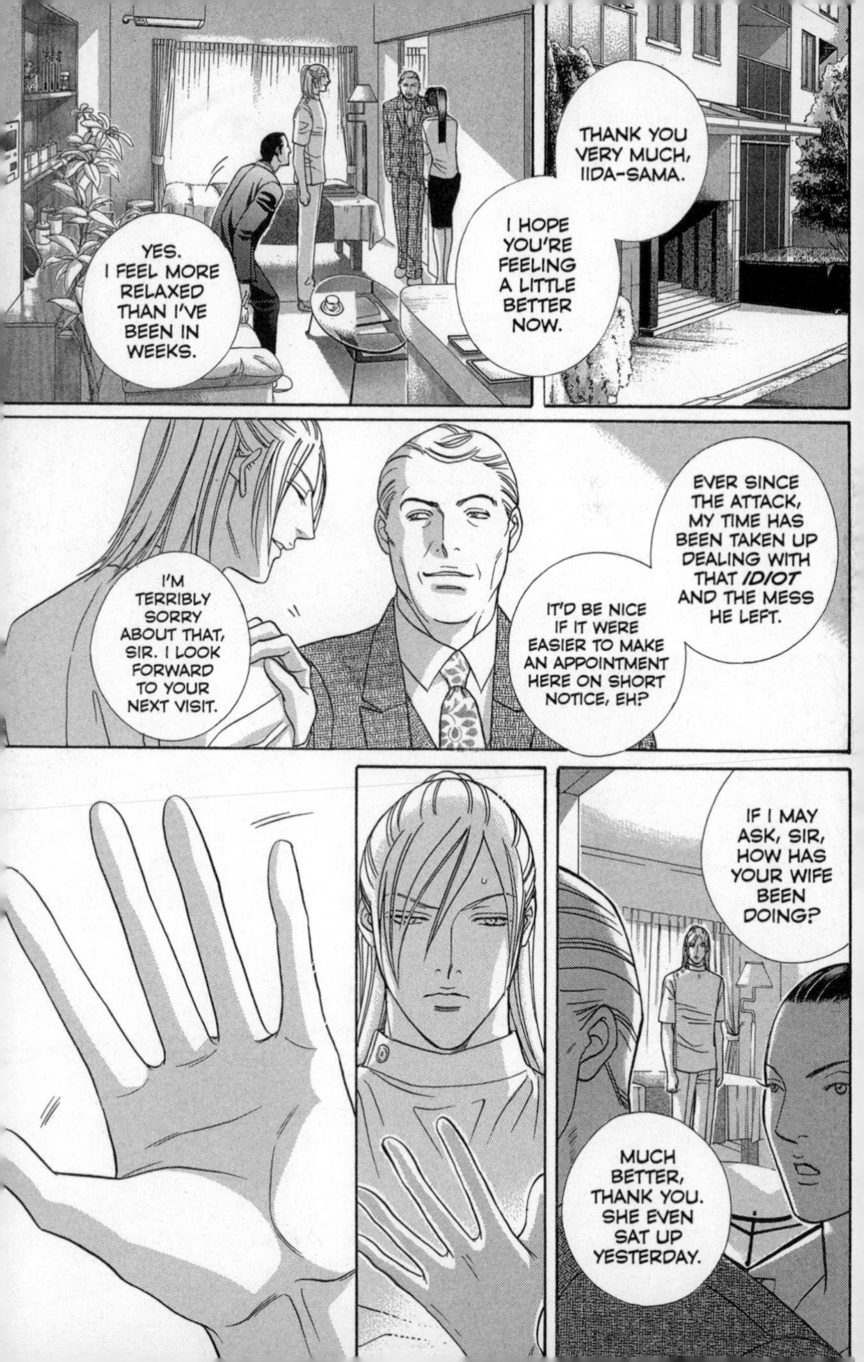
THANK YOU VERY MUCH, IIDA-SAMA.
I HOPE YOU'RE FEELING A LITTLE BETTER NOW.
YES. I FEEL MORE RELAXED THAN I'VE BEEN IN WEEKS.
EVER SINCE THE ATTACK, MY TIME HAS BEEN TAKEN UP DEALING WITH THAT *IDIOT* AND THE MESS HE LEFT.
IT'D BE NICE IF IT WERE EASIER TO MAKE AN APPOINTMENT HERE ON SHORT NOTICE, EH?
I'M TERRIBLY SORRY ABOUT THAT, SIR. I LOOK FORWARD TO YOUR NEXT VISIT.
IF I MAY ASK, SIR, HOW HAS YOUR WIFE BEEN DOING?
MUCH BETTER, THANK YOU. SHE EVEN SAT UP YESTERDAY.

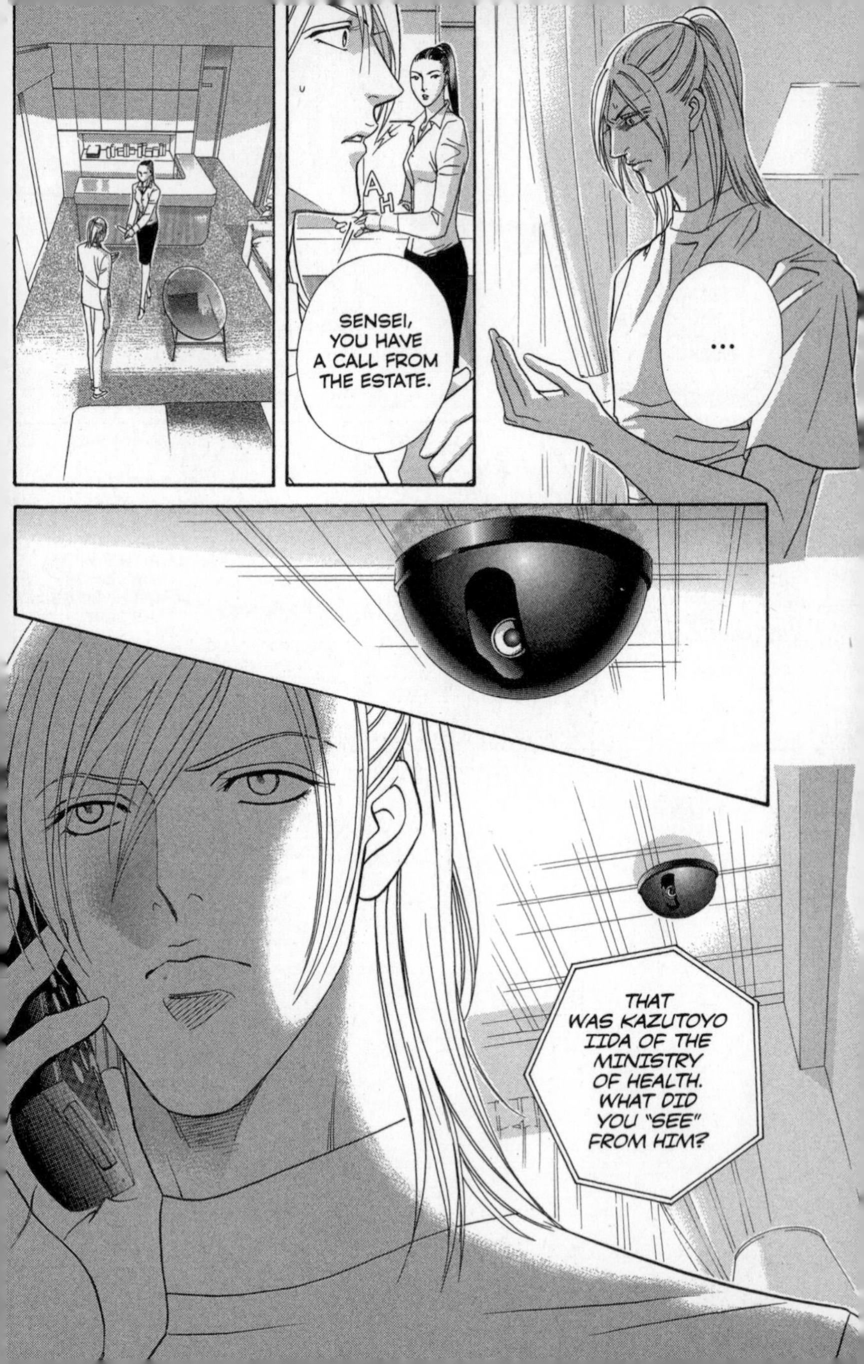
...
AH
SENSEI, YOU HAVE A CALL FROM THE ESTATE.
THAT WAS KAZUTOYO IIDA OF THE MINISTRY OF HEALTH. WHAT DID YOU "SEE" FROM HIM?

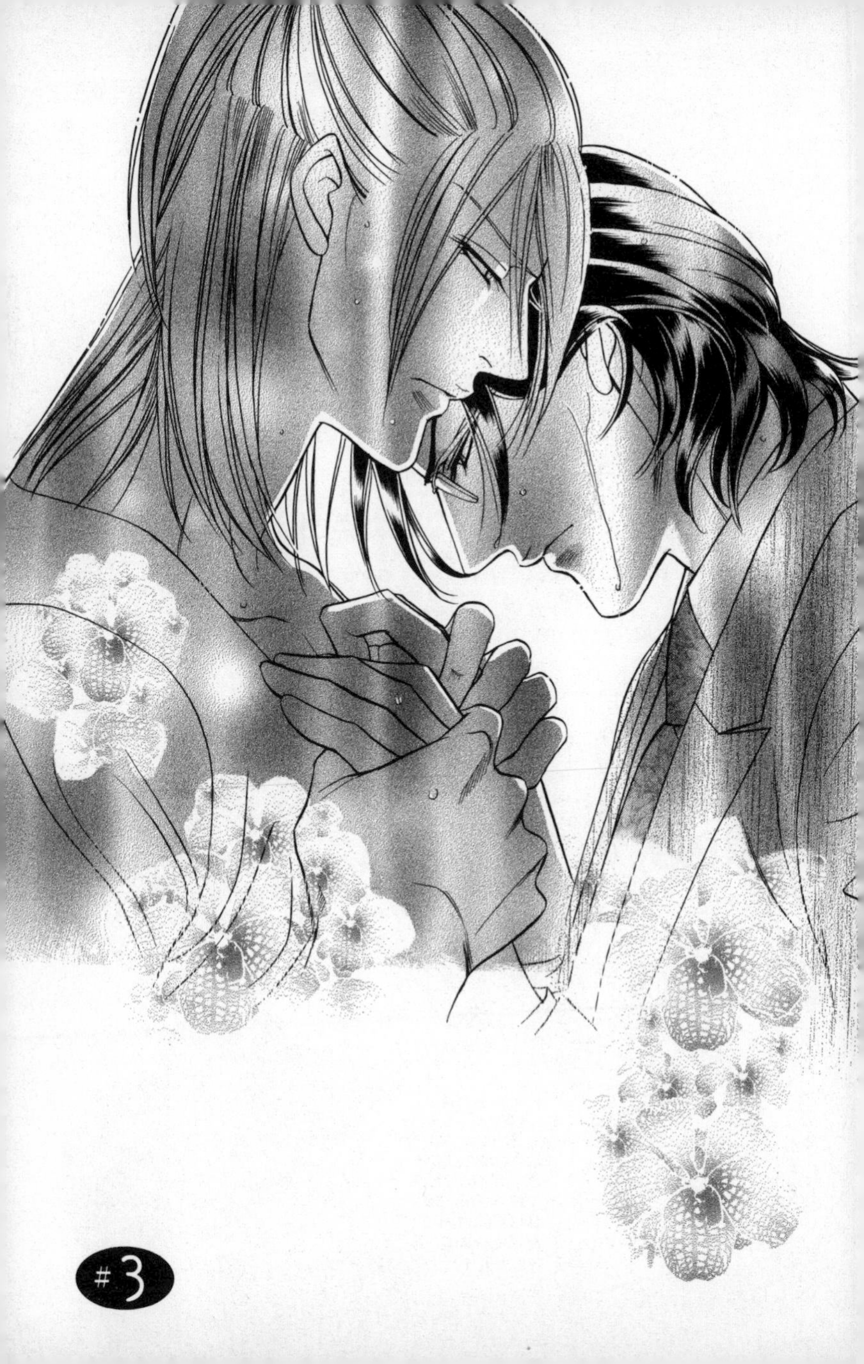
#3

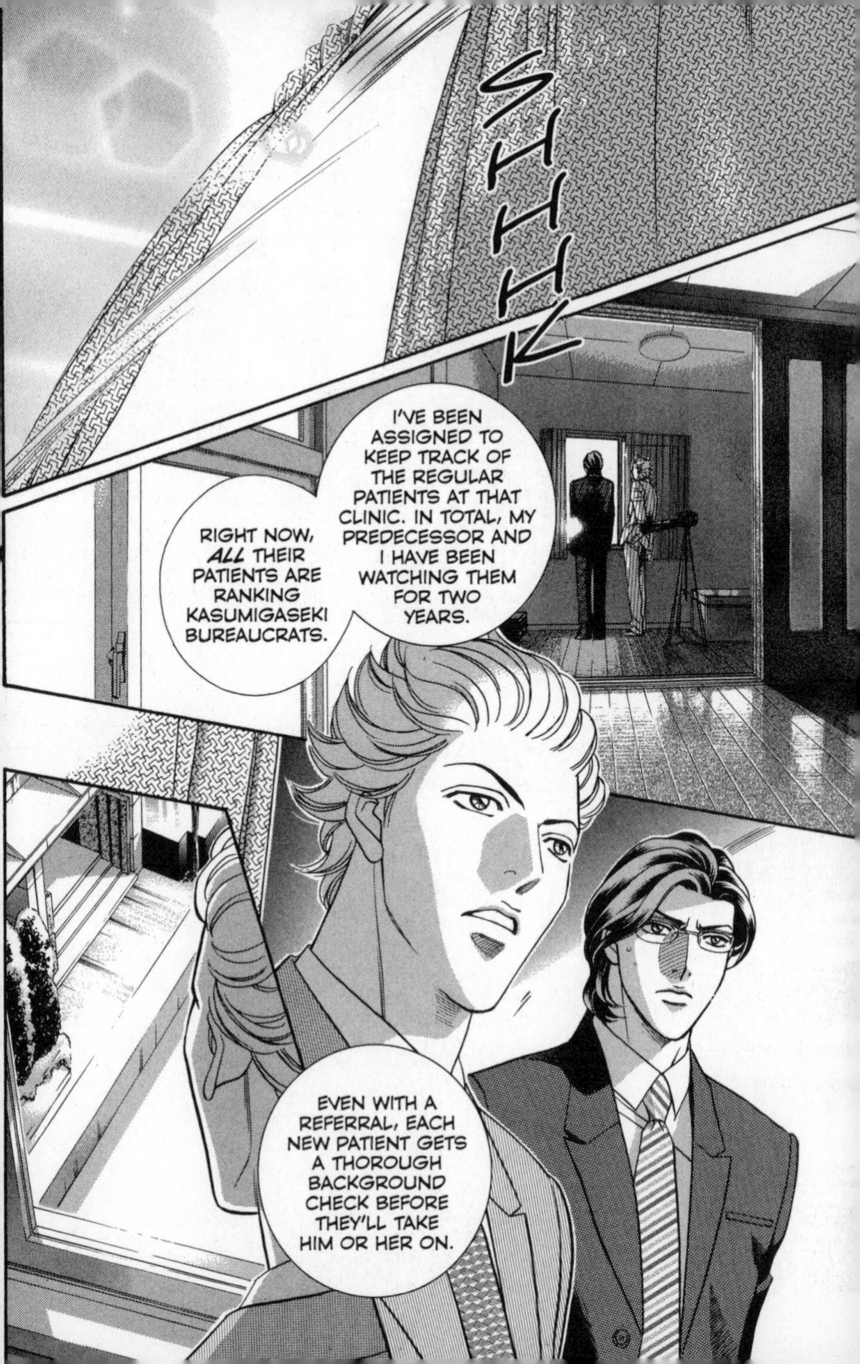
SHHHK
I'VE BEEN ASSIGNED TO KEEP TRACK OF THE REGULAR PATIENTS AT THAT CLINIC. IN TOTAL, MY PREDECESSOR AND I HAVE BEEN WATCHING THEM FOR TWO YEARS.
RIGHT NOW, ALL THEIR PATIENTS ARE RANKING KASUMIGASEKI BUREAUCRATS.
EVEN WITH A REFERRAL, EACH NEW PATIENT GETS A THOROUGH BACKGROUND CHECK BEFORE THEY'LL TAKE HIM OR HER ON.

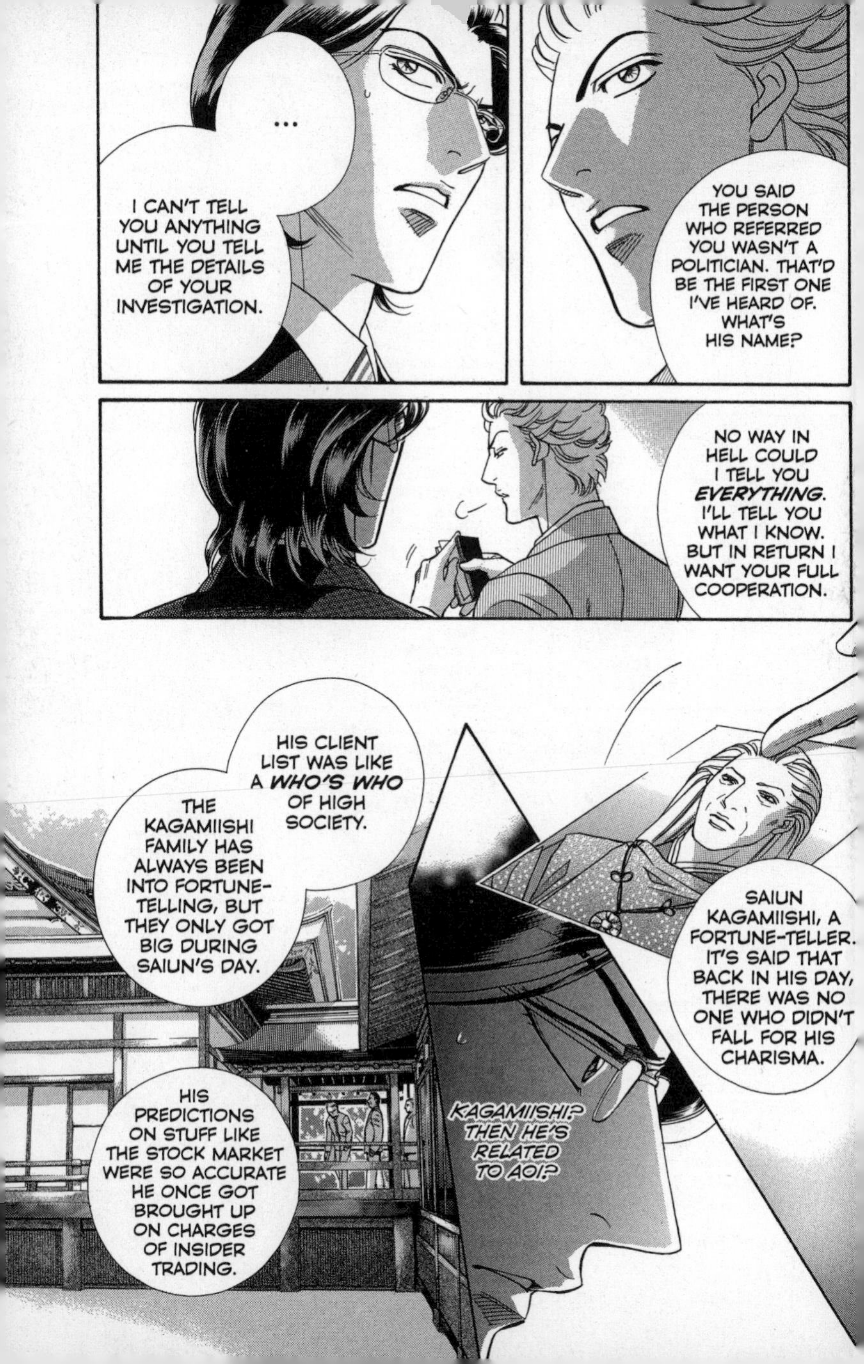
YOU SAID THE PERSON WHO REFERRED YOU WASN'T A POLITICIAN. THAT'D BE THE FIRST ONE I'VE HEARD OF. WHAT'S HIS NAME?
...
I CAN'T TELL YOU ANYTHING UNTIL YOU TELL ME THE DETAILS OF YOUR INVESTIGATION.
NO WAY IN HELL COULD I TELL YOU *EVERYTHING*. I'LL TELL YOU WHAT I KNOW. BUT IN RETURN I WANT YOUR FULL COOPERATION.
SAIUN KAGAMIISHI, A FORTUNE-TELLER. IT'S SAID THAT BACK IN HIS DAY, THERE WAS NO ONE WHO DIDN'T FALL FOR HIS CHARISMA.
KAGAMIISHI? THEN HE'S RELATED TO AOI?
HIS CLIENT LIST WAS LIKE A *WHO'S WHO* OF HIGH SOCIETY.
THE KAGAMIISHI FAMILY HAS ALWAYS BEEN INTO FORTUNE-TELLING, BUT THEY ONLY GOT BIG DURING SAIUN'S DAY.
HIS PREDICTIONS ON STUFF LIKE THE STOCK MARKET WERE SO ACCURATE HE ONCE GOT BROUGHT UP ON CHARGES OF INSIDER TRADING.

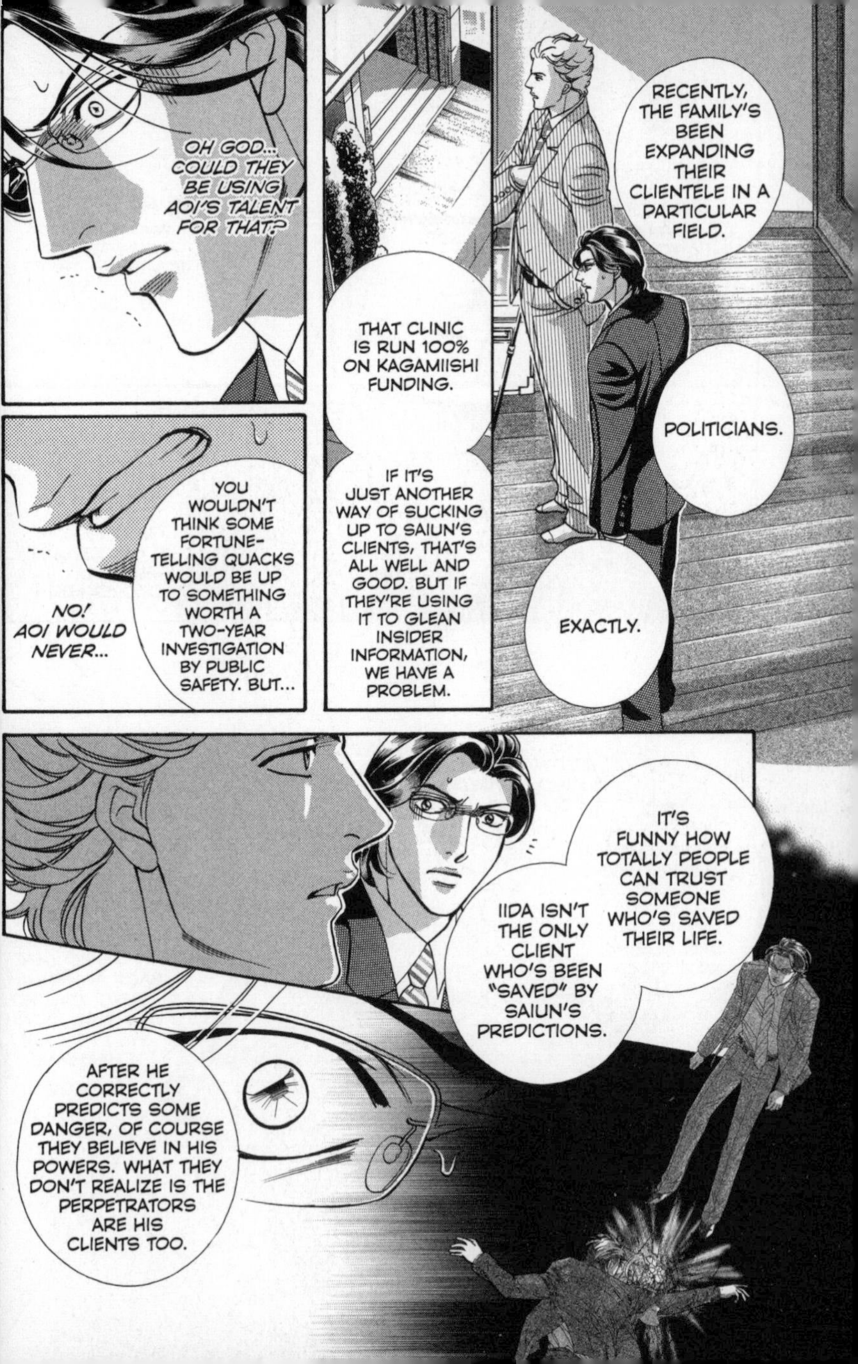
RECENTLY, THE FAMILY'S BEEN EXPANDING THEIR CLIENTELE IN A PARTICULAR FIELD.
POLITICIANS.
EXACTLY.
THAT CLINIC IS RUN 100% ON KAGAMIISHI FUNDING.
IF IT'S JUST ANOTHER WAY OF SUCKING UP TO SAIUN'S CLIENTS, THAT'S ALL WELL AND GOOD. BUT IF THEY'RE USING IT TO GLEAN INSIDER INFORMATION, WE HAVE A PROBLEM.
OH GOD... COULD THEY BE USING AOI'S TALENT FOR THAT?
YOU WOULDN'T THINK SOME FORTUNE-TELLING QUACKS WOULD BE UP TO SOMETHING WORTH A TWO-YEAR INVESTIGATION BY PUBLIC SAFETY. BUT...
NO! AOI WOULD NEVER...
IT'S FUNNY HOW TOTALLY PEOPLE CAN TRUST SOMEONE WHO'S SAVED THEIR LIFE.
IIDA ISN'T THE ONLY CLIENT WHO'S BEEN "SAVED" BY SAIUN'S PREDICTIONS.
AFTER HE CORRECTLY PREDICTS SOME DANGER, OF COURSE THEY BELIEVE IN HIS POWERS. WHAT THEY DON'T REALIZE IS THE PERPETRATORS ARE HIS CLIENTS TOO.

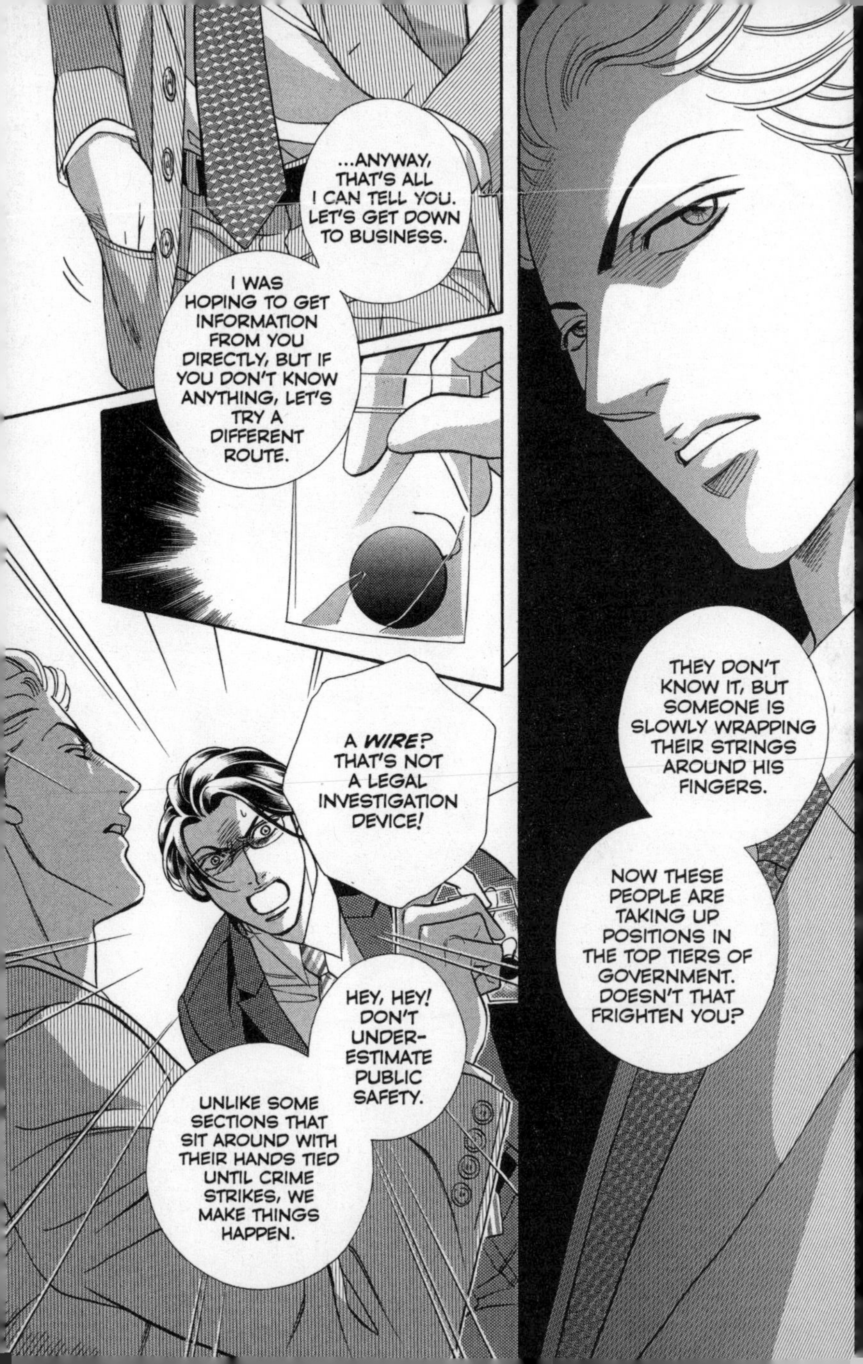
THEY DON'T KNOW IT, BUT SOMEONE IS SLOWLY WRAPPING THEIR STRINGS AROUND HIS FINGERS.
NOW THESE PEOPLE ARE TAKING UP POSITIONS IN THE TOP TIERS OF GOVERNMENT. DOESN'T THAT FRIGHTEN YOU?
...ANYWAY, THAT'S ALL I CAN TELL YOU. LET'S GET DOWN TO BUSINESS.
I WAS HOPING TO GET INFORMATION FROM YOU DIRECTLY, BUT IF YOU DON'T KNOW ANYTHING, LET'S TRY A DIFFERENT ROUTE.
A *WIRE*? THAT'S NOT A LEGAL INVESTIGATION DEVICE!
HEY, HEY! DON'T UNDER-ESTIMATE PUBLIC SAFETY.
UNLIKE SOME SECTIONS THAT SIT AROUND WITH THEIR HANDS TIED UNTIL CRIME STRIKES, WE MAKE THINGS HAPPEN.

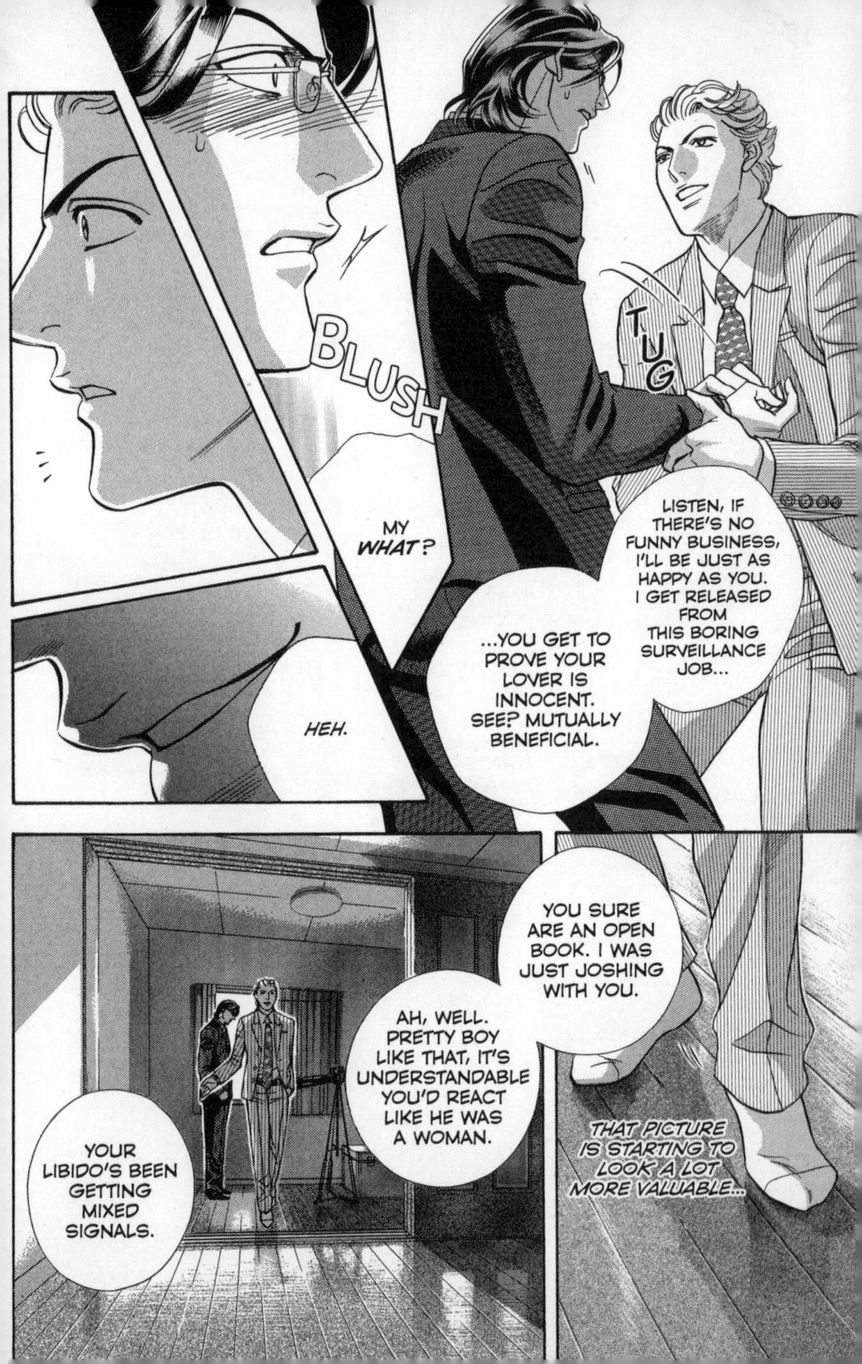
TUG
LISTEN, IF THERE'S NO FUNNY BUSINESS, I'LL BE JUST AS HAPPY AS YOU. I GET RELEASED FROM THIS BORING SURVEILLANCE JOB...
...YOU GET TO PROVE YOUR LOVER IS INNOCENT. SEE? MUTUALLY BENEFICIAL.
MY *WHAT*?
BLUSH
HEH.
YOU SURE ARE AN OPEN BOOK. I WAS JUST JOSHING WITH YOU.
THAT PICTURE IS STARTING TO LOOK A LOT MORE VALUABLE...
AH, WELL. PRETTY BOY LIKE THAT, IT'S UNDERSTANDABLE YOU'D REACT LIKE HE WAS A WOMAN.
YOUR LIBIDO'S BEEN GETTING MIXED SIGNALS.

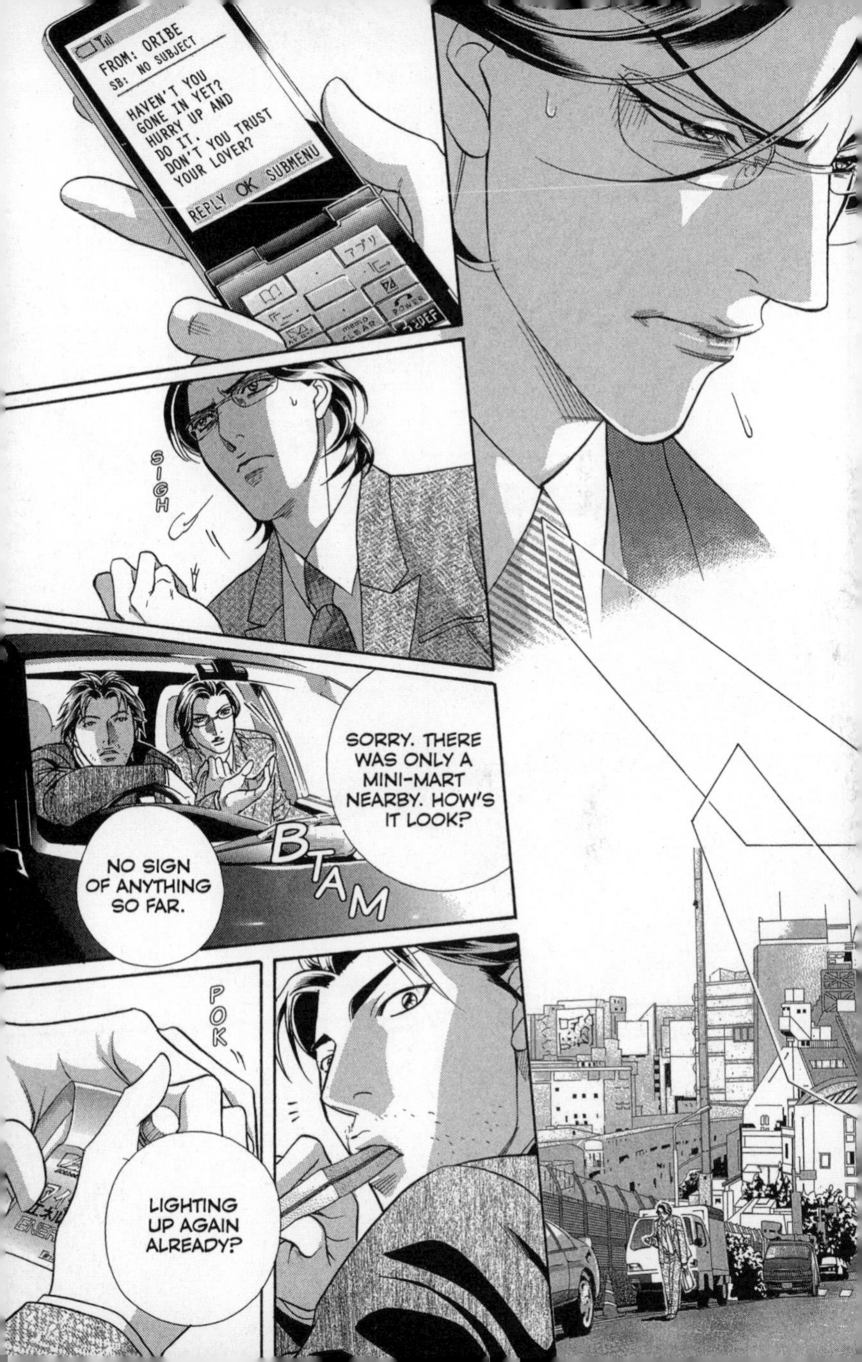
FROM: ORIBE
SB: NO SUBJECT
HAVEN'T YOU GONE IN YET? HURRY UP AND DO IT. DON'T YOU TRUST YOUR LOVER?
REPLY OK SUBMENU
SIGH
SORRY. THERE WAS ONLY A MINI-MART NEARBY. HOW'S IT LOOK?
BTAM
NO SIGN OF ANYTHING SO FAR.
POK
LIGHTING UP AGAIN ALREADY?

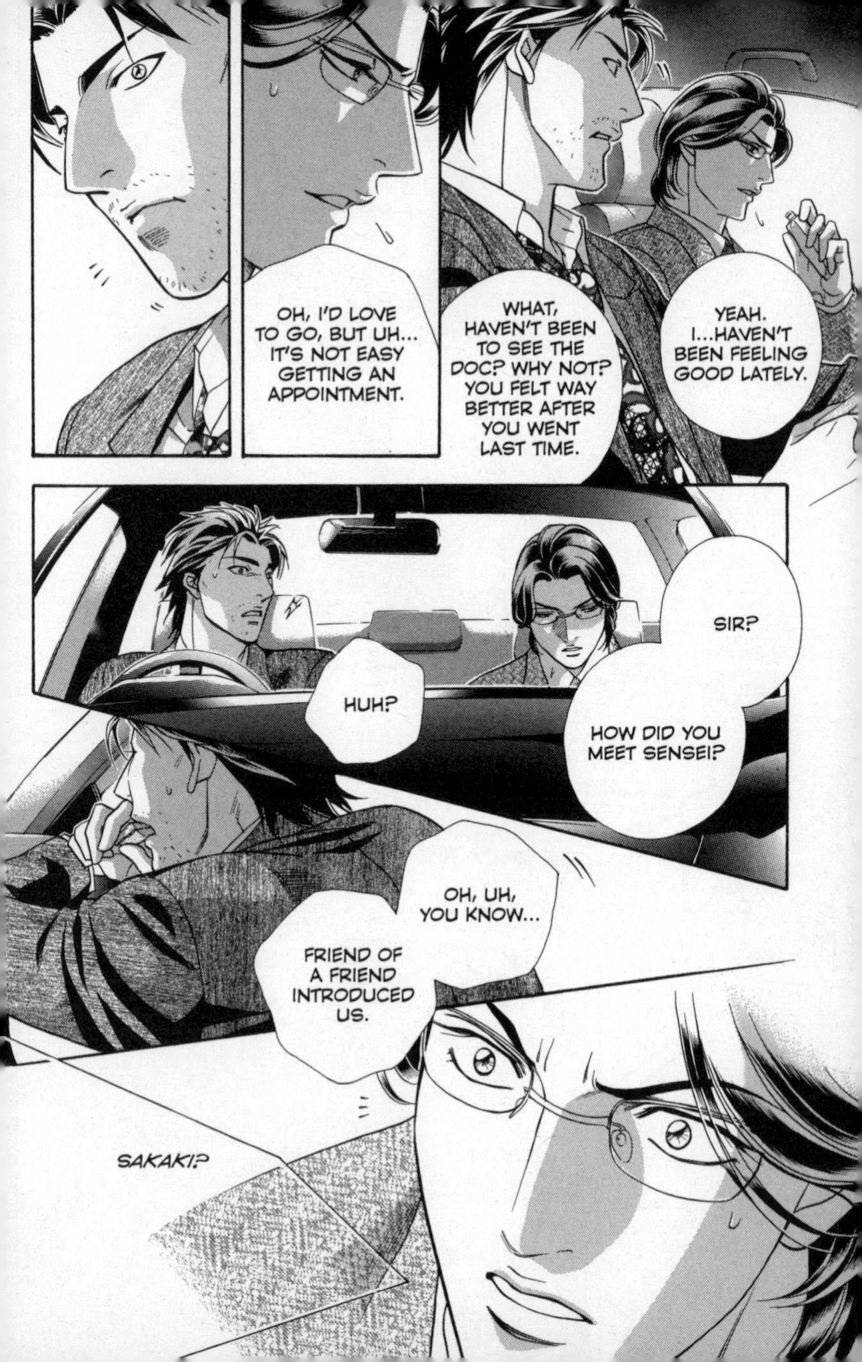
YEAH. I...HAVEN'T BEEN FEELING GOOD LATELY.
WHAT, HAVEN'T BEEN TO SEE THE DOC? WHY NOT? YOU FELT WAY BETTER AFTER YOU WENT LAST TIME.
OH, I'D LOVE TO GO, BUT UH... IT'S NOT EASY GETTING AN APPOINTMENT.
SIR?
HOW DID YOU MEET SENSEI?
HUH?
OH, UH, YOU KNOW...
FRIEND OF A FRIEND INTRODUCED US.
SAKAKI!?

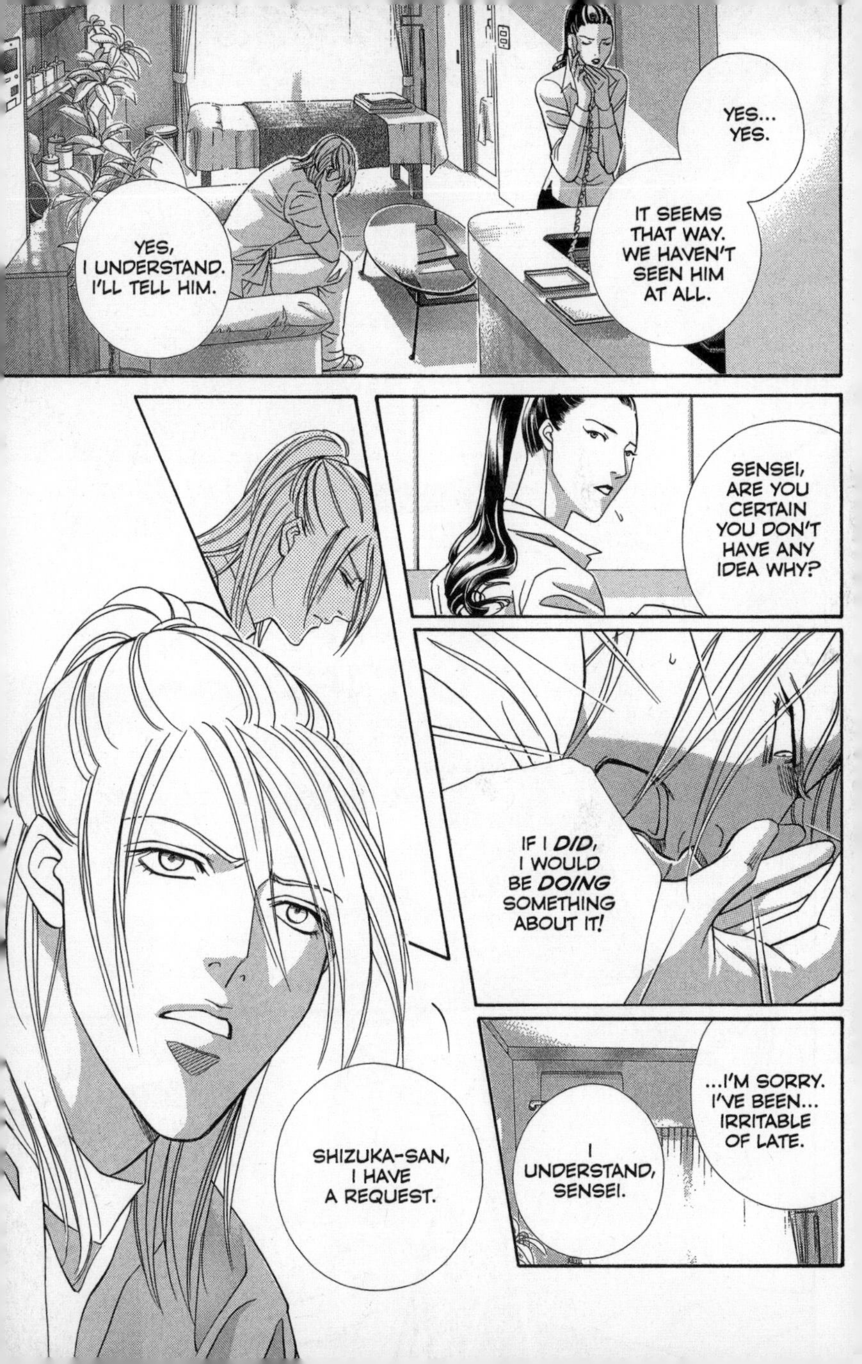
YES... YES.
IT SEEMS THAT WAY. WE HAVEN'T SEEN HIM AT ALL.
YES, I UNDERSTAND. I'LL TELL HIM.
SENSEI, ARE YOU CERTAIN YOU DON'T HAVE ANY IDEA WHY?
IF I *DID*, I WOULD BE *DOING* SOMETHING ABOUT IT!
...I'M SORRY. I'VE BEEN... IRRITABLE OF LATE.
I UNDERSTAND, SENSEI.
SHIZUKA-SAN, I HAVE A REQUEST.

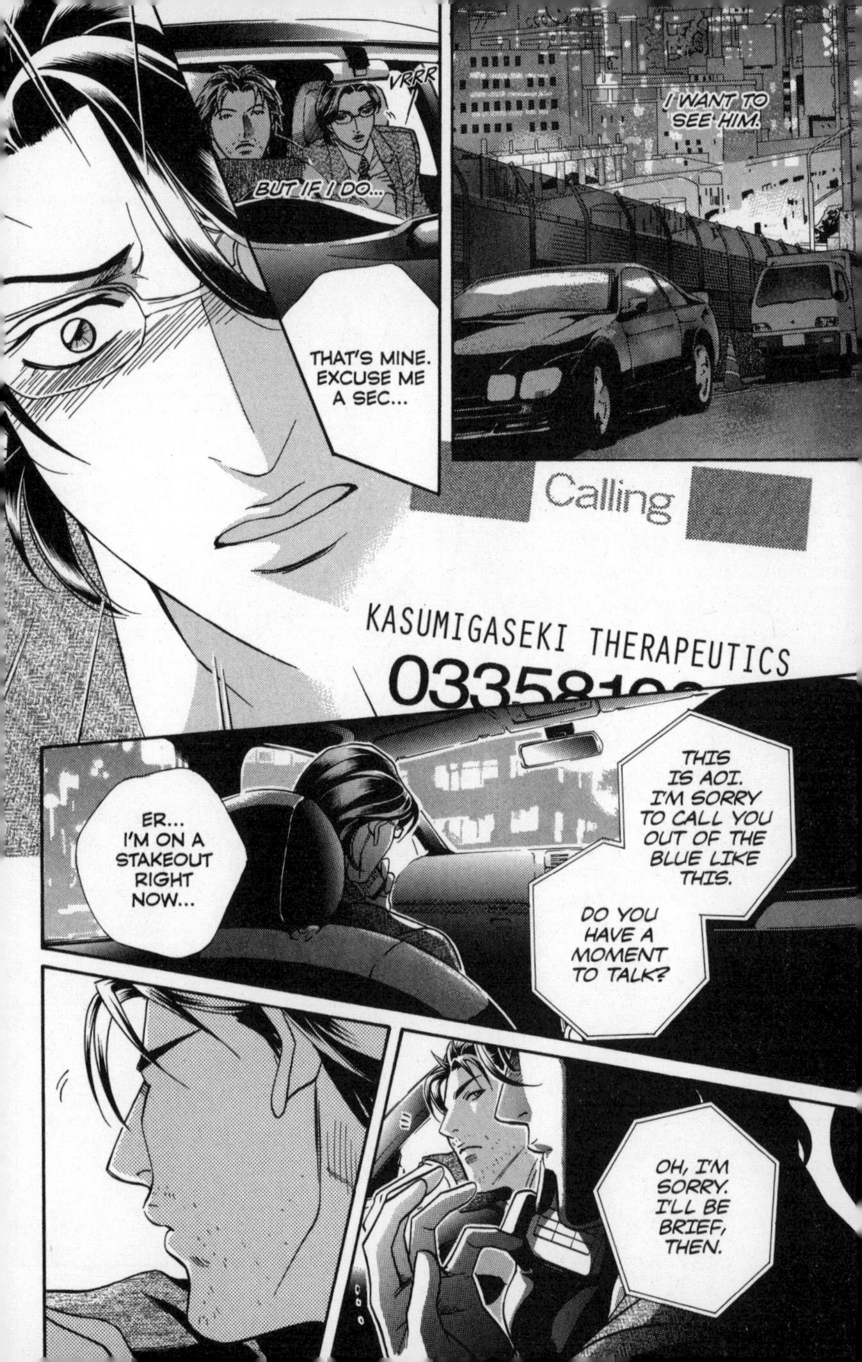
I WANT TO SEE HIM.
VRRR
BUT IF I DO...
THAT'S MINE. EXCUSE ME A SEC...
Calling
KASUMIGASEKI THERAPEUTICS
03358
THIS IS AOI. I'M SORRY TO CALL YOU OUT OF THE BLUE LIKE THIS.
DO YOU HAVE A MOMENT TO TALK?
ER... I'M ON A STAKEOUT RIGHT NOW...
OH, I'M SORRY. I'LL BE BRIEF, THEN.

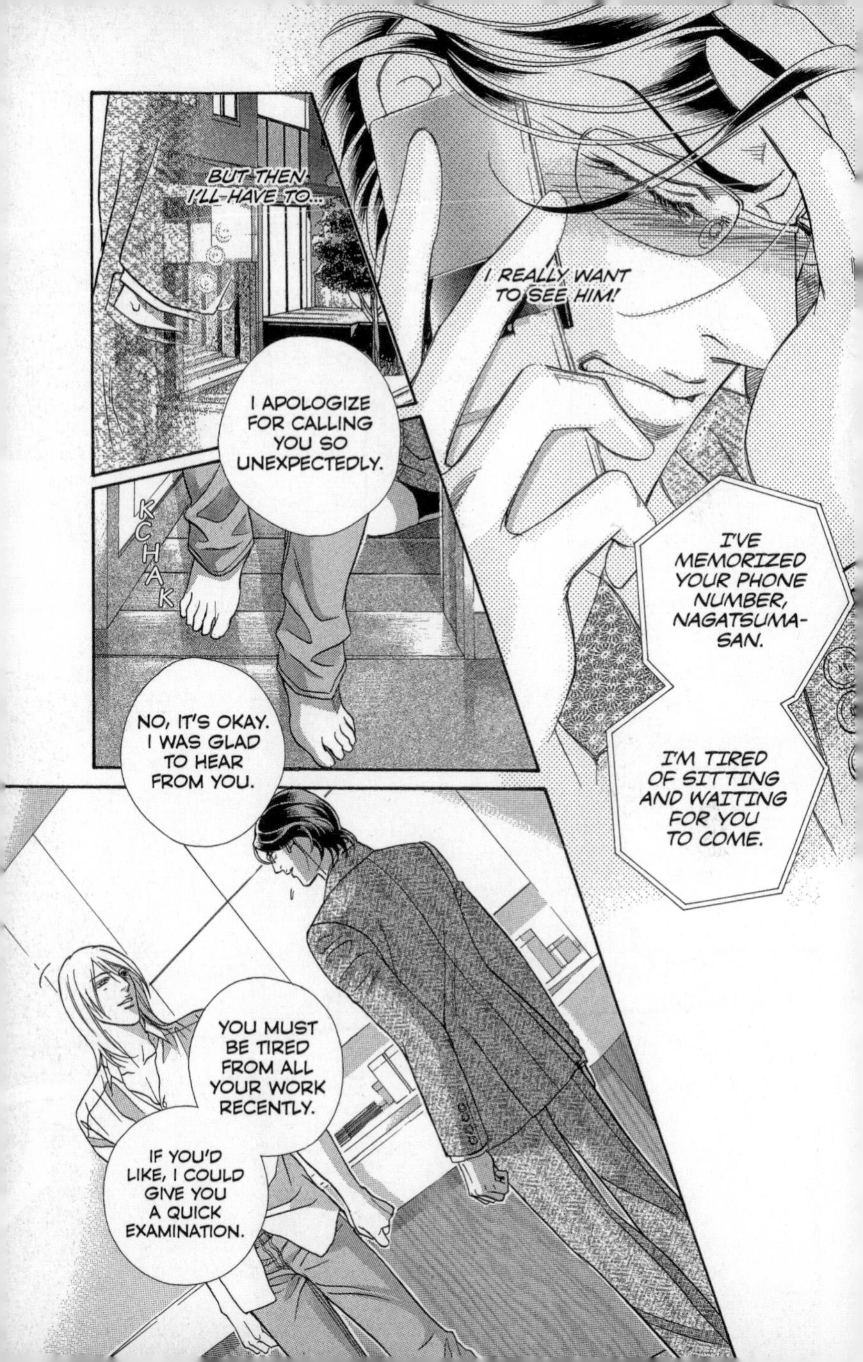
I REALLY WANT TO SEE HIM!
I'VE MEMORIZED YOUR PHONE NUMBER, NAGATSUMA-SAN.
I'M TIRED OF SITTING AND WAITING FOR YOU TO COME.
BUT THEN I'LL HAVE TO...
I APOLOGIZE FOR CALLING YOU SO UNEXPECTEDLY.
KCHAK
NO, IT'S OKAY. I WAS GLAD TO HEAR FROM YOU.
YOU MUST BE TIRED FROM ALL YOUR WORK RECENTLY.
IF YOU'D LIKE, I COULD GIVE YOU A QUICK EXAMINATION.

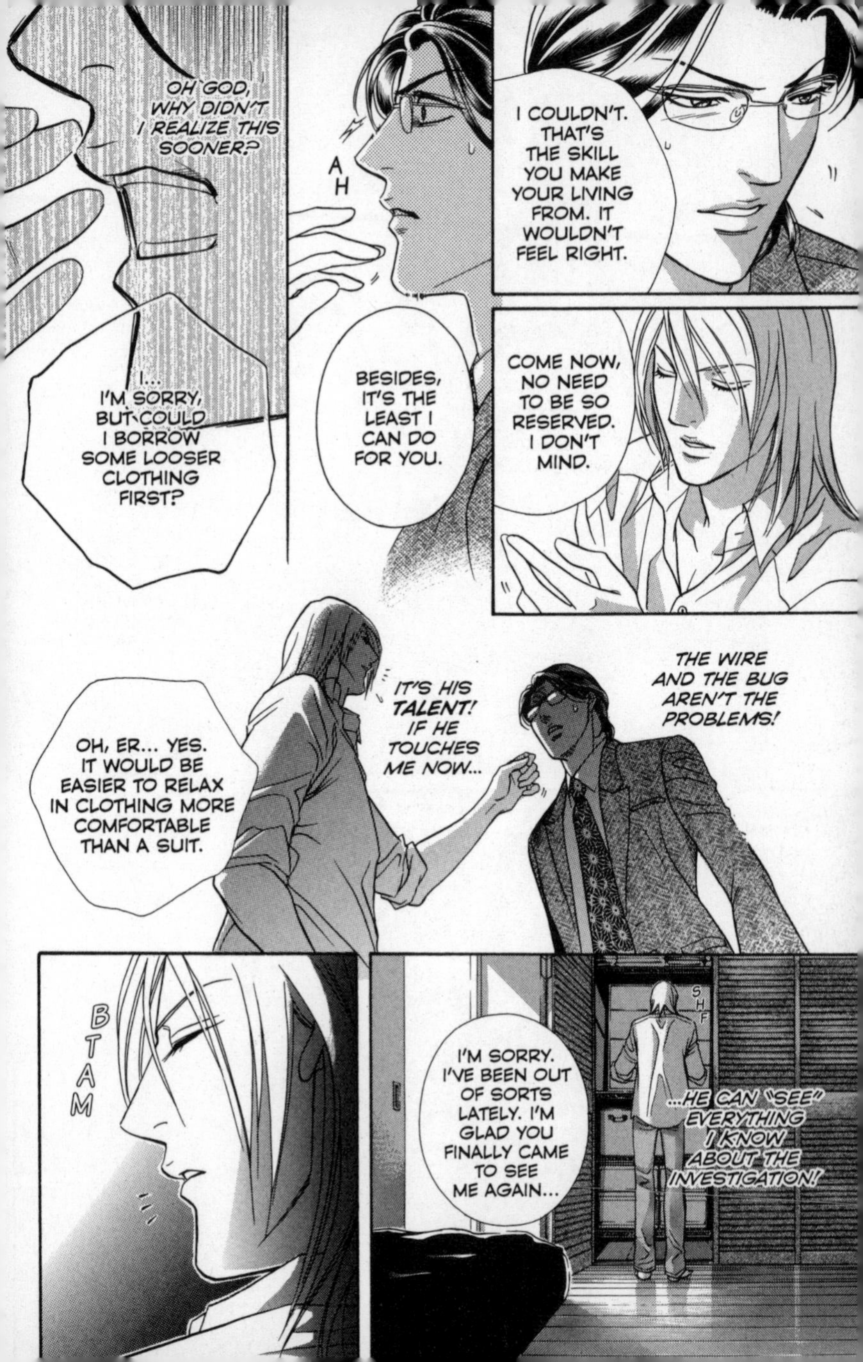
I COULDN'T. THAT'S THE SKILL YOU MAKE YOUR LIVING FROM. IT WOULDN'T FEEL RIGHT.
COME NOW, NO NEED TO BE SO RESERVED. I DON'T MIND.
AH
BESIDES, IT'S THE LEAST I CAN DO FOR YOU.
OH GOD, WHY DIDN'T I REALIZE THIS SOONER?
I... I'M SORRY, BUT COULD I BORROW SOME LOOSER CLOTHING FIRST?
THE WIRE AND THE BUG AREN'T THE PROBLEMS!
IT'S HIS *TALENT*! IF HE TOUCHES ME NOW...
OH, ER... YES. IT WOULD BE EASIER TO RELAX IN CLOTHING MORE COMFORTABLE THAN A SUIT.
SHF
...HE CAN "SEE" EVERYTHING I KNOW ABOUT THE INVESTIGATION!
I'M SORRY. I'VE BEEN OUT OF SORTS LATELY. I'M GLAD YOU FINALLY CAME TO SEE ME AGAIN...
BTAM

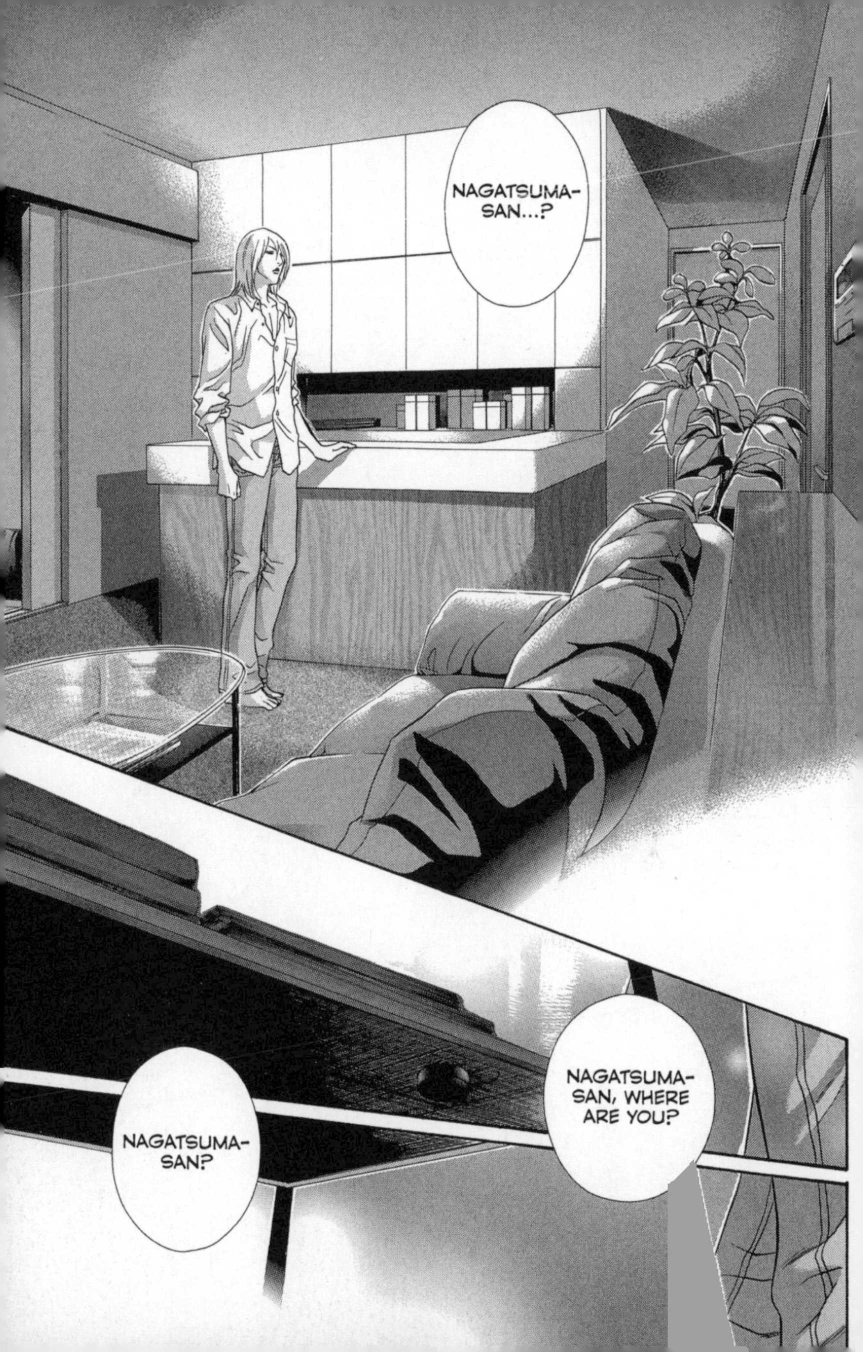
NAGATSUMA-SAN...?
NAGATSUMA-SAN, WHERE ARE YOU?
NAGATSUMA-SAN?

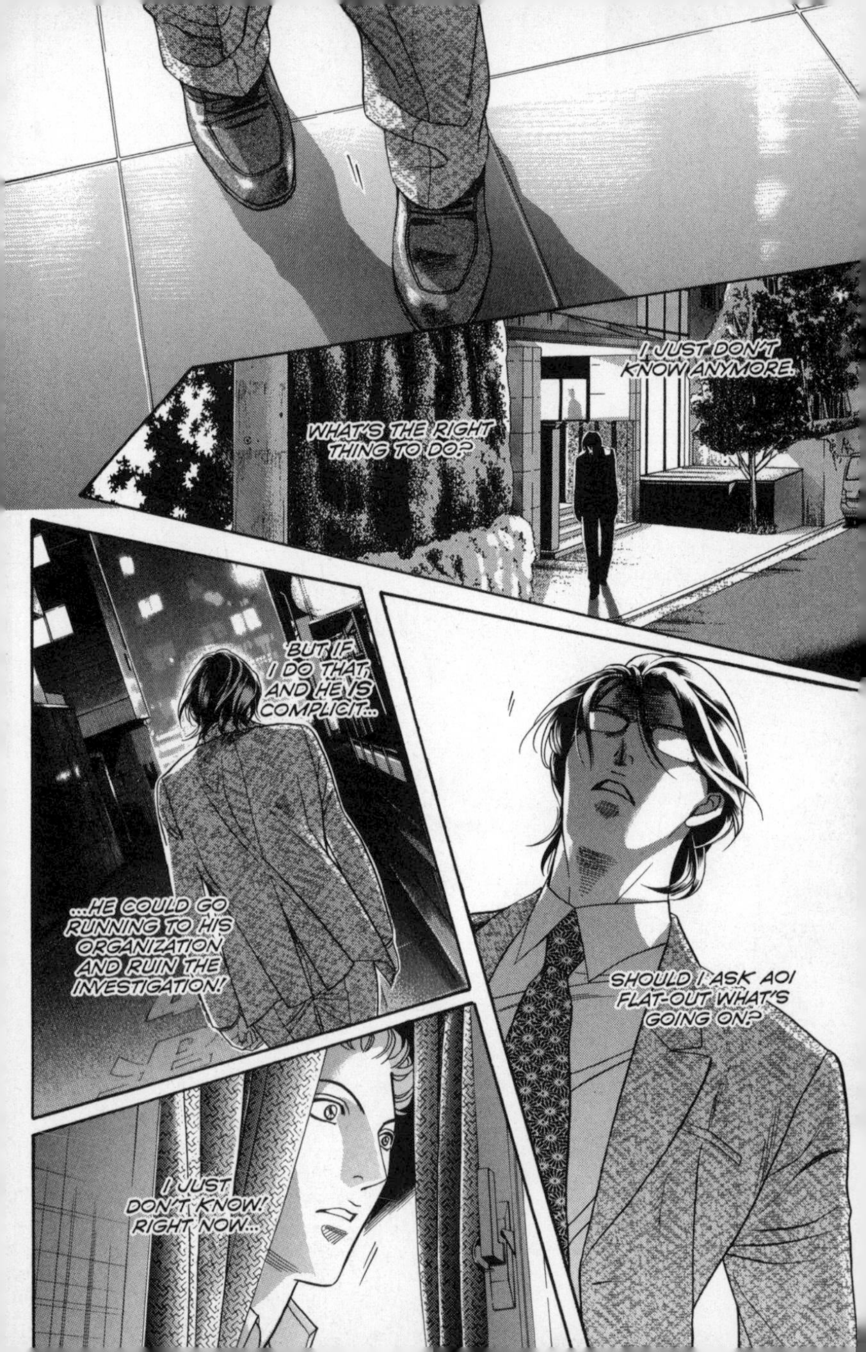
I JUST DON'T KNOW ANYMORE.
WHAT'S THE RIGHT THING TO DO?
SHOULD I ASK AOI FLAT-OUT WHAT'S GOING ON?
BUT IF I DO THAT, AND HE IS COMPLICIT...
...HE COULD GO RUNNING TO HIS ORGANIZATION AND RUIN THE INVESTIGATION!
I JUST DON'T KNOW! RIGHT NOW...

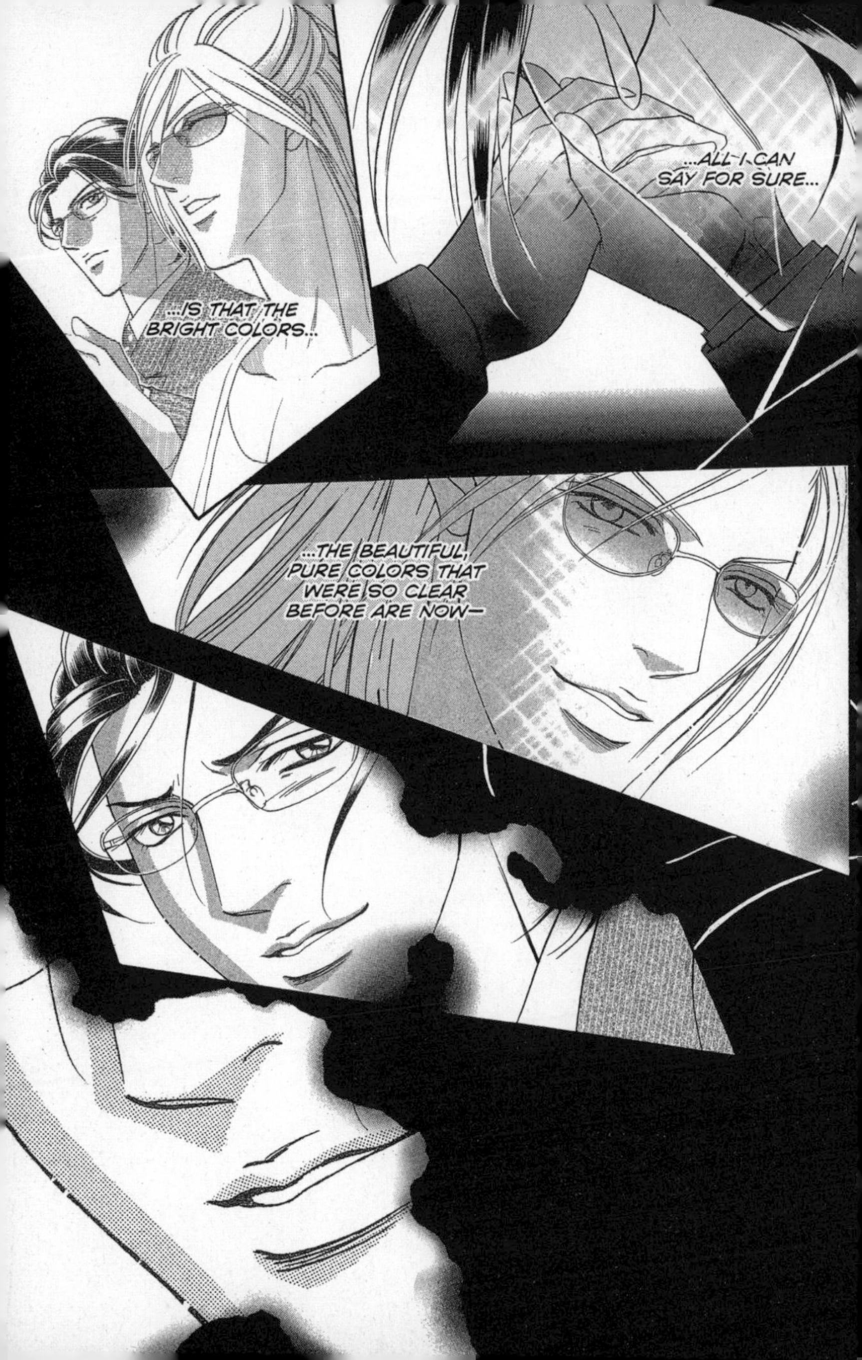
...ALL I CAN SAY FOR SURE...
...IS THAT THE BRIGHT COLORS...
...THE BEAUTIFUL, PURE COLORS THAT WERE SO CLEAR BEFORE ARE NOW—

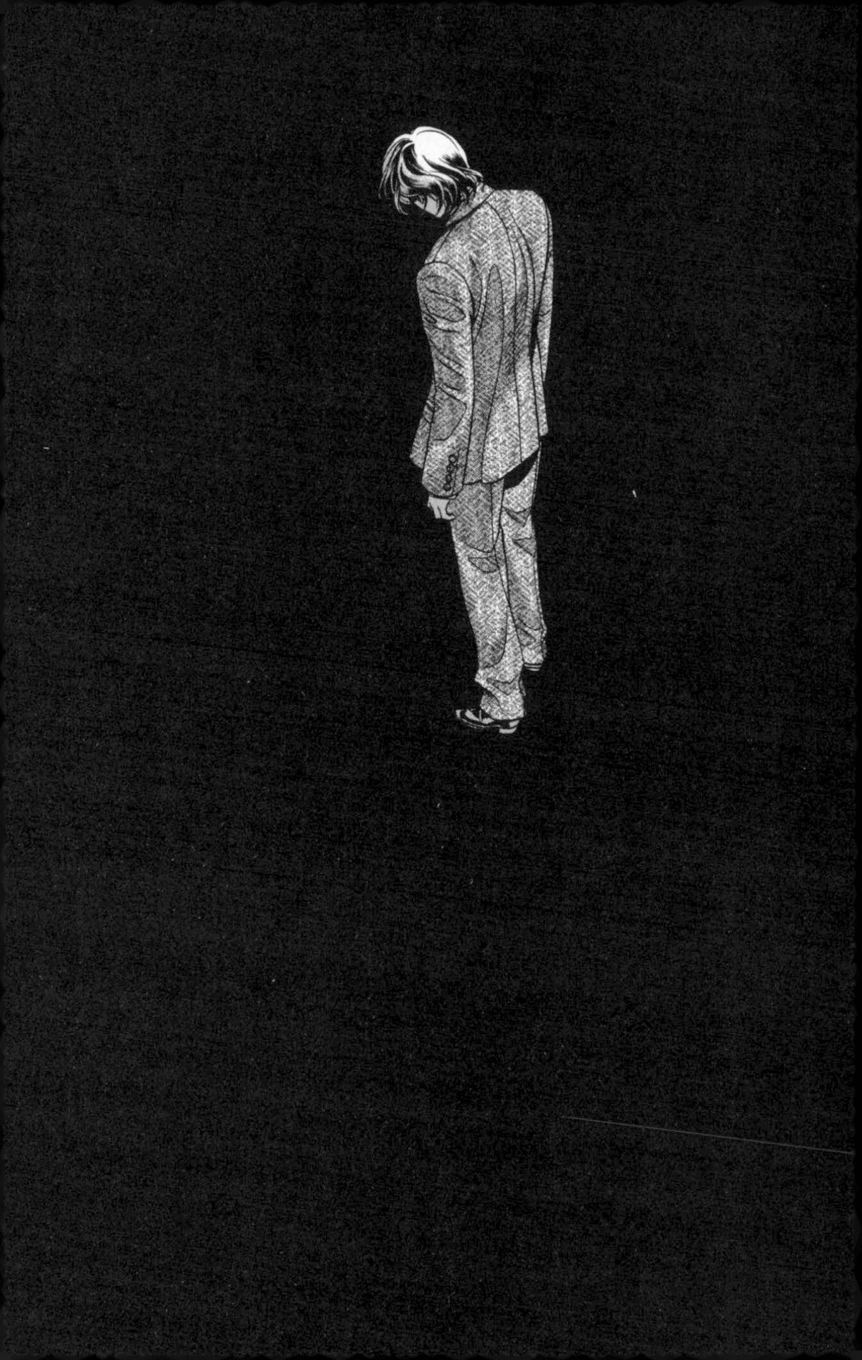

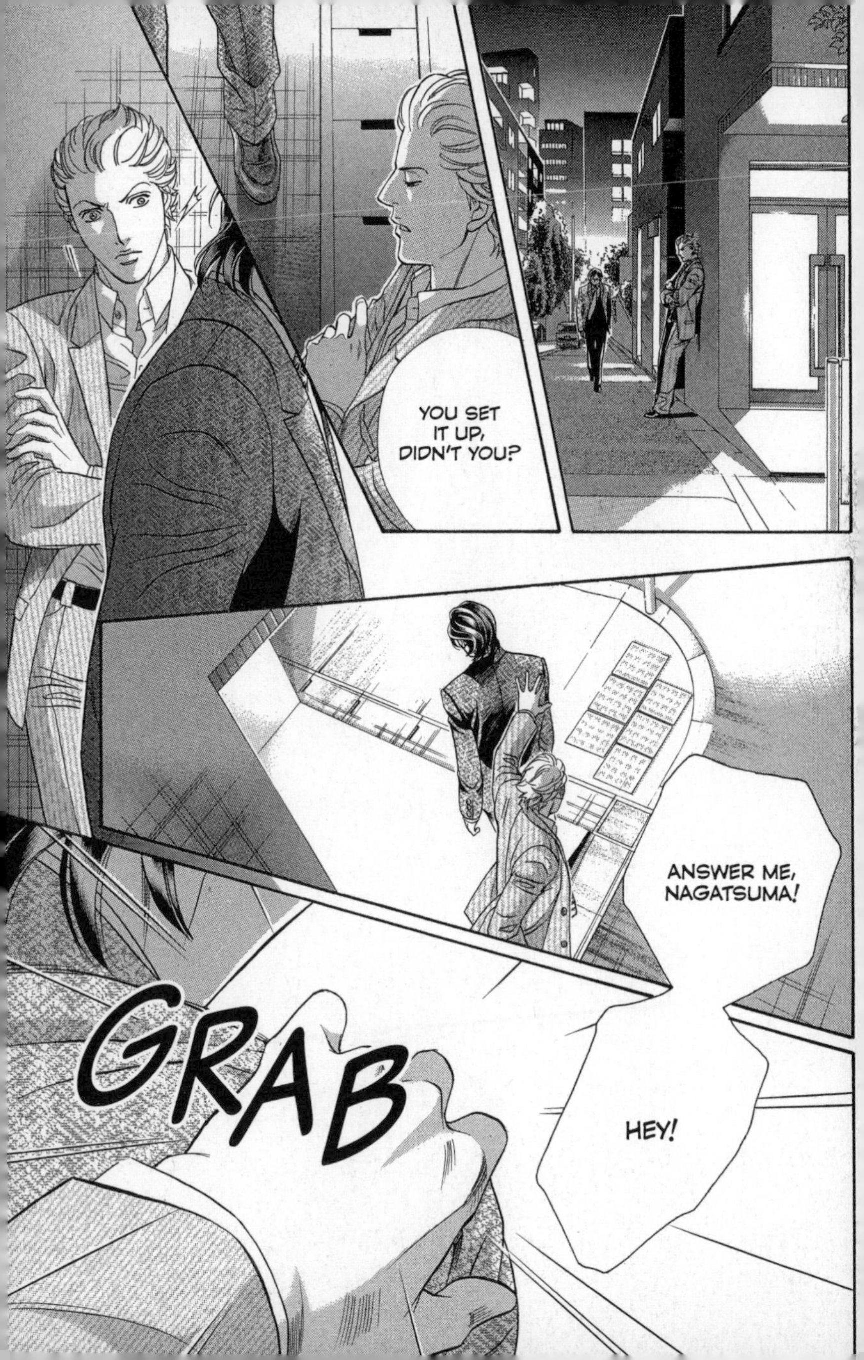
YOU SET IT UP, DIDN'T YOU?
ANSWER ME, NAGATSUMA!
HEY!
GRAB

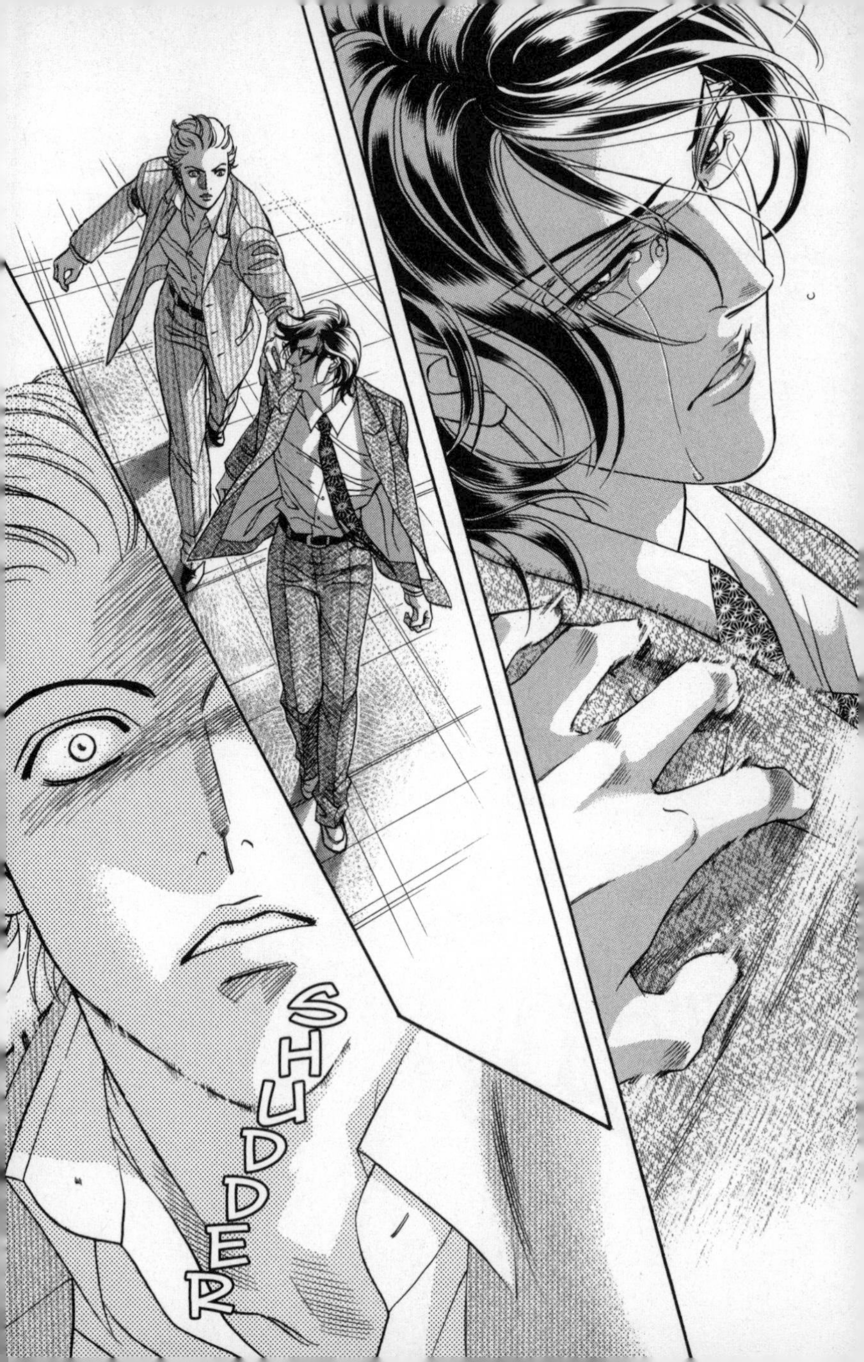
SHUDDER

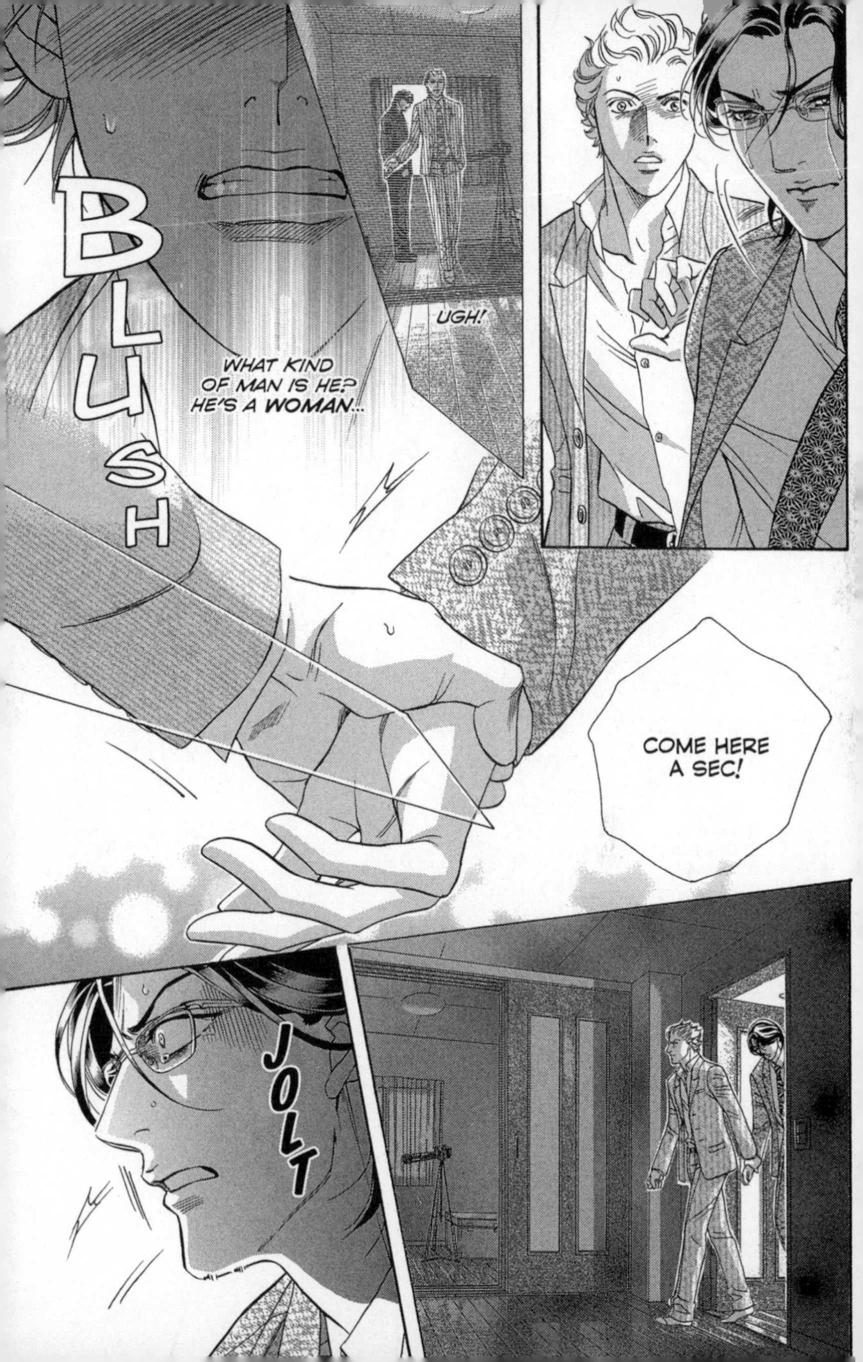
UGH!
WHAT KIND OF MAN IS HE? HE'S A WOMAN...
BLUSH
COME HERE A SEC!
JOLT

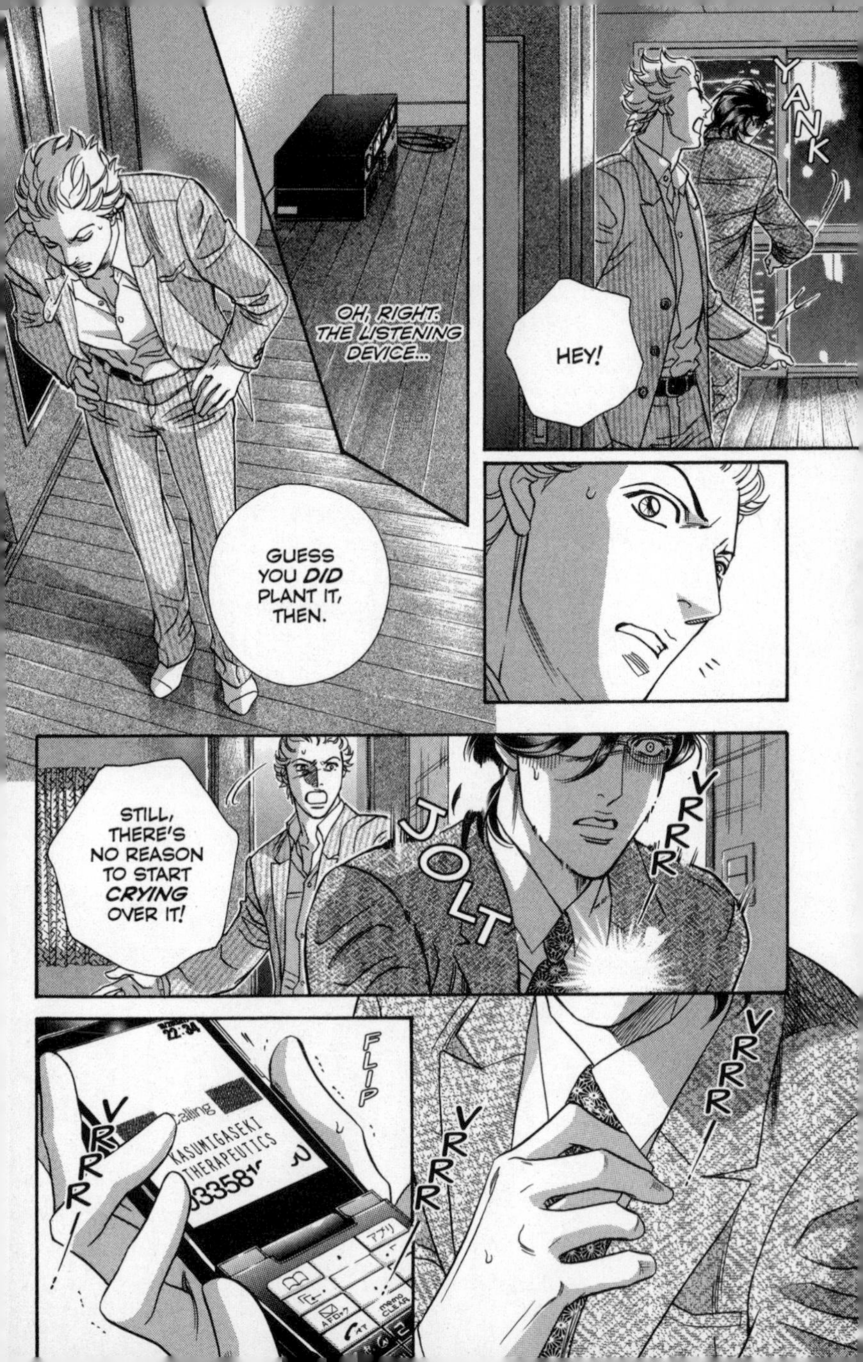
YANK
HEY!
OH, RIGHT. THE LISTENING DEVICE...
GUESS YOU *DID* PLANT IT, THEN.
VRRR
JOLT
STILL, THERE'S NO REASON TO START *CRYING* OVER IT!
VRRRR
VRRRR
FLIP
22:34
Calling
KASUMIGASEKI THERAPEUTICS
03358
VRRRR

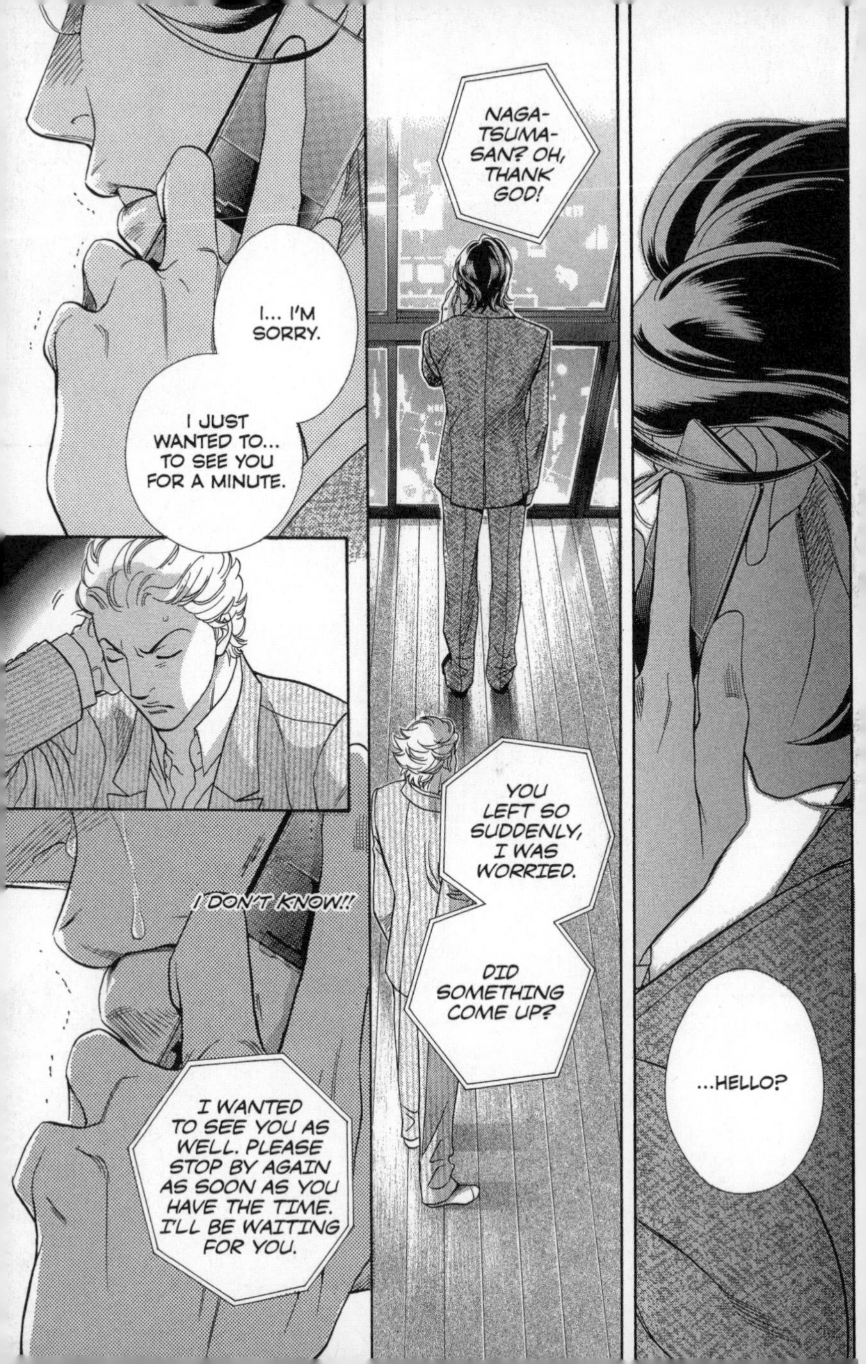
...HELLO?
NAGA-TSUMA-SAN? OH, THANK GOD!
YOU LEFT SO SUDDENLY, I WAS WORRIED.
DID SOMETHING COME UP?
I... I'M SORRY.
I JUST WANTED TO... TO SEE YOU FOR A MINUTE.
I DON'T KNOW!!
I WANTED TO SEE YOU AS WELL. PLEASE STOP BY AGAIN AS SOON AS YOU HAVE THE TIME. I'LL BE WAITING FOR YOU.

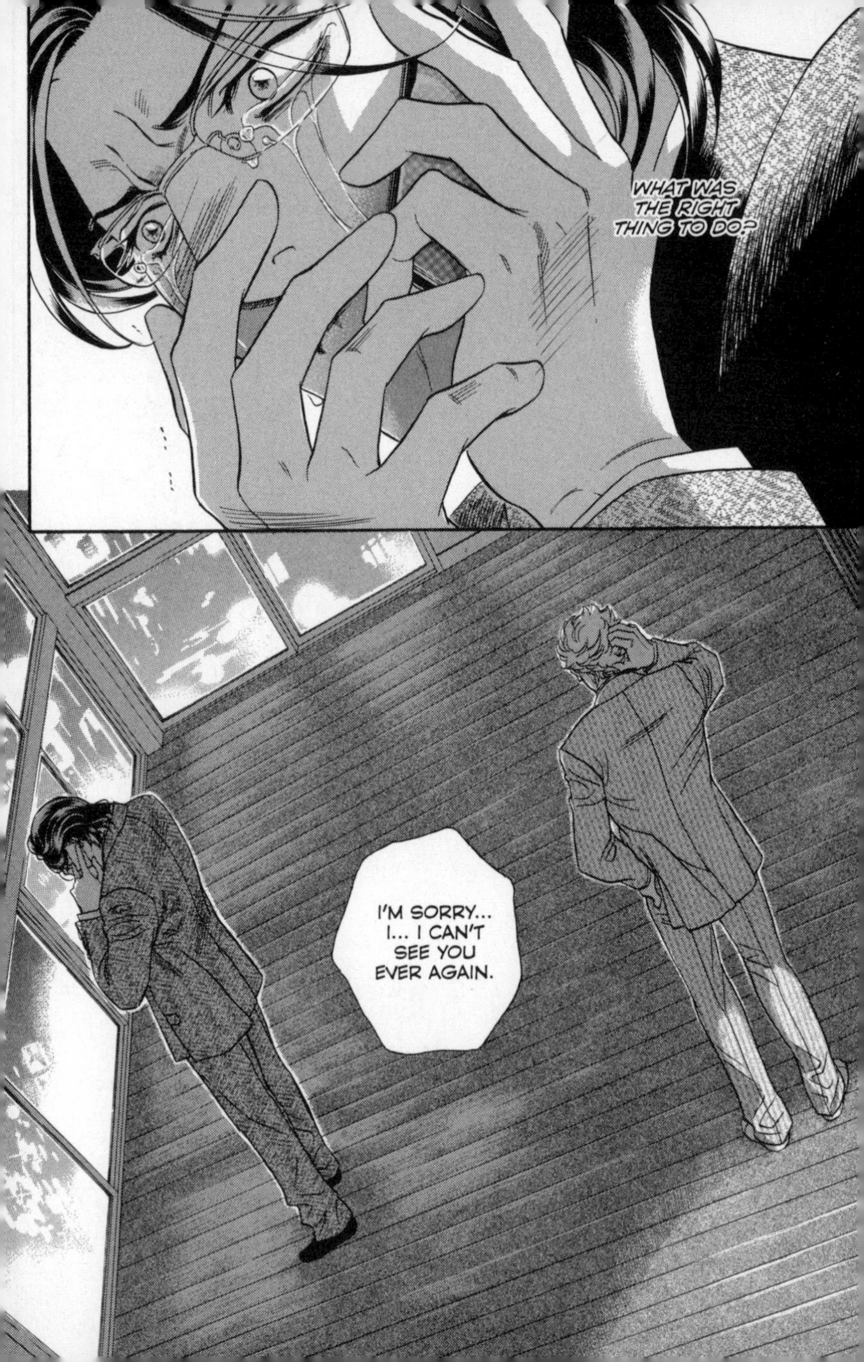
WHAT WAS THE RIGHT THING TO DO?
I'M SORRY... I... I CAN'T SEE YOU EVER AGAIN.

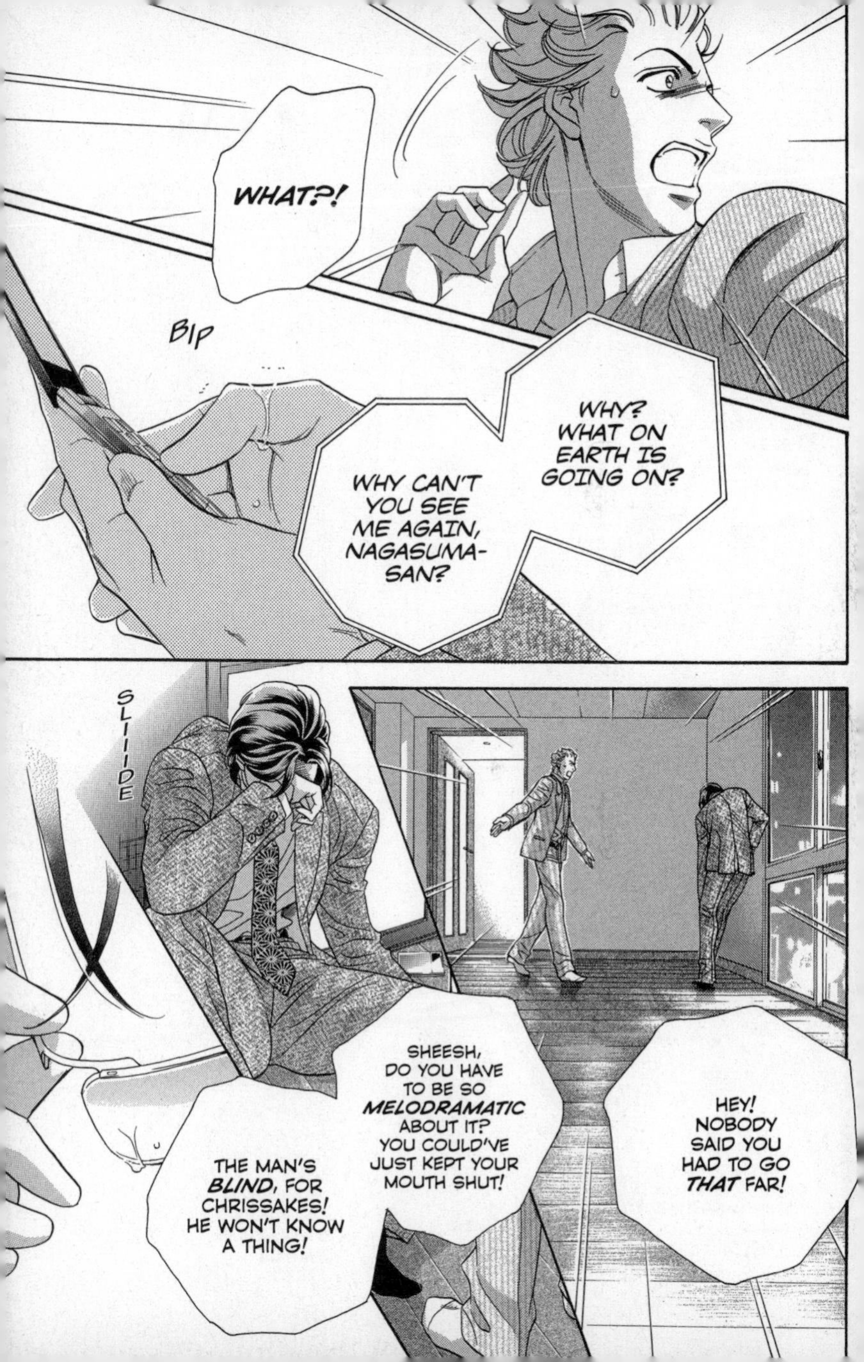
WHAT?!
WHY? WHAT ON EARTH IS GOING ON?
WHY CAN'T YOU SEE ME AGAIN, NAGASUMA-SAN?
BIP
HEY! NOBODY SAID YOU HAD TO GO THAT FAR!
SHEESH, DO YOU HAVE TO BE SO MELODRAMATIC ABOUT IT? YOU COULD'VE JUST KEPT YOUR MOUTH SHUT!
THE MAN'S BLIND, FOR CHRISSAKES! HE WON'T KNOW A THING!
SLIIIDE

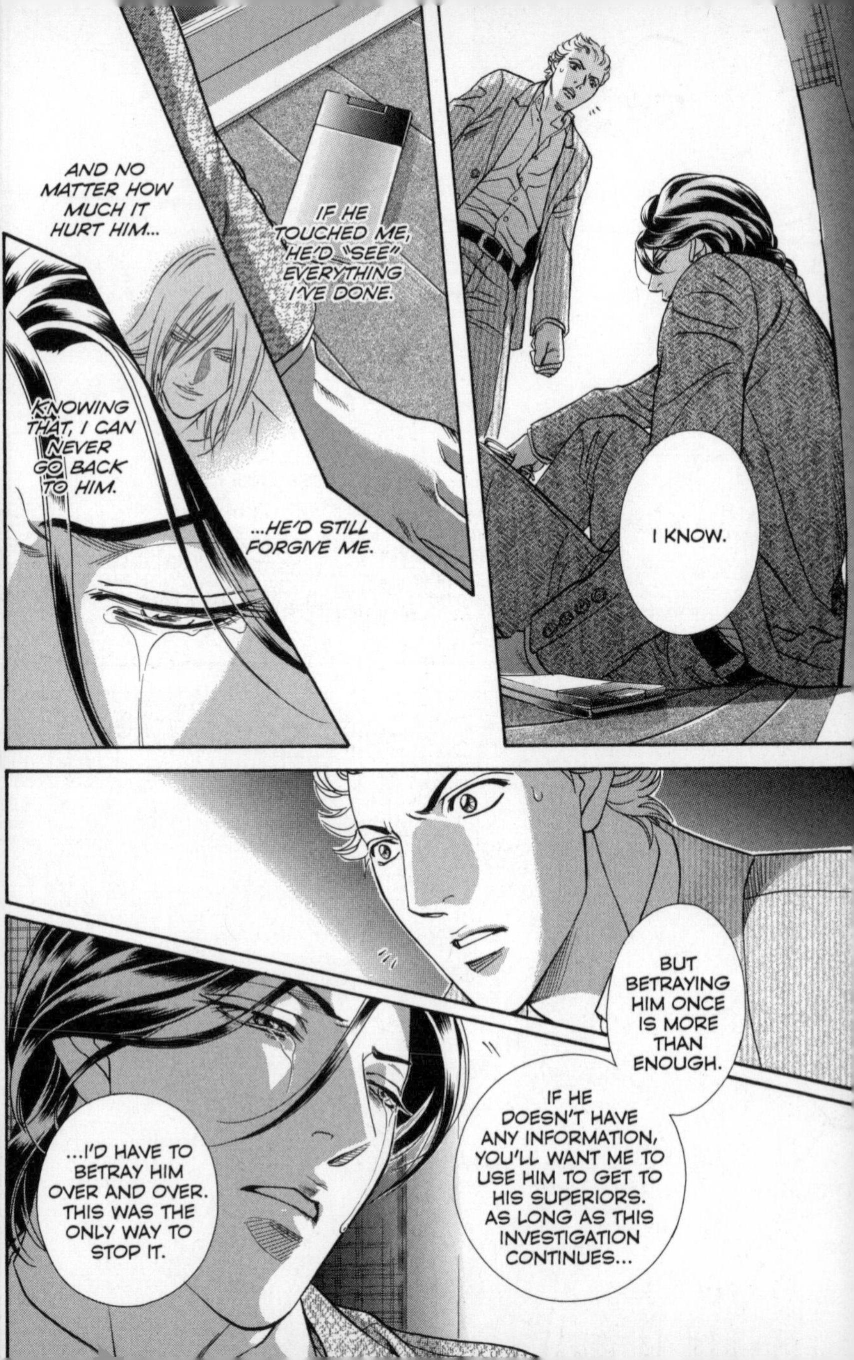
I KNOW.
IF HE TOUCHED ME, HE'D "SEE" EVERYTHING I'VE DONE.
AND NO MATTER HOW MUCH IT HURT HIM...
...HE'D STILL FORGIVE ME.
KNOWING THAT, I CAN NEVER GO BACK TO HIM.
BUT BETRAYING HIM ONCE IS MORE THAN ENOUGH.
IF HE DOESN'T HAVE ANY INFORMATION, YOU'LL WANT ME TO USE HIM TO GET TO HIS SUPERIORS. AS LONG AS THIS INVESTIGATION CONTINUES...
...I'D HAVE TO BETRAY HIM OVER AND OVER. THIS WAS THE ONLY WAY TO STOP IT.

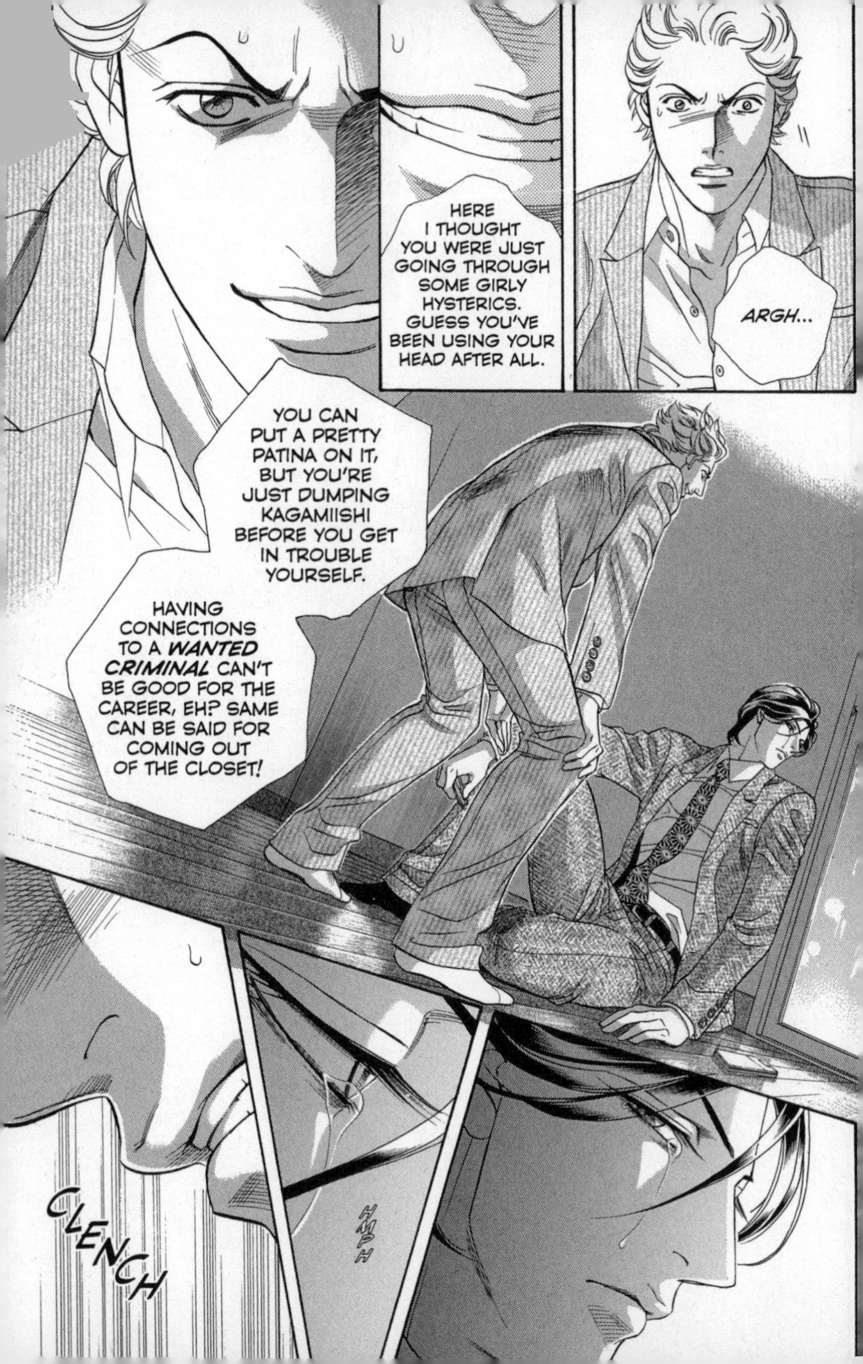

ARGH...
HERE I THOUGHT YOU WERE JUST GOING THROUGH SOME GIRLY HYSTERICS. GUESS YOU'VE BEEN USING YOUR HEAD AFTER ALL.
YOU CAN PUT A PRETTY PATINA ON IT, BUT YOU'RE JUST DUMPING KAGAMIISHI BEFORE YOU GET IN TROUBLE YOURSELF.
HAVING CONNECTIONS TO A ***WANTED CRIMINAL*** CAN'T BE GOOD FOR THE CAREER, EH? SAME CAN BE SAID FOR COMING OUT OF THE CLOSET!
HMPH
CLENCH

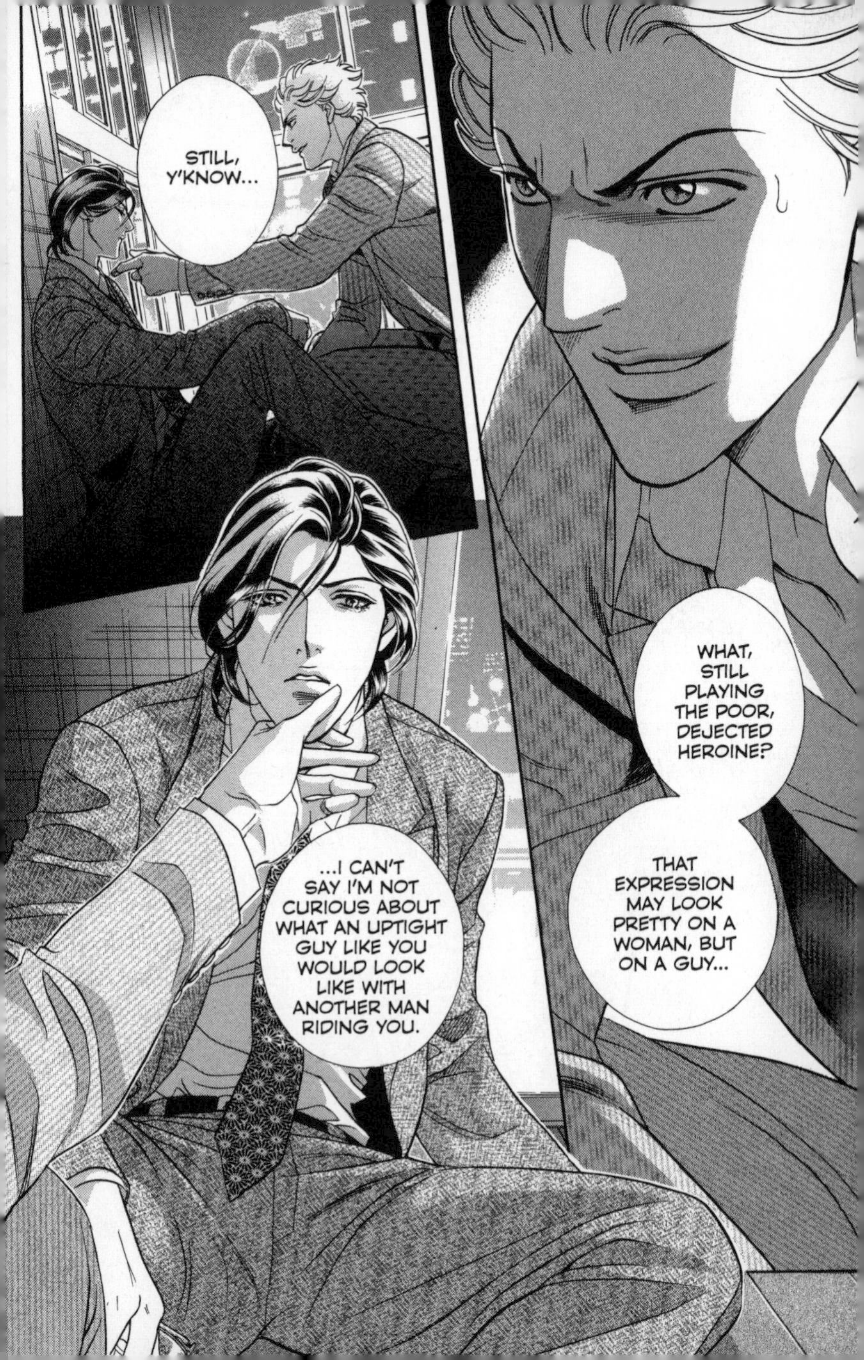
WHAT, STILL PLAYING THE POOR, DEJECTED HEROINE?
THAT EXPRESSION MAY LOOK PRETTY ON A WOMAN, BUT ON A GUY...
STILL, Y'KNOW...
...I CAN'T SAY I'M NOT CURIOUS ABOUT WHAT AN UPTIGHT GUY LIKE YOU WOULD LOOK LIKE WITH ANOTHER MAN RIDING YOU.

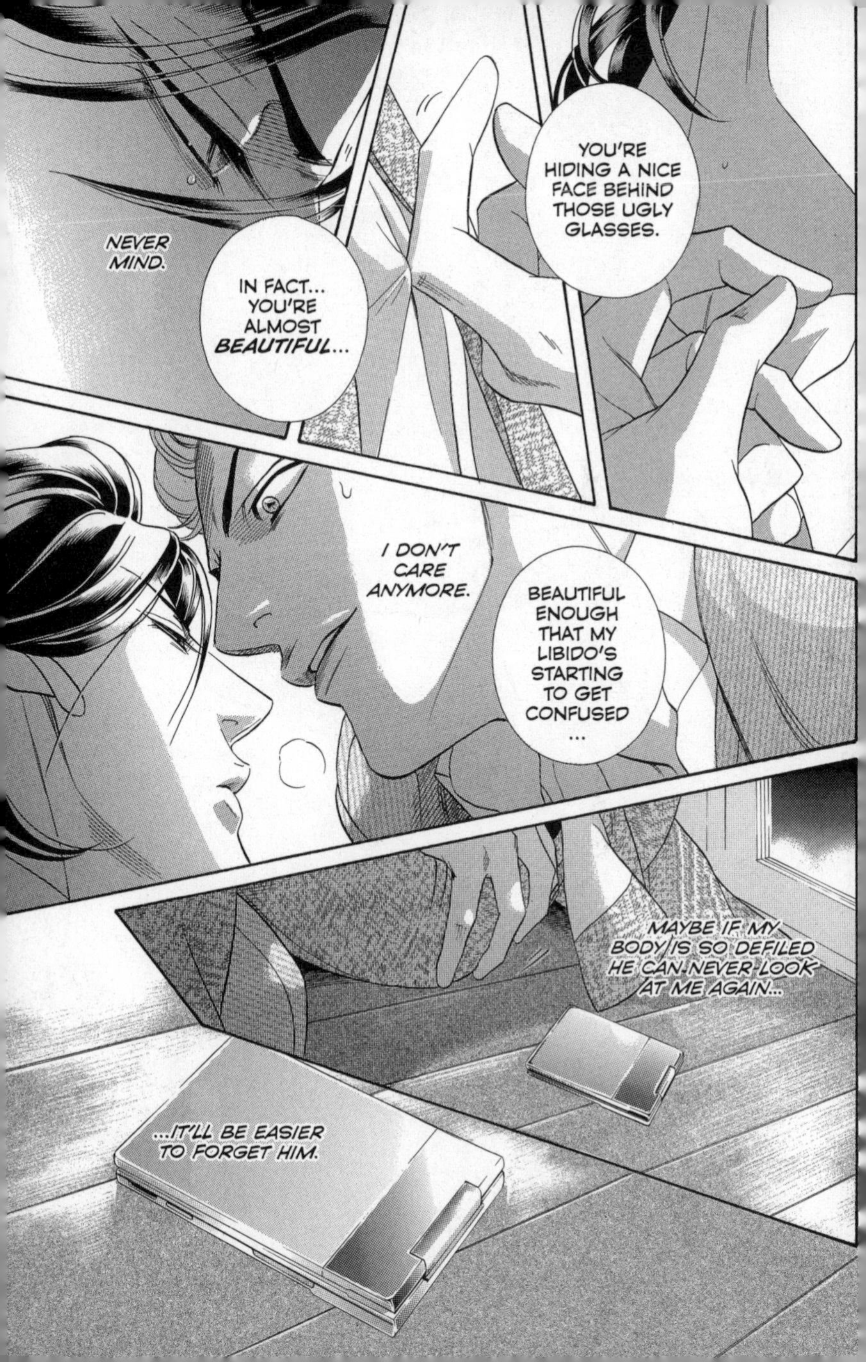
YOU'RE HIDING A NICE FACE BEHIND THOSE UGLY GLASSES.
IN FACT... YOU'RE ALMOST *BEAUTIFUL*...
NEVER MIND.
BEAUTIFUL ENOUGH THAT MY LIBIDO'S STARTING TO GET CONFUSED ...
I DON'T CARE ANYMORE.
MAYBE IF MY BODY IS SO DEFILED HE CAN NEVER LOOK AT ME AGAIN...
...IT'LL BE EASIER TO FORGET HIM.

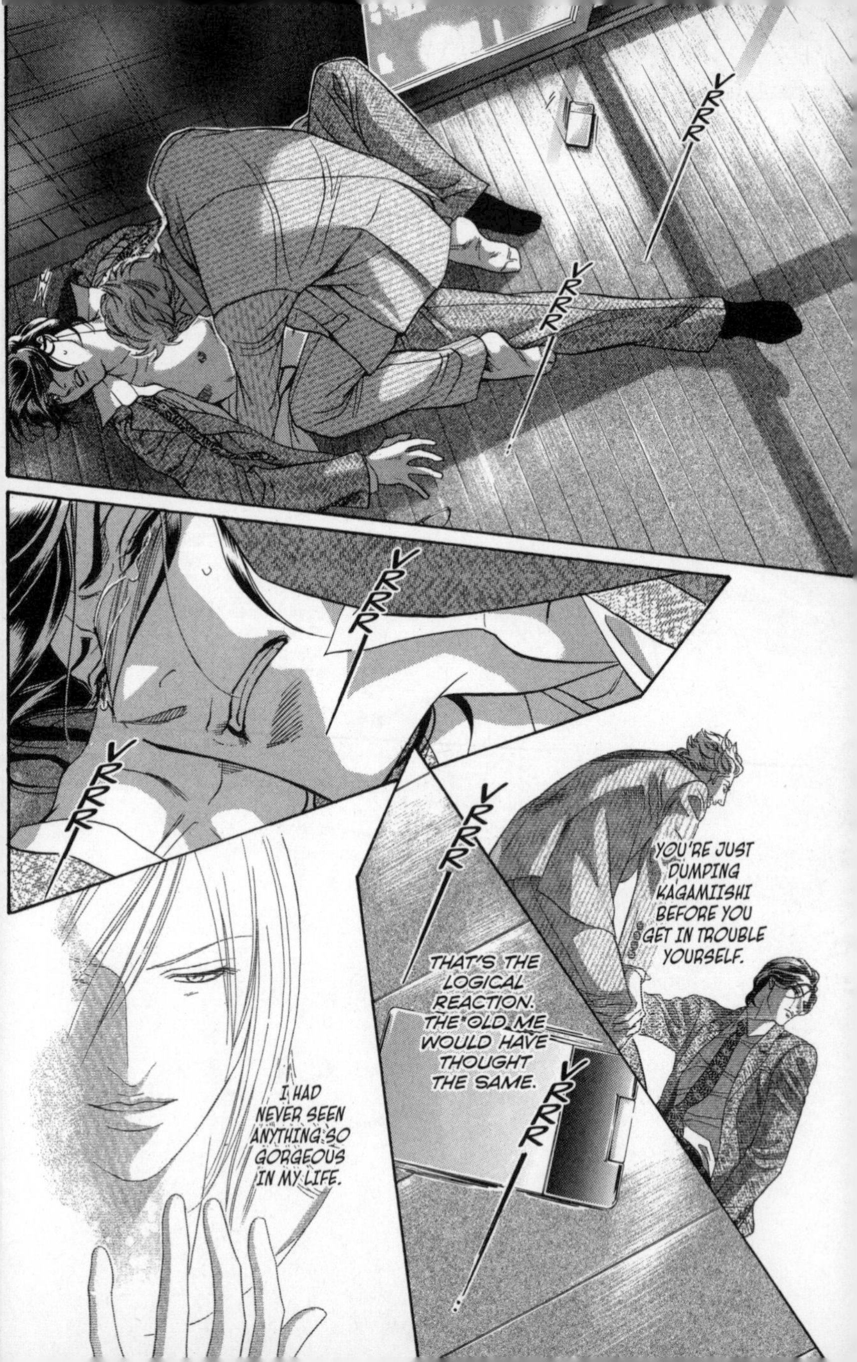
VRRR
VRRR
VRRR
VRRR
YOU'RE JUST DUMPING KAGAMIISHI BEFORE YOU GET IN TROUBLE YOURSELF.
VRRR
THAT'S THE LOGICAL REACTION. THE OLD ME WOULD HAVE THOUGHT THE SAME.
VRRR
I HAD NEVER SEEN ANYTHING SO GORGEOUS IN MY LIFE.

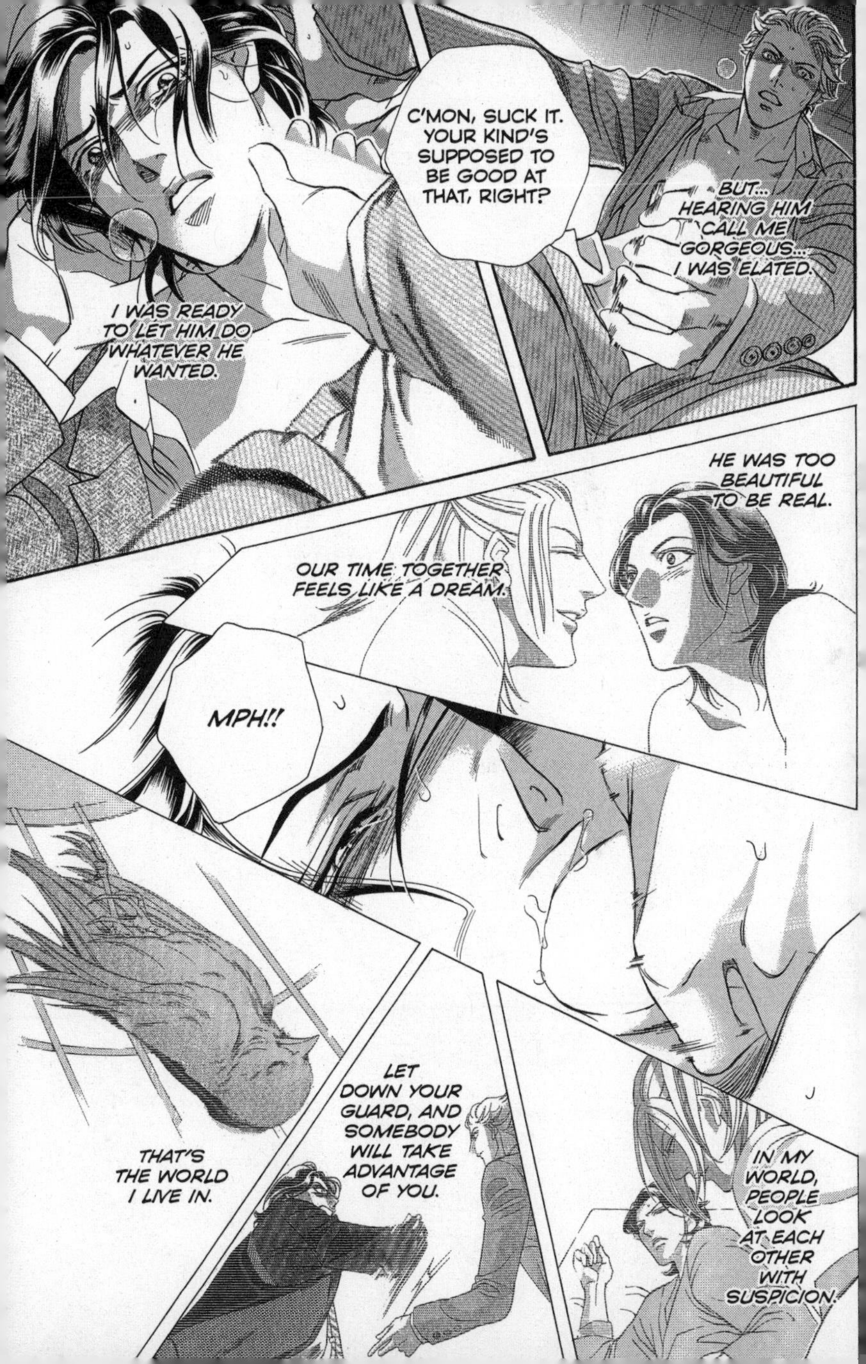
BUT... HEARING HIM CALL ME GORGEOUS... I WAS ELATED.
C'MON, SUCK IT. YOUR KIND'S SUPPOSED TO BE GOOD AT THAT, RIGHT?
I WAS READY TO LET HIM DO WHATEVER HE WANTED.
HE WAS TOO BEAUTIFUL TO BE REAL.
OUR TIME TOGETHER FEELS LIKE A DREAM.
MPH!!
IN MY WORLD, PEOPLE LOOK AT EACH OTHER WITH SUSPICION.
LET DOWN YOUR GUARD, AND SOMEBODY WILL TAKE ADVANTAGE OF YOU.
THAT'S THE WORLD I LIVE IN.

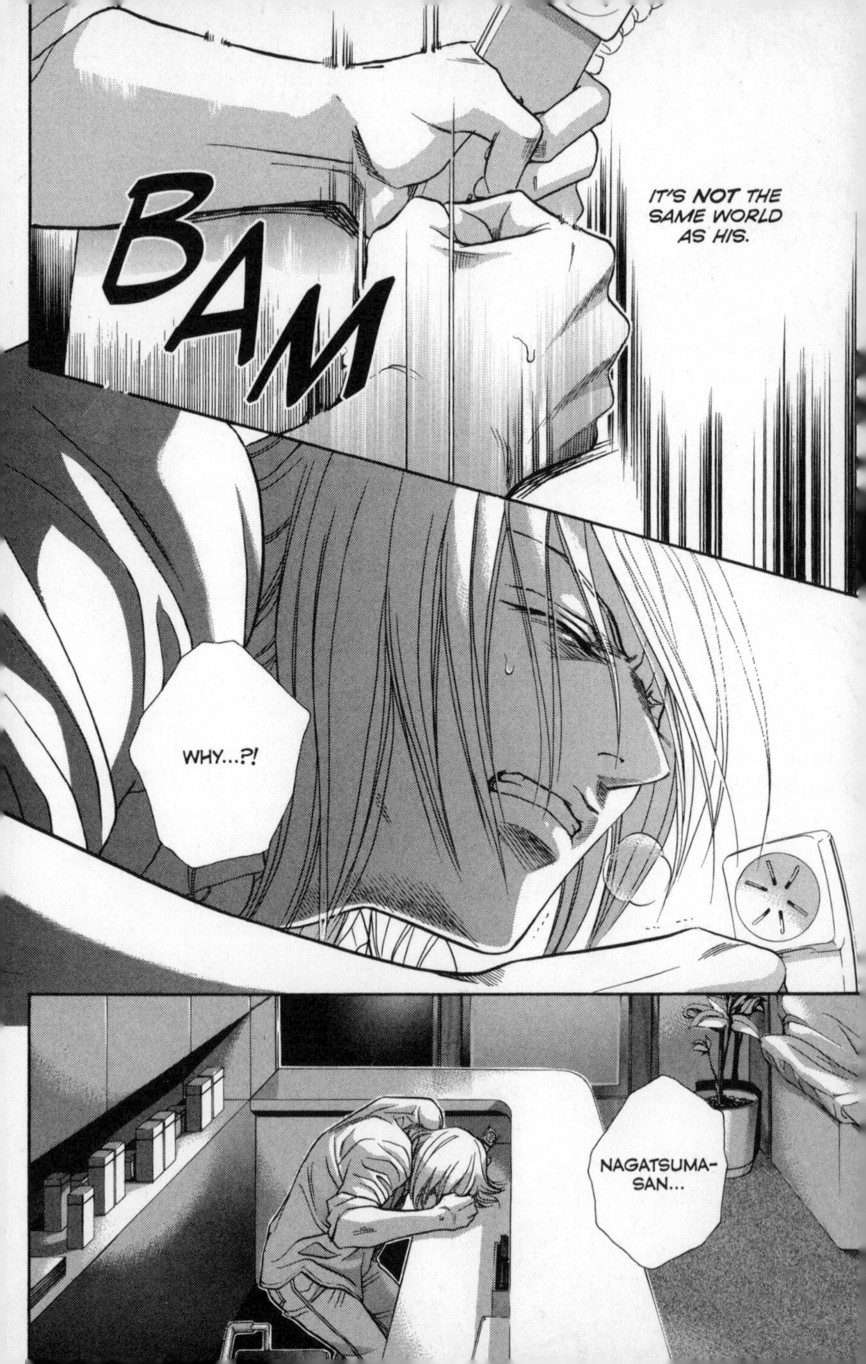
IT'S NOT THE SAME WORLD AS HIS.
BAM
WHY...?!
NAGATSUMA-SAN...

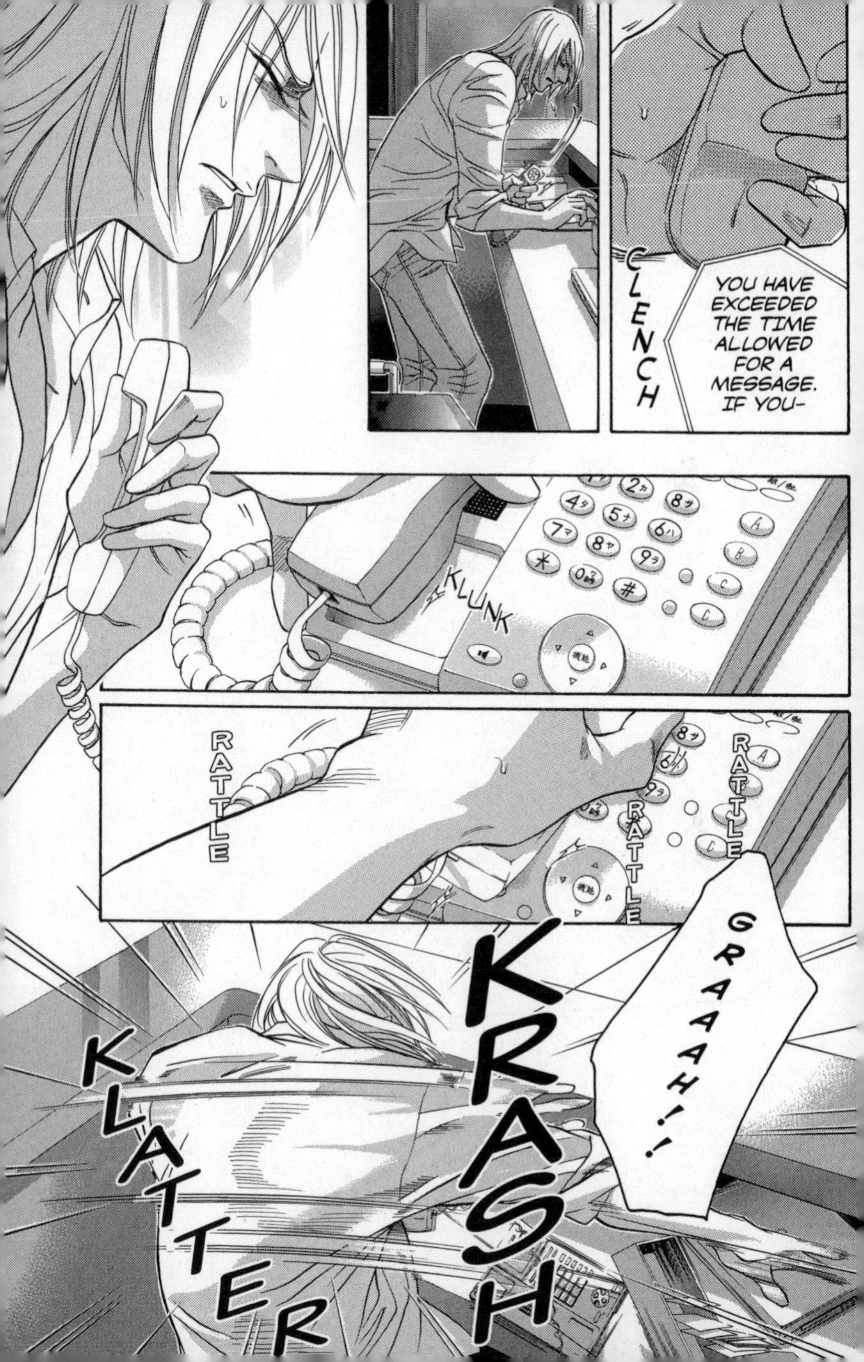
YOU HAVE EXCEEDED THE TIME ALLOWED FOR A MESSAGE. IF YOU-
CLENCH
KLUNK
RATTLE
RATTLE
RATTLE
GRAAAAH!!
KRASH
KLATTER

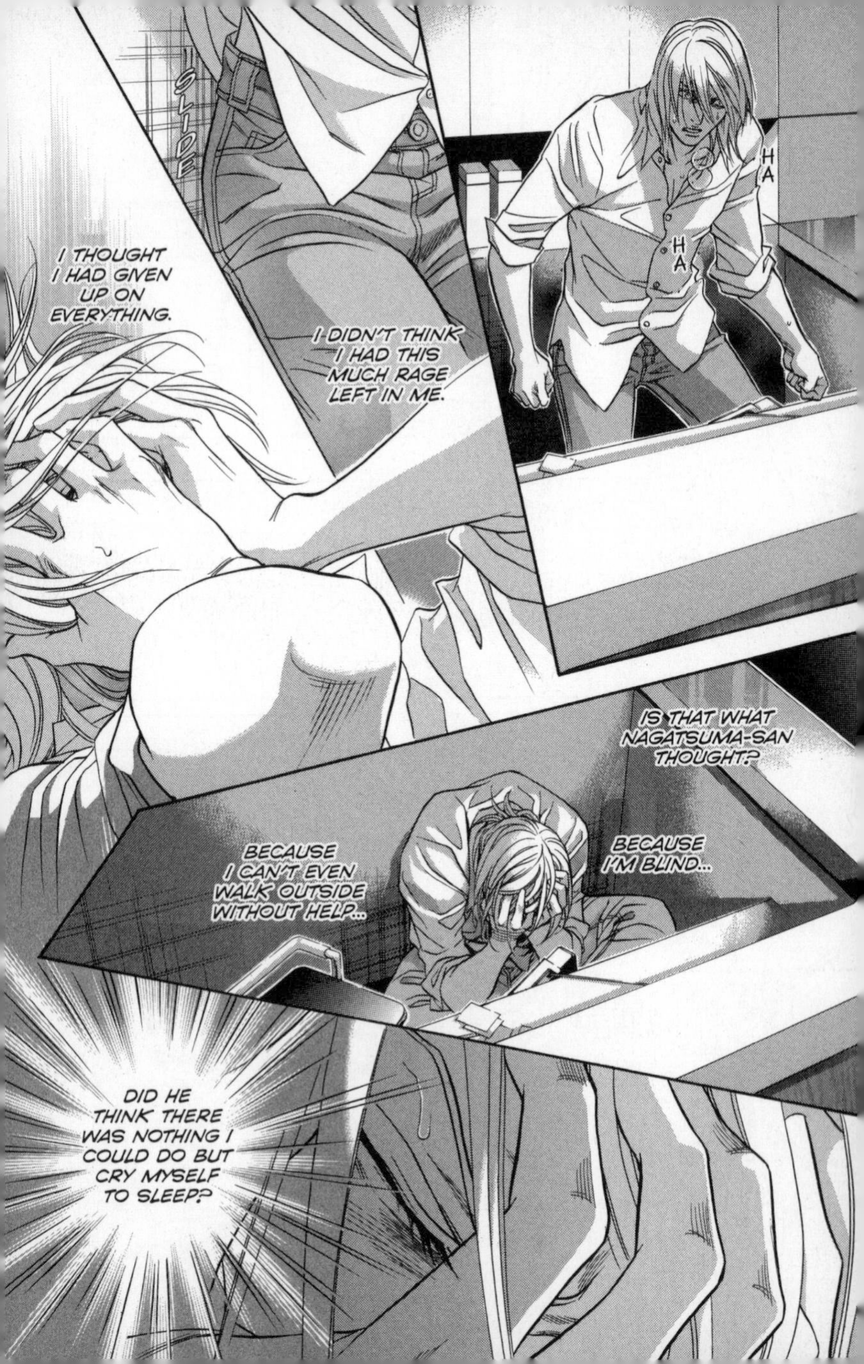
HA
HA
SLIDE
I THOUGHT I HAD GIVEN UP ON EVERYTHING.
I DIDN'T THINK I HAD THIS MUCH RAGE LEFT IN ME.
IS THAT WHAT NAGATSUMA-SAN THOUGHT?
BECAUSE I'M BLIND...
BECAUSE I CAN'T EVEN WALK OUTSIDE WITHOUT HELP...
DID HE THINK THERE WAS NOTHING I COULD DO BUT CRY MYSELF TO SLEEP?

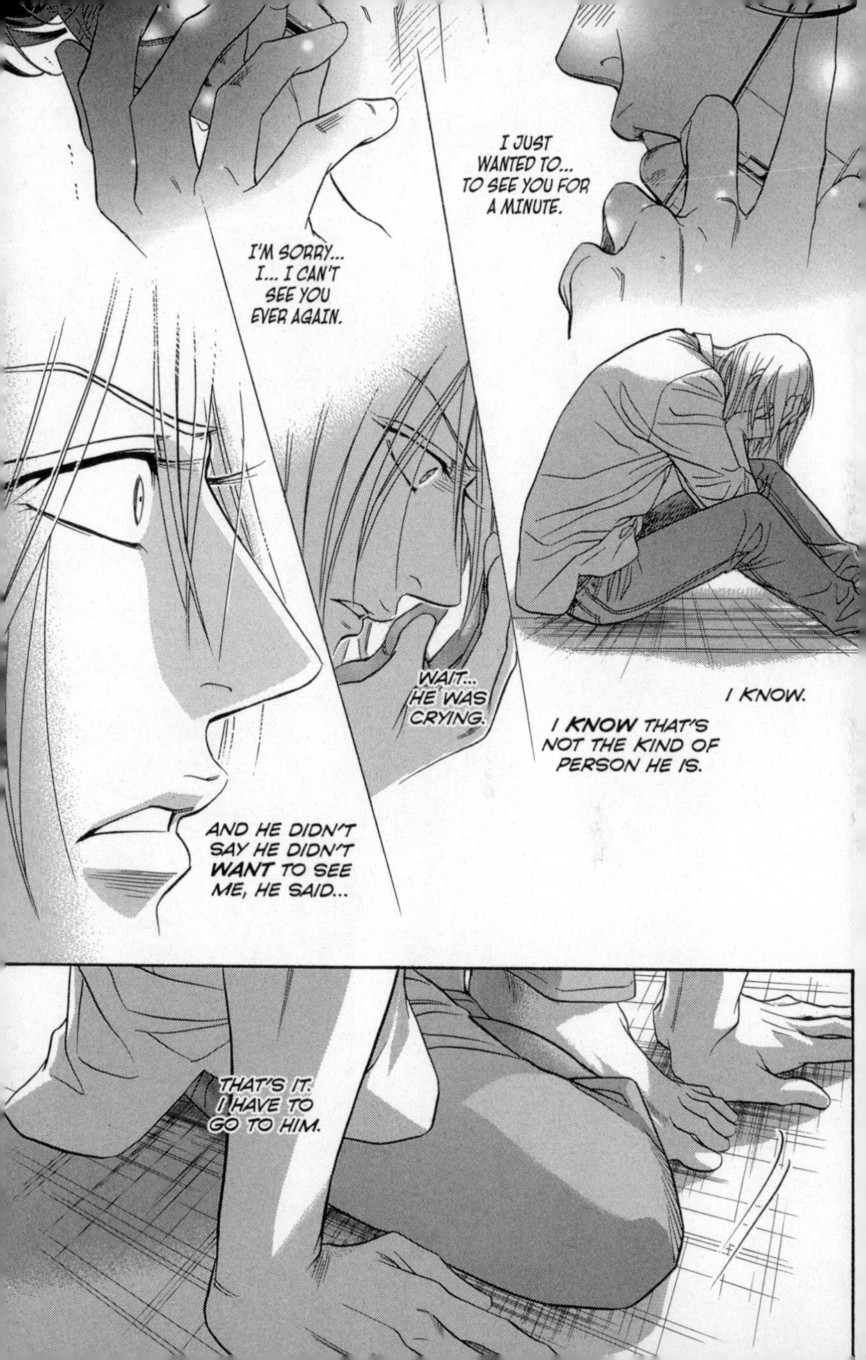
I JUST WANTED TO... TO SEE YOU FOR A MINUTE.
I'M SORRY... I... I CAN'T SEE YOU EVER AGAIN.
I KNOW.
I **KNOW** THAT'S NOT THE KIND OF PERSON HE IS.
WAIT... HE WAS CRYING.
AND HE DIDN'T SAY HE DIDN'T **WANT** TO SEE ME, HE SAID...
THAT'S IT. I HAVE TO GO TO HIM.

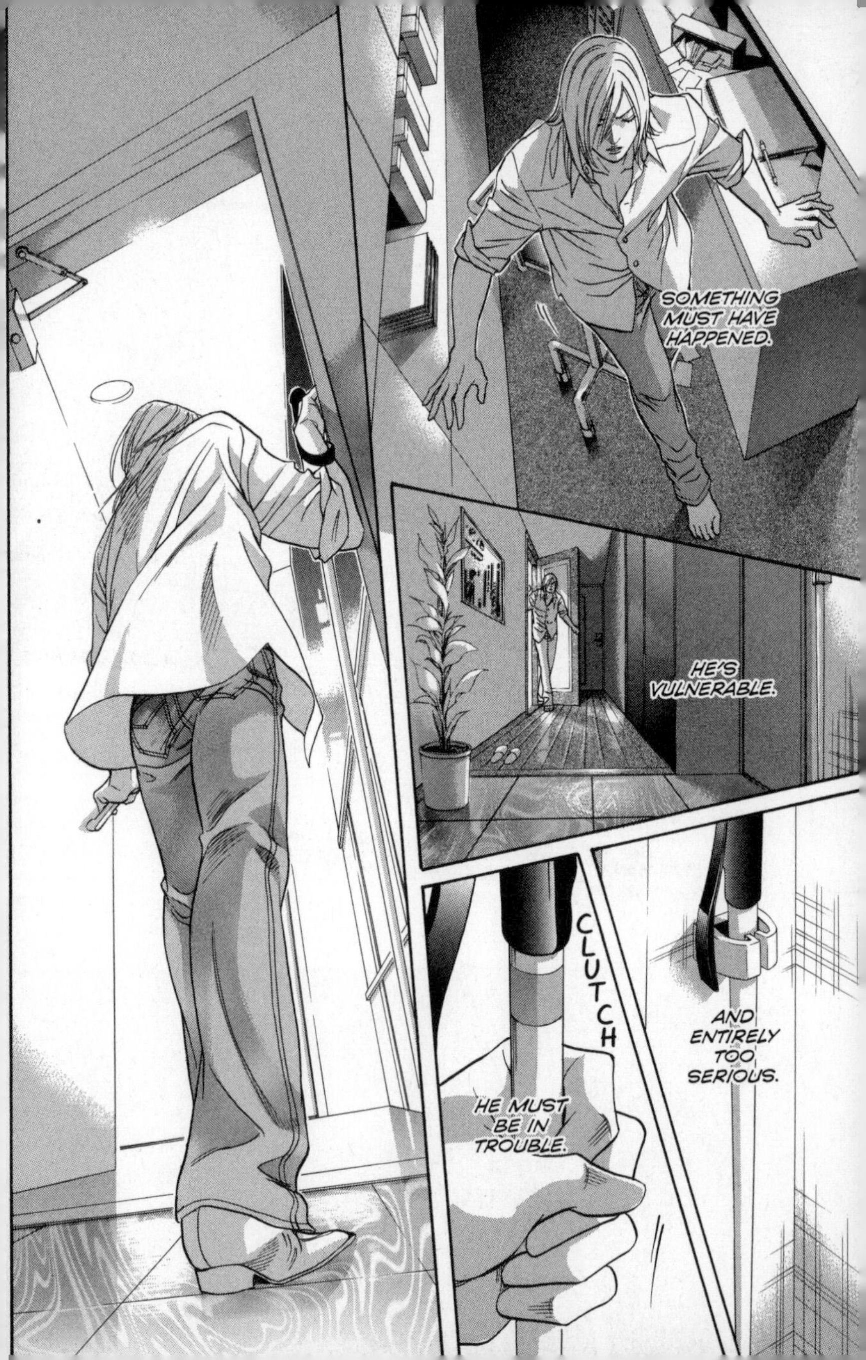
SOMETHING MUST HAVE HAPPENED.
HE'S VULNERABLE.
AND ENTIRELY TOO SERIOUS.
CLUTCH
HE MUST BE IN TROUBLE.

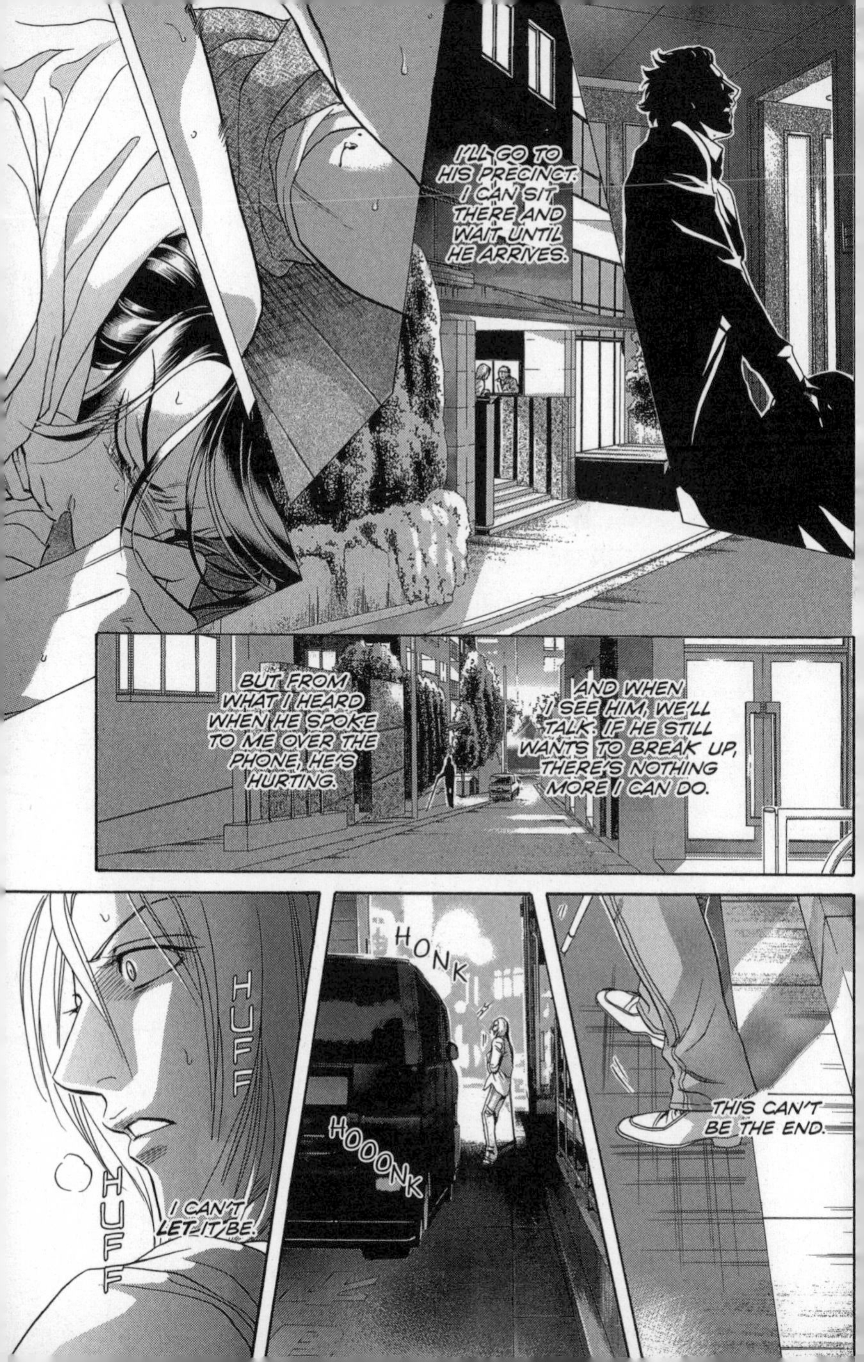
I'LL GO TO HIS PRECINCT. I CAN SIT THERE AND WAIT UNTIL HE ARRIVES.
AND WHEN I SEE HIM, WE'LL TALK. IF HE STILL WANTS TO BREAK UP, THERE'S NOTHING MORE I CAN DO.
BUT FROM WHAT I HEARD WHEN HE SPOKE TO ME OVER THE PHONE, HE'S HURTING.
THIS CAN'T BE THE END.
HONK
HOOOONK
HUFF
HUFF
I CAN'T LET IT BE.

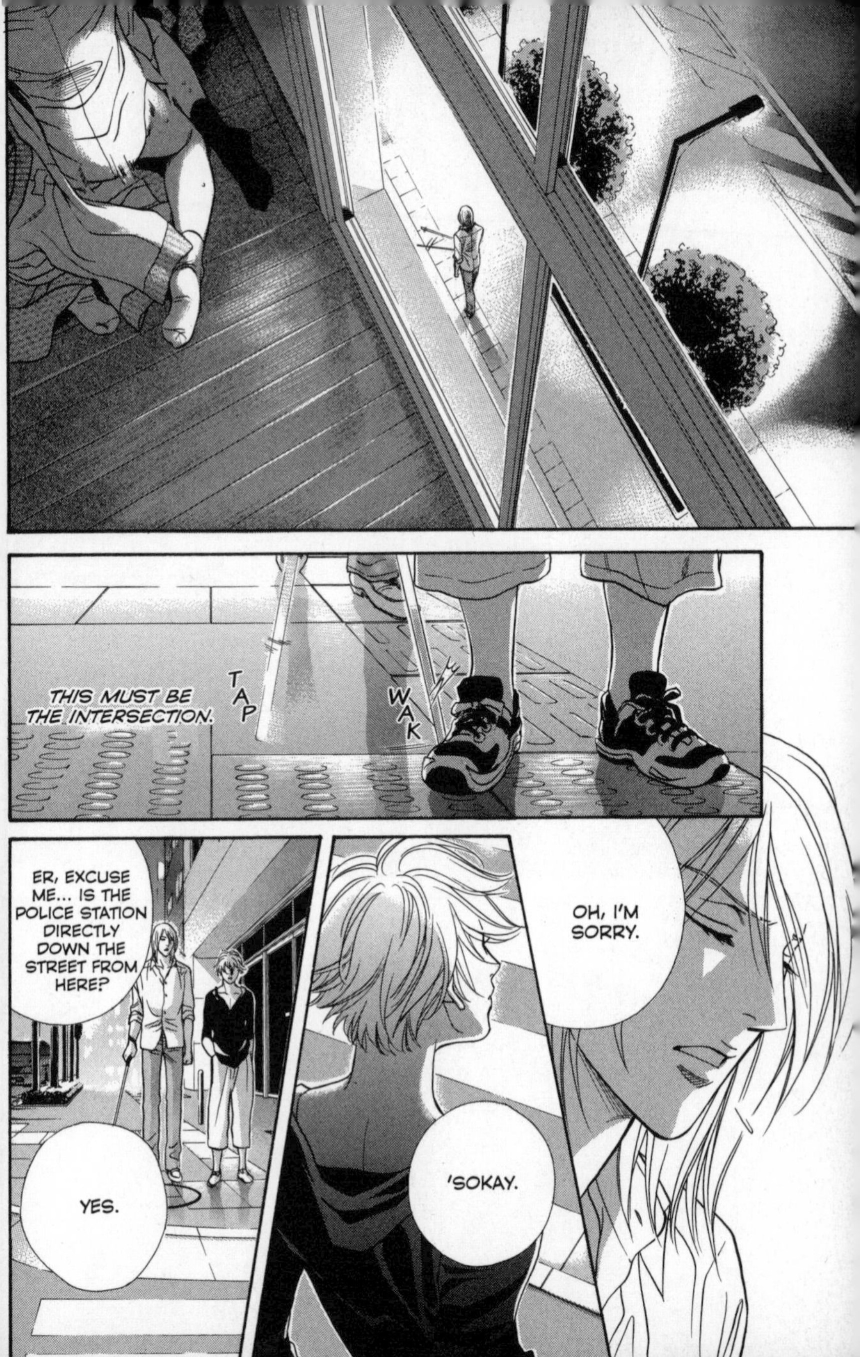
WAK
TAP
THIS MUST BE THE INTERSECTION.
OH, I'M SORRY.
'SOKAY.
ER, EXCUSE ME... IS THE POLICE STATION DIRECTLY DOWN THE STREET FROM HERE?
YES.

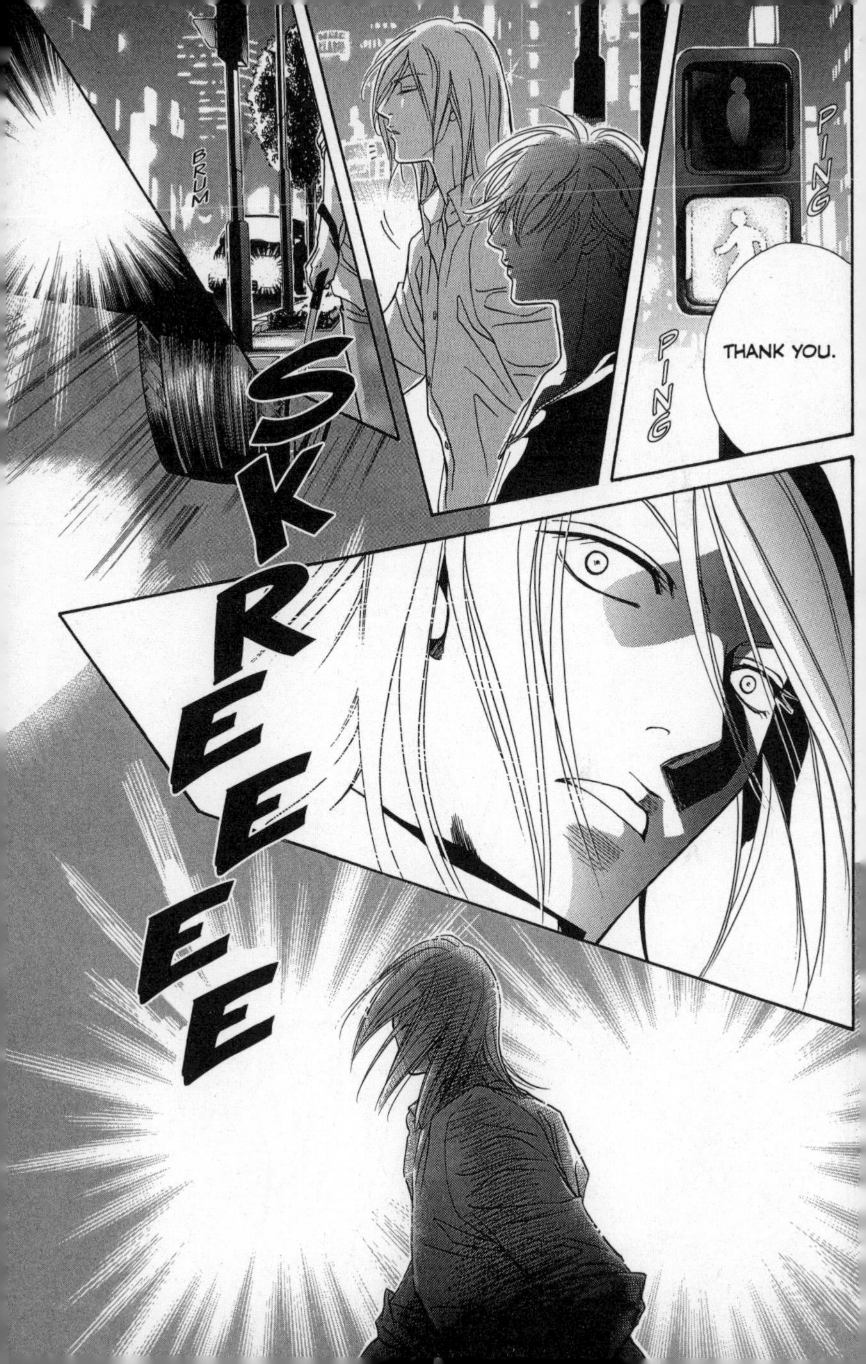
PING
THANK YOU.
PING
BRUM
SKREEEE

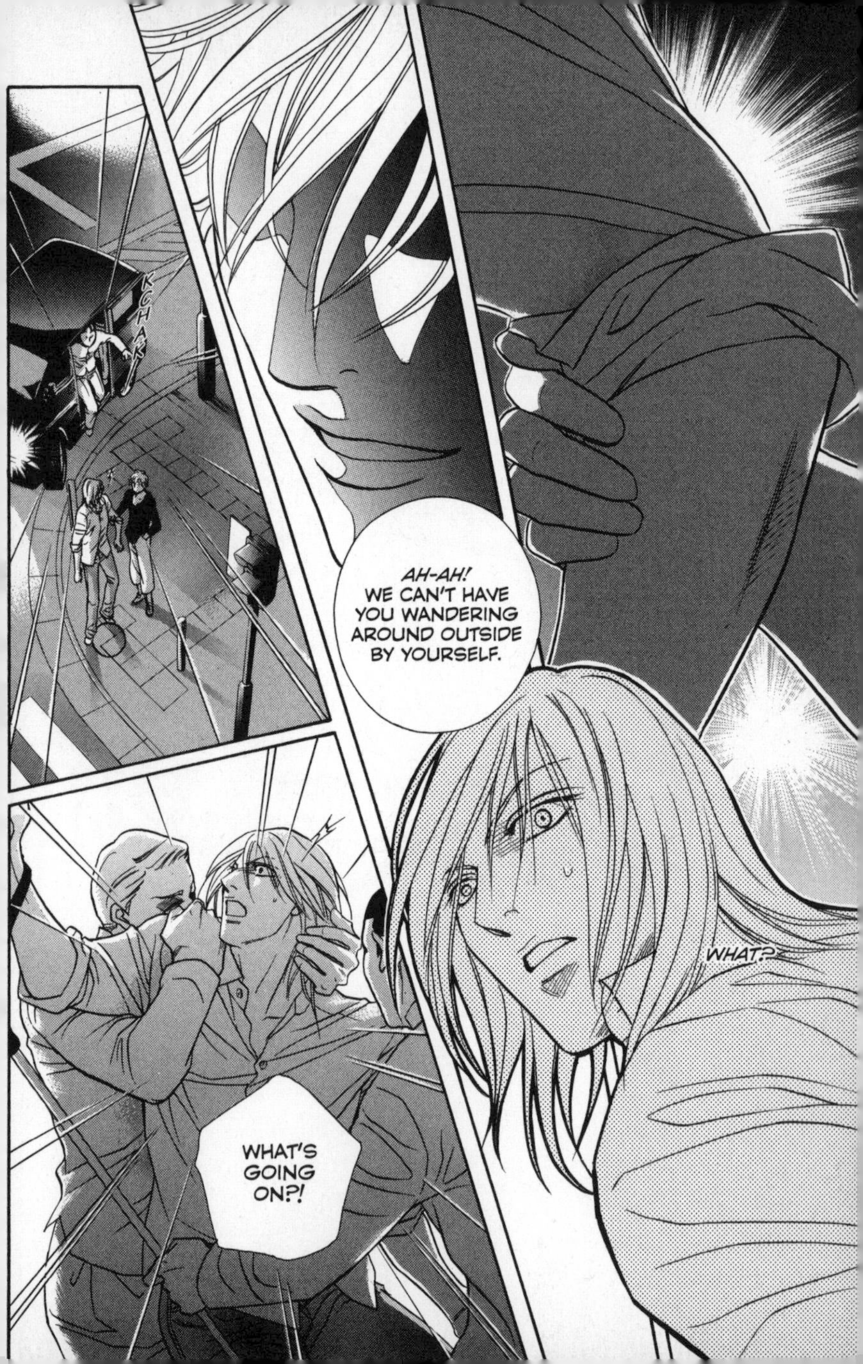
KCHAK
AH-AH! WE CAN'T HAVE YOU WANDERING AROUND OUTSIDE BY YOURSELF.
WHAT?
WHAT'S GOING ON?!

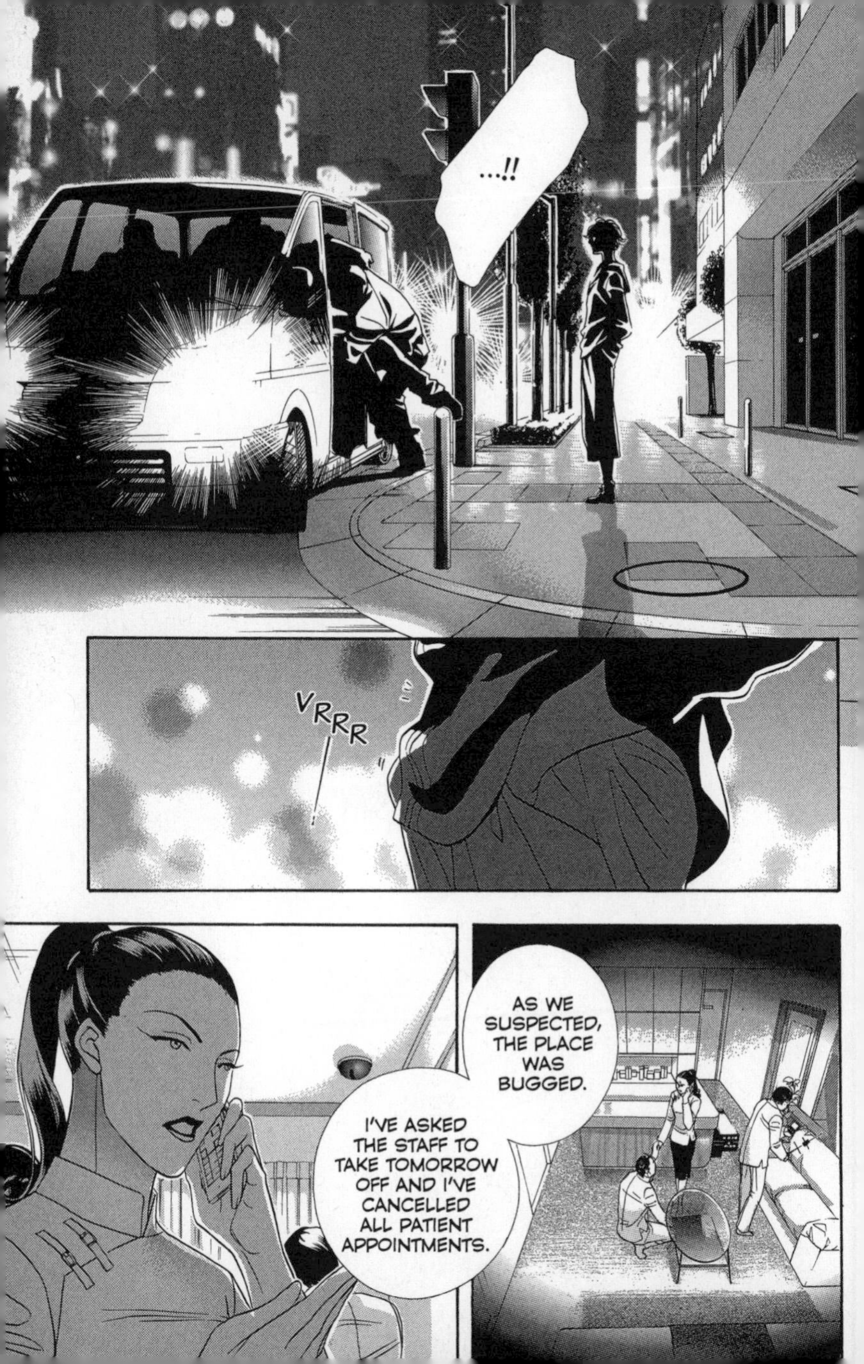
...!!
VRRR
AS WE SUSPECTED, THE PLACE WAS BUGGED.
I'VE ASKED THE STAFF TO TAKE TOMORROW OFF AND I'VE CANCELLED ALL PATIENT APPOINTMENTS.

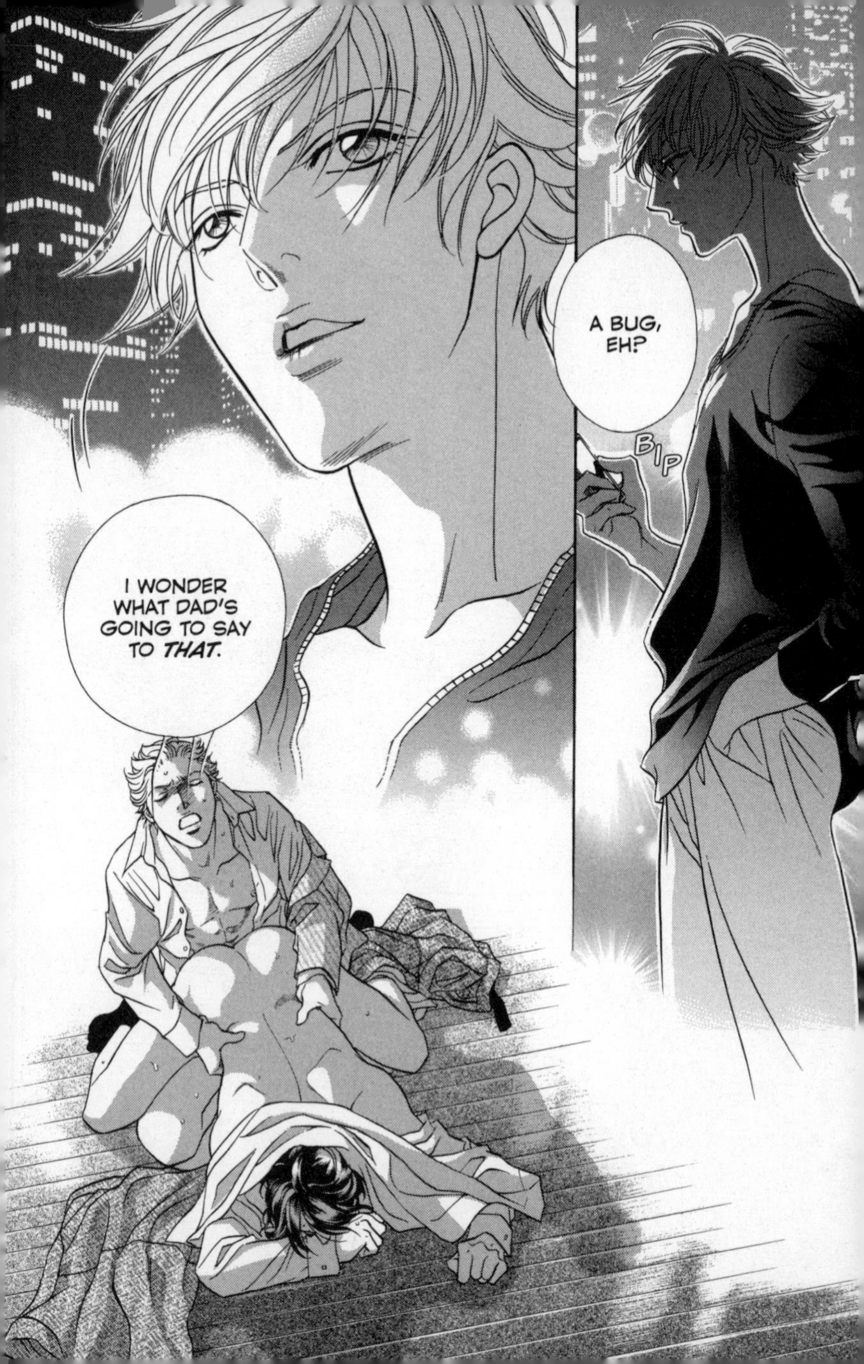
A BUG, EH?
BIP
I WONDER WHAT DAD'S GOING TO SAY TO *THAT*.

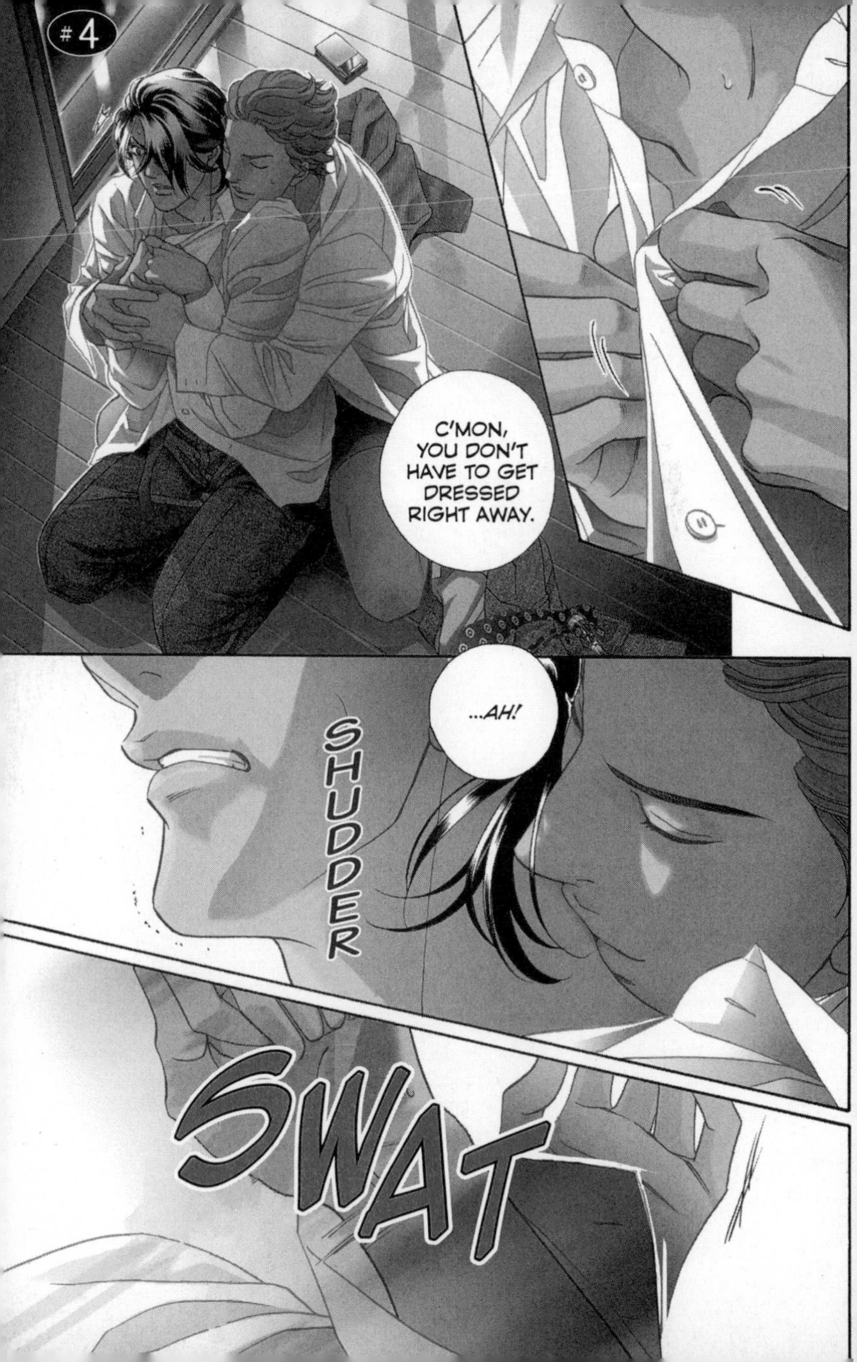
#4
C'MON, YOU DON'T HAVE TO GET DRESSED RIGHT AWAY.
...AH!
SHUDDER
SWAT

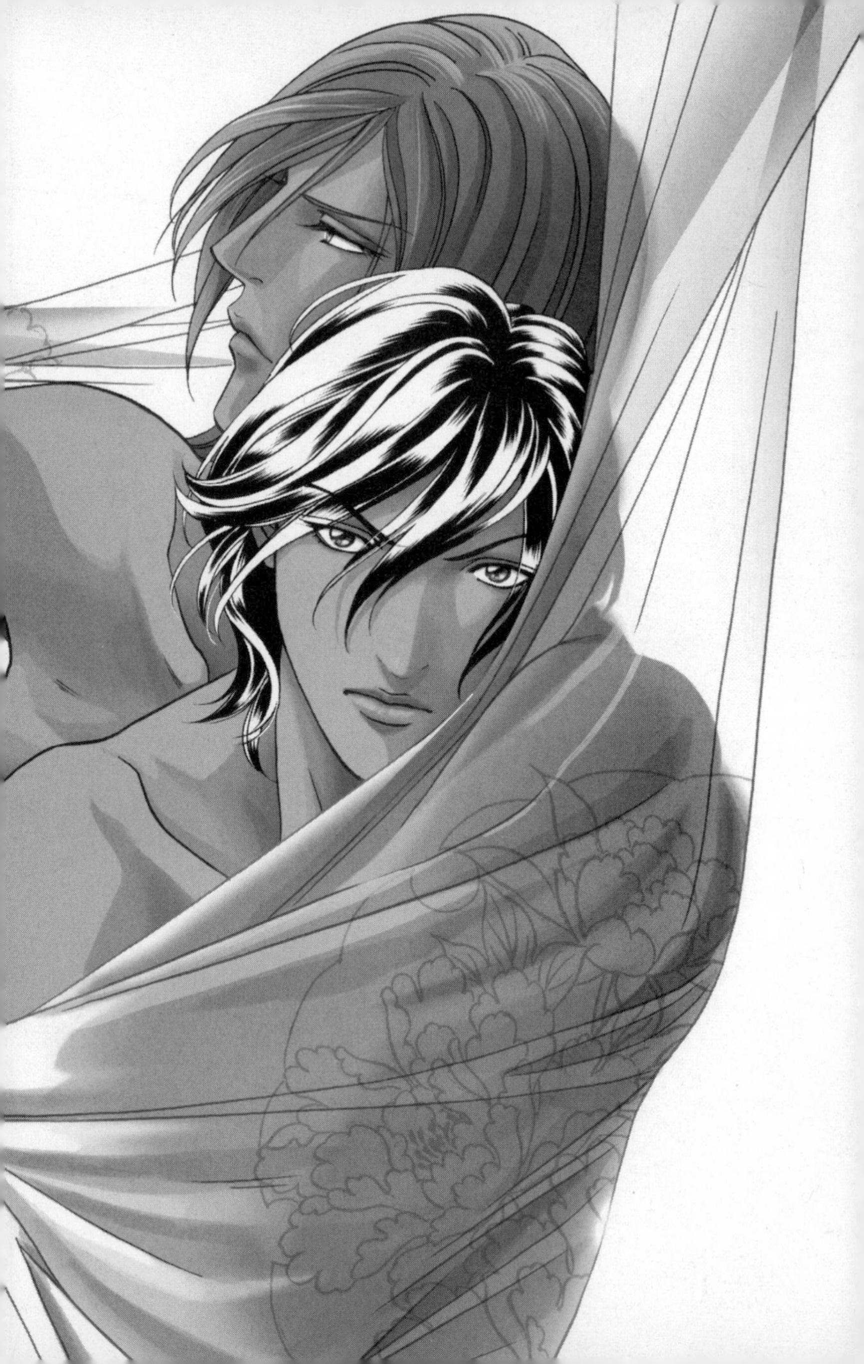

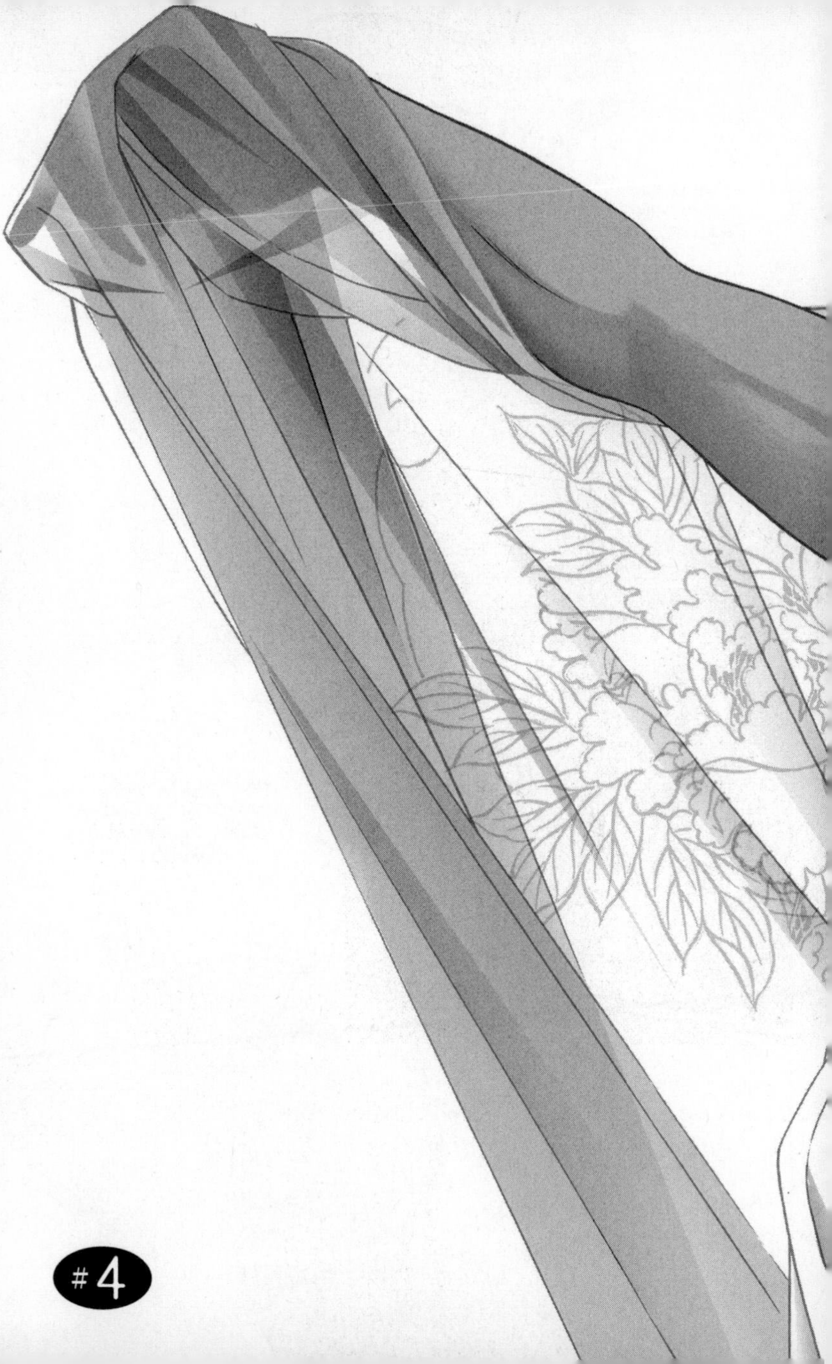

#4

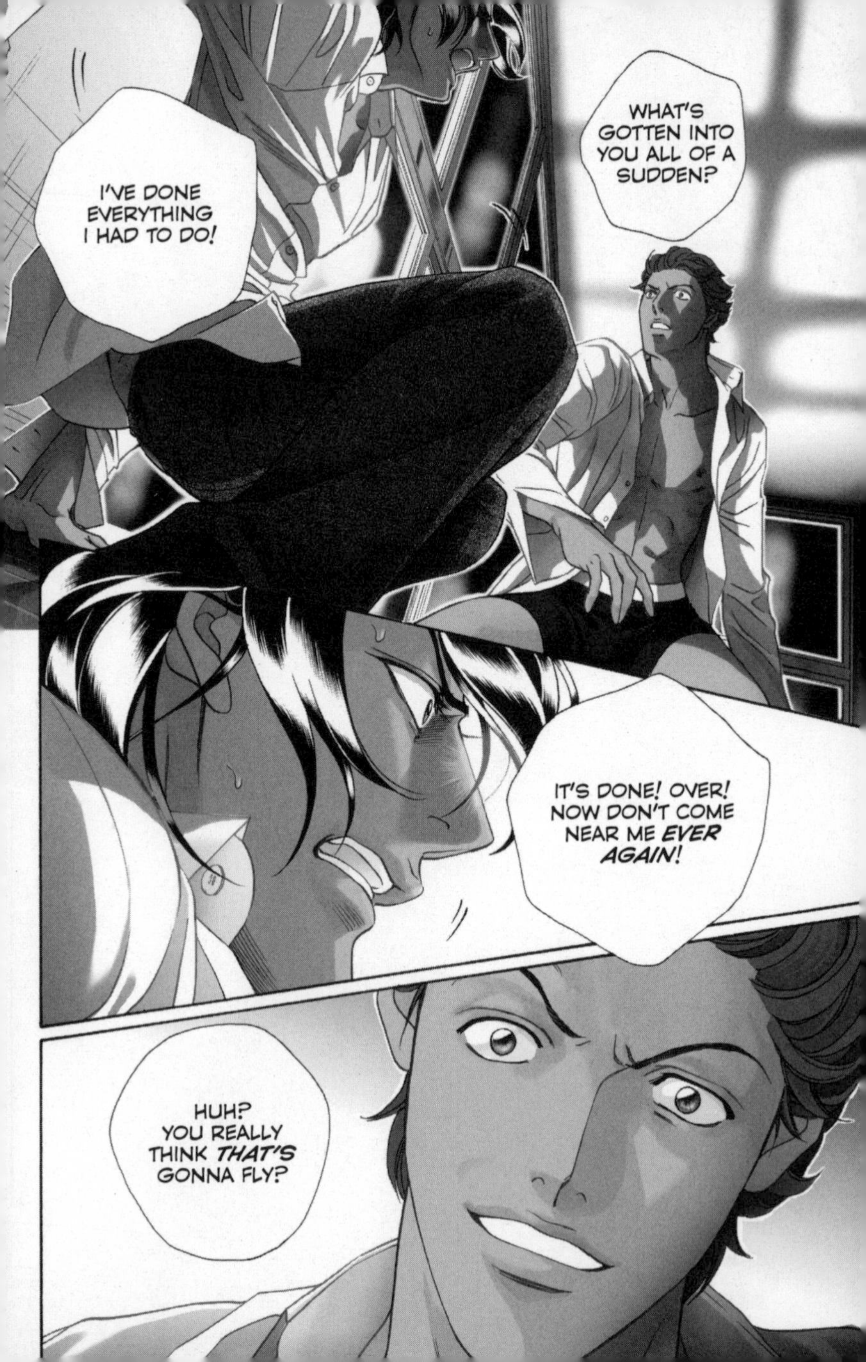
WHAT'S GOTTEN INTO YOU ALL OF A SUDDEN?
I'VE DONE EVERYTHING I HAD TO DO!
IT'S DONE! OVER! NOW DON'T COME NEAR ME *EVER AGAIN*!
HUH? YOU REALLY THINK *THAT'S* GONNA FLY?

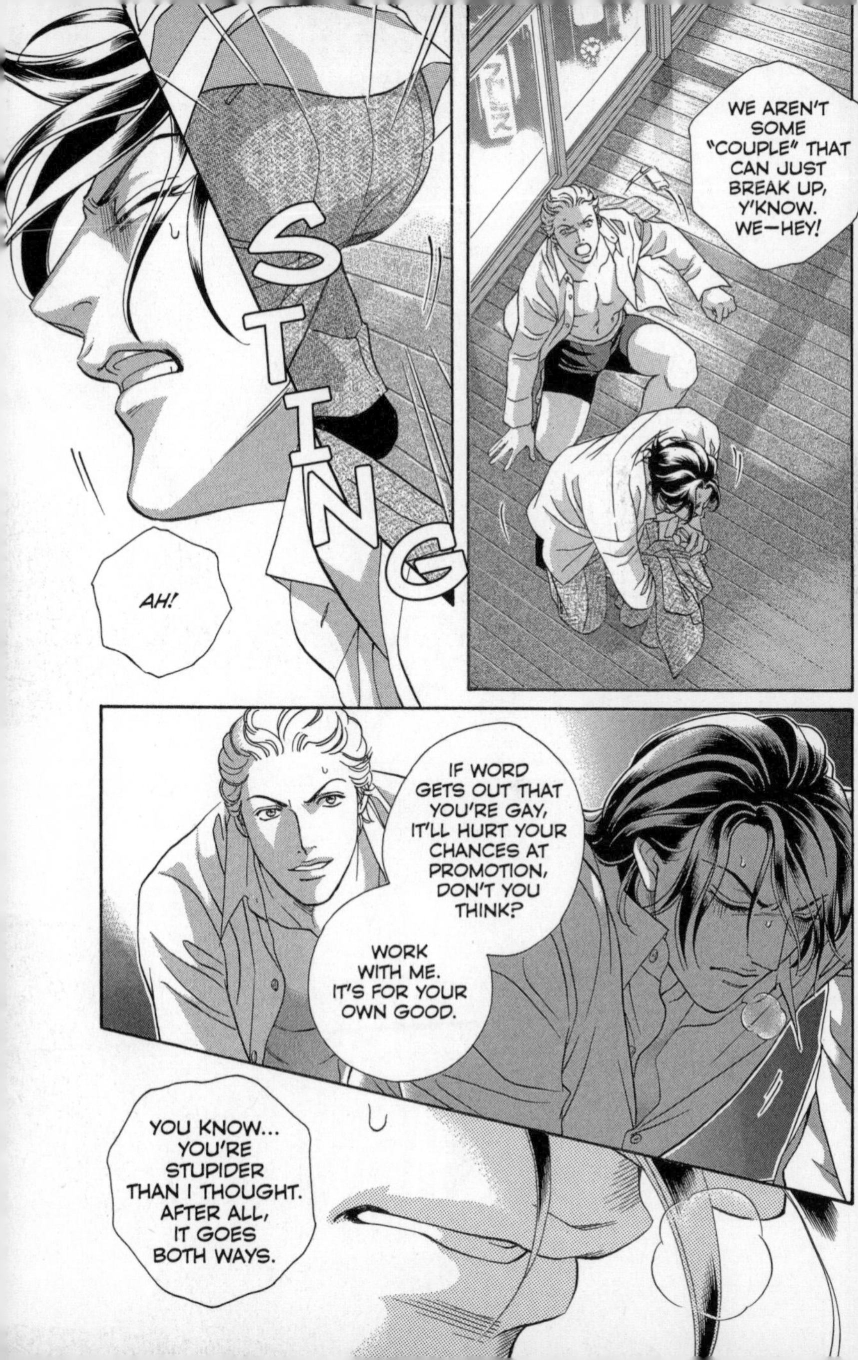
WE AREN'T SOME "COUPLE" THAT CAN JUST BREAK UP, Y'KNOW. WE—HEY!
STING
AH!
IF WORD GETS OUT THAT YOU'RE GAY, IT'LL HURT YOUR CHANCES AT PROMOTION, DON'T YOU THINK?
WORK WITH ME. IT'S FOR YOUR OWN GOOD.
YOU KNOW... YOU'RE STUPIDER THAN I THOUGHT. AFTER ALL, IT GOES BOTH WAYS.

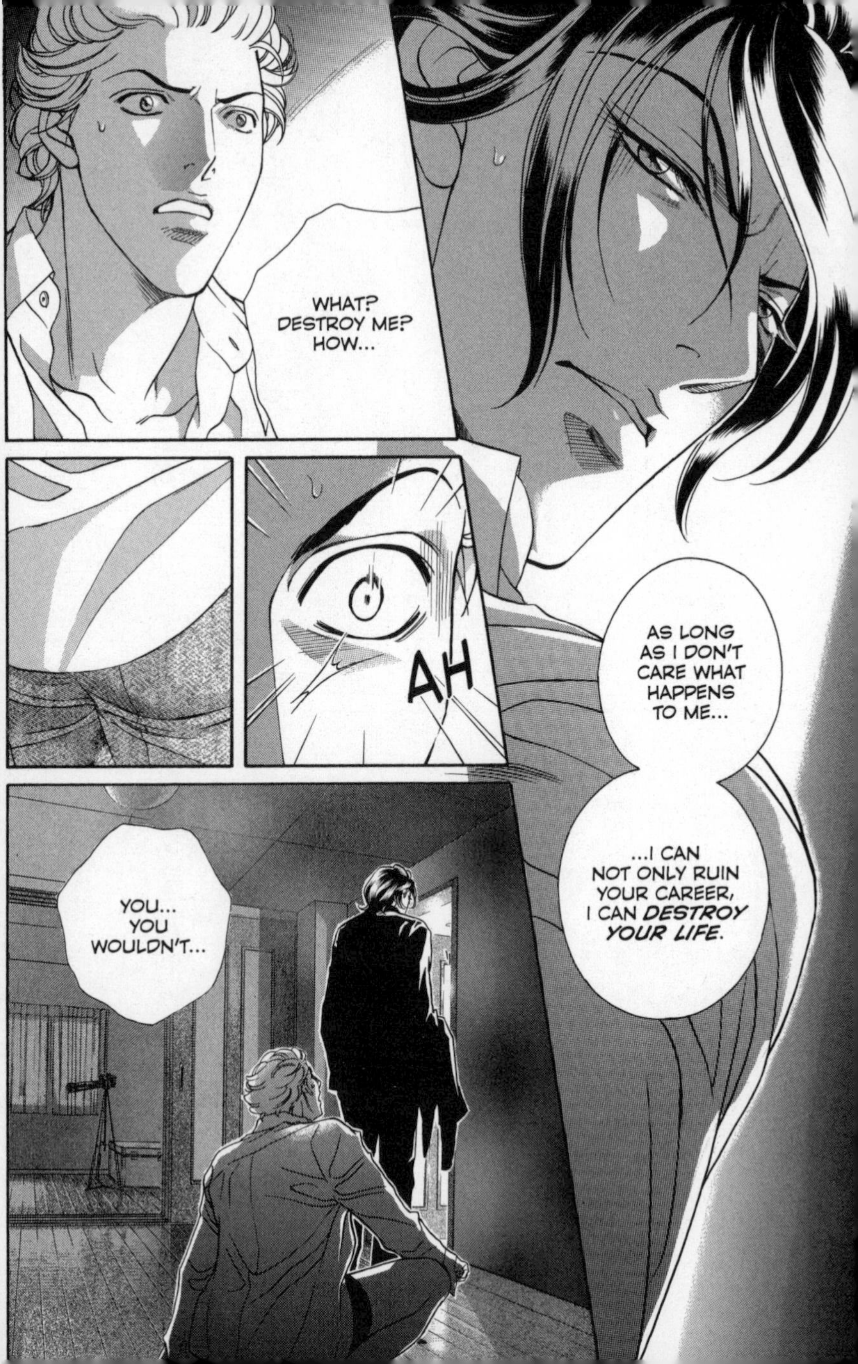
WHAT? DESTROY ME? HOW...
AS LONG AS I DON'T CARE WHAT HAPPENS TO ME...
...I CAN NOT ONLY RUIN YOUR CAREER, I CAN *DESTROY YOUR LIFE*.
AH
YOU... YOU WOULDN'T...

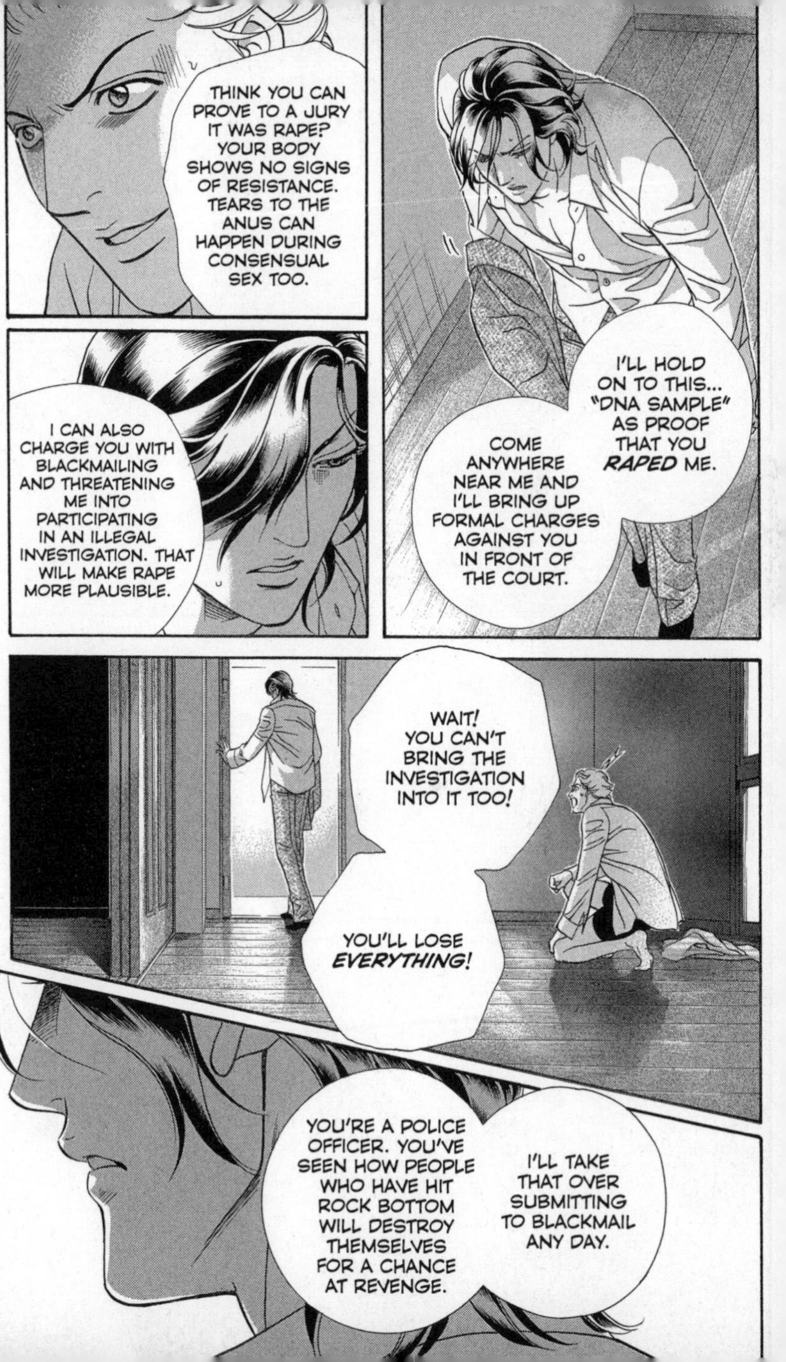

I'LL HOLD ON TO THIS... "DNA SAMPLE" AS PROOF THAT YOU *RAPED* ME.
COME ANYWHERE NEAR ME AND I'LL BRING UP FORMAL CHARGES AGAINST YOU IN FRONT OF THE COURT.
THINK YOU CAN PROVE TO A JURY IT WAS RAPE? YOUR BODY SHOWS NO SIGNS OF RESISTANCE. TEARS TO THE ANUS CAN HAPPEN DURING CONSENSUAL SEX TOO.
I CAN ALSO CHARGE YOU WITH BLACKMAILING AND THREATENING ME INTO PARTICIPATING IN AN ILLEGAL INVESTIGATION. THAT WILL MAKE RAPE MORE PLAUSIBLE.
WAIT! YOU CAN'T BRING THE INVESTIGATION INTO IT TOO!
YOU'LL LOSE *EVERYTHING*!
I'LL TAKE THAT OVER SUBMITTING TO BLACKMAIL ANY DAY.
YOU'RE A POLICE OFFICER. YOU'VE SEEN HOW PEOPLE WHO HAVE HIT ROCK BOTTOM WILL DESTROY THEMSELVES FOR A CHANCE AT REVENGE.

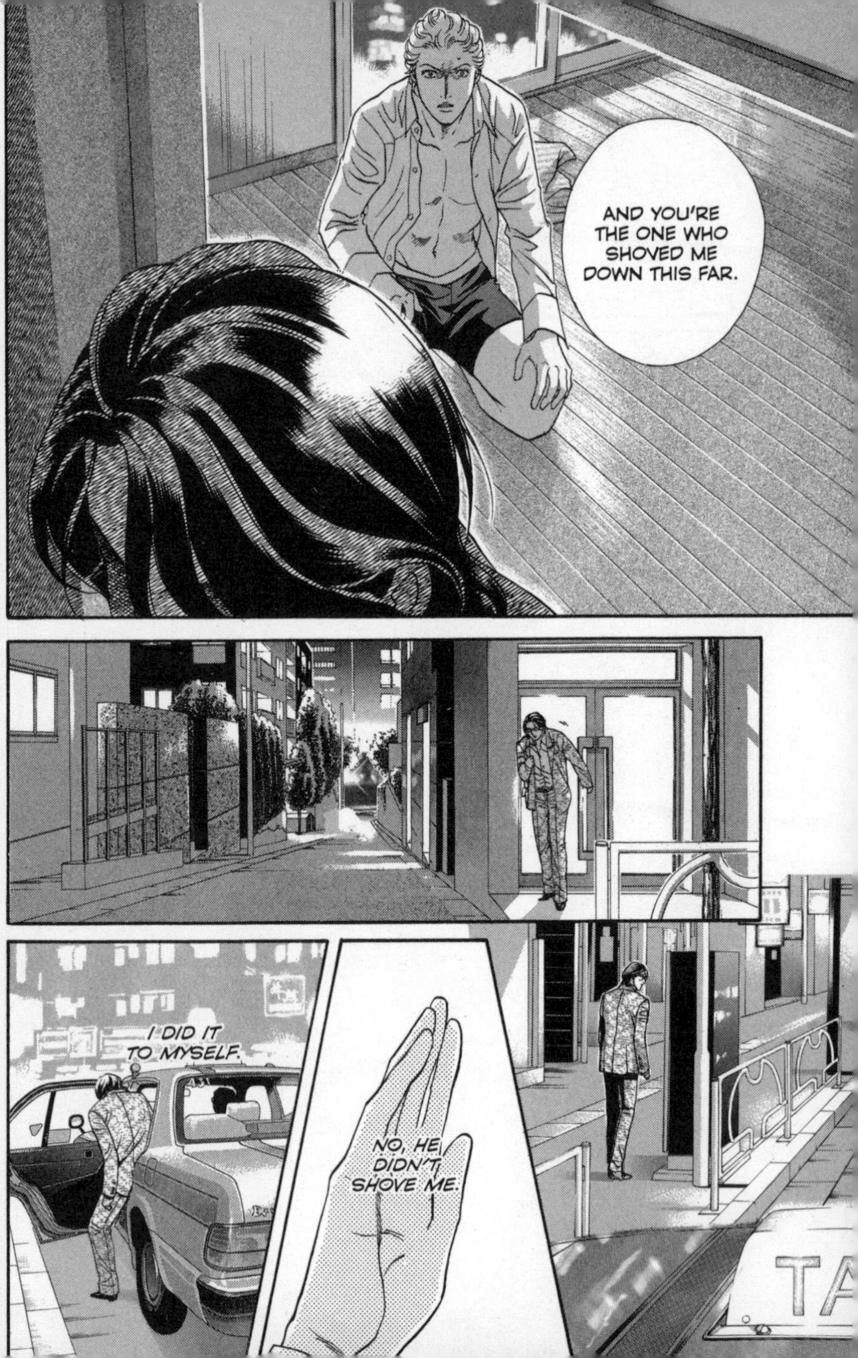
AND YOU'RE THE ONE WHO SHOVED ME DOWN THIS FAR.
NO, HE DIDN'T SHOVE ME.
I DID IT TO MYSELF.

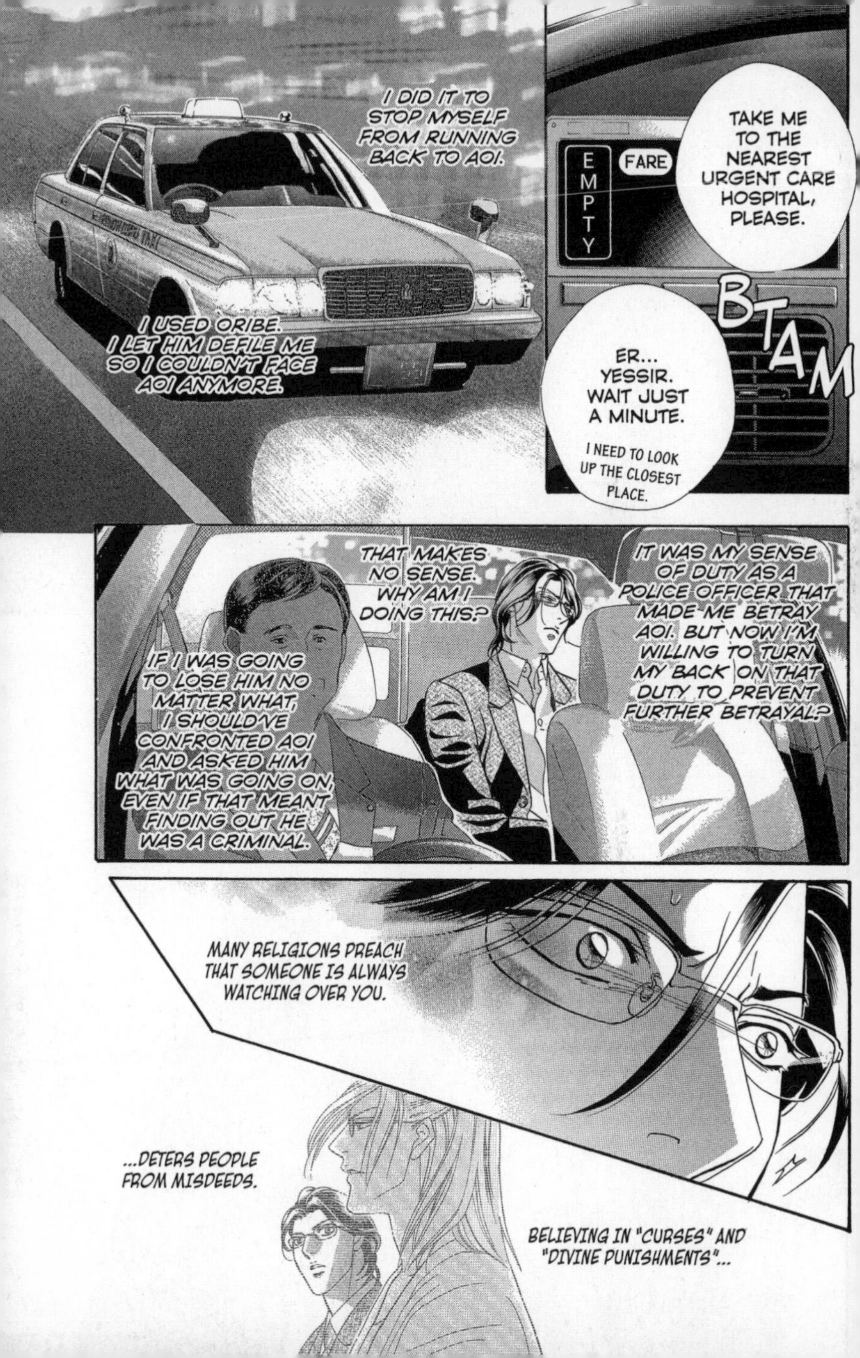
TAKE ME TO THE NEAREST URGENT CARE HOSPITAL, PLEASE.
EMPTY
FARE
BTAM
ER... YESSIR. WAIT JUST A MINUTE.
I NEED TO LOOK UP THE CLOSEST PLACE.
I DID IT TO STOP MYSELF FROM RUNNING BACK TO AOI.
I USED ORIBE. I LET HIM DEFILE ME SO I COULDN'T FACE AOI ANYMORE.
IT WAS MY SENSE OF DUTY AS A POLICE OFFICER THAT MADE ME BETRAY AOI. BUT NOW I'M WILLING TO TURN MY BACK ON THAT DUTY TO PREVENT FURTHER BETRAYAL?
THAT MAKES NO SENSE. WHY AM I DOING THIS?
IF I WAS GOING TO LOSE HIM NO MATTER WHAT, I SHOULD'VE CONFRONTED AOI AND ASKED HIM WHAT WAS GOING ON, EVEN IF THAT MEANT FINDING OUT HE WAS A CRIMINAL.
MANY RELIGIONS PREACH THAT SOMEONE IS ALWAYS WATCHING OVER YOU.
BELIEVING IN "CURSES" AND "DIVINE PUNISHMENTS"...
...DETERS PEOPLE FROM MISDEEDS.

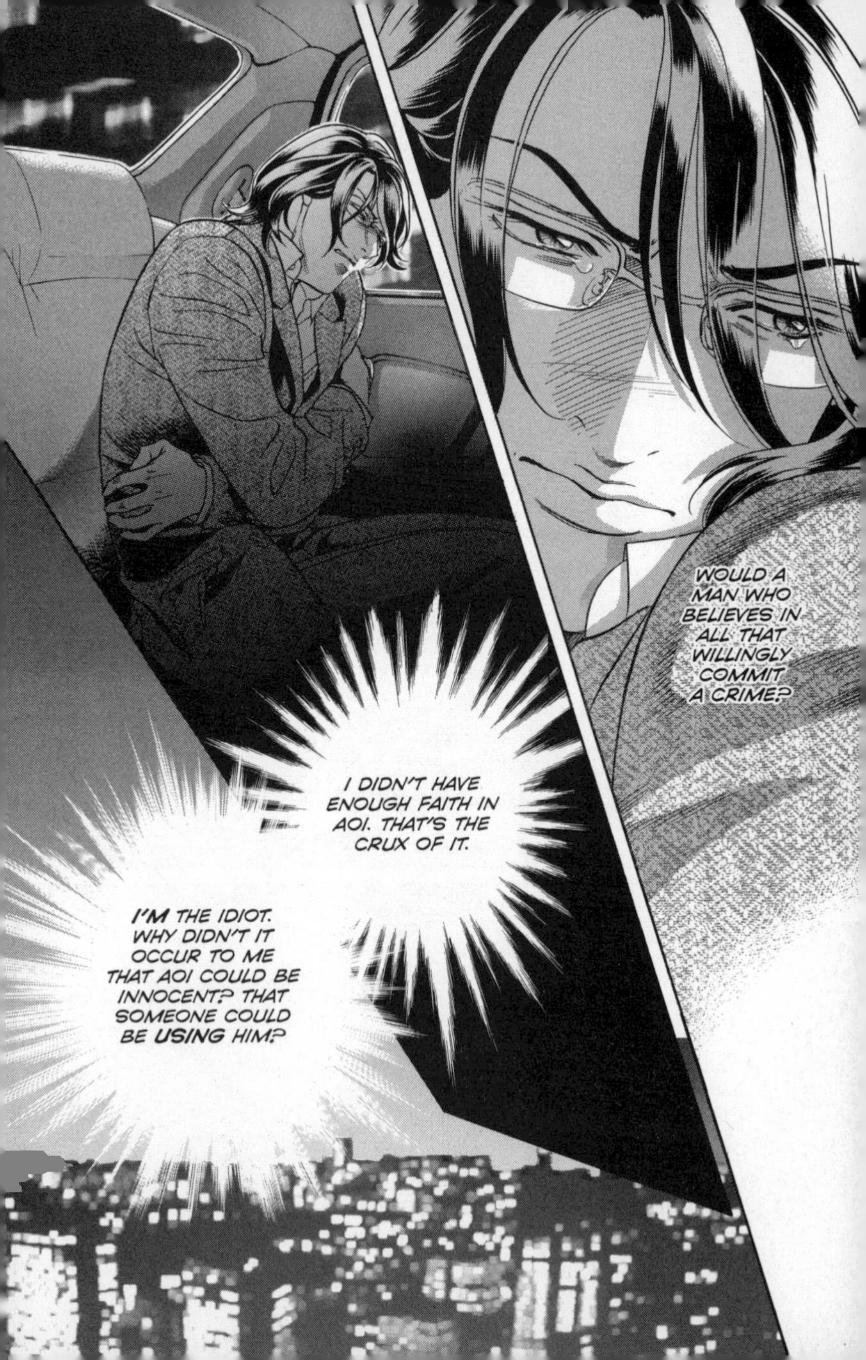
WOULD A MAN WHO BELIEVES IN ALL THAT WILLINGLY COMMIT A CRIME?
I DIDN'T HAVE ENOUGH FAITH IN AOI. THAT'S THE CRUX OF IT.
I'M THE IDIOT. WHY DIDN'T IT OCCUR TO ME THAT AOI COULD BE INNOCENT? THAT SOMEONE COULD BE USING HIM?

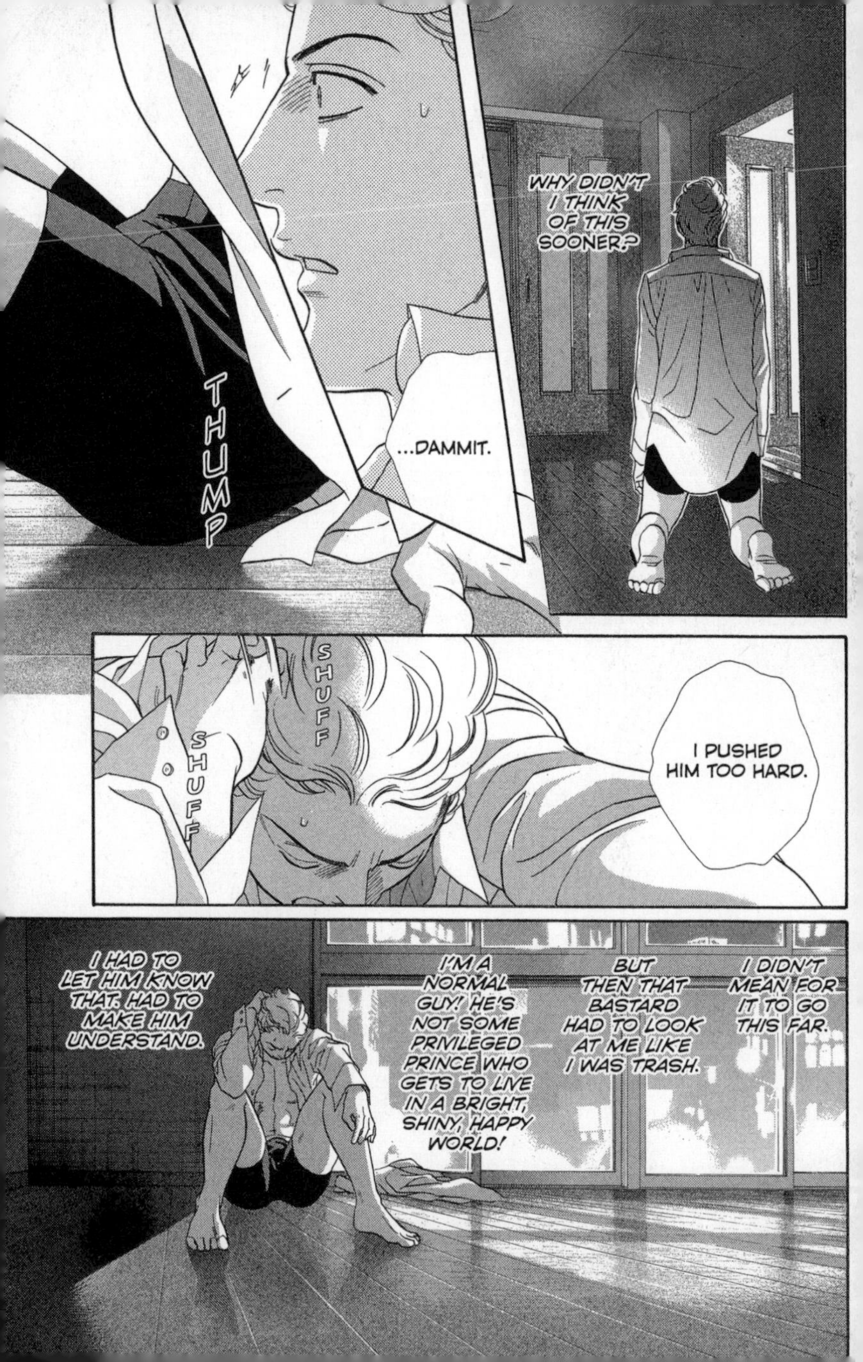

WHY DIDN'T I THINK OF THIS SOONER?
THUMP
...DAMMIT.
I PUSHED HIM TOO HARD.
SHUFF
SHUFF
I DIDN'T MEAN FOR IT TO GO THIS FAR.
BUT THEN THAT BASTARD HAD TO LOOK AT ME LIKE I WAS TRASH.
I'M A NORMAL GUY! HE'S NOT SOME PRIVILEGED PRINCE WHO GETS TO LIVE IN A BRIGHT, SHINY, HAPPY WORLD!
I HAD TO LET HIM KNOW THAT. HAD TO MAKE HIM UNDERSTAND.

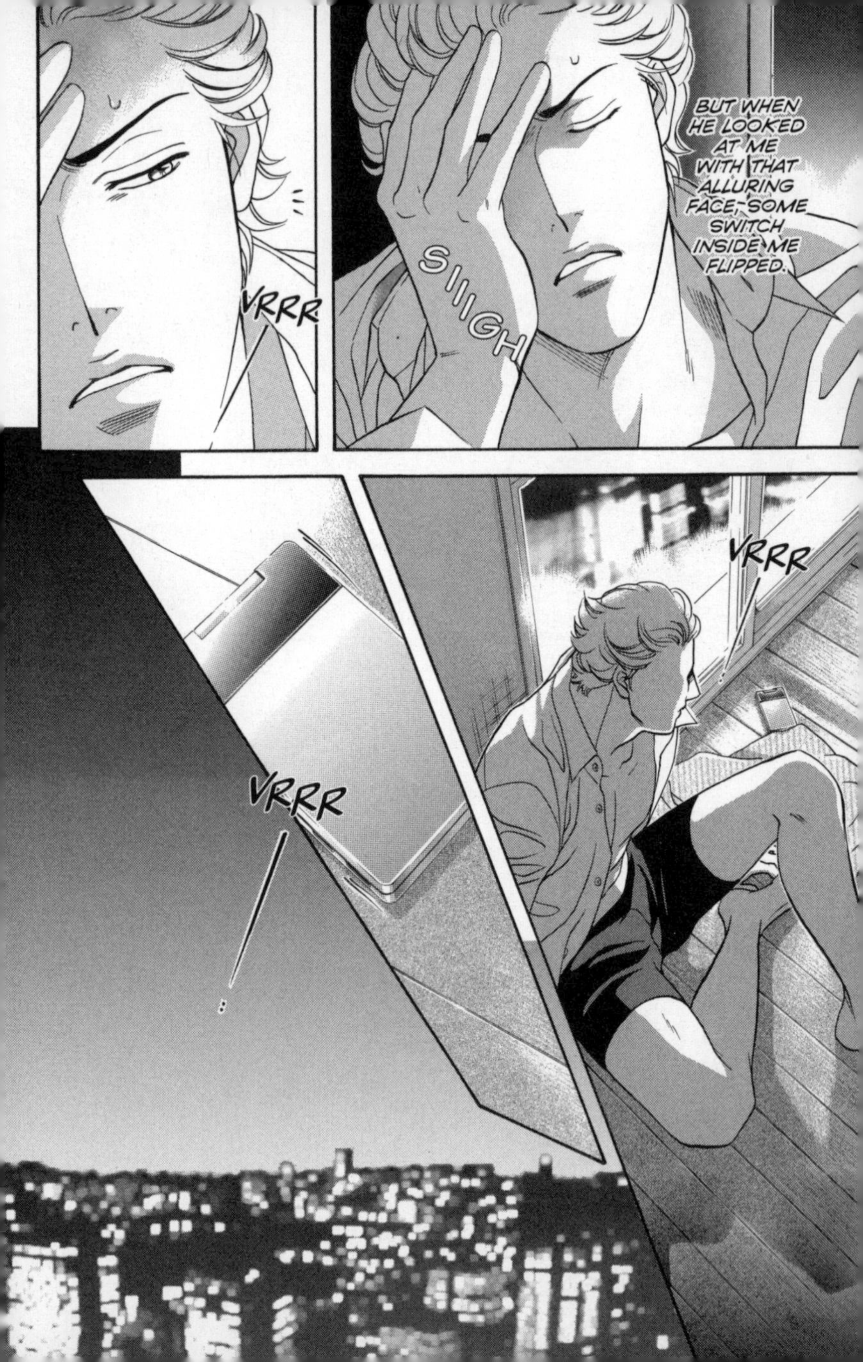
BUT WHEN HE LOOKED AT ME WITH THAT ALLURING FACE, SOME SWITCH INSIDE ME FLIPPED.
SIIIGH
VRRR
VRRR
VRRR

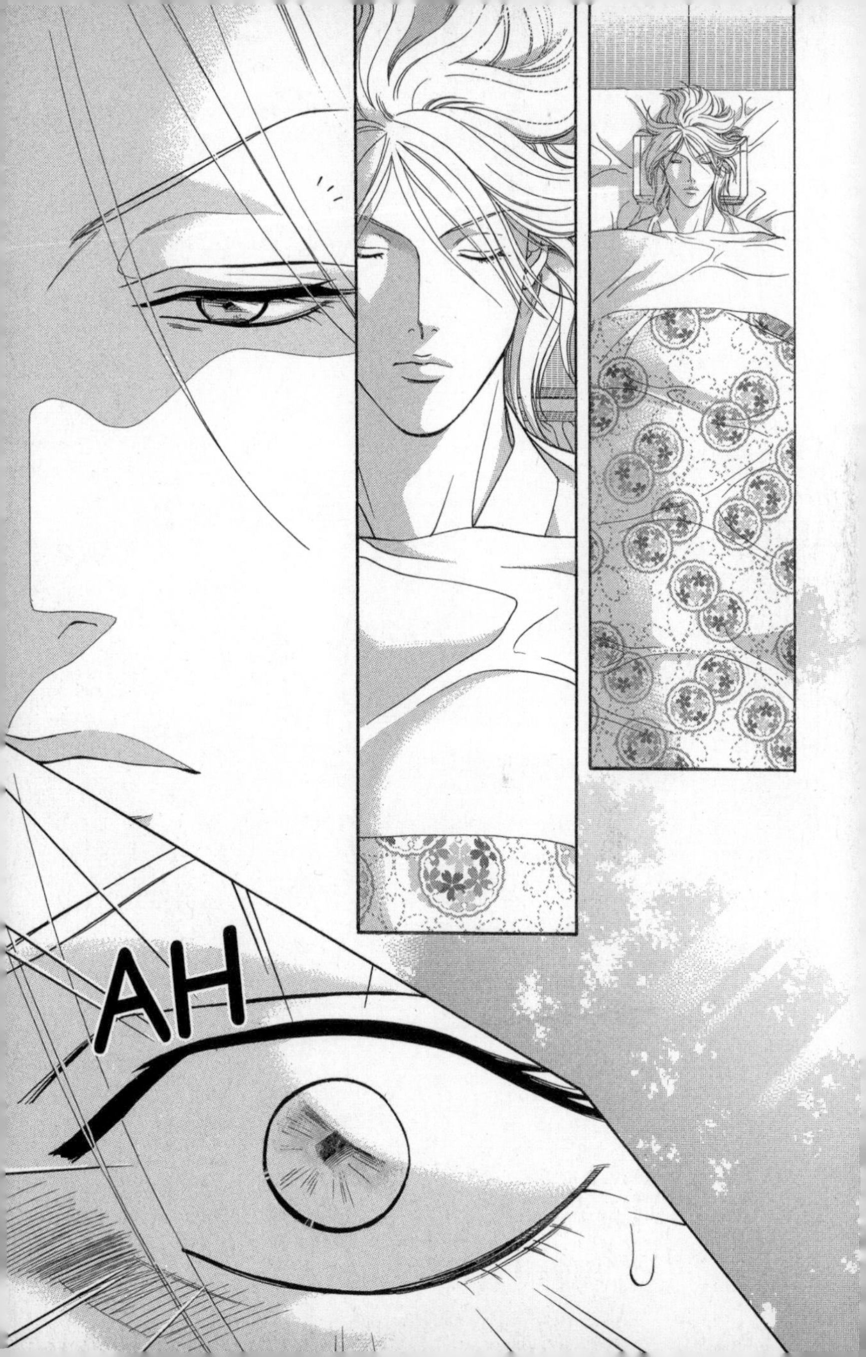
AH

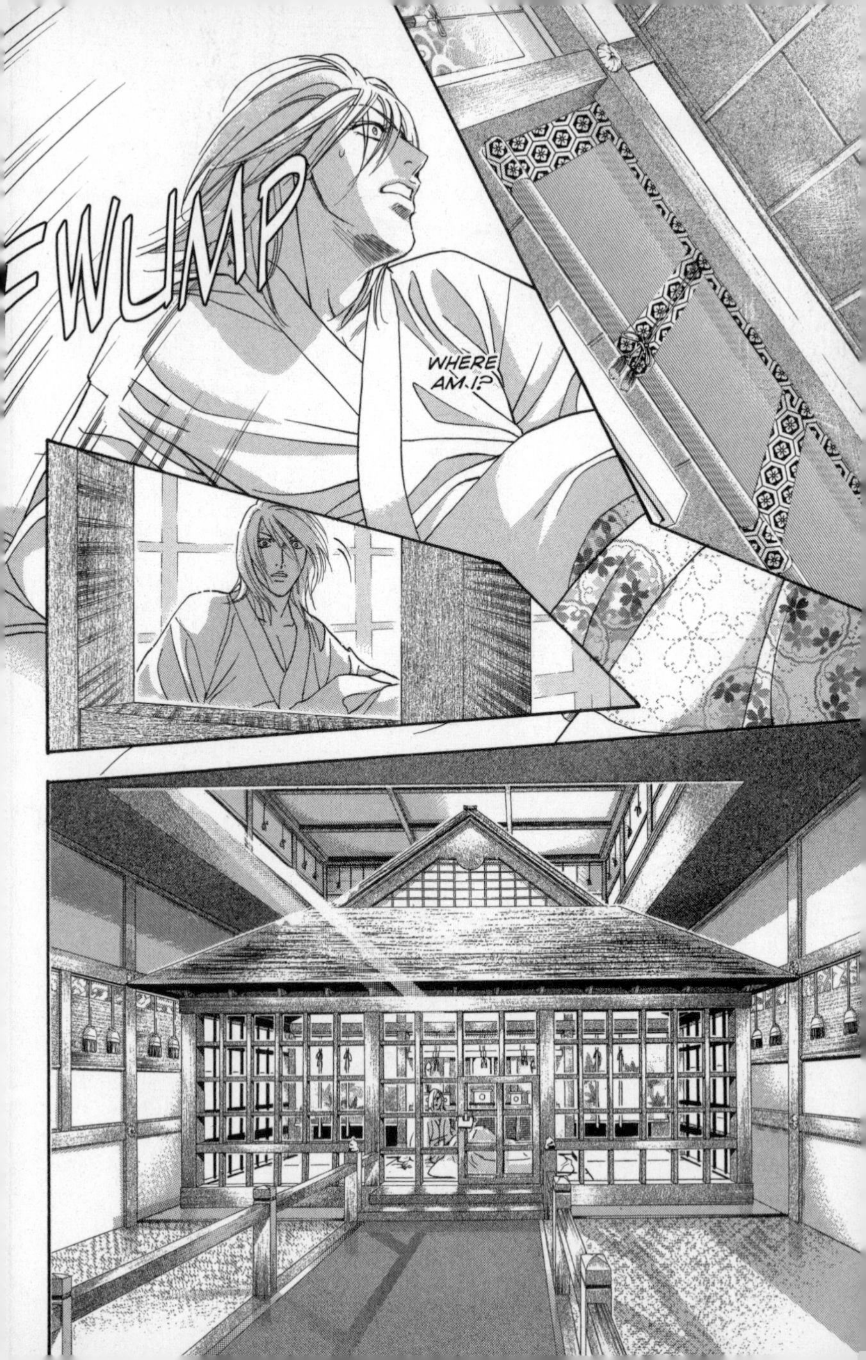
FWUMP
WHERE AM I?

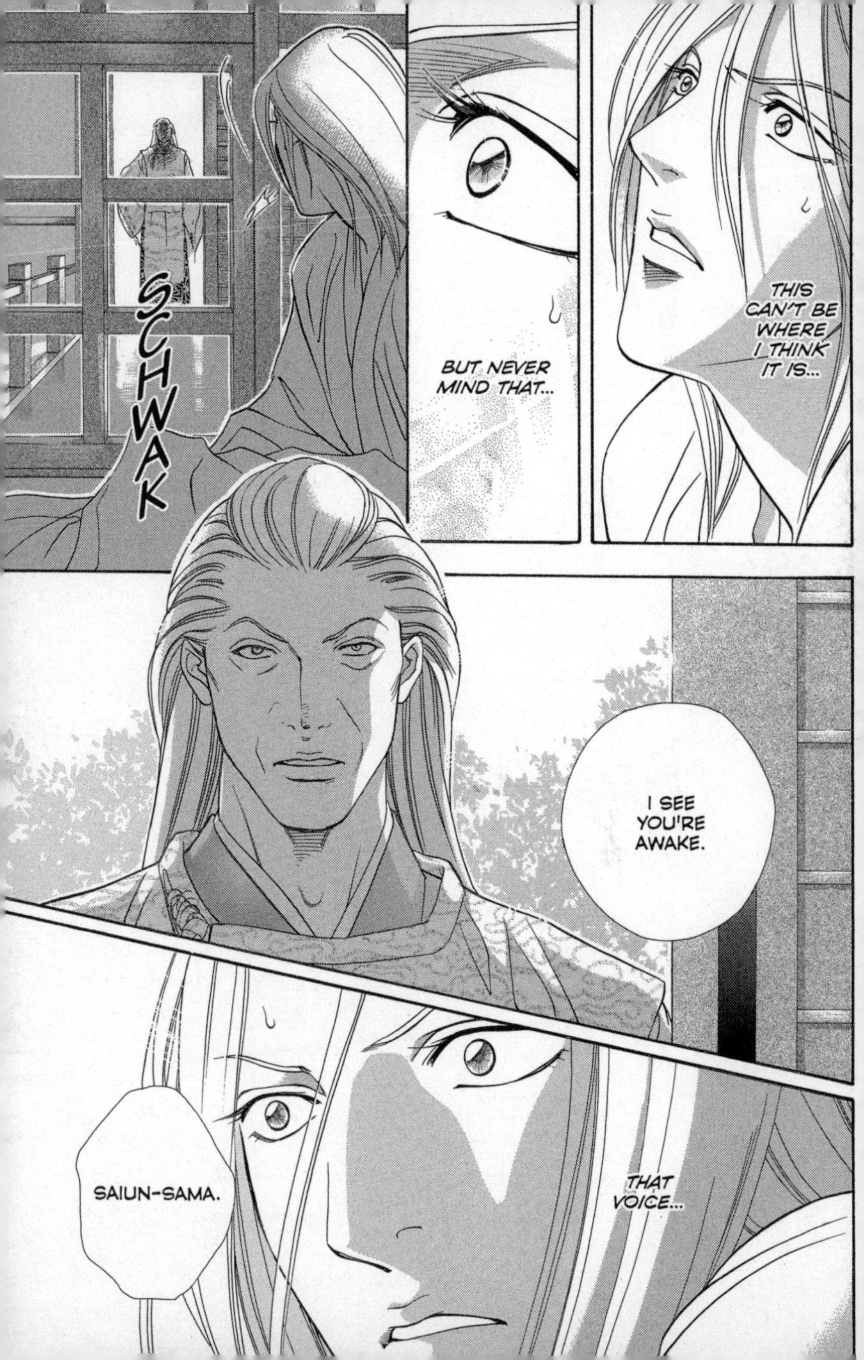
THIS CAN'T BE WHERE I THINK IT IS...
BUT NEVER MIND THAT...
SCHWAK
I SEE YOU'RE AWAKE.
THAT VOICE...
SAIUN-SAMA.

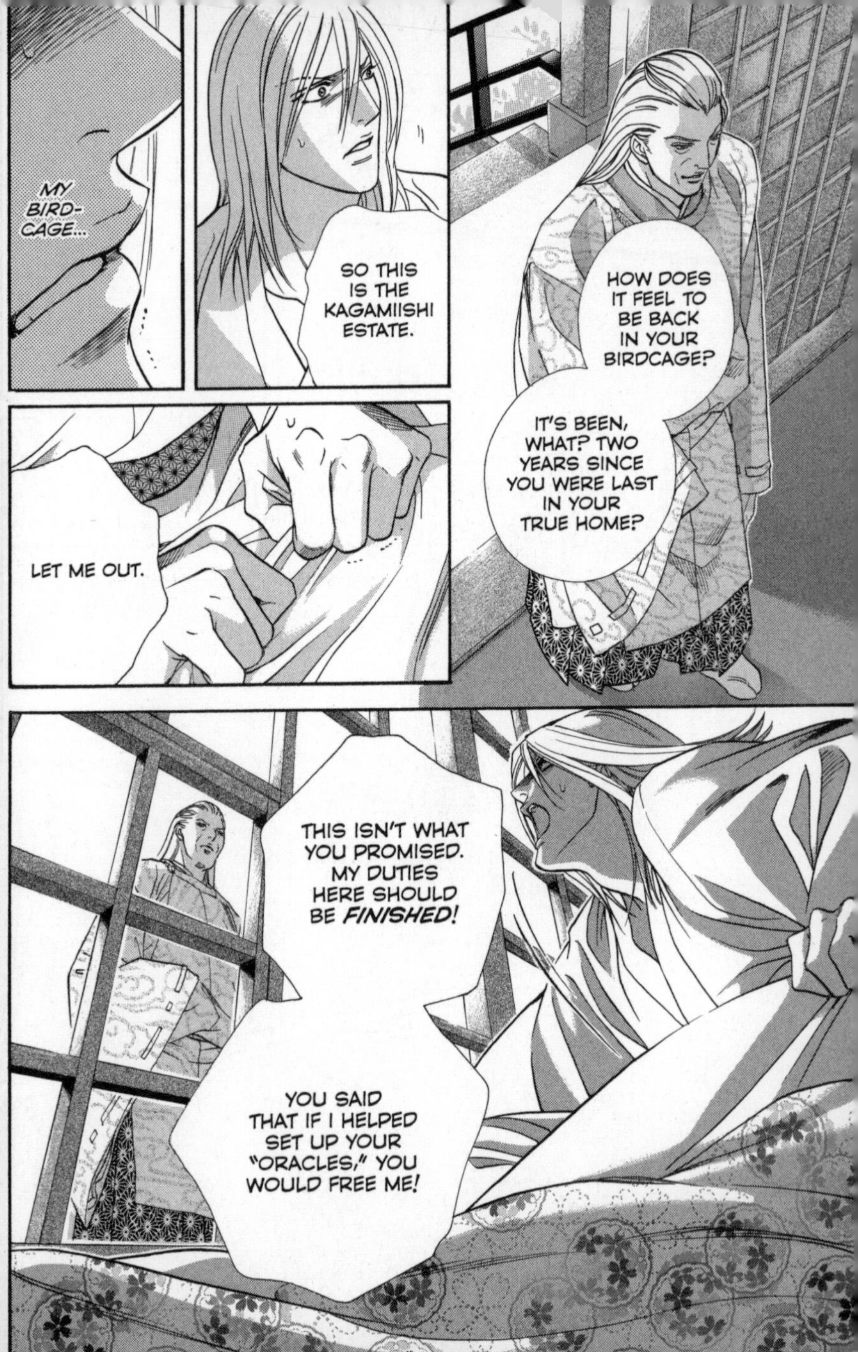
HOW DOES IT FEEL TO BE BACK IN YOUR BIRDCAGE?
IT'S BEEN, WHAT? TWO YEARS SINCE YOU WERE LAST IN YOUR TRUE HOME?
SO THIS IS THE KAGAMIISHI ESTATE.
MY BIRD-CAGE...
LET ME OUT.
THIS ISN'T WHAT YOU PROMISED. MY DUTIES HERE SHOULD BE *FINISHED*!
YOU SAID THAT IF I HELPED SET UP YOUR "ORACLES," YOU WOULD FREE ME!

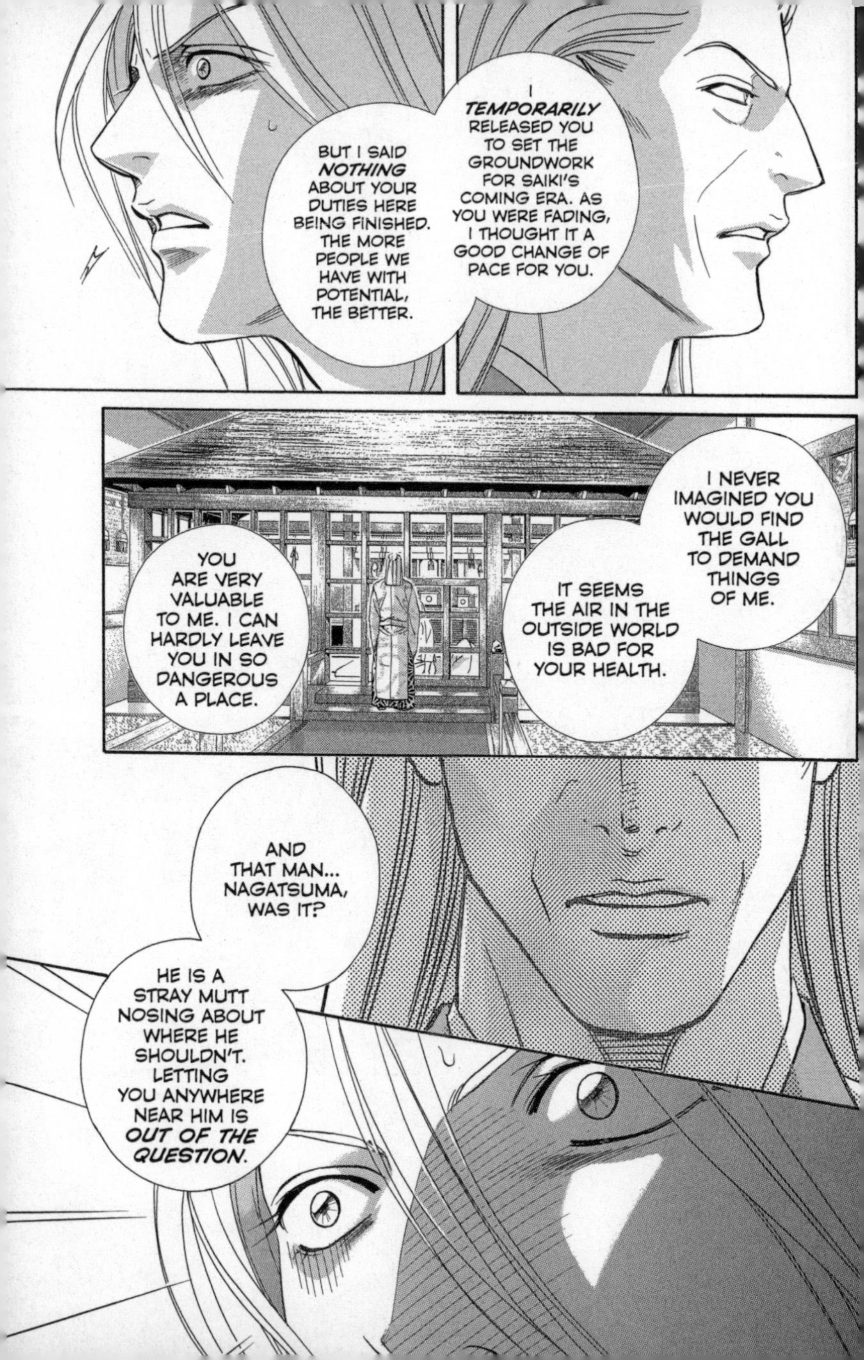
I *TEMPORARILY* RELEASED YOU TO SET THE GROUNDWORK FOR SAIKI'S COMING ERA. AS YOU WERE FADING, I THOUGHT IT A GOOD CHANGE OF PACE FOR YOU.
BUT I SAID *NOTHING* ABOUT YOUR DUTIES HERE BEING FINISHED. THE MORE PEOPLE WE HAVE WITH POTENTIAL, THE BETTER.
I NEVER IMAGINED YOU WOULD FIND THE GALL TO DEMAND THINGS OF ME.
IT SEEMS THE AIR IN THE OUTSIDE WORLD IS BAD FOR YOUR HEALTH.
YOU ARE VERY VALUABLE TO ME. I CAN HARDLY LEAVE YOU IN SO DANGEROUS A PLACE.
AND THAT MAN... NAGATSUMA, WAS IT?
HE IS A STRAY MUTT NOSING ABOUT WHERE HE SHOULDN'T. LETTING YOU ANYWHERE NEAR HIM IS *OUT OF THE QUESTION*.

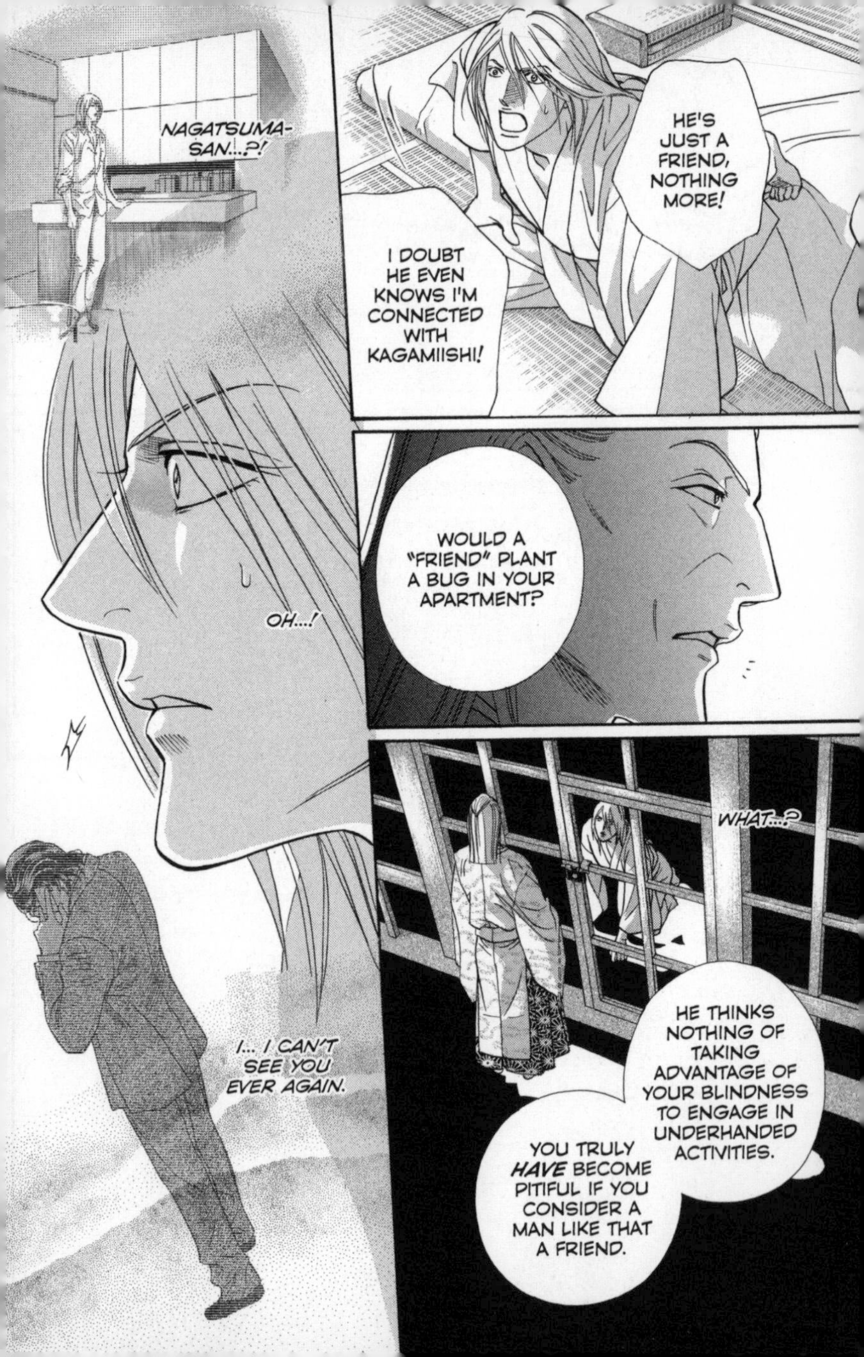
HE'S JUST A FRIEND, NOTHING MORE!
I DOUBT HE EVEN KNOWS I'M CONNECTED WITH KAGAMIISHI!
WOULD A "FRIEND" PLANT A BUG IN YOUR APARTMENT?
WHAT...?
HE THINKS NOTHING OF TAKING ADVANTAGE OF YOUR BLINDNESS TO ENGAGE IN UNDERHANDED ACTIVITIES.
YOU TRULY HAVE BECOME PITIFUL IF YOU CONSIDER A MAN LIKE THAT A FRIEND.
NAGATSUMA-SAN...?!
OH...!
I... I CAN'T SEE YOU EVER AGAIN.

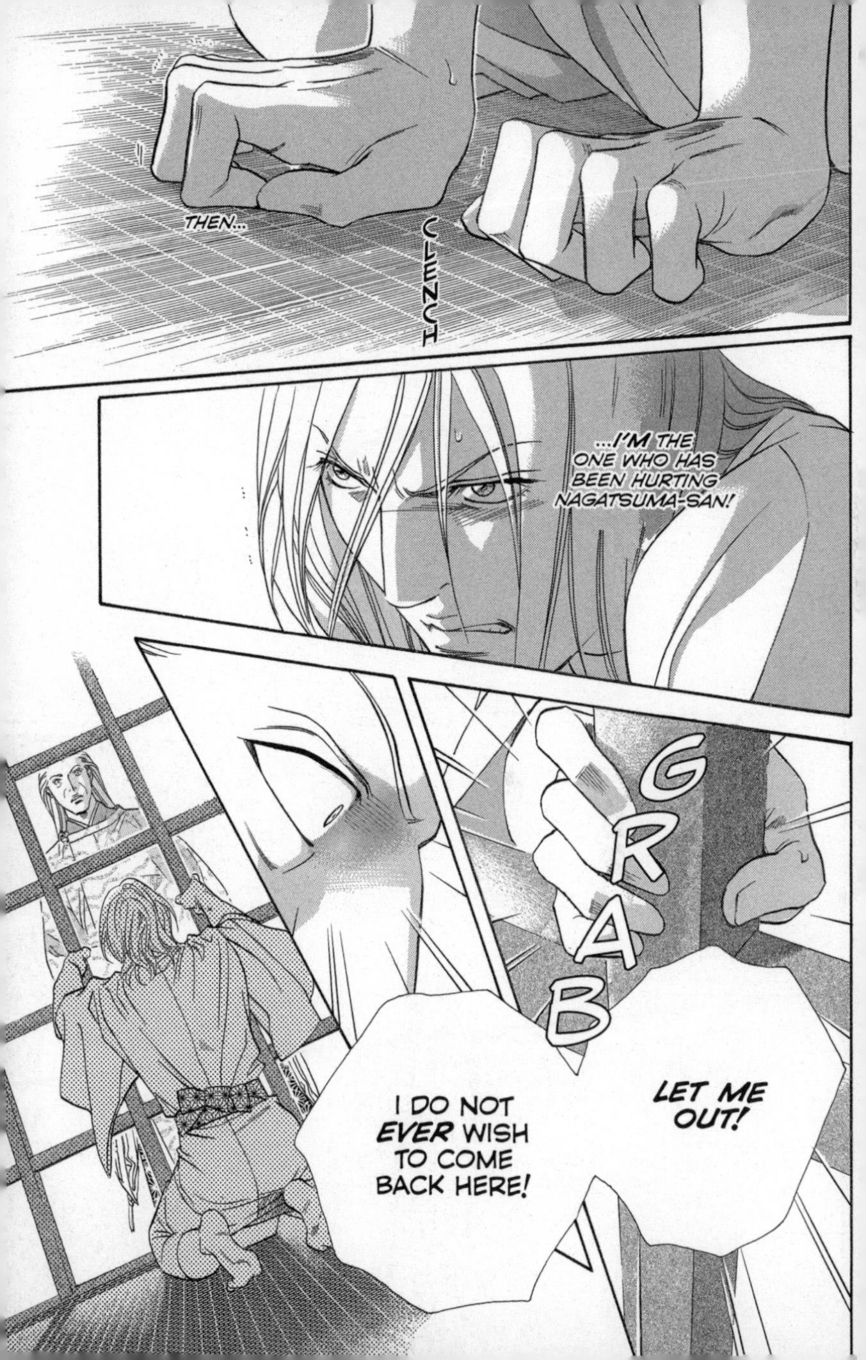
CLENCH
THEN...
...I'M THE ONE WHO HAS BEEN HURTING NAGATSUMA-SAN!
GRAB
LET ME OUT!
I DO NOT EVER WISH TO COME BACK HERE!

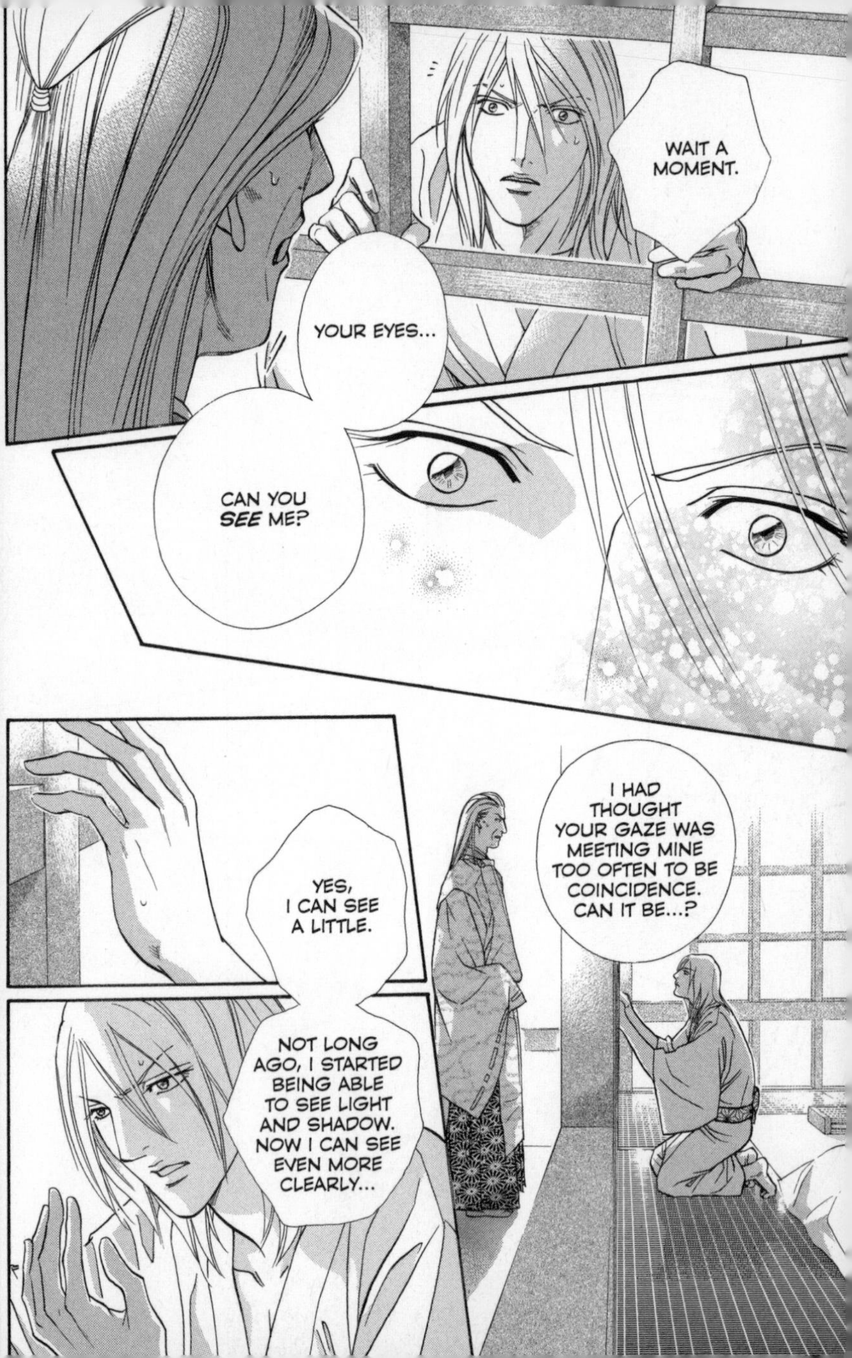
WAIT A MOMENT.
YOUR EYES...
CAN YOU *SEE* ME?
I HAD THOUGHT YOUR GAZE WAS MEETING MINE TOO OFTEN TO BE COINCIDENCE. CAN IT BE...?
YES, I CAN SEE A LITTLE.
NOT LONG AGO, I STARTED BEING ABLE TO SEE LIGHT AND SHADOW. NOW I CAN SEE EVEN MORE CLEARLY...

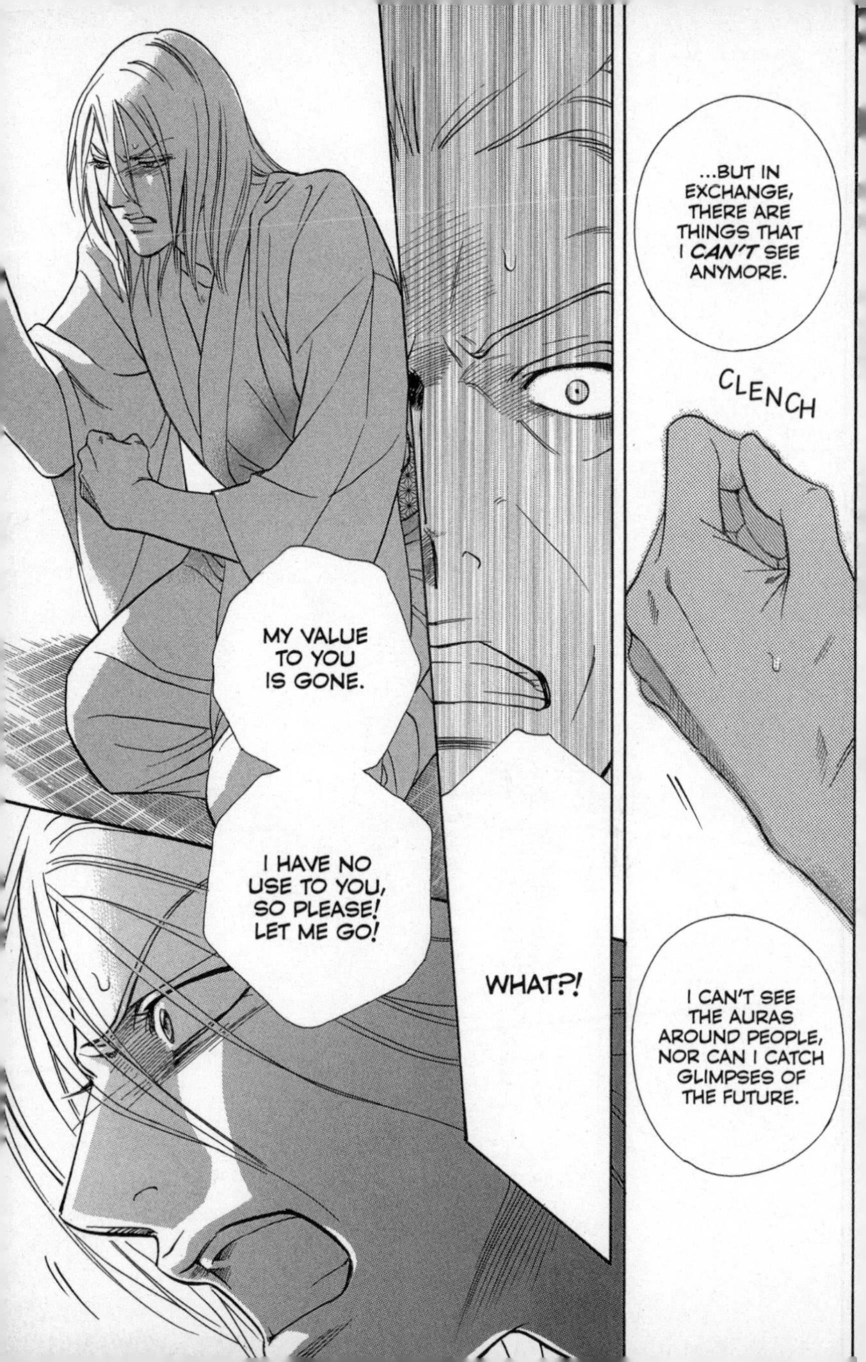
...BUT IN EXCHANGE, THERE ARE THINGS THAT I *CAN'T* SEE ANYMORE.
CLENCH
I CAN'T SEE THE AURAS AROUND PEOPLE, NOR CAN I CATCH GLIMPSES OF THE FUTURE.
MY VALUE TO YOU IS GONE.
I HAVE NO USE TO YOU, SO PLEASE! LET ME GO!
WHAT?!

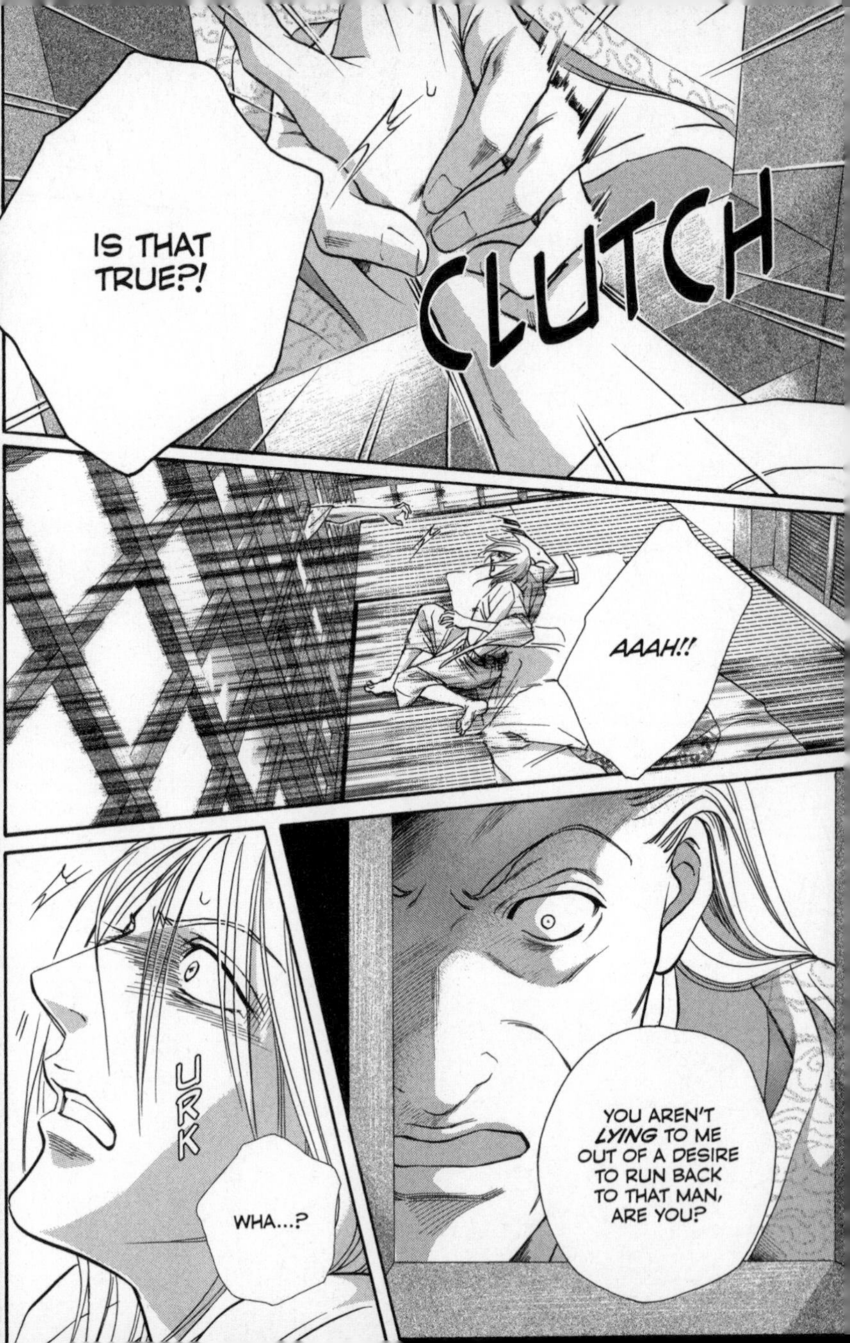
IS THAT TRUE?!
CLUTCH
AAAH!!
YOU AREN'T LYING TO ME OUT OF A DESIRE TO RUN BACK TO THAT MAN, ARE YOU?
URK
WHA...?

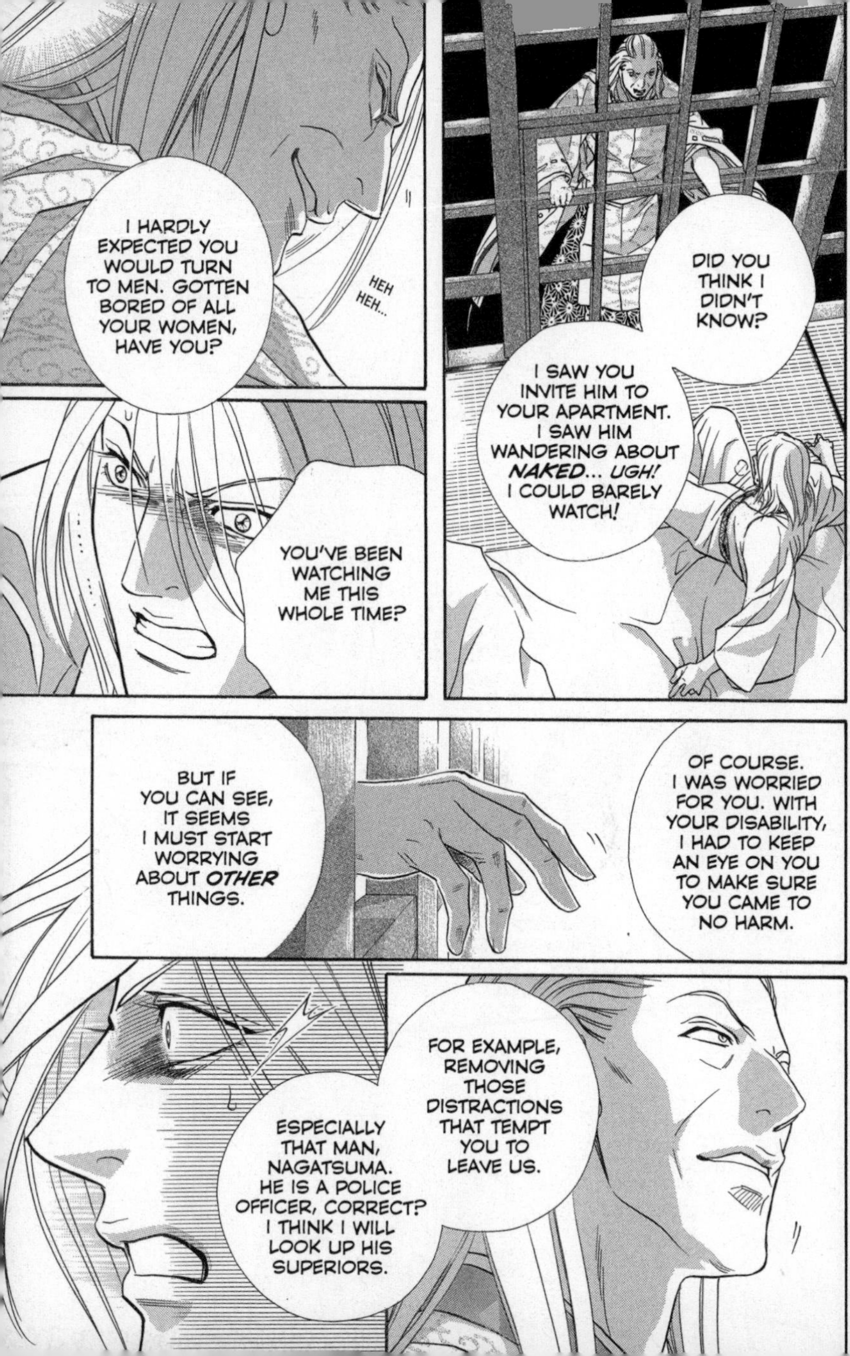
DID YOU THINK I DIDN'T KNOW?
I SAW YOU INVITE HIM TO YOUR APARTMENT. I SAW HIM WANDERING ABOUT *NAKED*... *UGH!* I COULD BARELY WATCH!
I HARDLY EXPECTED YOU WOULD TURN TO MEN. GOTTEN BORED OF ALL YOUR WOMEN, HAVE YOU?
HEH HEH...
YOU'VE BEEN WATCHING ME THIS WHOLE TIME?
OF COURSE. I WAS WORRIED FOR YOU. WITH YOUR DISABILITY, I HAD TO KEEP AN EYE ON YOU TO MAKE SURE YOU CAME TO NO HARM.
BUT IF YOU CAN SEE, IT SEEMS I MUST START WORRYING ABOUT *OTHER* THINGS.
FOR EXAMPLE, REMOVING THOSE DISTRACTIONS THAT TEMPT YOU TO LEAVE US.
ESPECIALLY THAT MAN, NAGATSUMA. HE IS A POLICE OFFICER, CORRECT? I THINK I WILL LOOK UP HIS SUPERIORS.

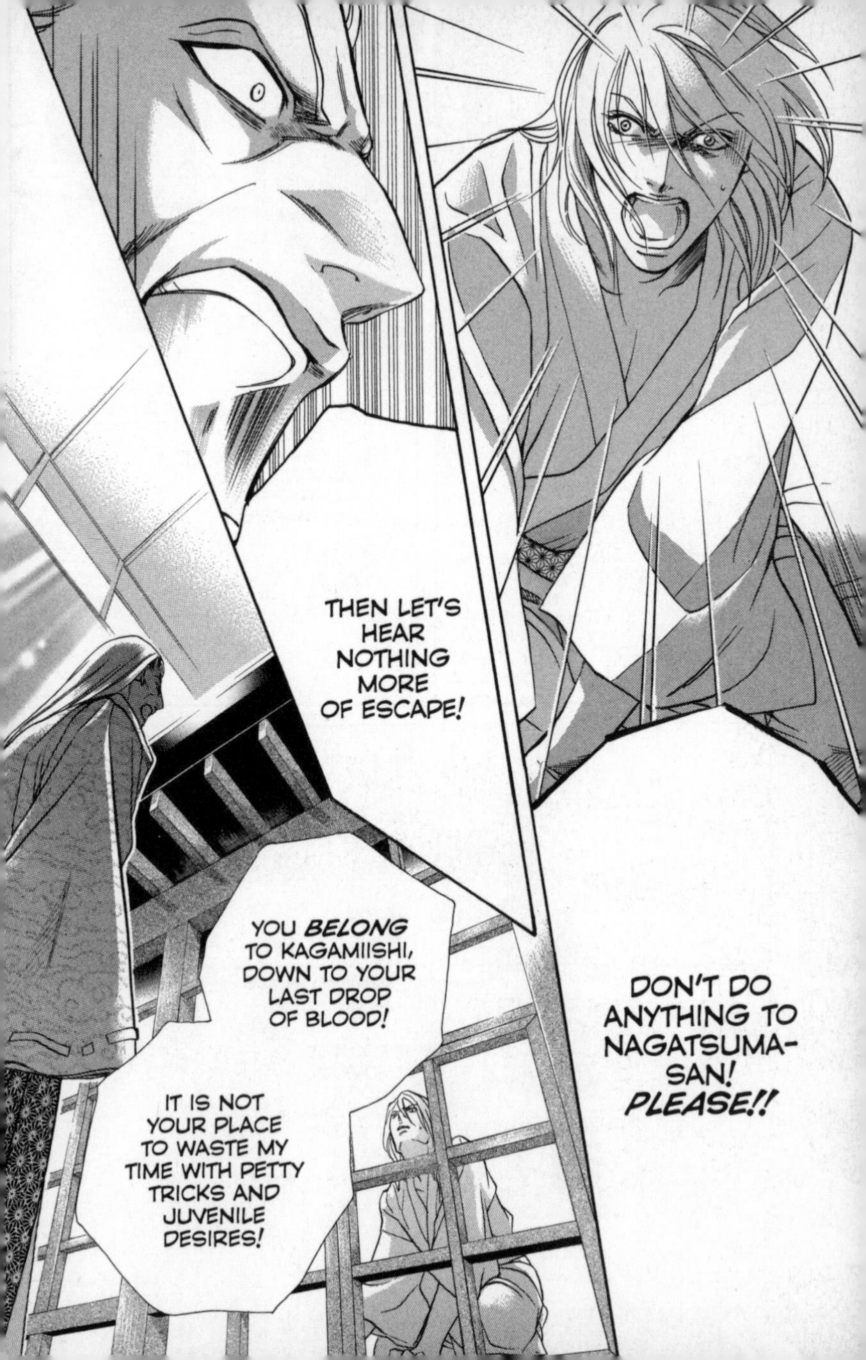

DON'T DO ANYTHING TO NAGATSUMA-SAN! *PLEASE!!*
THEN LET'S HEAR NOTHING MORE OF ESCAPE!
YOU *BELONG* TO KAGAMIISHI, DOWN TO YOUR LAST DROP OF BLOOD!
IT IS NOT YOUR PLACE TO WASTE MY TIME WITH PETTY TRICKS AND JUVENILE DESIRES!

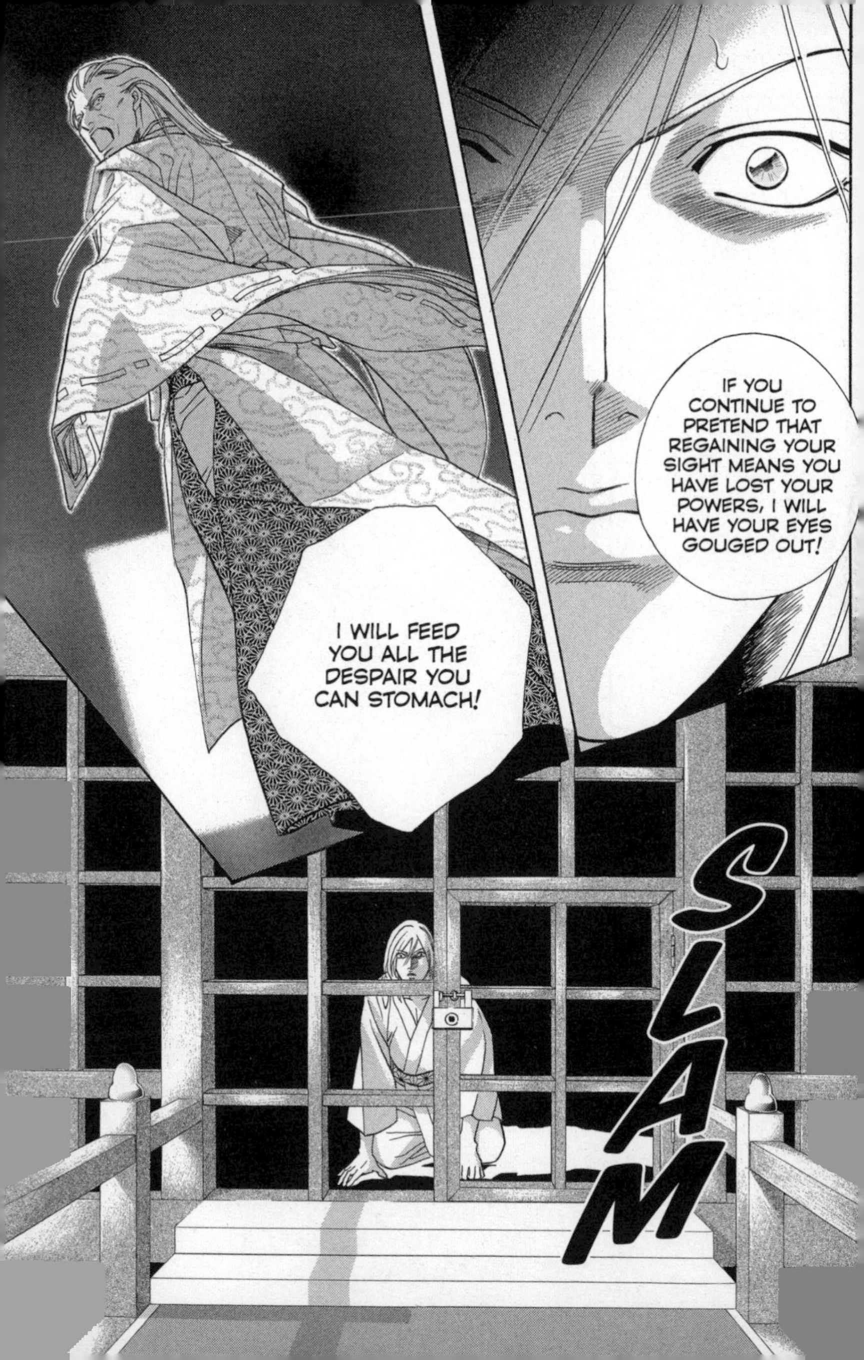
IF YOU CONTINUE TO PRETEND THAT REGAINING YOUR SIGHT MEANS YOU HAVE LOST YOUR POWERS, I WILL HAVE YOUR EYES GOUGED OUT!
I WILL FEED YOU ALL THE DESPAIR YOU CAN STOMACH!
SLAM

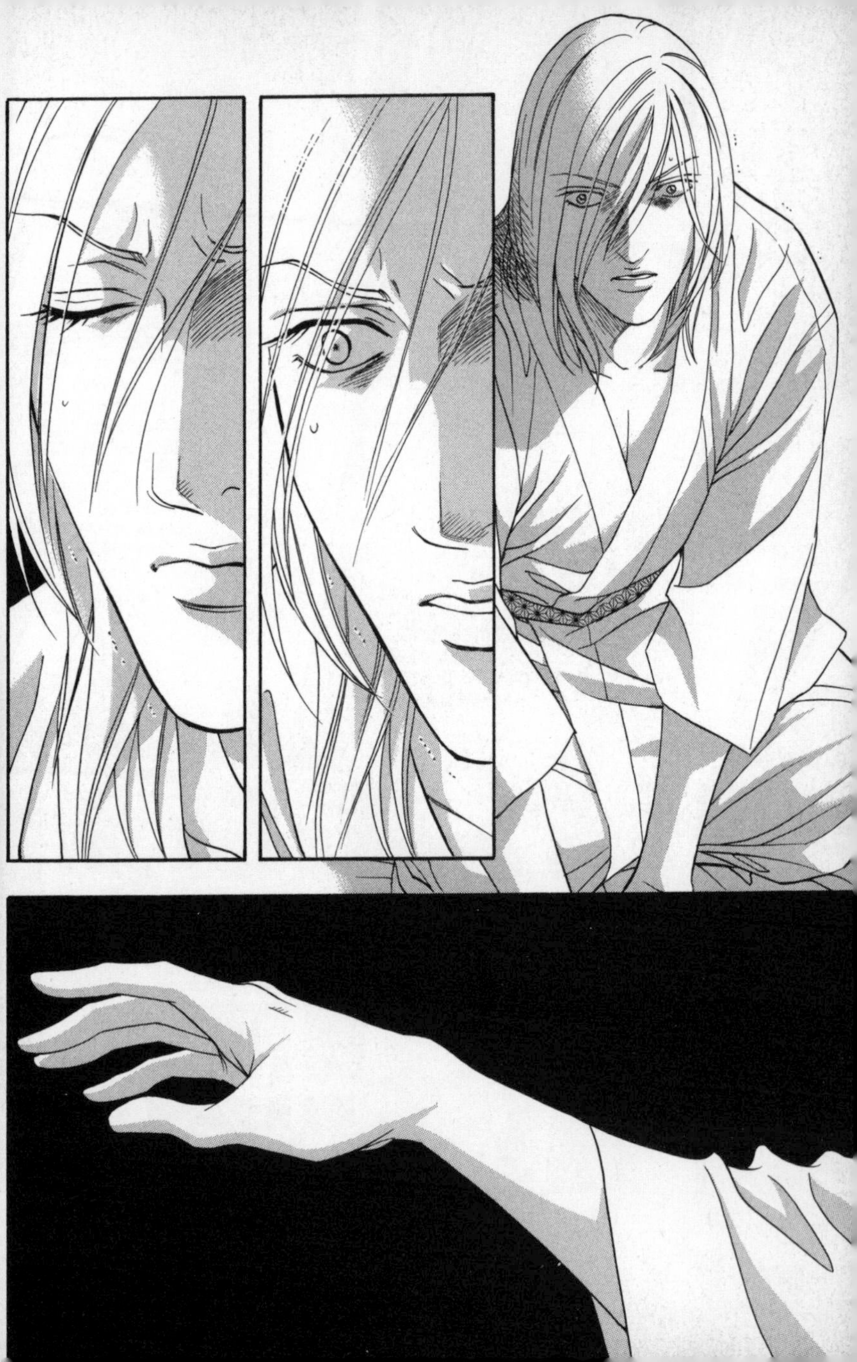

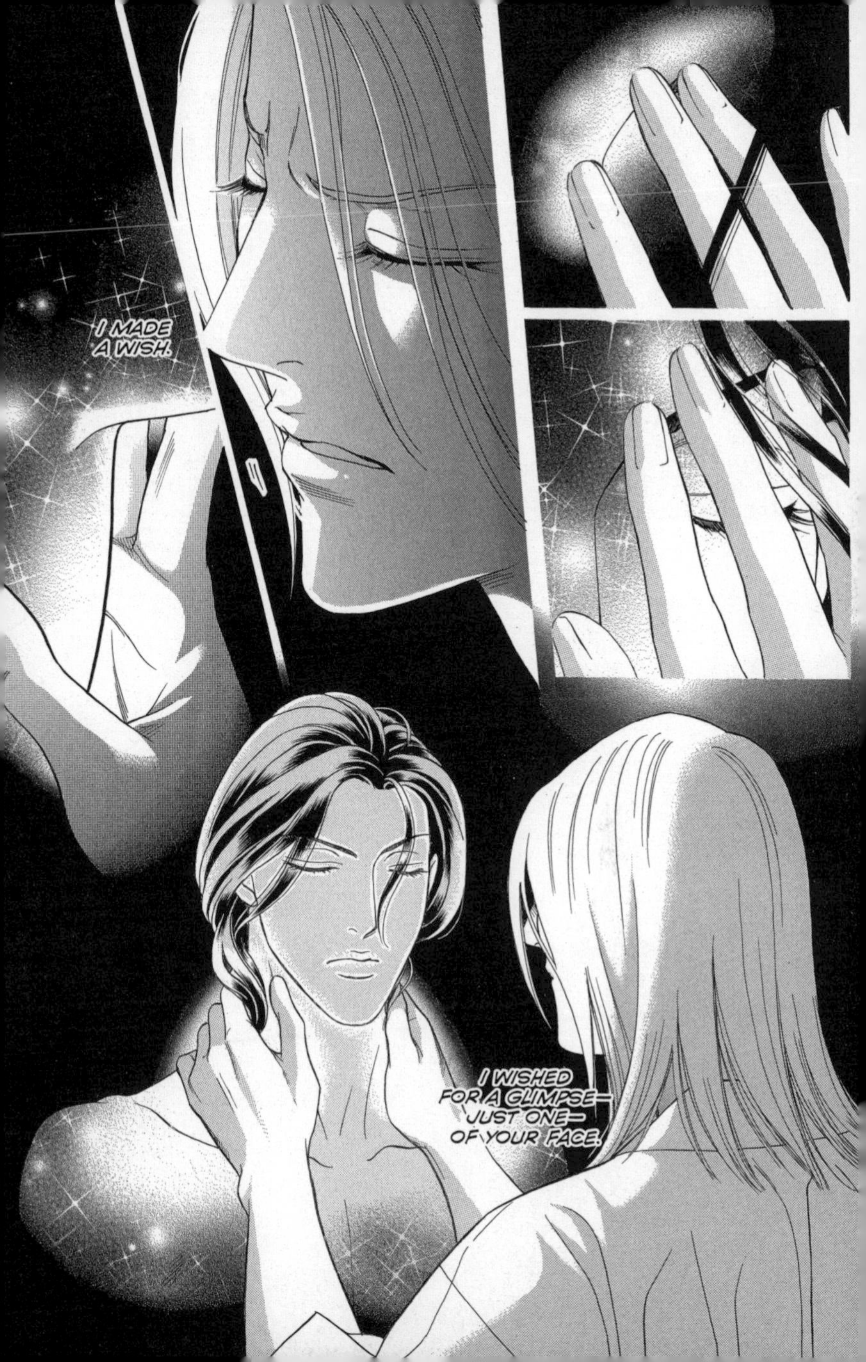
I MADE A WISH.
I WISHED FOR A GLIMPSE— JUST ONE— OF YOUR FACE.

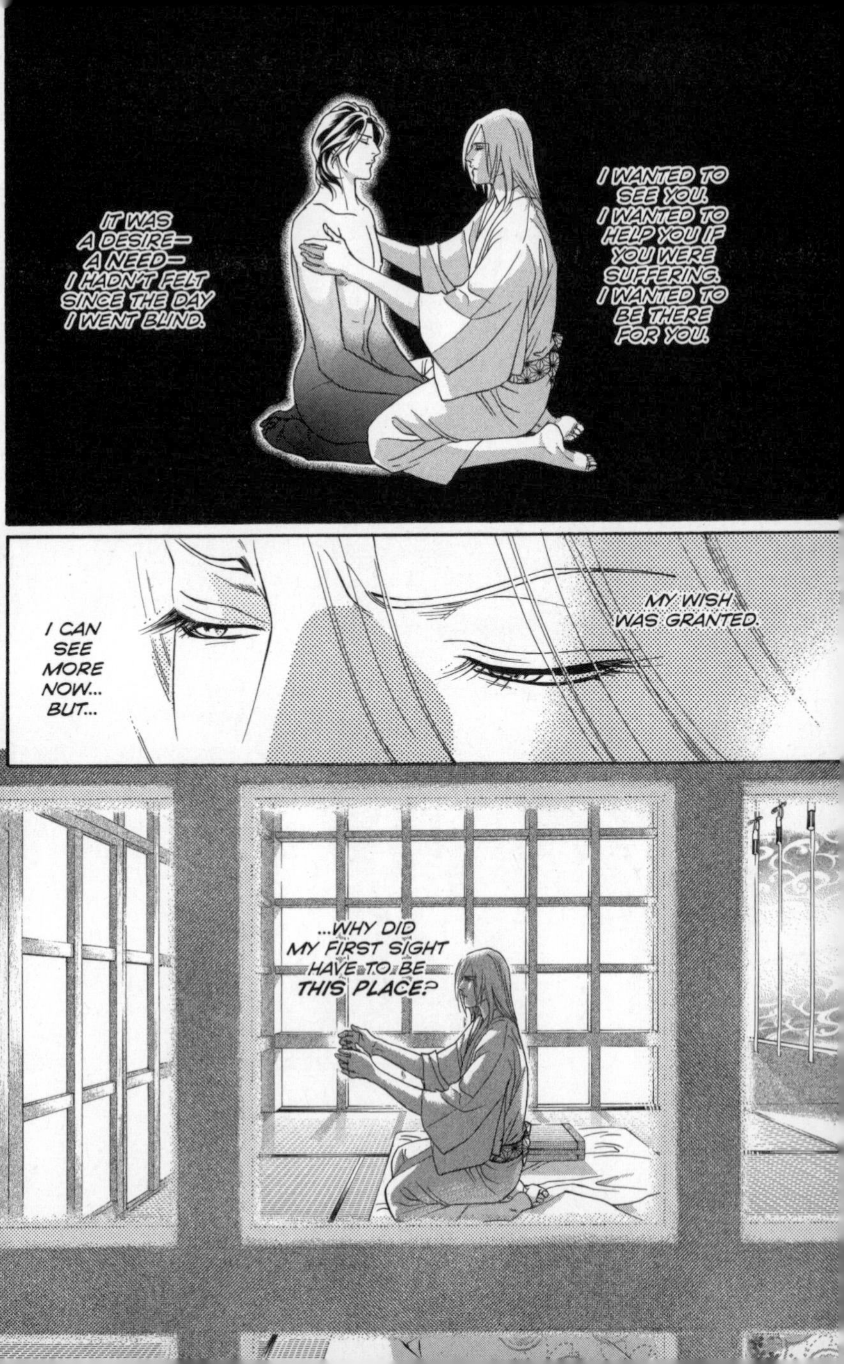
I WANTED TO SEE YOU. I WANTED TO HELP YOU IF YOU WERE SUFFERING. I WANTED TO BE THERE FOR YOU.
IT WAS A DESIRE— A NEED— I HADN'T FELT SINCE THE DAY I WENT BLIND.
MY WISH WAS GRANTED.
I CAN SEE MORE NOW... BUT...
...WHY DID MY FIRST SIGHT HAVE TO BE THIS PLACE?

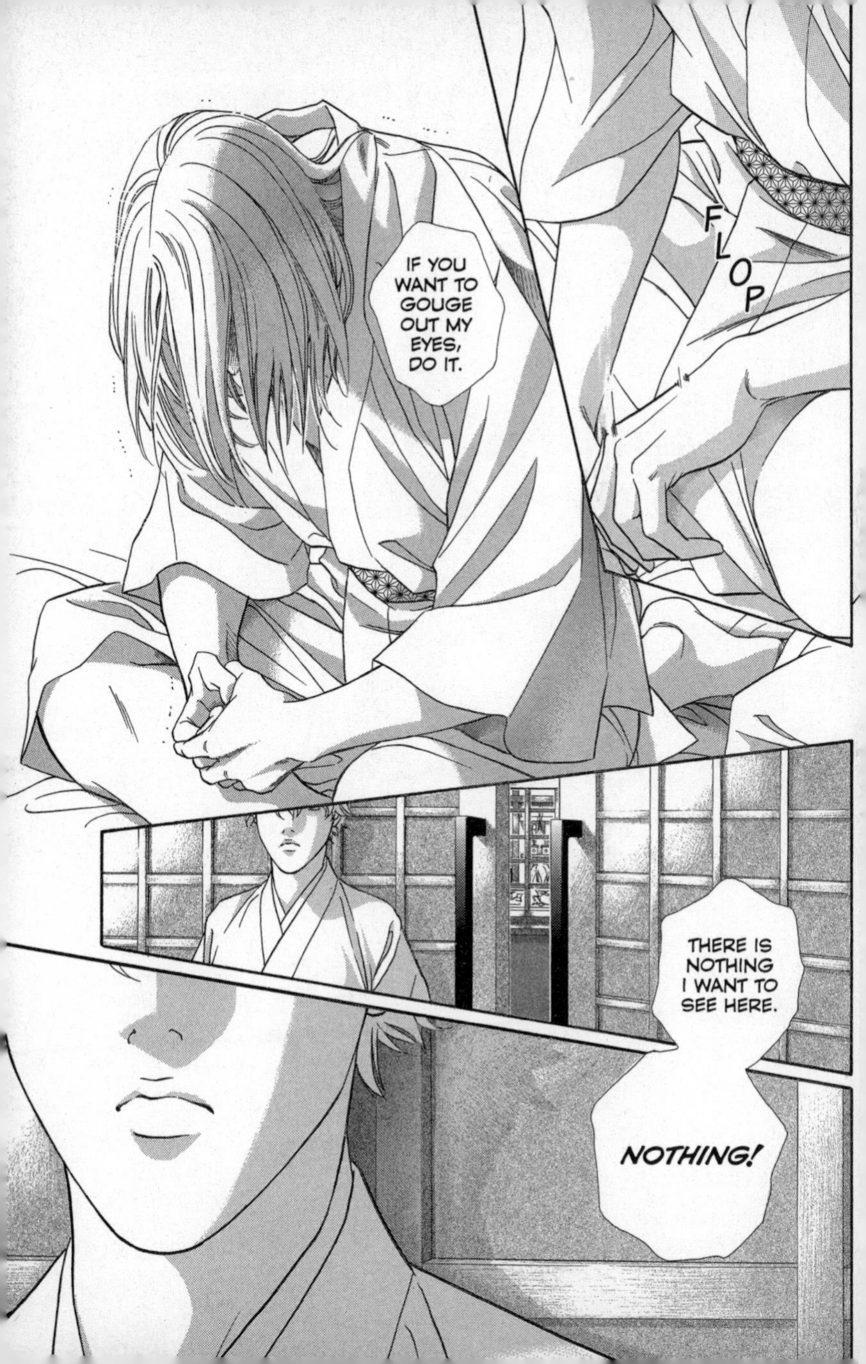
FLOP
IF YOU WANT TO GOUGE OUT MY EYES, DO IT.
THERE IS NOTHING I WANT TO SEE HERE.
NOTHING!

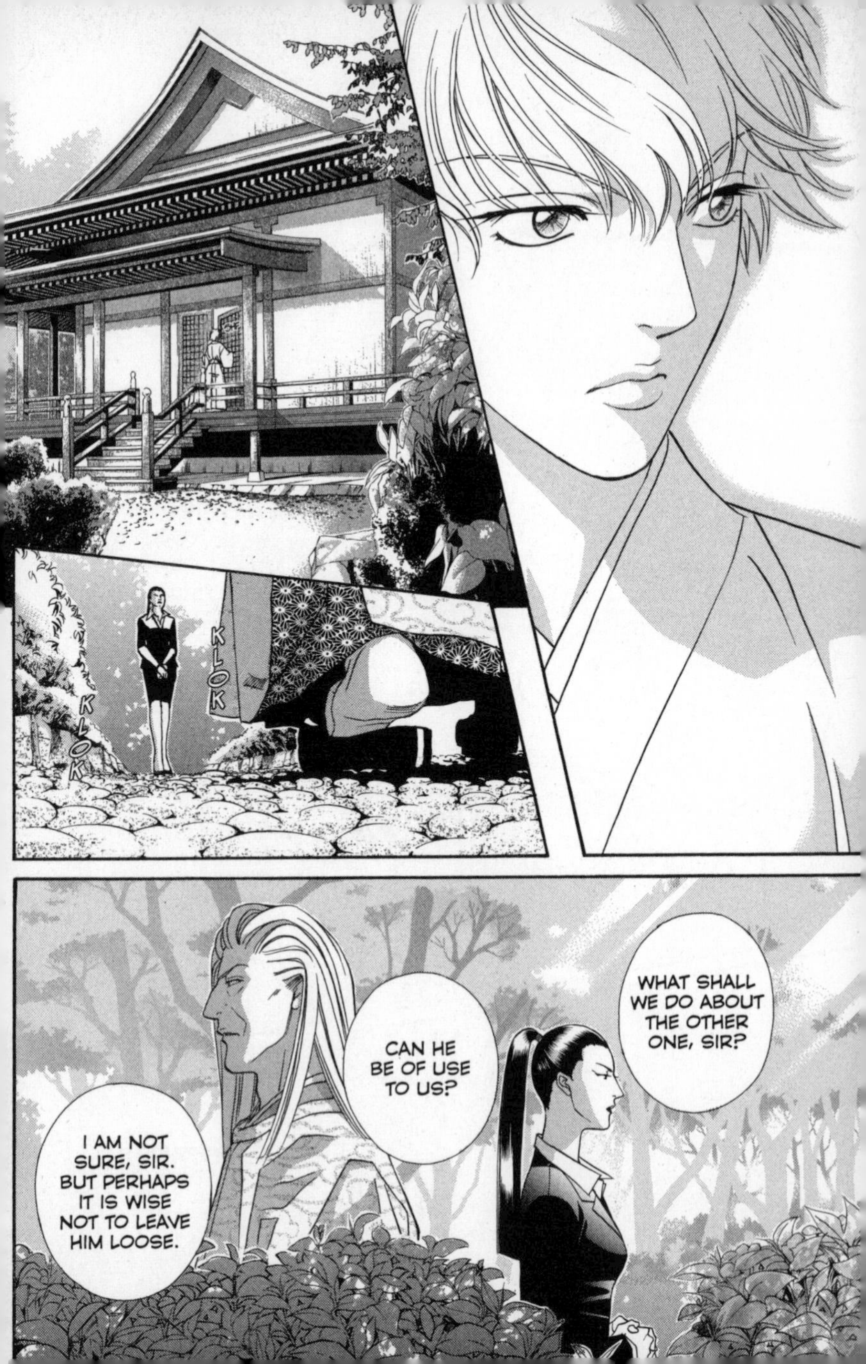
KLOK
KLOK
WHAT SHALL WE DO ABOUT THE OTHER ONE, SIR?
CAN HE BE OF USE TO US?
I AM NOT SURE, SIR. BUT PERHAPS IT IS WISE NOT TO LEAVE HIM LOOSE.

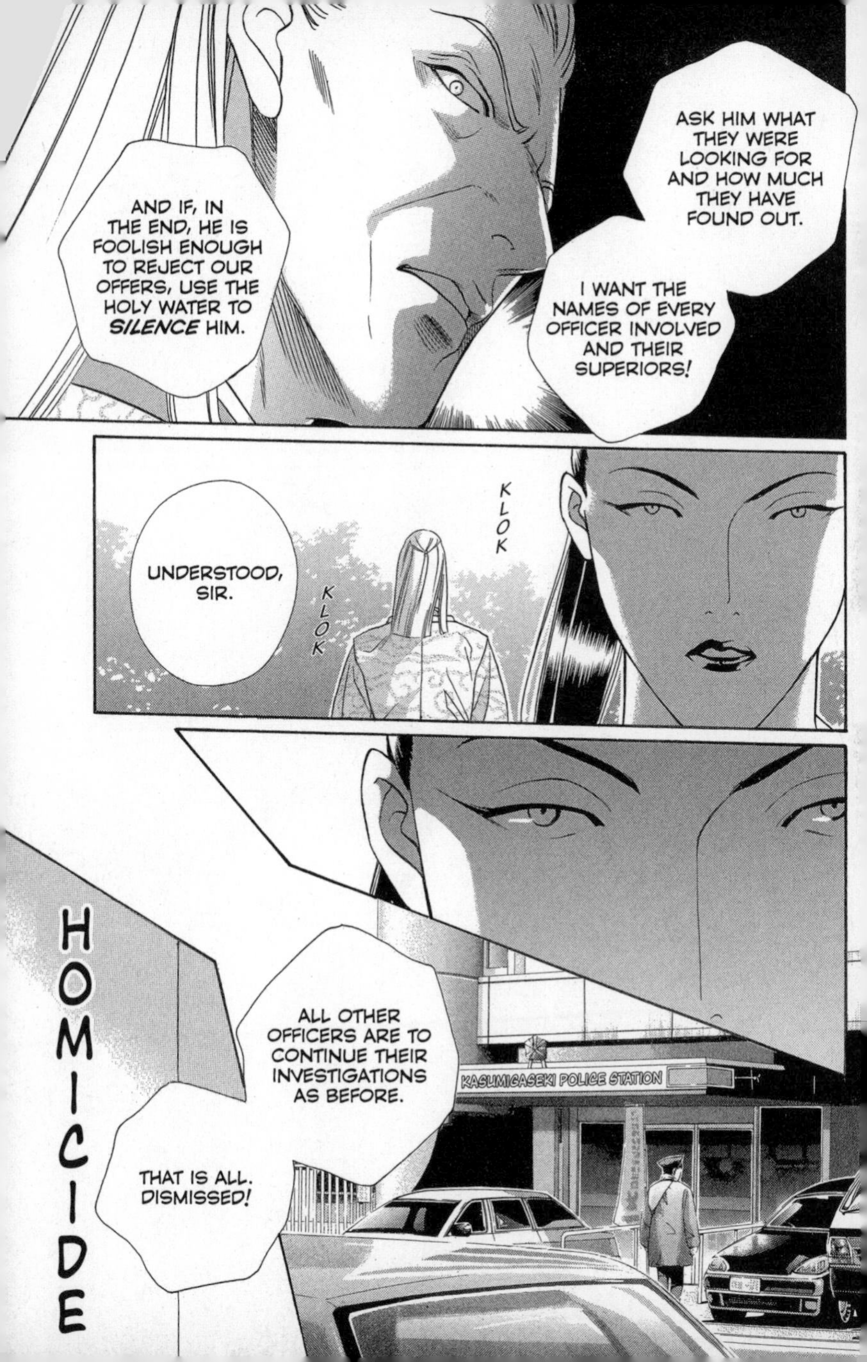
ASK HIM WHAT THEY WERE LOOKING FOR AND HOW MUCH THEY HAVE FOUND OUT.
I WANT THE NAMES OF EVERY OFFICER INVOLVED AND THEIR SUPERIORS!
AND IF, IN THE END, HE IS FOOLISH ENOUGH TO REJECT OUR OFFERS, USE THE HOLY WATER TO *SILENCE* HIM.
KLOK
KLOK
UNDERSTOOD, SIR.
KASUMIGASEKI POLICE STATION
ALL OTHER OFFICERS ARE TO CONTINUE THEIR INVESTIGATIONS AS BEFORE.
THAT IS ALL. DISMISSED!
HOMICIDE

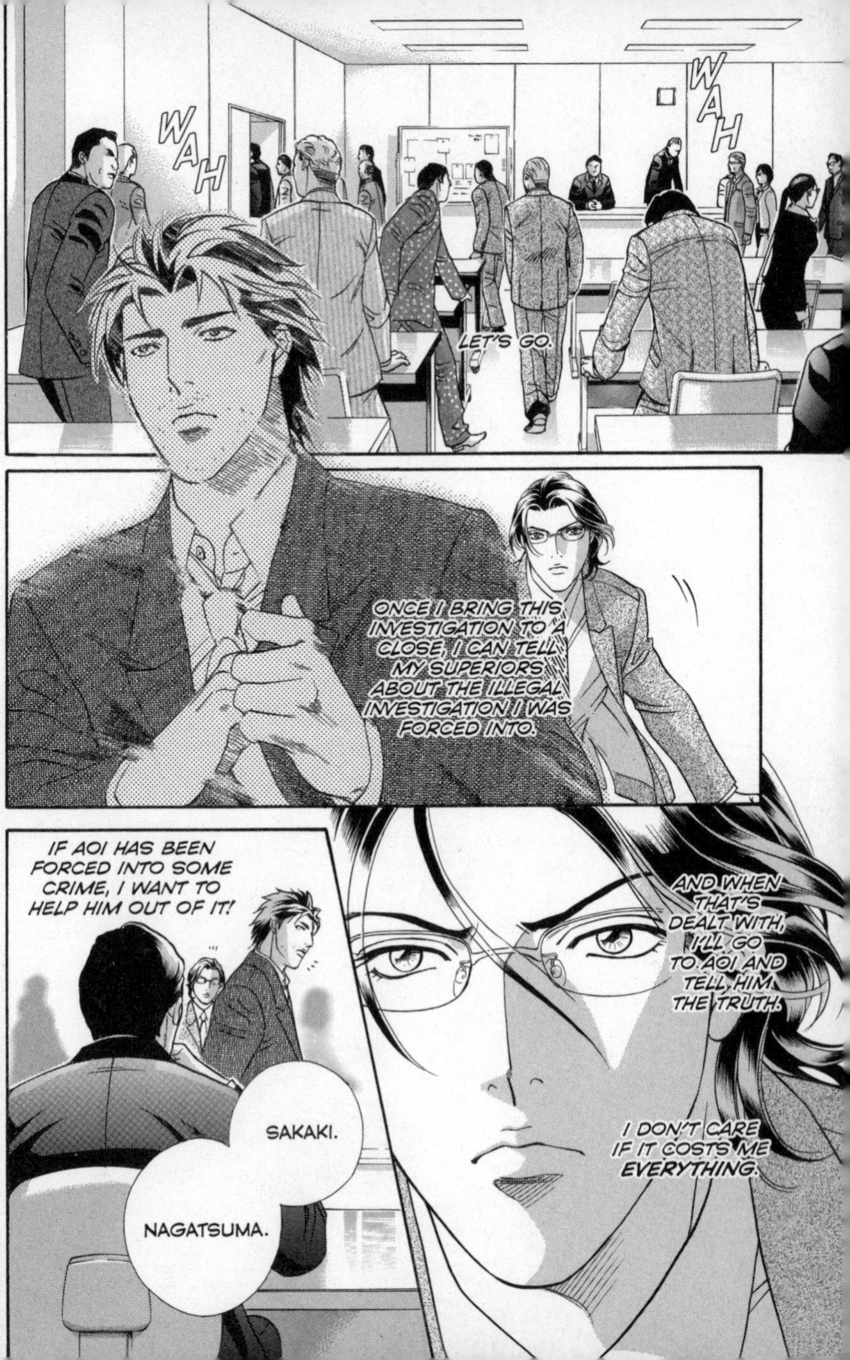
WAH
WAH
LET'S GO.
ONCE I BRING THIS INVESTIGATION TO A CLOSE, I CAN TELL MY SUPERIORS ABOUT THE ILLEGAL INVESTIGATION I WAS FORCED INTO.
AND WHEN THAT'S DEALT WITH, I'LL GO TO AOI AND TELL HIM THE TRUTH.
I DON'T CARE IF IT COSTS ME EVERYTHING.
IF AOI HAS BEEN FORCED INTO SOME CRIME, I WANT TO HELP HIM OUT OF IT!
SAKAKI.
NAGATSUMA.

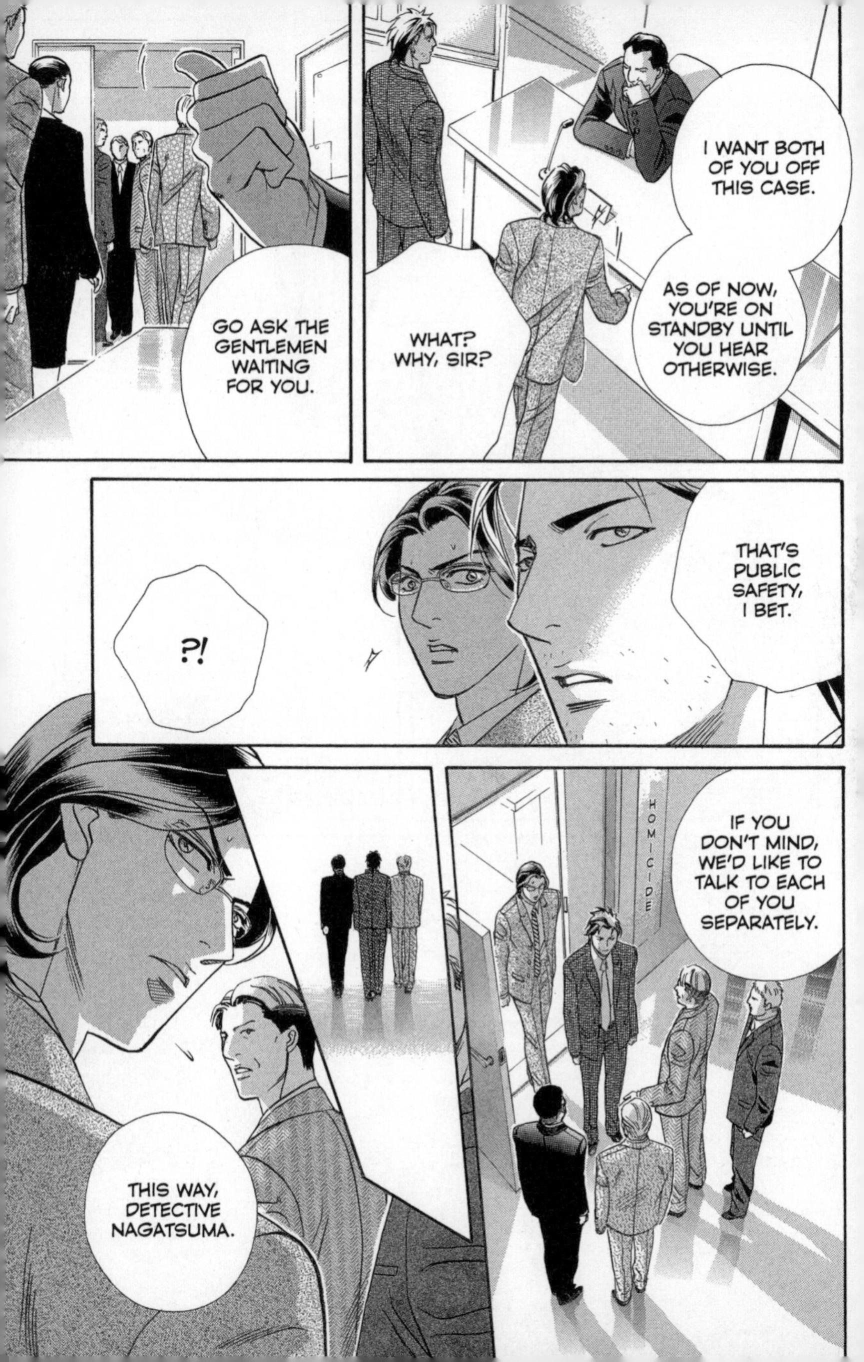
I WANT BOTH OF YOU OFF THIS CASE.
AS OF NOW, YOU'RE ON STANDBY UNTIL YOU HEAR OTHERWISE.
WHAT? WHY, SIR?
GO ASK THE GENTLEMEN WAITING FOR YOU.
THAT'S PUBLIC SAFETY, I BET.
?!
HOMICIDE
IF YOU DON'T MIND, WE'D LIKE TO TALK TO EACH OF YOU SEPARATELY.
THIS WAY, DETECTIVE NAGATSUMA.

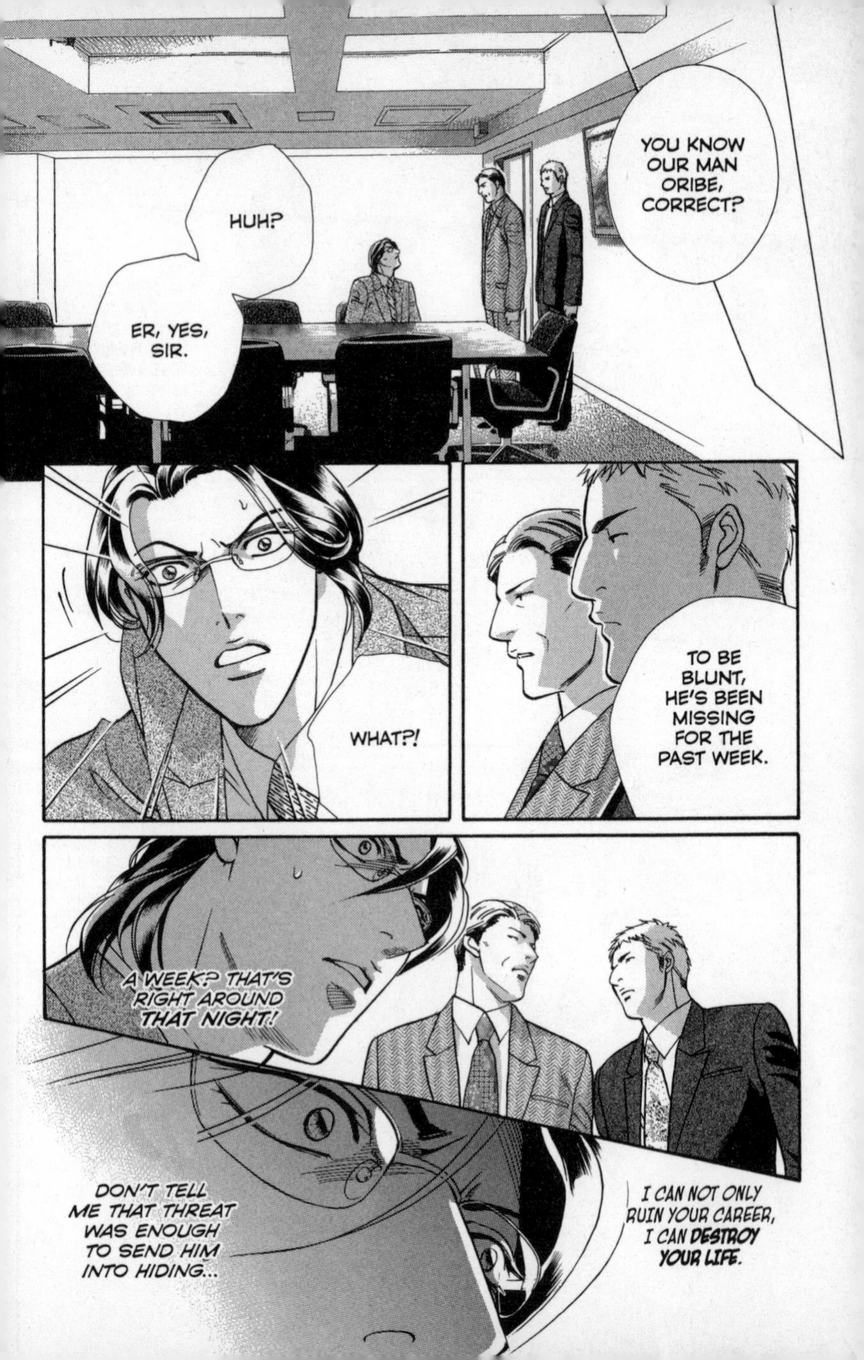
YOU KNOW OUR MAN ORIBE, CORRECT?
HUH?
ER, YES, SIR.
TO BE BLUNT, HE'S BEEN MISSING FOR THE PAST WEEK.
WHAT?!
A WEEK? THAT'S RIGHT AROUND THAT NIGHT!
I CAN NOT ONLY RUIN YOUR CAREER, I CAN DESTROY YOUR LIFE.
DON'T TELL ME THAT THREAT WAS ENOUGH TO SEND HIM INTO HIDING...

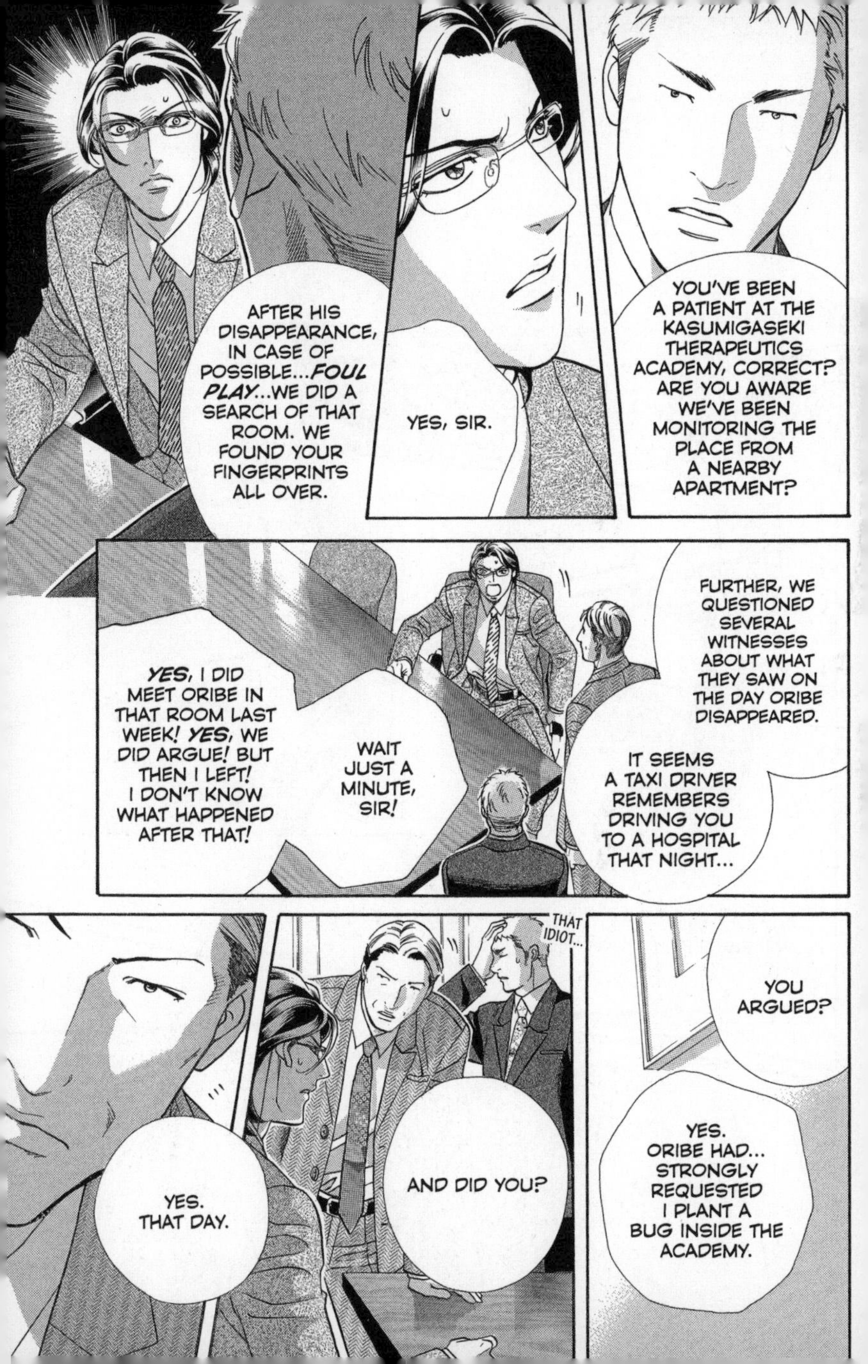
YOU'VE BEEN A PATIENT AT THE KASUMIGASEKI THERAPEUTICS ACADEMY, CORRECT? ARE YOU AWARE WE'VE BEEN MONITORING THE PLACE FROM A NEARBY APARTMENT?
YES, SIR.
AFTER HIS DISAPPEARANCE, IN CASE OF POSSIBLE...*FOUL PLAY*...WE DID A SEARCH OF THAT ROOM. WE FOUND YOUR FINGERPRINTS ALL OVER.
FURTHER, WE QUESTIONED SEVERAL WITNESSES ABOUT WHAT THEY SAW ON THE DAY ORIBE DISAPPEARED.
IT SEEMS A TAXI DRIVER REMEMBERS DRIVING YOU TO A HOSPITAL THAT NIGHT...
WAIT JUST A MINUTE, SIR!
YES, I DID MEET ORIBE IN THAT ROOM LAST WEEK! *YES*, WE DID ARGUE! BUT THEN I LEFT! I DON'T KNOW WHAT HAPPENED AFTER THAT!
YOU ARGUED?
YES. ORIBE HAD... STRONGLY REQUESTED I PLANT A BUG INSIDE THE ACADEMY.
THAT IDIOT...
AND DID YOU?
YES. THAT DAY.

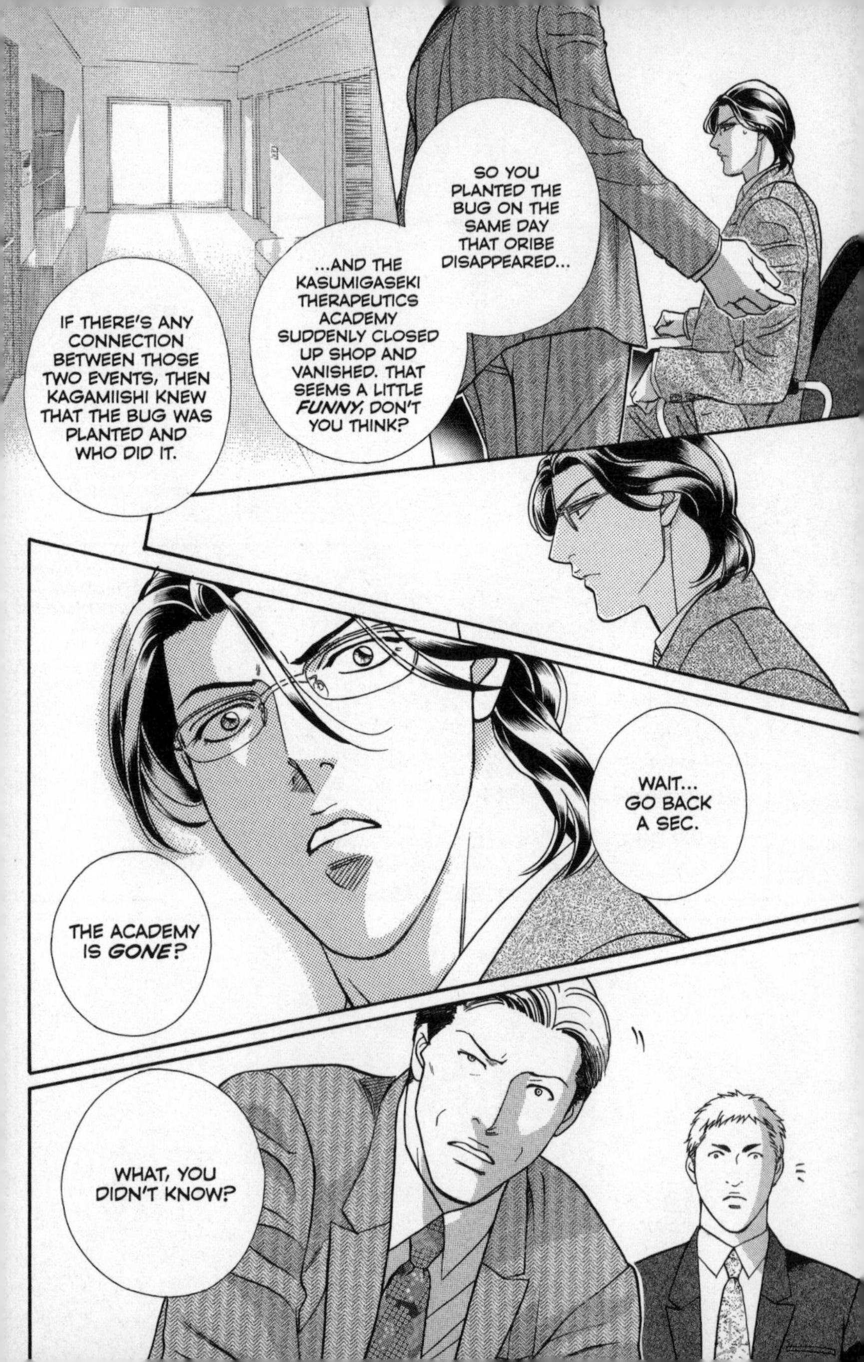
SO YOU PLANTED THE BUG ON THE SAME DAY THAT ORIBE DISAPPEARED...
...AND THE KASUMIGASEKI THERAPEUTICS ACADEMY SUDDENLY CLOSED UP SHOP AND VANISHED. THAT SEEMS A LITTLE *FUNNY*, DON'T YOU THINK?
IF THERE'S ANY CONNECTION BETWEEN THOSE TWO EVENTS, THEN KAGAMIISHI KNEW THAT THE BUG WAS PLANTED AND WHO DID IT.
WAIT... GO BACK A SEC.
THE ACADEMY IS *GONE*?
WHAT, YOU DIDN'T KNOW?

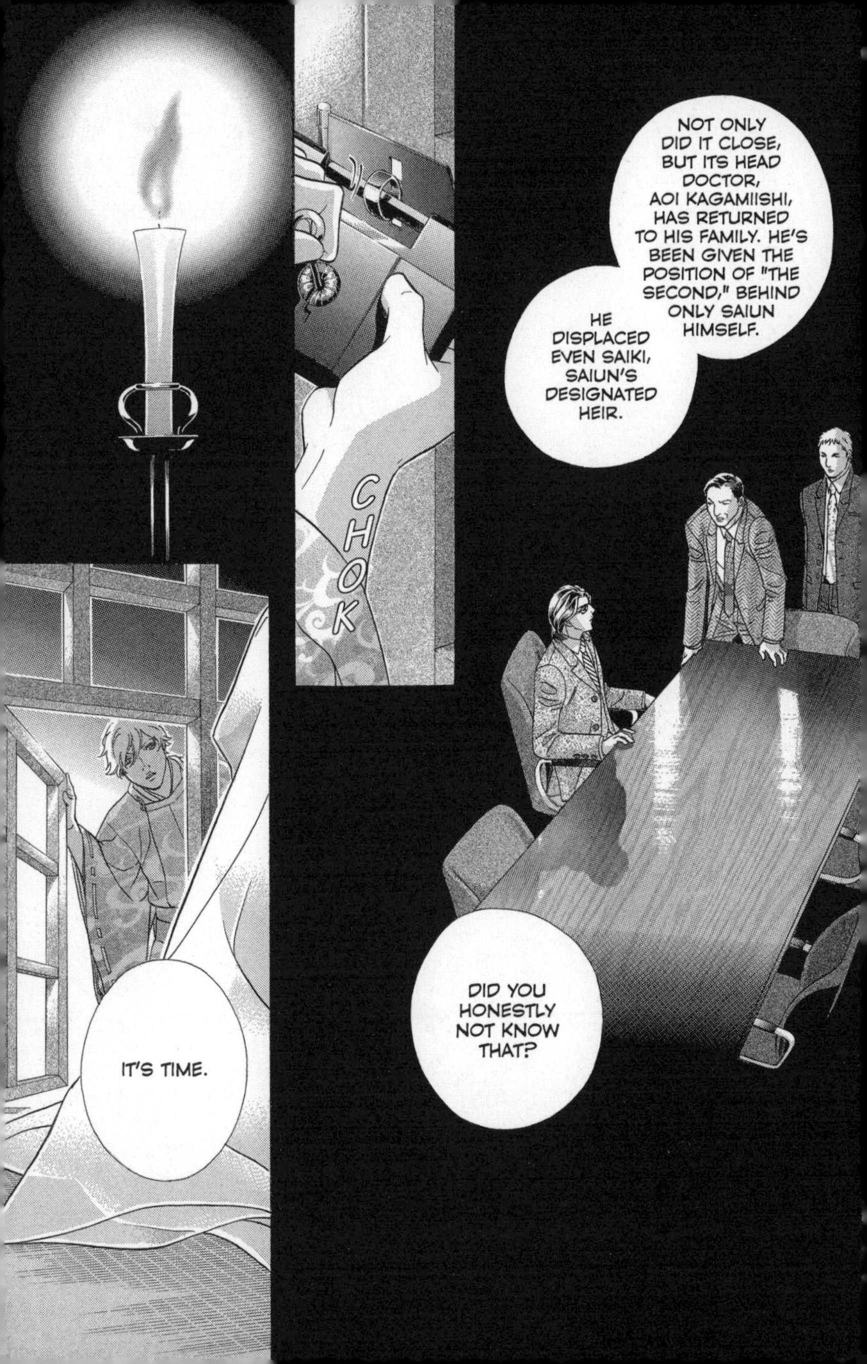
NOT ONLY DID IT CLOSE, BUT ITS HEAD DOCTOR, AOI KAGAMIISHI, HAS RETURNED TO HIS FAMILY. HE'S BEEN GIVEN THE POSITION OF "THE SECOND," BEHIND ONLY SAIUN HIMSELF.
HE DISPLACED EVEN SAIKI, SAIUN'S DESIGNATED HEIR.
DID YOU HONESTLY NOT KNOW THAT?
CHOK
IT'S TIME.

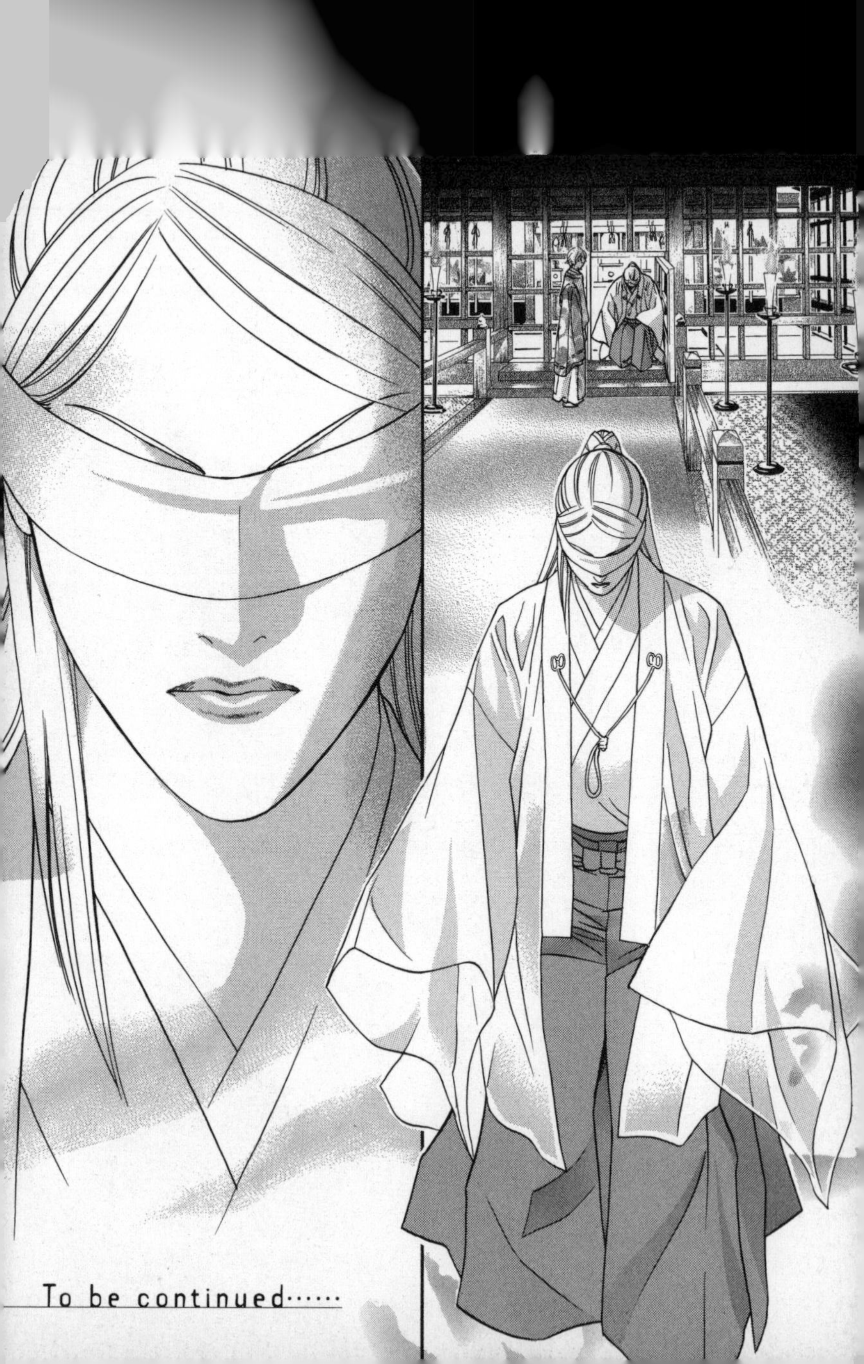
To be continued……

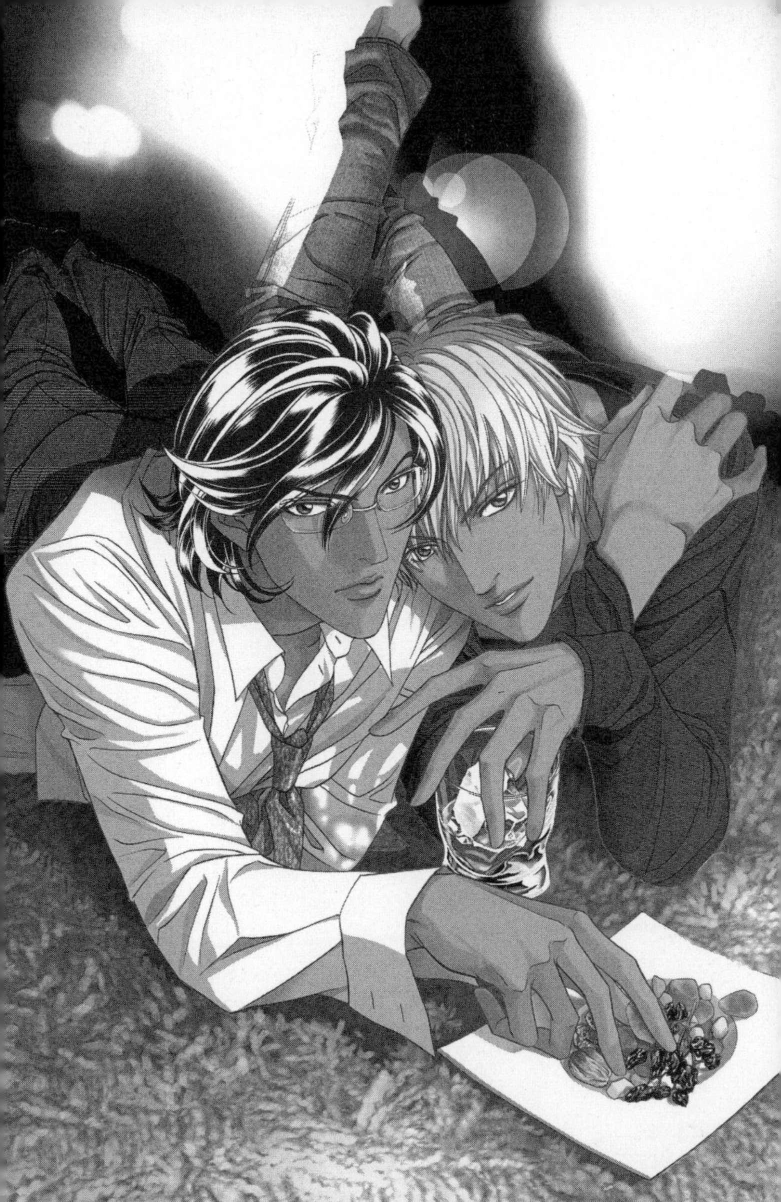

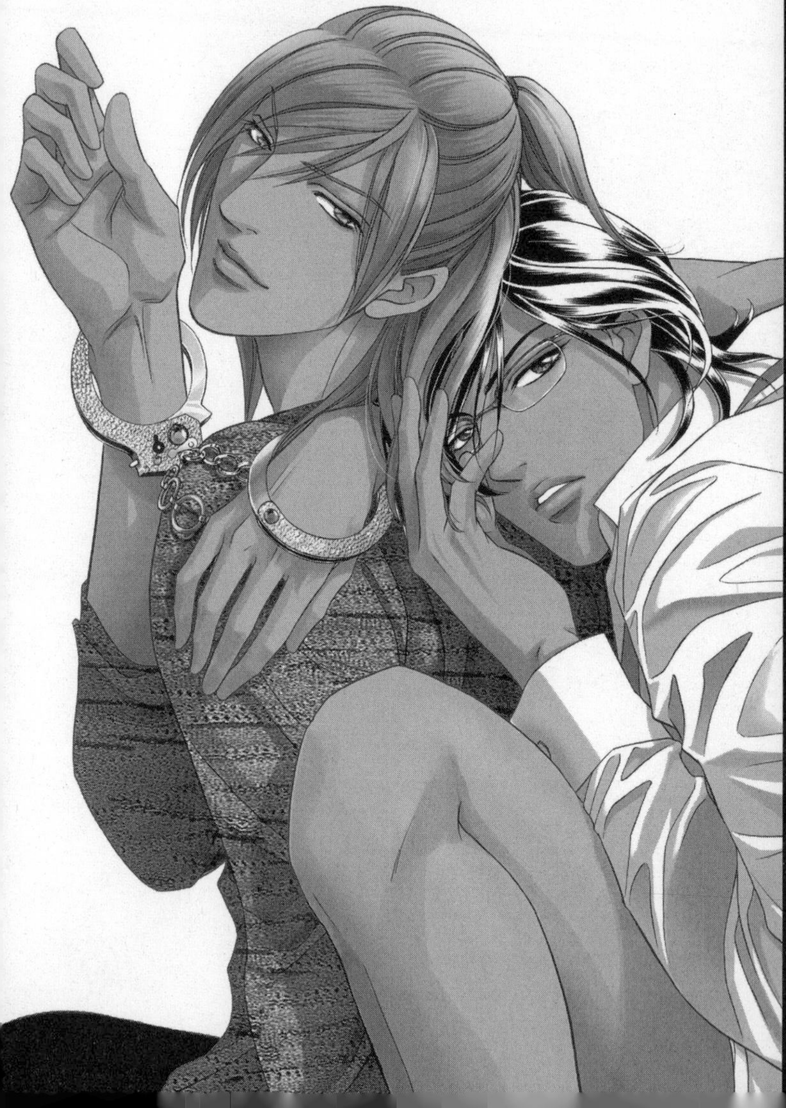

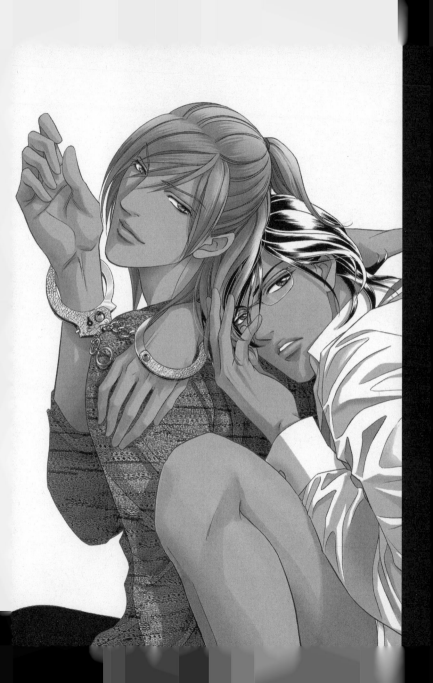

About the Author

Youka Nitta made her publishing debut with *Groupie* in 1995 and since then has become one of the most prolific and popular yaoi creators worldwide. Her most well-known series, *Embracing Love*, has been adapted into both a drama CD and an anime series. Born on March 8th in Fukui Prefecture, she's a Pisces with blood type B. Her hobbies include walking and going to the theater.

Spiritual Police

Volume 1

SuBLime Manga Edition

Story and Art by **Youka Nitta**

Translation—**Adrienne Beck**
Touch-up Art and Lettering—**WOWMAX Media**
Cover and Graphic Design—**Yukiko Whitley**
Editor—**Shaenon K. Garrity**

First published in Japan in 2012 by SHINSHOKAN Co., Ltd.

Printed in the U.S.A.

Published by SuBLime Manga
P.O. Box 77010
San Francisco, CA 94107

10 9 8 7 6 5 4 3 2 1
First printing, November 2013

M
MATURE

PARENTAL ADVISORY
SPIRITUAL POLICE is rated M for Mature and is recommended for adults. This volume contains mature themes and frank depictions of sexuality.

SUBLIME
www.SuBLimeManga.com

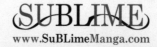

For more information

on all our products, along with the most up-to-date news on releases, series announcements, and contests, please visit us at:

SUBLIME

MANGA

These construction workers like to play with their tools!

Punch Up!

Story & Art by Shiuko KANO

Architect Motoharu Maki is hanging out at the construction site ogling a particular hunky, well-toned construction worker when he is unexpectedly reunited with his lost cat, Shinobu. The reunion is all thanks to Kouta Ohki, a foul-mouthed young ironworker who found and cared for the lost cat. Unfortunately for Kouta, this act of kindness led to his eviction! When Motoharu agrees to take in young Kouta, will he be able to tame this feisty stray? Includes a bonus *Play Boy Blues* side story.

SUBLIME

Punch↑ ① © 2006 Shiuko Kano/Libre Publishing